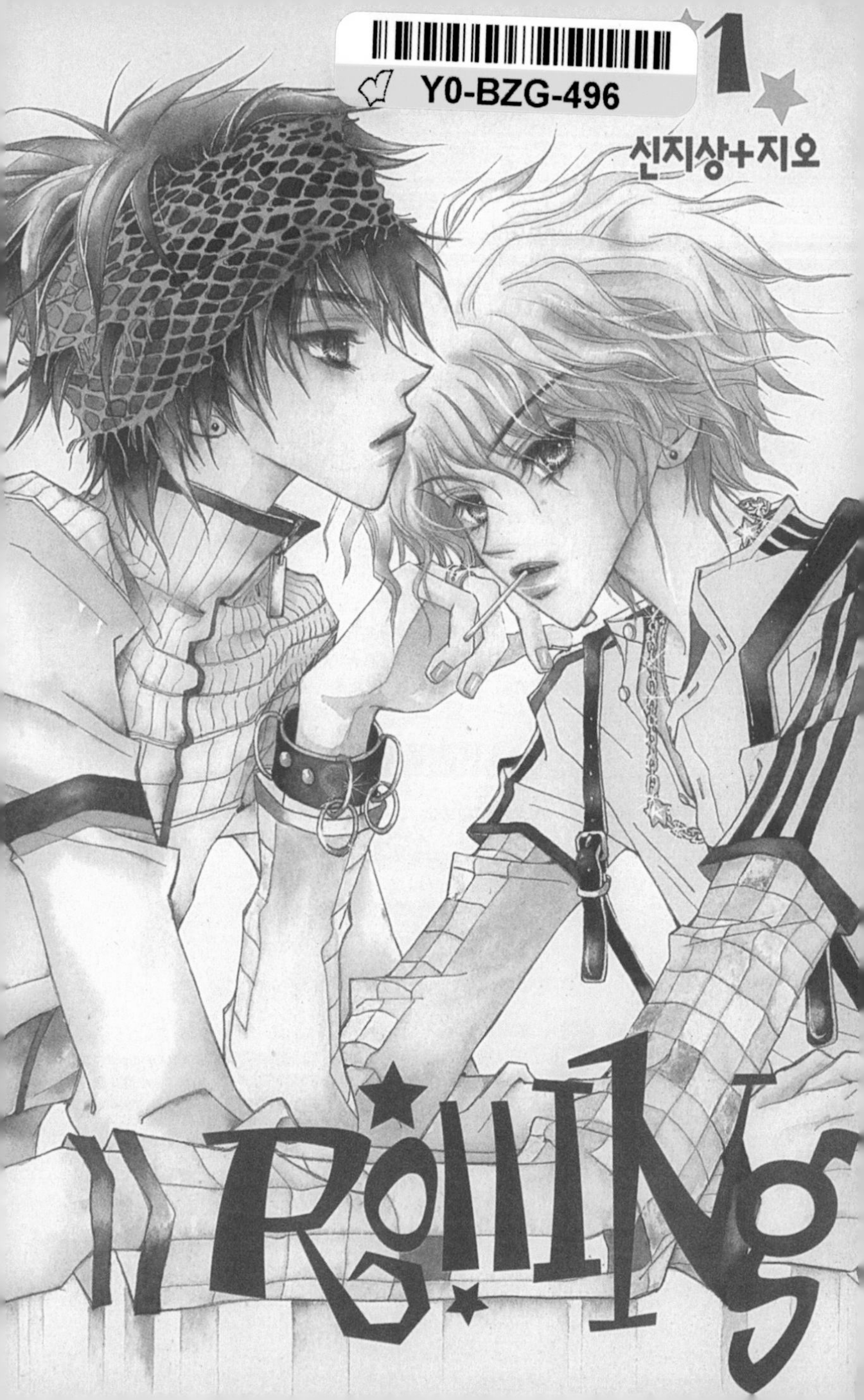
1
신지상+지오
Rolling

Rolling Vol.1
Story by Ji-sang Sin
Art by Geo

Translation - Soo-Kyung Kim
English Adaptation - Liz Forbes
Copy Editor - Jessica Chavez
Retouch and Lettering - Star Print Brokers
Production Artist - Jennifer M. Sanchez
Cover Design - Chelsea Windlinger

Editor - Hyun Joo Kim
Digital Imaging Manager - Chris Buford
Pre-Production Supervisor - Lucas Rivera
Production Manager - Elisabeth Brizzi
Managing Editor - Vy Nguyen
Creative Director - Anne Marie Horne
Editor-in-Chief - Rob Tokar
Publisher - Mike Kiley
President and C.O.O. - John Parker
C.E.O. and Chief Creative Officer - Stu Levy

A  Manga

TOKYOPOP Inc.
5900 Wilshire Blvd. Suite 2000
Los Angeles, CA 90036

E-mail: info@TOKYOPOP.com
Come visit us online at www.TOKYOPOP.com

© 2004 Ji-sang SIN, Geo, DAIWON C.I. Inc.
All Rights Reserved.
First published in Korea in 2004 by DAIWON C.I. Inc. English
translation rights in North America, UK, NZ, and Australia
arranged by DAIWON C.I. Inc. through Topaz Agency.
English text copyright © 2008 TOKYOPOP Inc.

All rights reserved. No portion of this book may be
reproduced or transmitted in any form or by any means
without written permission from the copyright holders.
This manga is a work of fiction. Any resemblance to
actual events or locales or persons, living or dead, is
entirely coincidental.

ISBN: 978-1-4278-0961-2

First TOKYOPOP printing: July 2008
10 9 8 7 6 5 4 3 2 1
Printed in the USA

Story By
Ji-sang Sin
Art by
Geo

HAMBURG // LONDON // LOS ANGELES // TOKYO

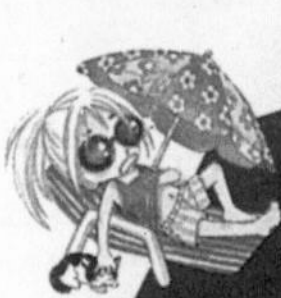

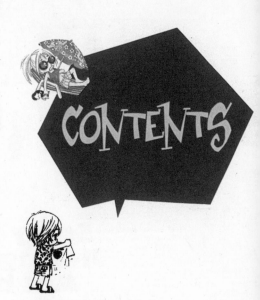

CONTENTS

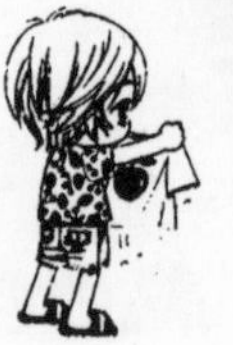

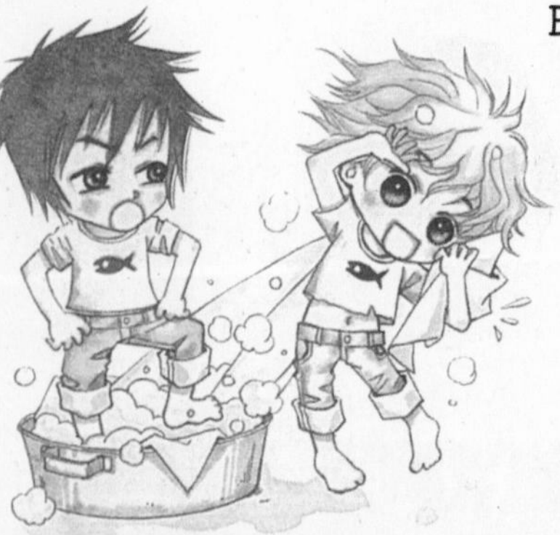

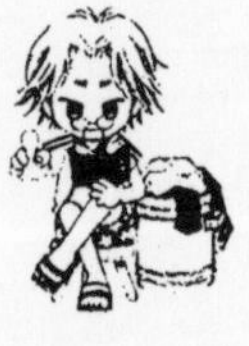

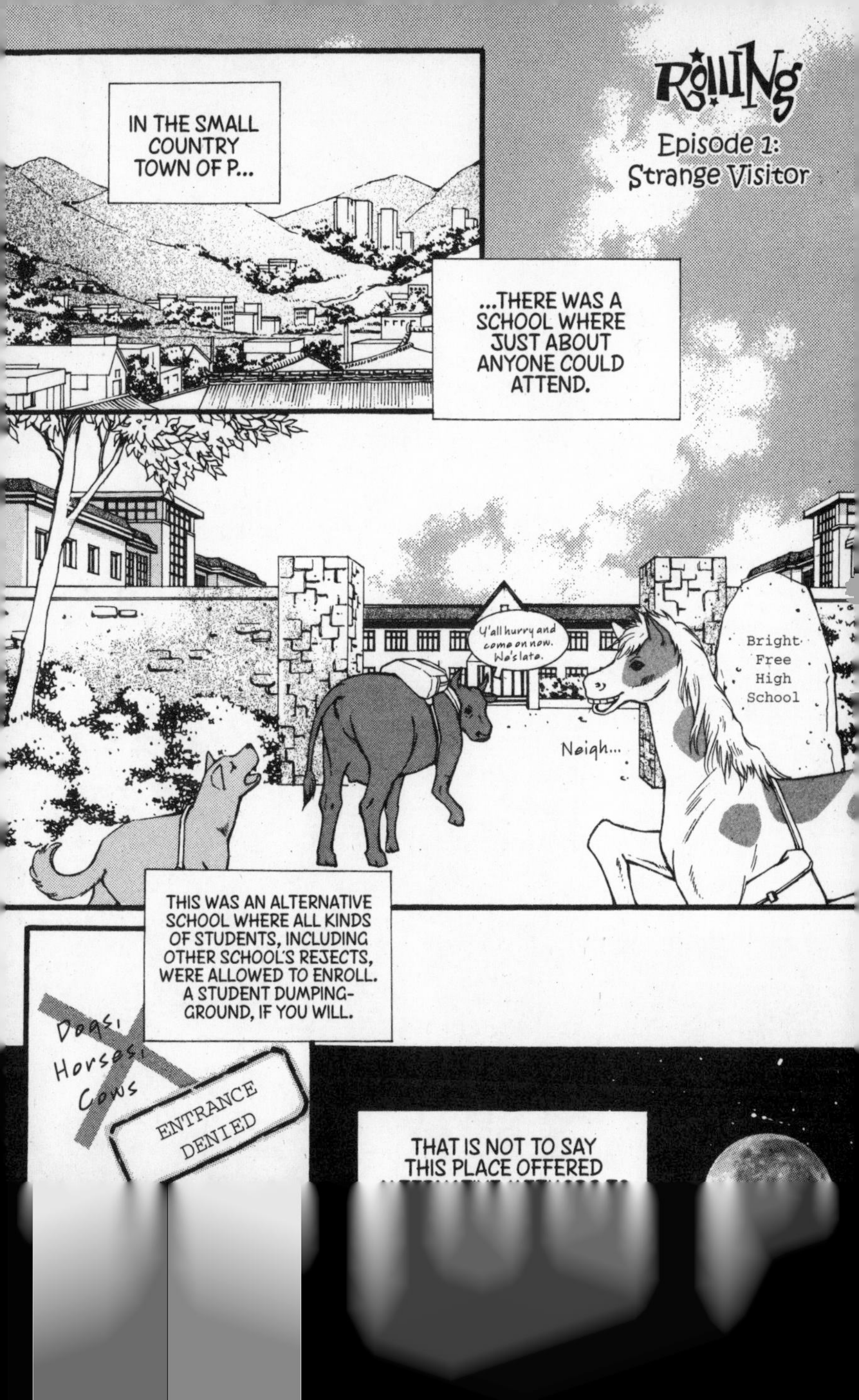

Rolling
Episode 1: Strange Visitor
IN THE SMALL COUNTRY TOWN OF P...
...THERE WAS A SCHOOL WHERE JUST ABOUT ANYONE COULD ATTEND.
Y'all hurry and come on now. We's late.
Bright Free High School
Neigh...
THIS WAS AN ALTERNATIVE SCHOOL WHERE ALL KINDS OF STUDENTS, INCLUDING OTHER SCHOOL'S REJECTS, WERE ALLOWED TO ENROLL. A STUDENT DUMPING-GROUND, IF YOU WILL.
Dogs, Horses, Cows
ENTRANCE DENIED
THAT IS NOT TO SAY THIS PLACE OFFERED

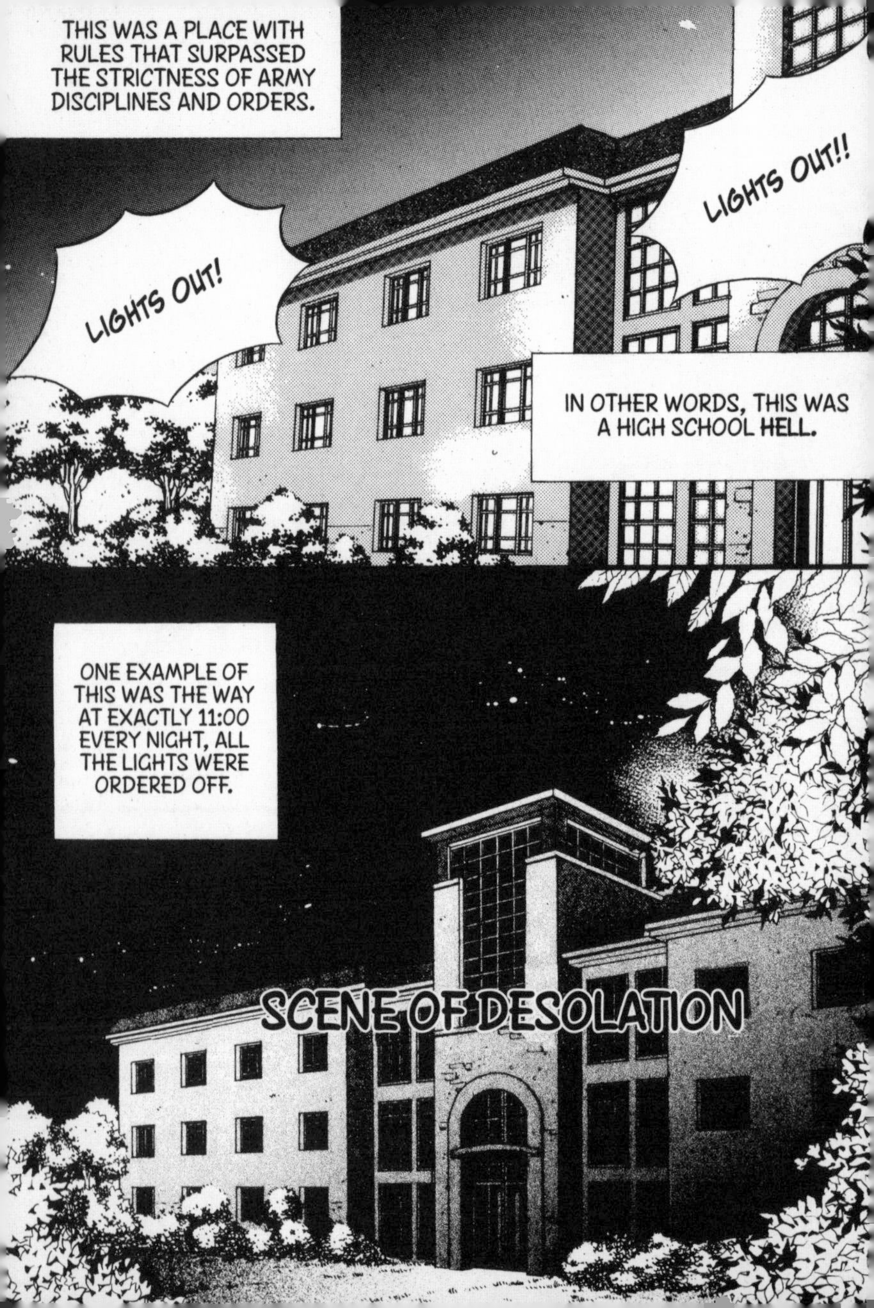
THIS WAS A PLACE WITH RULES THAT SURPASSED THE STRICTNESS OF ARMY DISCIPLINES AND ORDERS.
LIGHTS OUT!
LIGHTS OUT!!
IN OTHER WORDS, THIS WAS A HIGH SCHOOL HELL.
ONE EXAMPLE OF THIS WAS THE WAY AT EXACTLY 11:00 EVERY NIGHT, ALL THE LIGHTS WERE ORDERED OFF.
SCENE OF DESOLATION

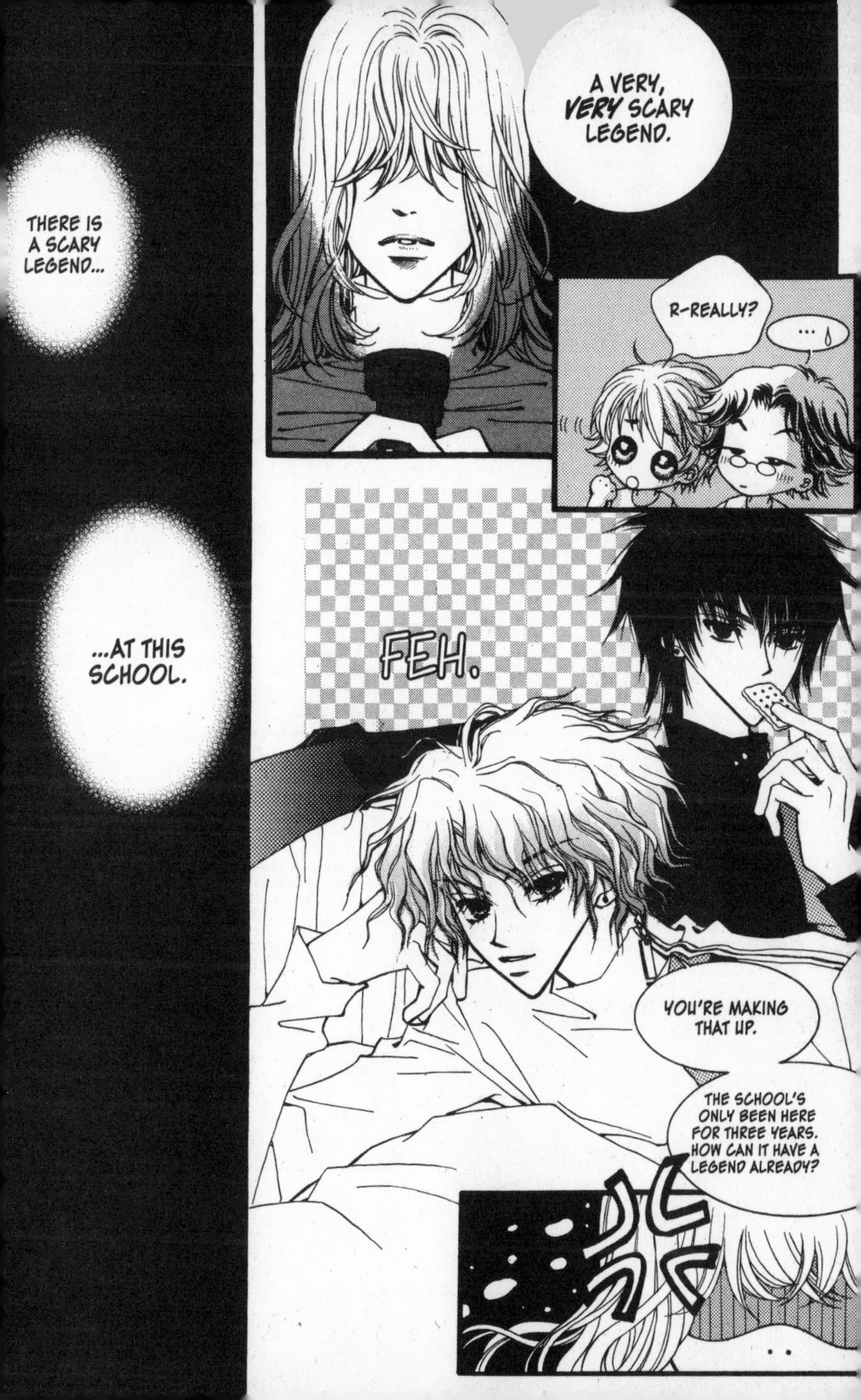
THERE IS A SCARY LEGEND...
...AT THIS SCHOOL.
A VERY, VERY SCARY LEGEND.
R-REALLY?
...
FEH.
YOU'RE MAKING THAT UP.
THE SCHOOL'S ONLY BEEN HERE FOR THREE YEARS. HOW CAN IT HAVE A LEGEND ALREADY?
..

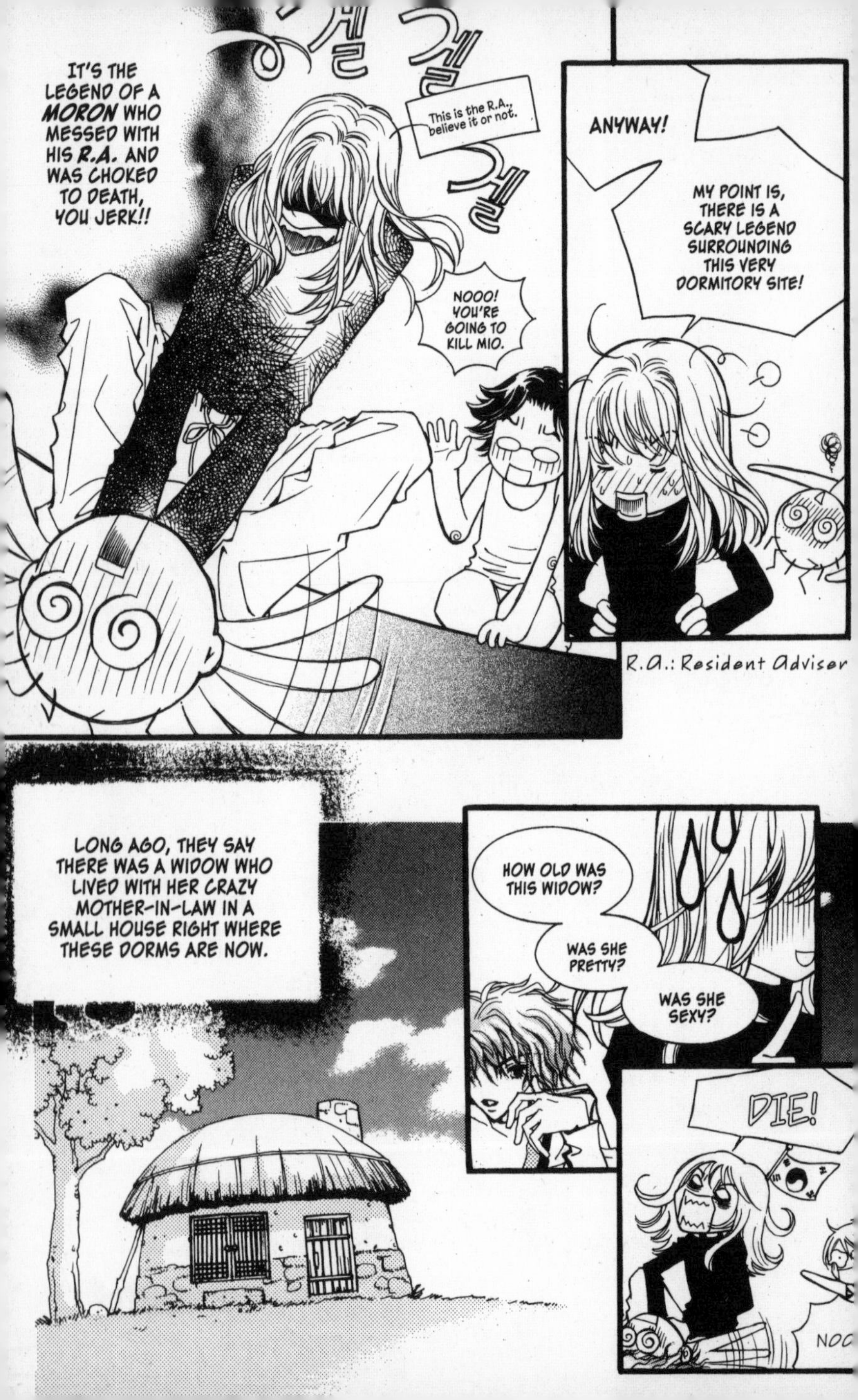
IT'S THE LEGEND OF A MORON WHO MESSED WITH HIS R.A. AND WAS CHOKED TO DEATH, YOU JERK!!
This is the R.A., believe it or not.
NOOO! YOU'RE GOING TO KILL MIO.
ANYWAY!
MY POINT IS, THERE IS A SCARY LEGEND SURROUNDING THIS VERY DORMITORY SITE!
R.A.: Resident Adviser
LONG AGO, THEY SAY THERE WAS A WIDOW WHO LIVED WITH HER CRAZY MOTHER-IN-LAW IN A SMALL HOUSE RIGHT WHERE THESE DORMS ARE NOW.
HOW OLD WAS THIS WIDOW?
WAS SHE PRETTY?
WAS SHE SEXY?
DIE!

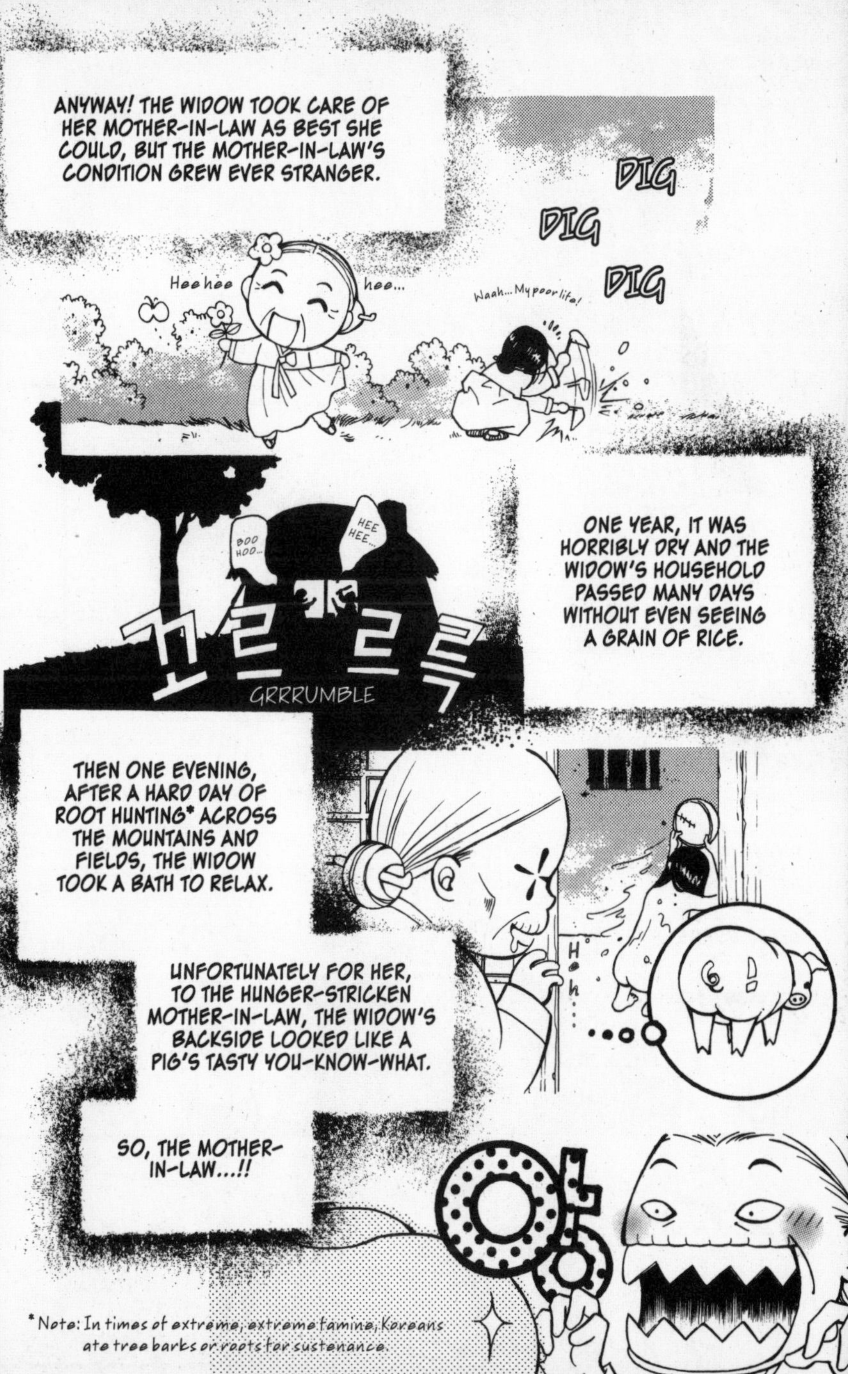
ANYWAY! THE WIDOW TOOK CARE OF HER MOTHER-IN-LAW AS BEST SHE COULD, BUT THE MOTHER-IN-LAW'S CONDITION GREW EVER STRANGER.
Heehee hee...
Waah... My poor life!
DIG
DIG
DIG
BOO HOO...
HEE HEE...
꼬르르륵
GRRRUMBLE
ONE YEAR, IT WAS HORRIBLY DRY AND THE WIDOW'S HOUSEHOLD PASSED MANY DAYS WITHOUT EVEN SEEING A GRAIN OF RICE.
THEN ONE EVENING, AFTER A HARD DAY OF ROOT HUNTING* ACROSS THE MOUNTAINS AND FIELDS, THE WIDOW TOOK A BATH TO RELAX.
UNFORTUNATELY FOR HER, TO THE HUNGER-STRICKEN MOTHER-IN-LAW, THE WIDOW'S BACKSIDE LOOKED LIKE A PIG'S TASTY YOU-KNOW-WHAT.
Heh...
SO, THE MOTHER-IN-LAW...!!
아

*Note: In times of extreme, extreme famine, Koreans ate tree barks or roots for sustenance.

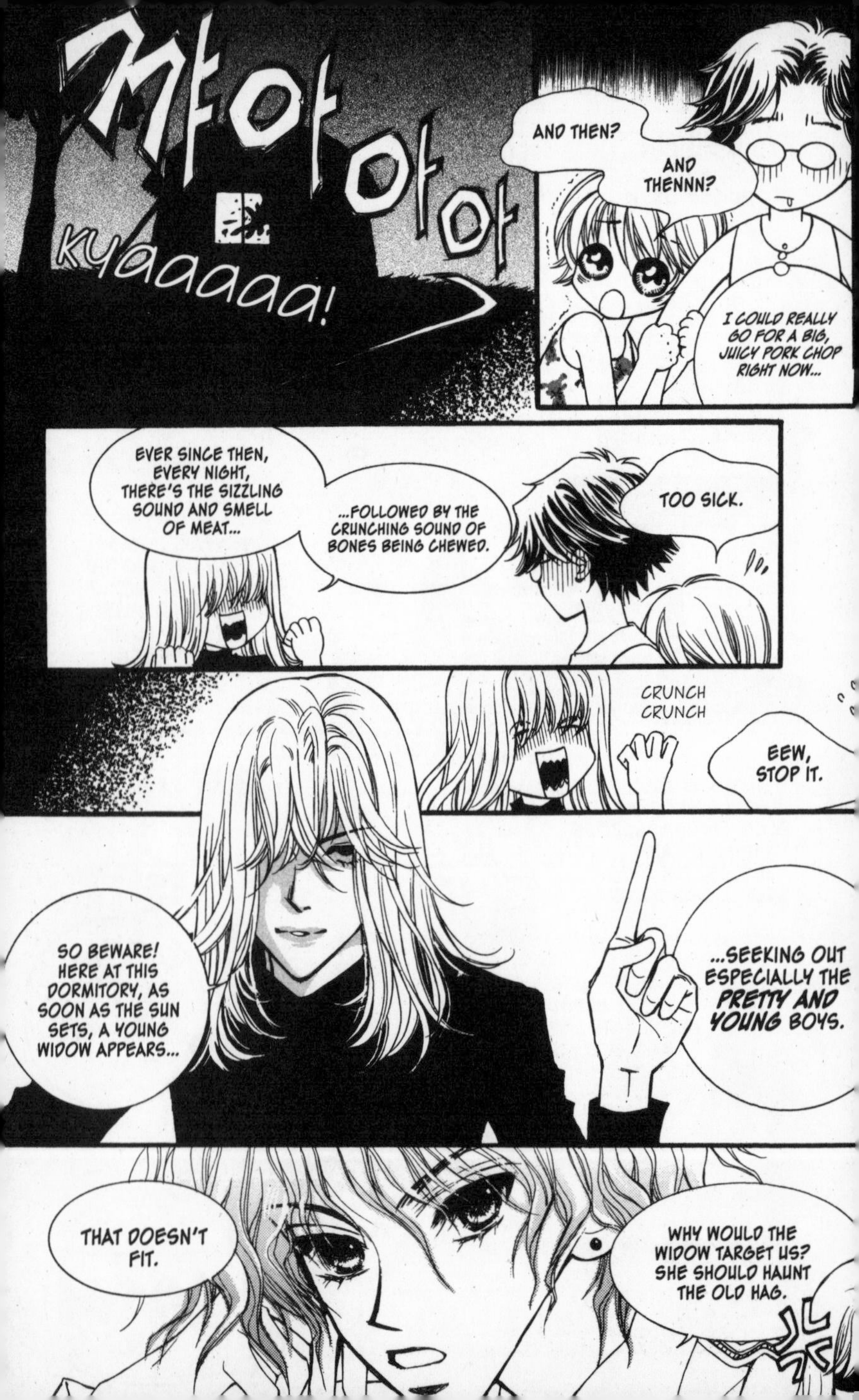

꺄아아아
kyaaaaaa!
AND THEN?
AND THENNN?
I COULD REALLY GO FOR A BIG, JUICY PORK CHOP RIGHT NOW...
EVER SINCE THEN, EVERY NIGHT, THERE'S THE SIZZLING SOUND AND SMELL OF MEAT...
...FOLLOWED BY THE CRUNCHING SOUND OF BONES BEING CHEWED.
TOO SICK.
CRUNCH CRUNCH
EEW, STOP IT.
SO BEWARE! HERE AT THIS DORMITORY, AS SOON AS THE SUN SETS, A YOUNG WIDOW APPEARS...
...SEEKING OUT ESPECIALLY THE ***PRETTY AND YOUNG*** BOYS.
THAT DOESN'T FIT.
WHY WOULD THE WIDOW TARGET US? SHE SHOULD HAUNT THE OLD HAG.

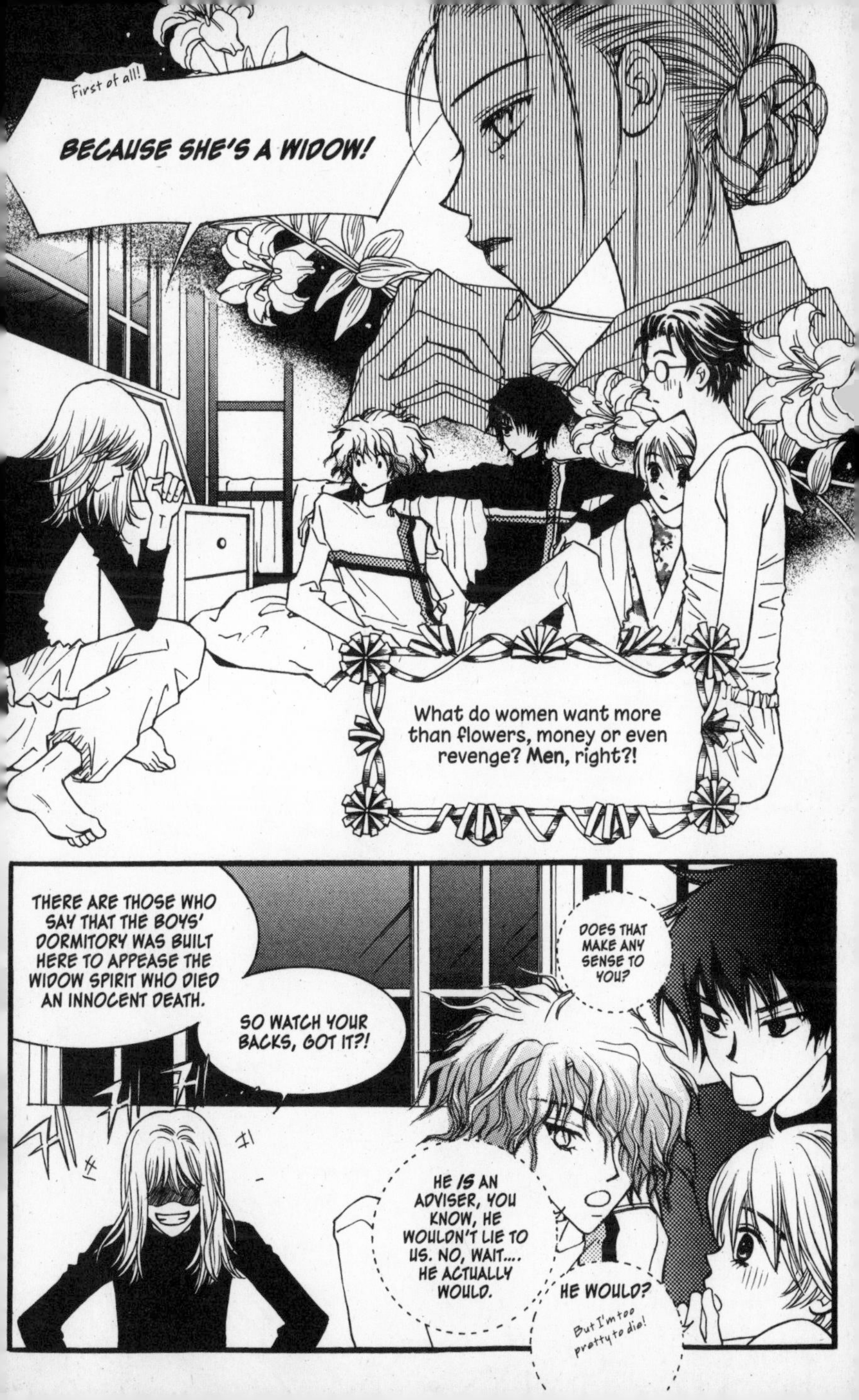
First of all!
BECAUSE SHE'S A WIDOW!
What do women want more than flowers, money or even revenge? Men, right?!
THERE ARE THOSE WHO SAY THAT THE BOYS' DORMITORY WAS BUILT HERE TO APPEASE THE WIDOW SPIRIT WHO DIED AN INNOCENT DEATH.
SO WATCH YOUR BACKS, GOT IT?!
DOES THAT MAKE ANY SENSE TO YOU?
HE IS AN ADVISER, YOU KNOW, HE WOULDN'T LIE TO US. NO, WAIT.... HE ACTUALLY WOULD.
HE WOULD?
But I'm too pretty to die!

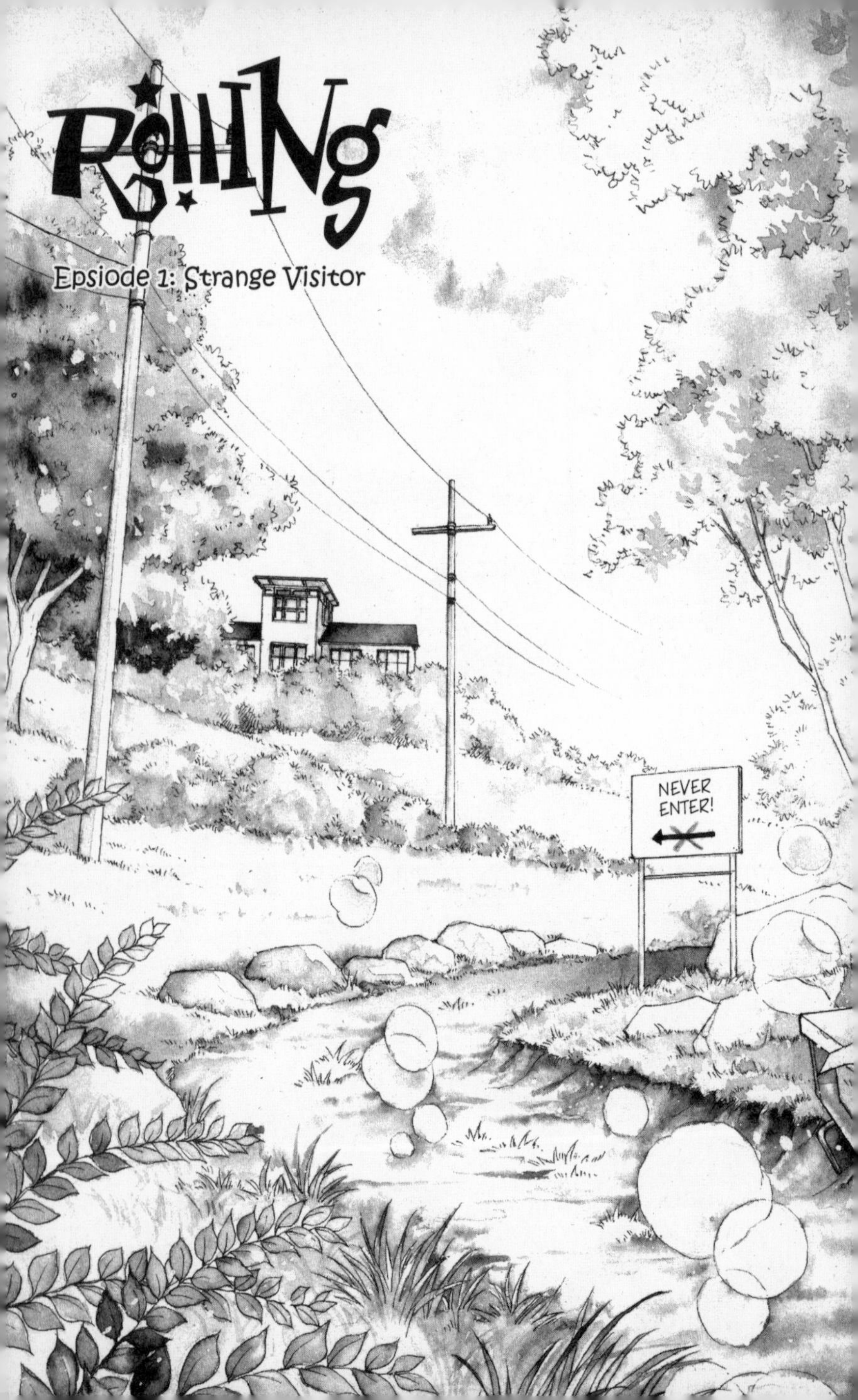
Rolling
Epsiode 1: Strange Visitor
NEVER ENTER!

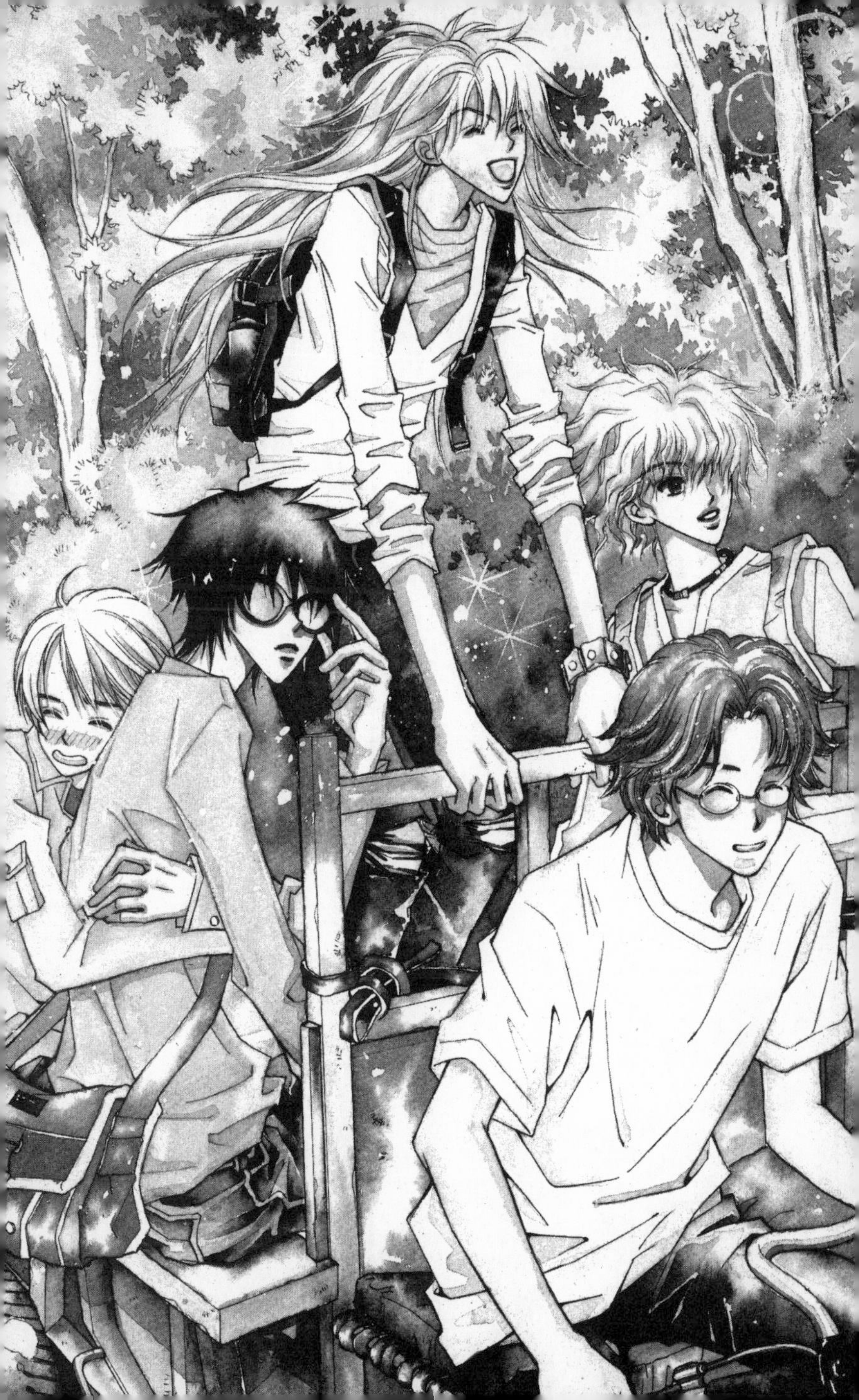

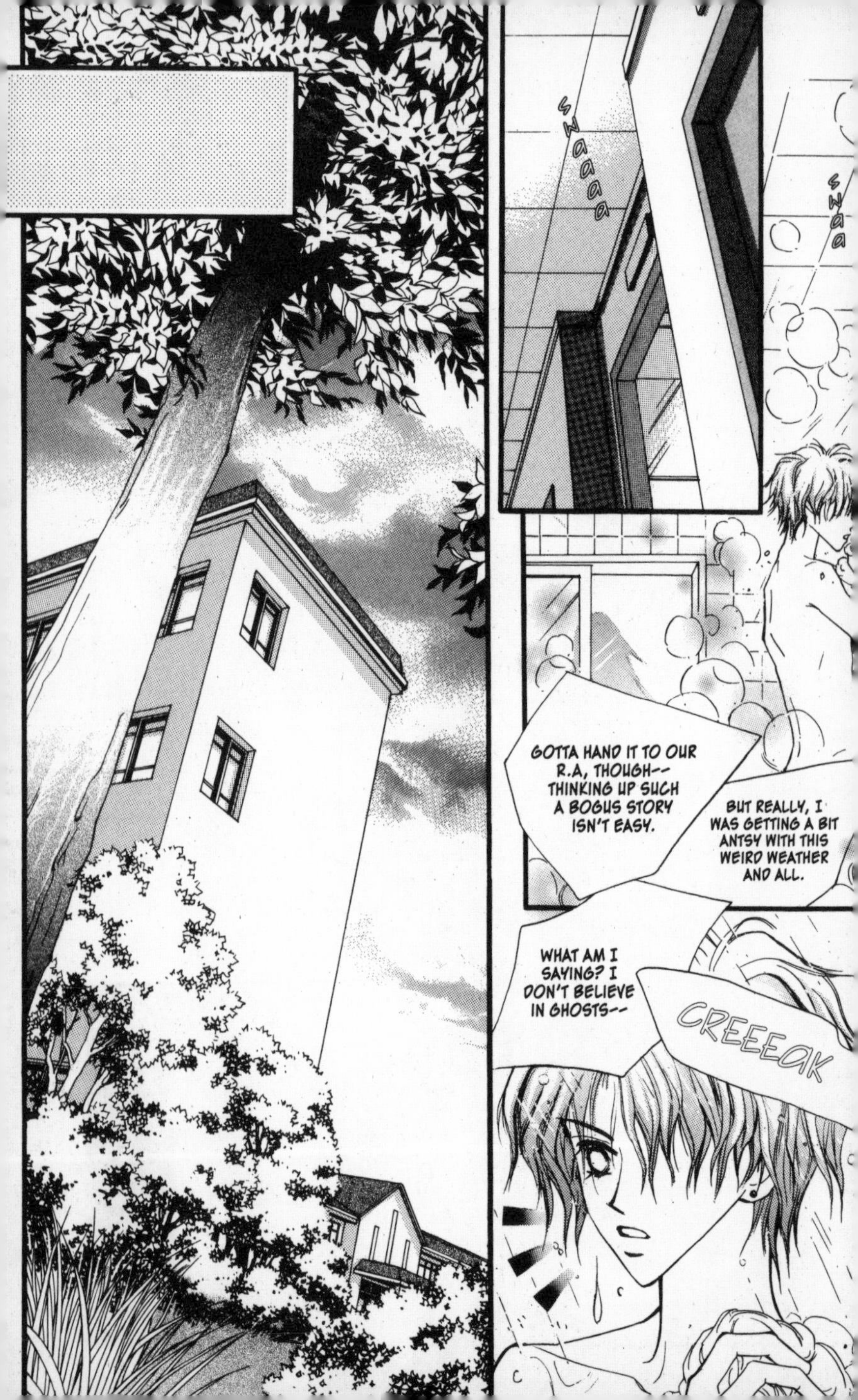
swaaaa
swaa
GOTTA HAND IT TO OUR R.A, THOUGH--THINKING UP SUCH A BOGUS STORY ISN'T EASY.
BUT REALLY, I WAS GETTING A BIT ANTSY WITH THIS WEIRD WEATHER AND ALL.
WHAT AM I SAYING? I DON'T BELIEVE IN GHOSTS--
CREEEAK

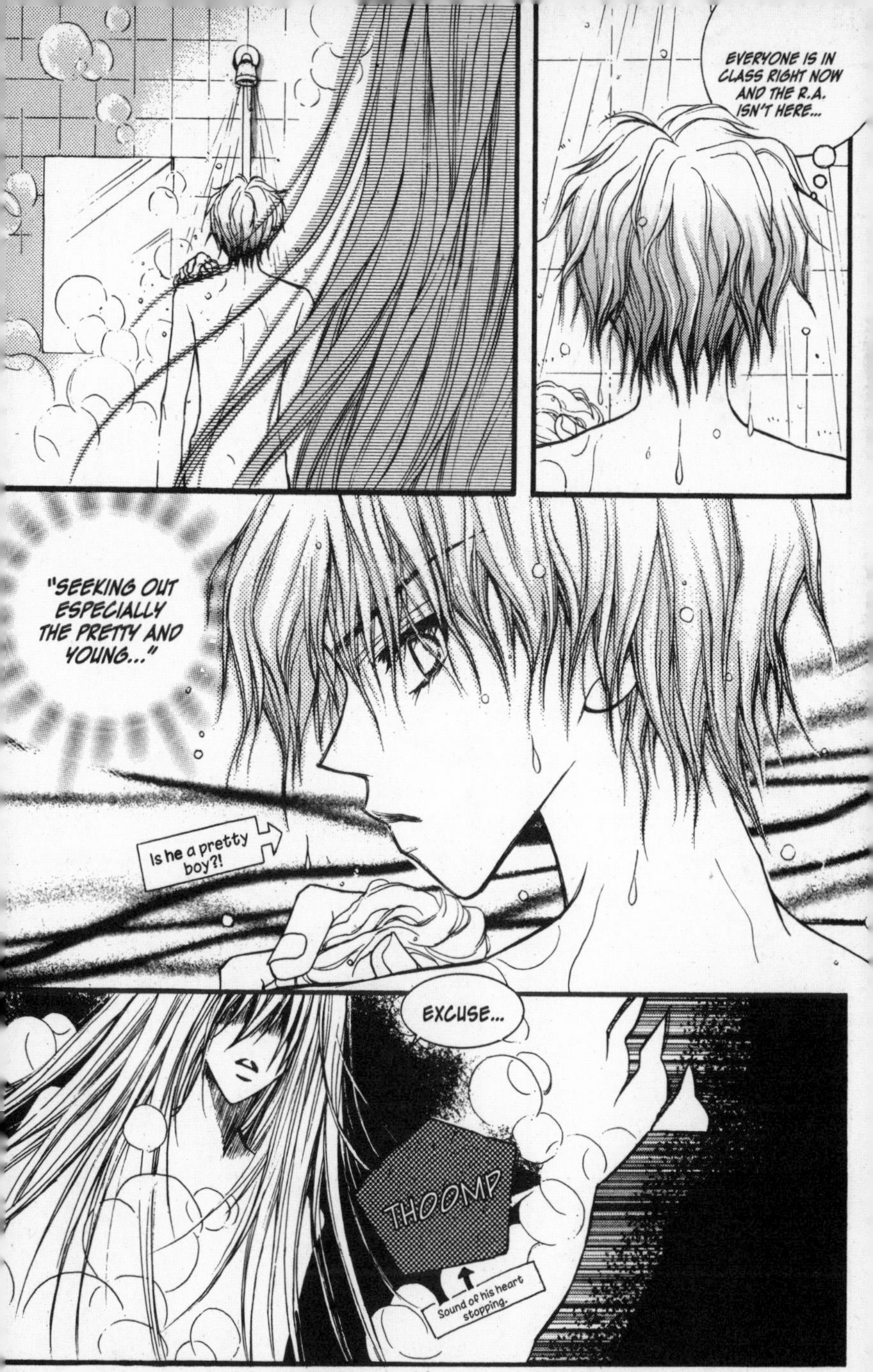
EVERYONE IS IN CLASS RIGHT NOW AND THE R.A. ISN'T HERE...
"SEEKING OUT ESPECIALLY THE PRETTY AND YOUNG..."
Is he a pretty boy?!
EXCUSE...
THOOMP
Sound of his heart stopping.

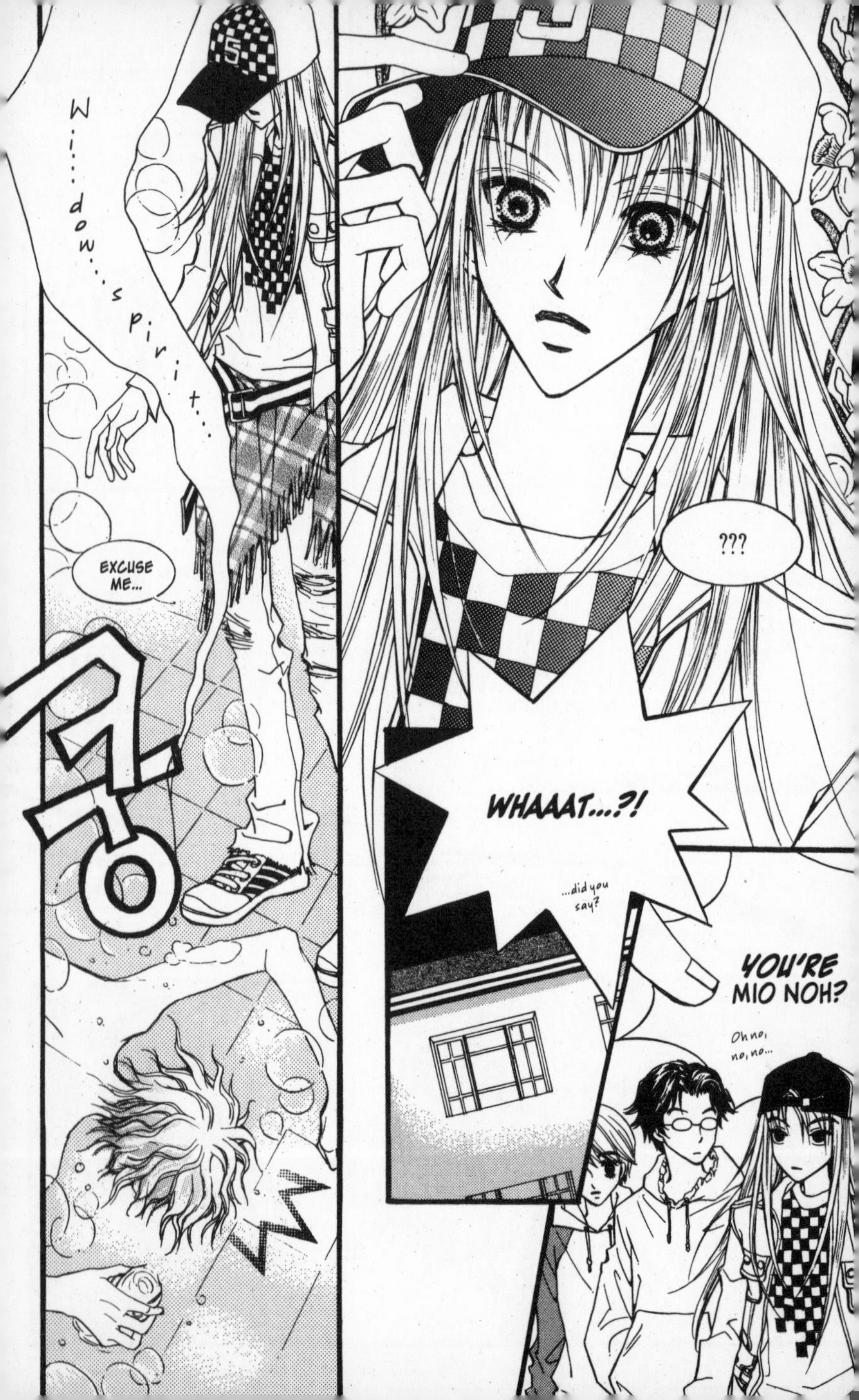
W...i...dow...spirit...
EXCUSE ME...
???
WHAAAT...?!
...did you say?
YOU'RE MIO NOH?
Oh no, no, no...

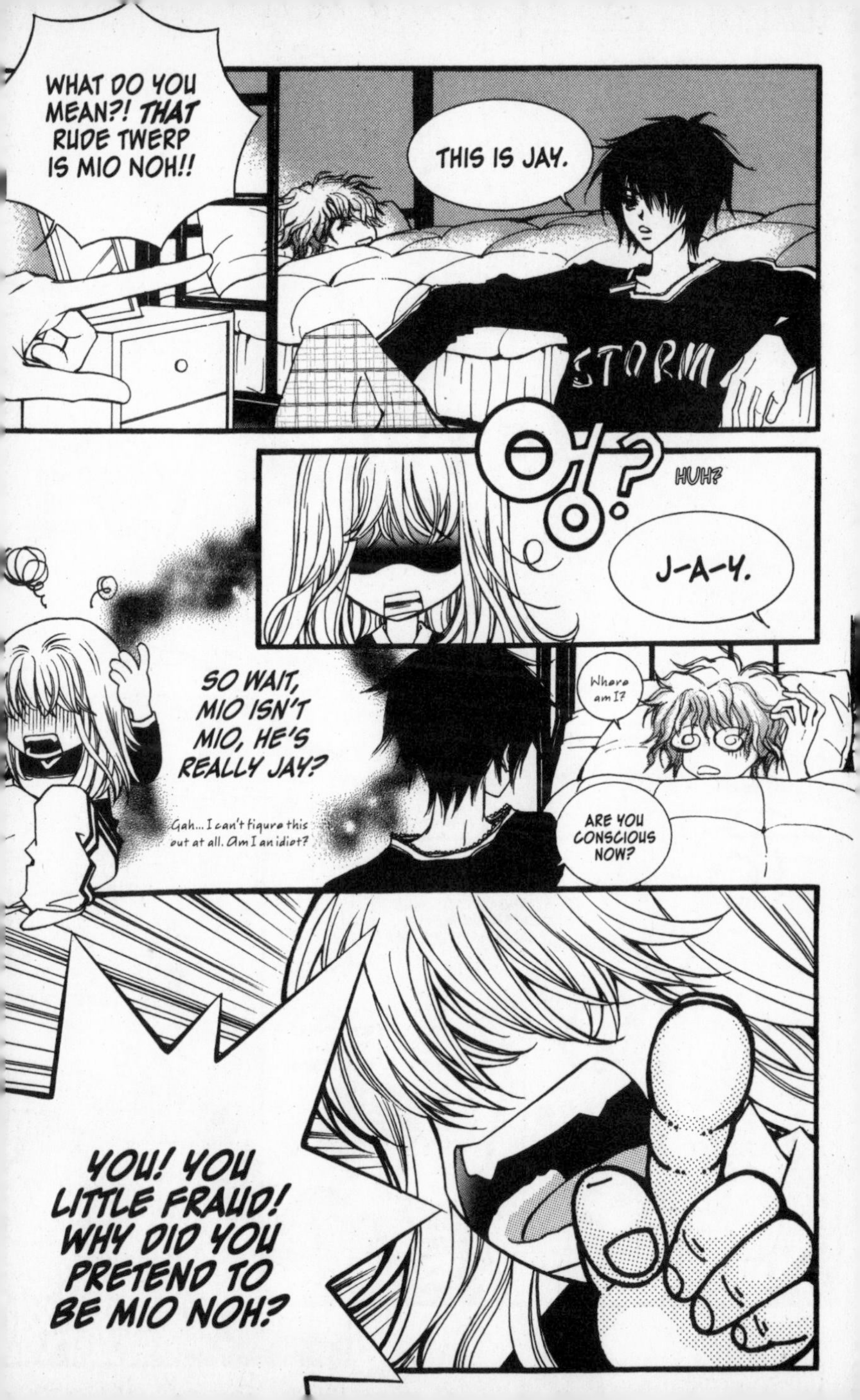
WHAT DO YOU MEAN?! THAT RUDE TWERP IS MIO NOH!!
THIS IS JAY.
어?
HUH?
J-A-Y.
SO WAIT, MIO ISN'T MIO, HE'S REALLY JAY?
Gah... I can't figure this out at all. Am I an idiot?
Where am I?
ARE YOU CONSCIOUS NOW?
YOU! YOU LITTLE FRAUD! WHY DID YOU PRETEND TO BE MIO NOH?

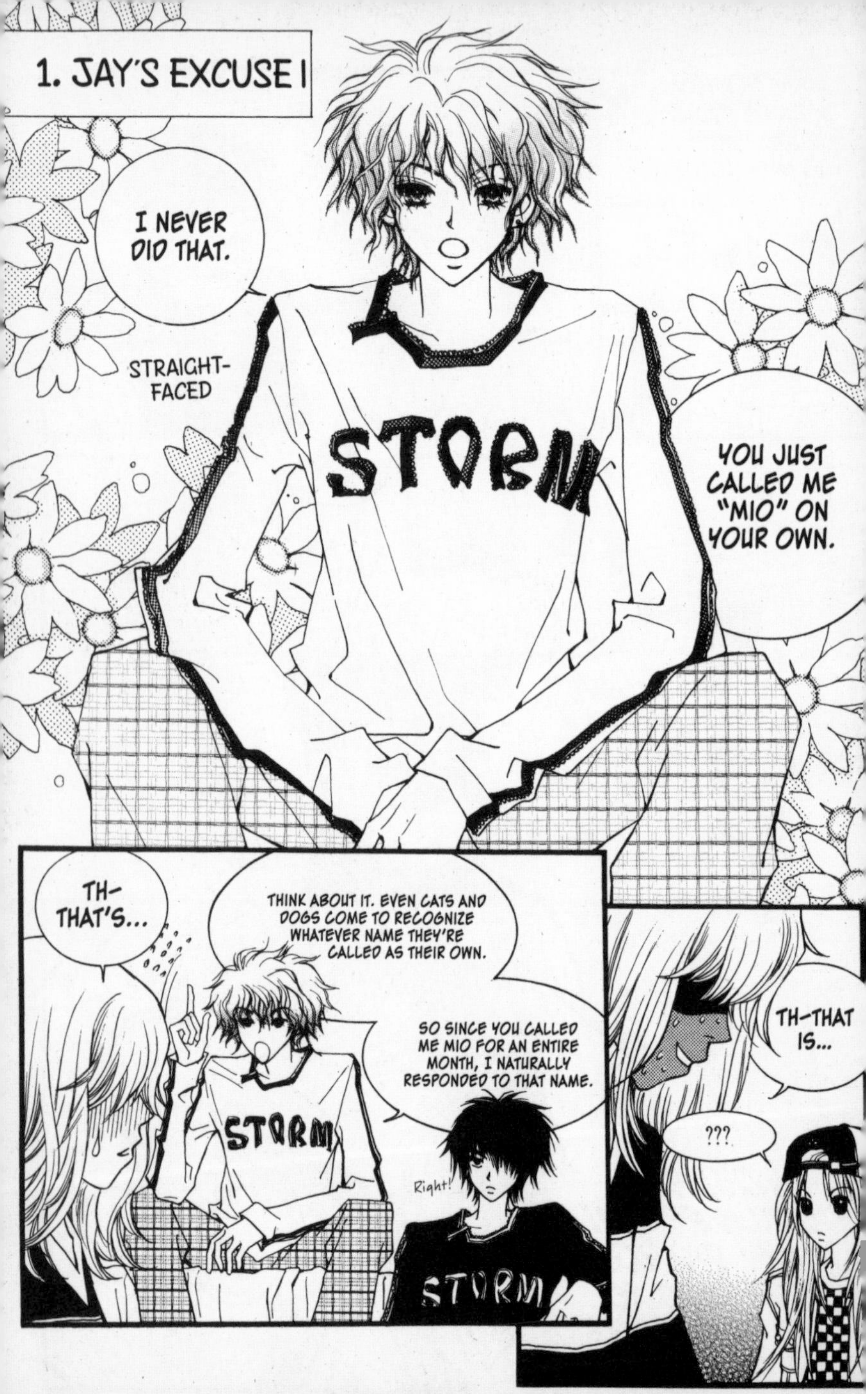
1. JAY'S EXCUSE 1
I NEVER DID THAT.
STRAIGHT-FACED
YOU JUST CALLED ME "MIO" ON YOUR OWN.
TH-THAT'S...
THINK ABOUT IT. EVEN CATS AND DOGS COME TO RECOGNIZE WHATEVER NAME THEY'RE CALLED AS THEIR OWN.
SO SINCE YOU CALLED ME MIO FOR AN ENTIRE MONTH, I NATURALLY RESPONDED TO THAT NAME.
Right!
TH-THAT IS...
???

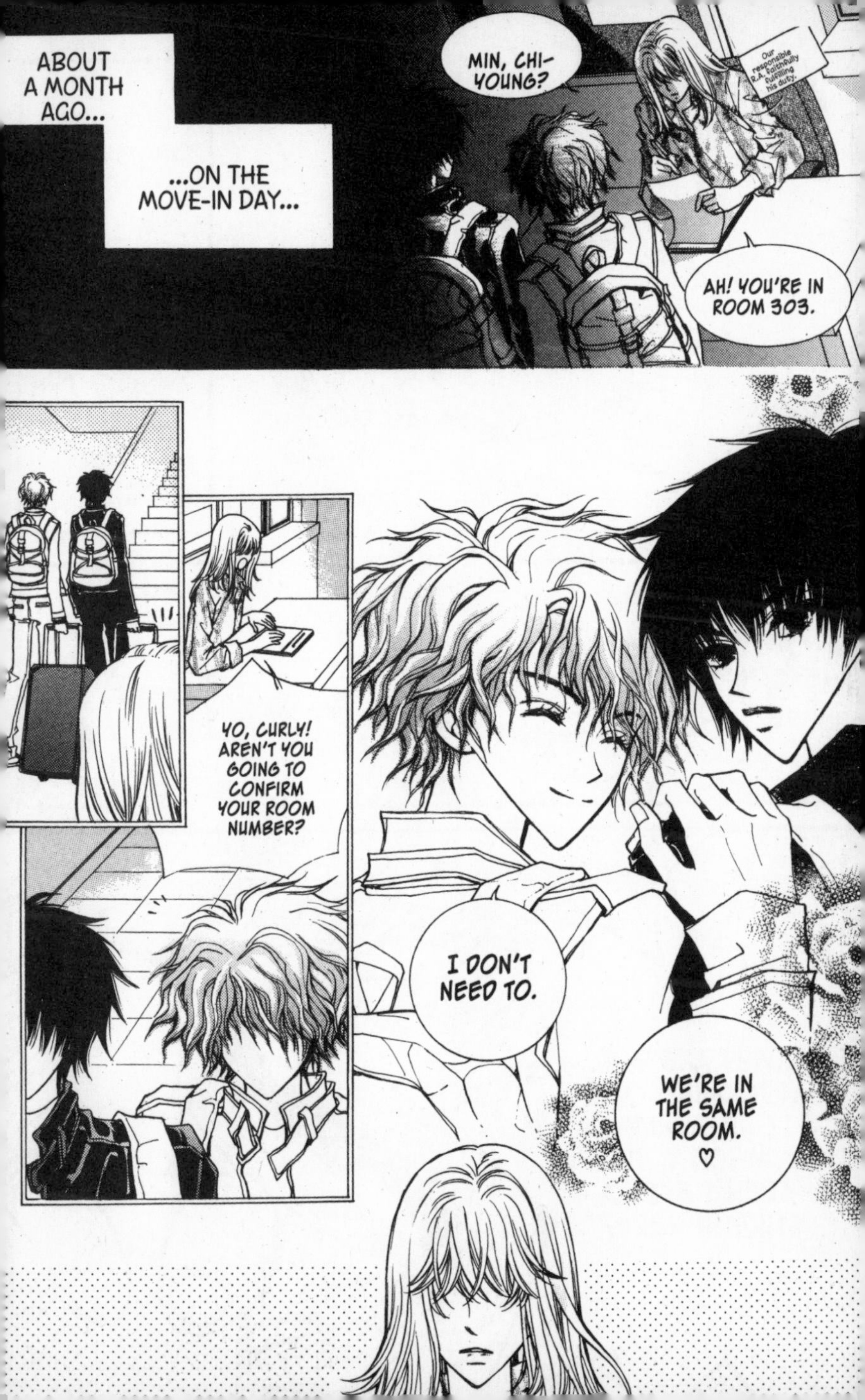
ABOUT A MONTH AGO...
...ON THE MOVE-IN DAY...
MIN, CHI-YOUNG?
Our responsible R.A. faithfully fulfilling his duty.
AH! YOU'RE IN ROOM 303.
YO, CURLY! AREN'T YOU GOING TO CONFIRM YOUR ROOM NUMBER?
I DON'T NEED TO.
WE'RE IN THE SAME ROOM. ♡

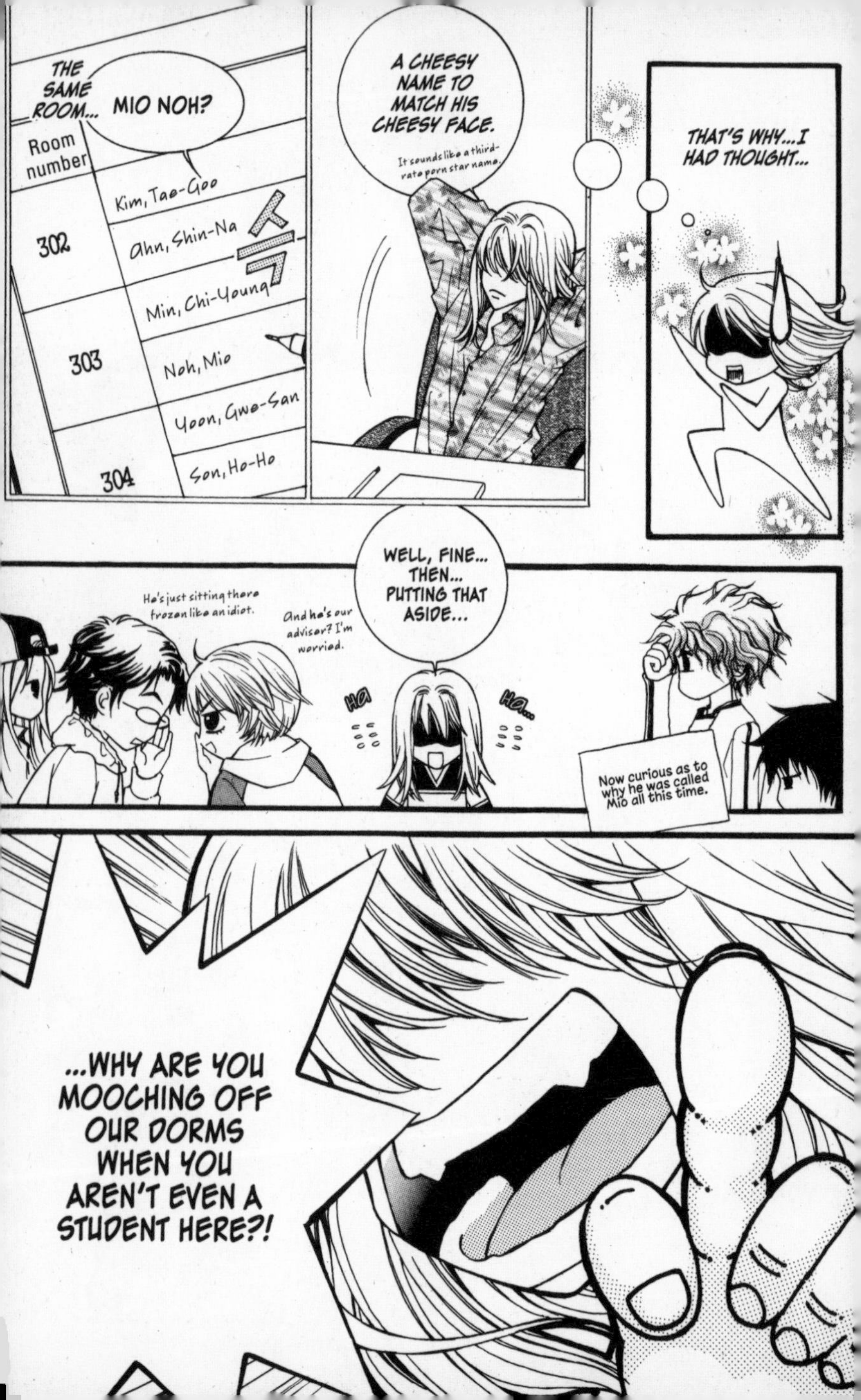
THE SAME ROOM...
MIO NOH?
Room number
302
Kim, Tae-Goo
Ahn, Shin-Na
Min, Chi-Young
303
Noh, Mio
Yoon, Gwe-San
304
Son, Ho-Ho
A CHEESY NAME TO MATCH HIS CHEESY FACE.
It sounds like a third-rate porn star name.
THAT'S WHY...I HAD THOUGHT...
He's just sitting there frozen like an idiot.
And he's our advisor? I'm worried.
WELL, FINE... THEN... PUTTING THAT ASIDE...
HA
HA...
Now curious as to why he was called Mio all this time.
...WHY ARE YOU MOOCHING OFF OUR DORMS WHEN YOU AREN'T EVEN A STUDENT HERE?!

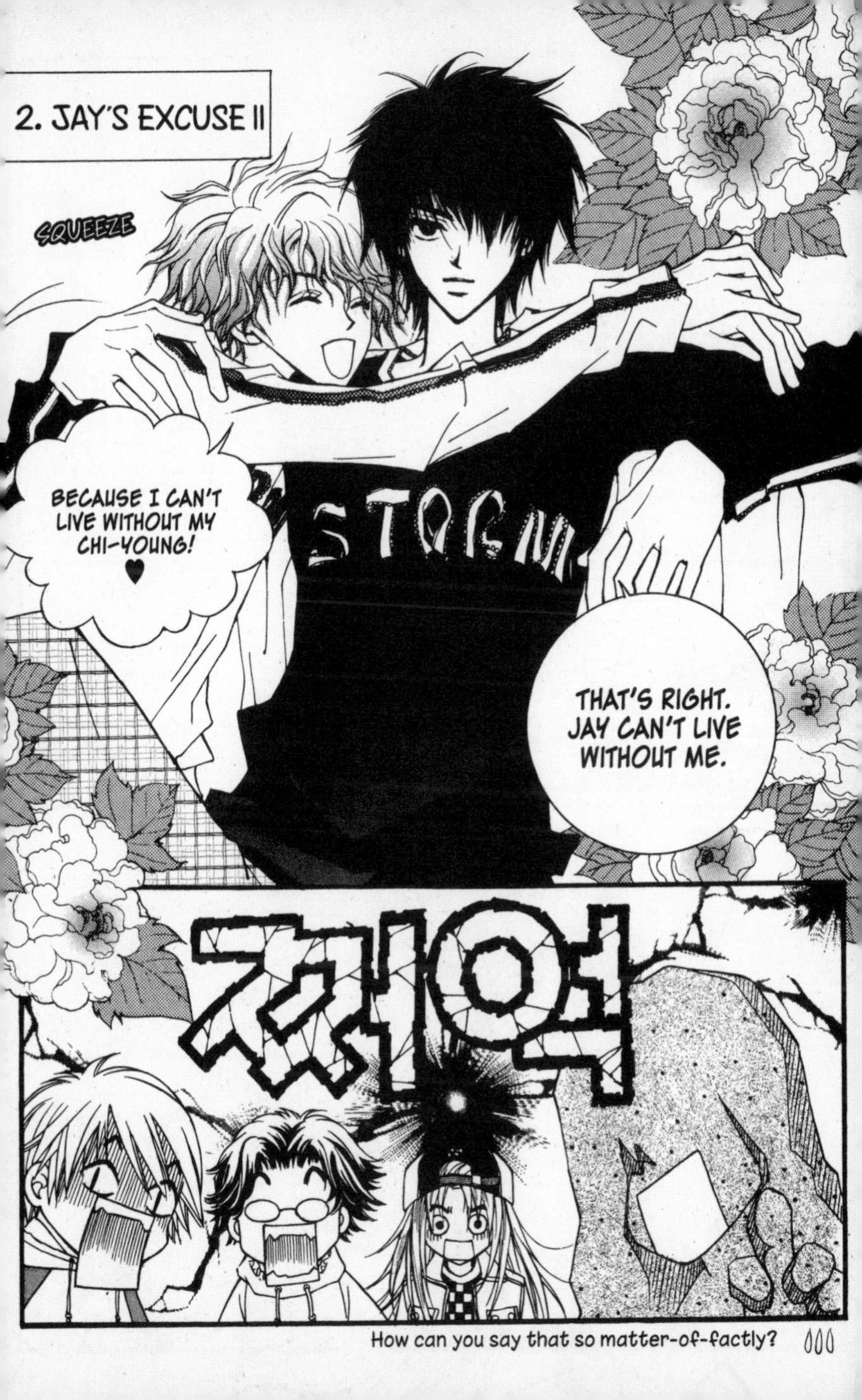
2. JAY'S EXCUSE II
SQUEEZE
BECAUSE I CAN'T LIVE WITHOUT MY CHI-YOUNG! ♥
THAT'S RIGHT. JAY CAN'T LIVE WITHOUT ME.
How can you say that so matter-of-factly?

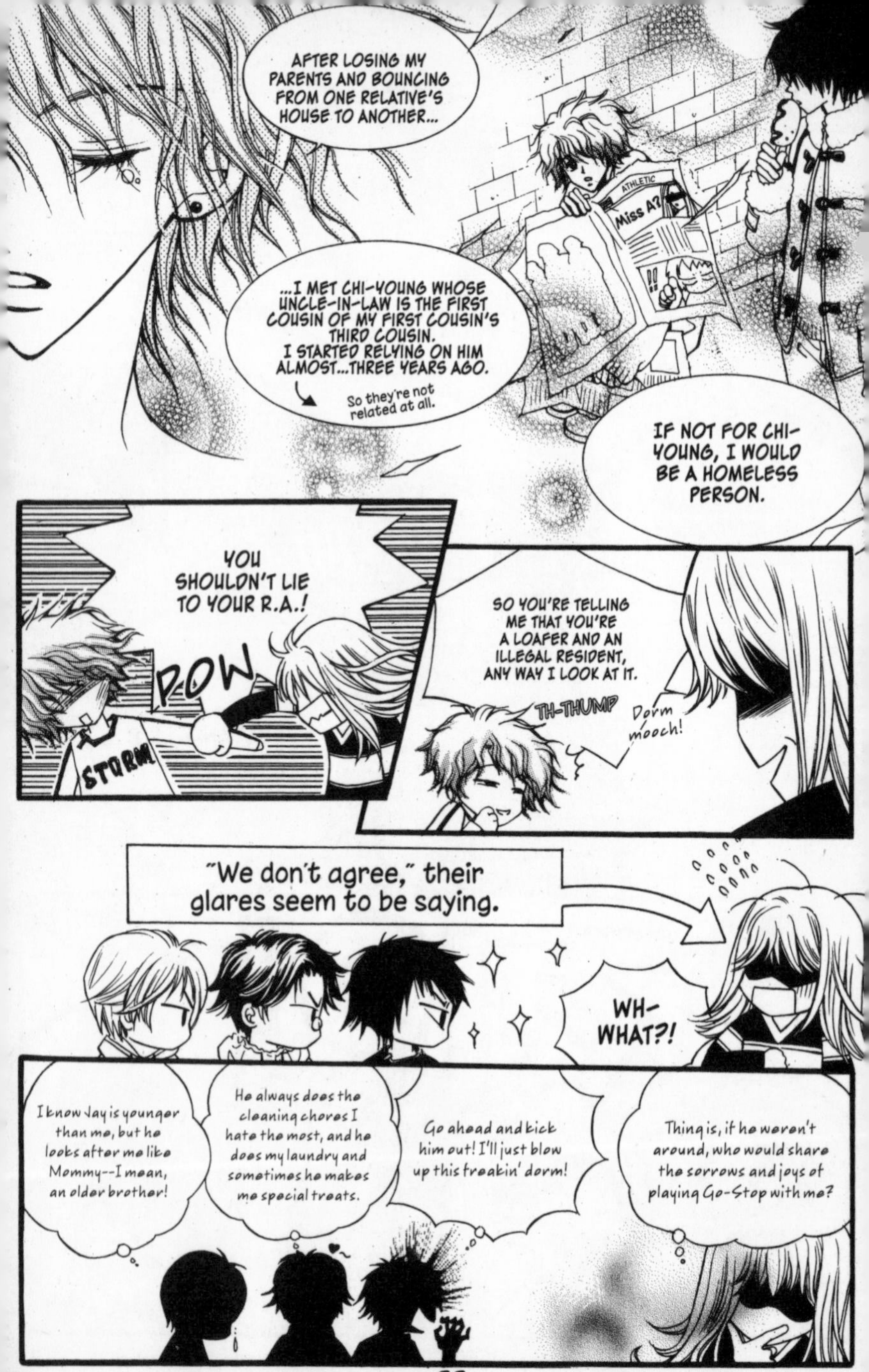
AFTER LOSING MY PARENTS AND BOUNCING FROM ONE RELATIVE'S HOUSE TO ANOTHER...
ATHLETIC
Miss A?
!!
...I MET CHI-YOUNG WHOSE UNCLE-IN-LAW IS THE FIRST COUSIN OF MY FIRST COUSIN'S THIRD COUSIN. I STARTED RELYING ON HIM ALMOST...THREE YEARS AGO.
So they're not related at all.
IF NOT FOR CHI-YOUNG, I WOULD BE A HOMELESS PERSON.
YOU SHOULDN'T LIE TO YOUR R.A.!
POW
STORM
SO YOU'RE TELLING ME THAT YOU'RE A LOAFER AND AN ILLEGAL RESIDENT, ANY WAY I LOOK AT IT.
TH-THUMP
Dorm mooch!
"We don't agree," their glares seem to be saying.
WH-WHAT?!
I know Jay is younger than me, but he looks after me like Mommy--I mean, an older brother!
He always does the cleaning chores I hate the most, and he does my laundry and sometimes he makes me special treats.
Go ahead and kick him out! I'll just blow up this freakin' dorm!
Thing is, if he weren't around, who would share the sorrows and joys of playing Go-Stop with me?

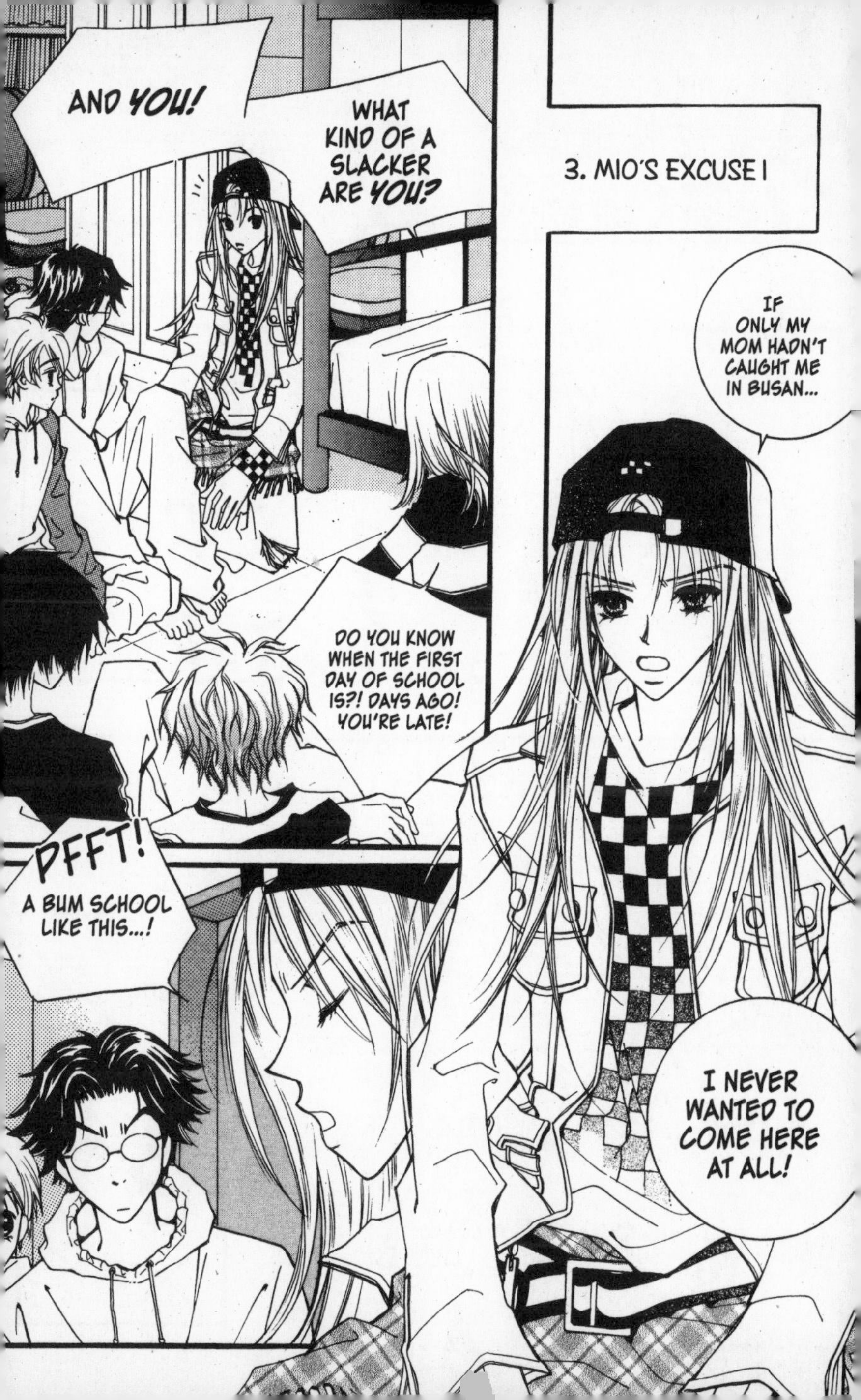
AND YOU!
WHAT KIND OF A SLACKER ARE YOU?
DO YOU KNOW WHEN THE FIRST DAY OF SCHOOL IS?! DAYS AGO! YOU'RE LATE!
PFFT!
A BUM SCHOOL LIKE THIS...!
3. MIO'S EXCUSE I
IF ONLY MY MOM HADN'T CAUGHT ME IN BUSAN...
I NEVER WANTED TO COME HERE AT ALL!

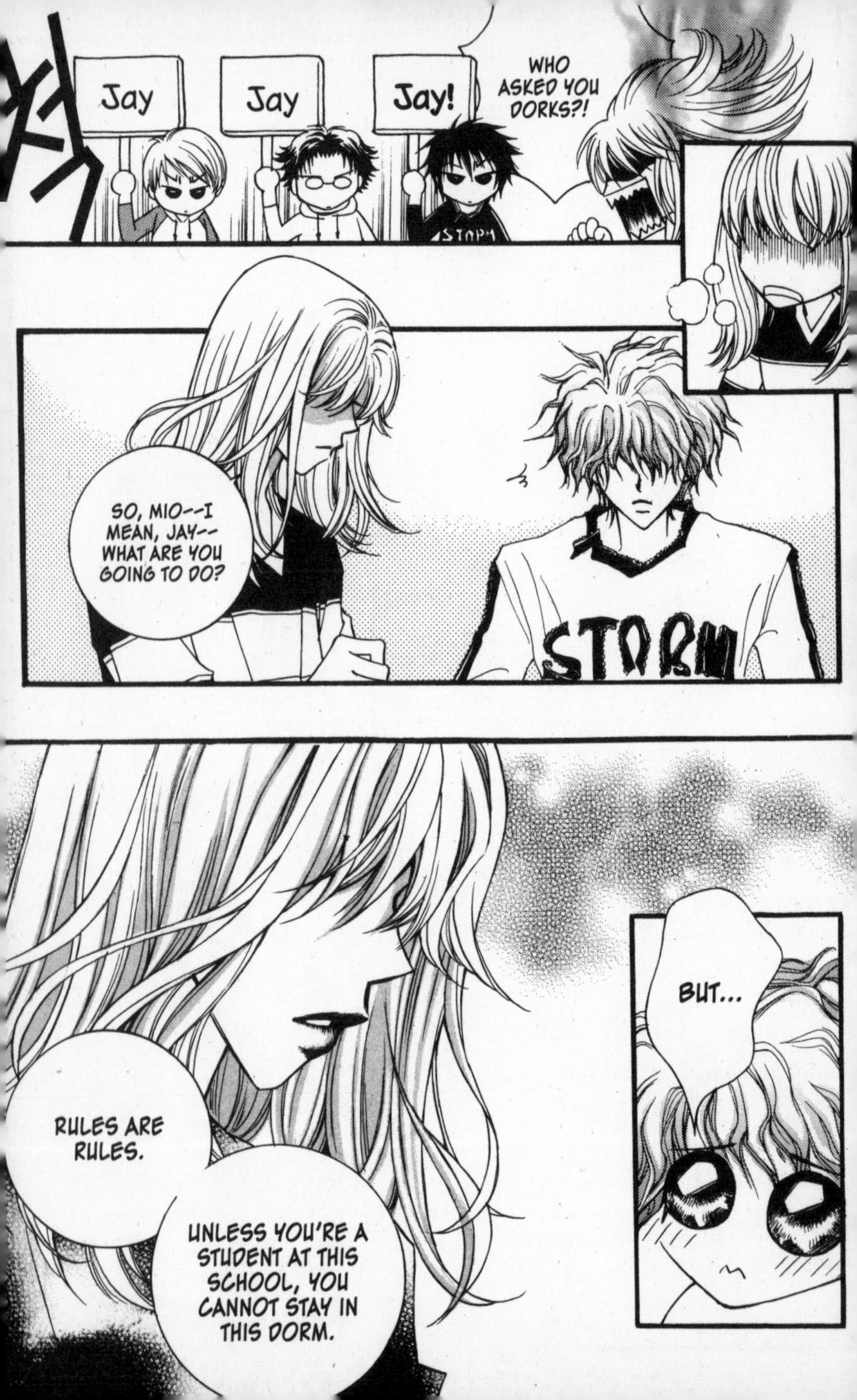
Jay
Jay
Jay!
WHO ASKED YOU DORKS?!
SO, MIO--I MEAN, JAY--WHAT ARE YOU GOING TO DO?
RULES ARE RULES.
UNLESS YOU'RE A STUDENT AT THIS SCHOOL, YOU CANNOT STAY IN THIS DORM.
BUT...

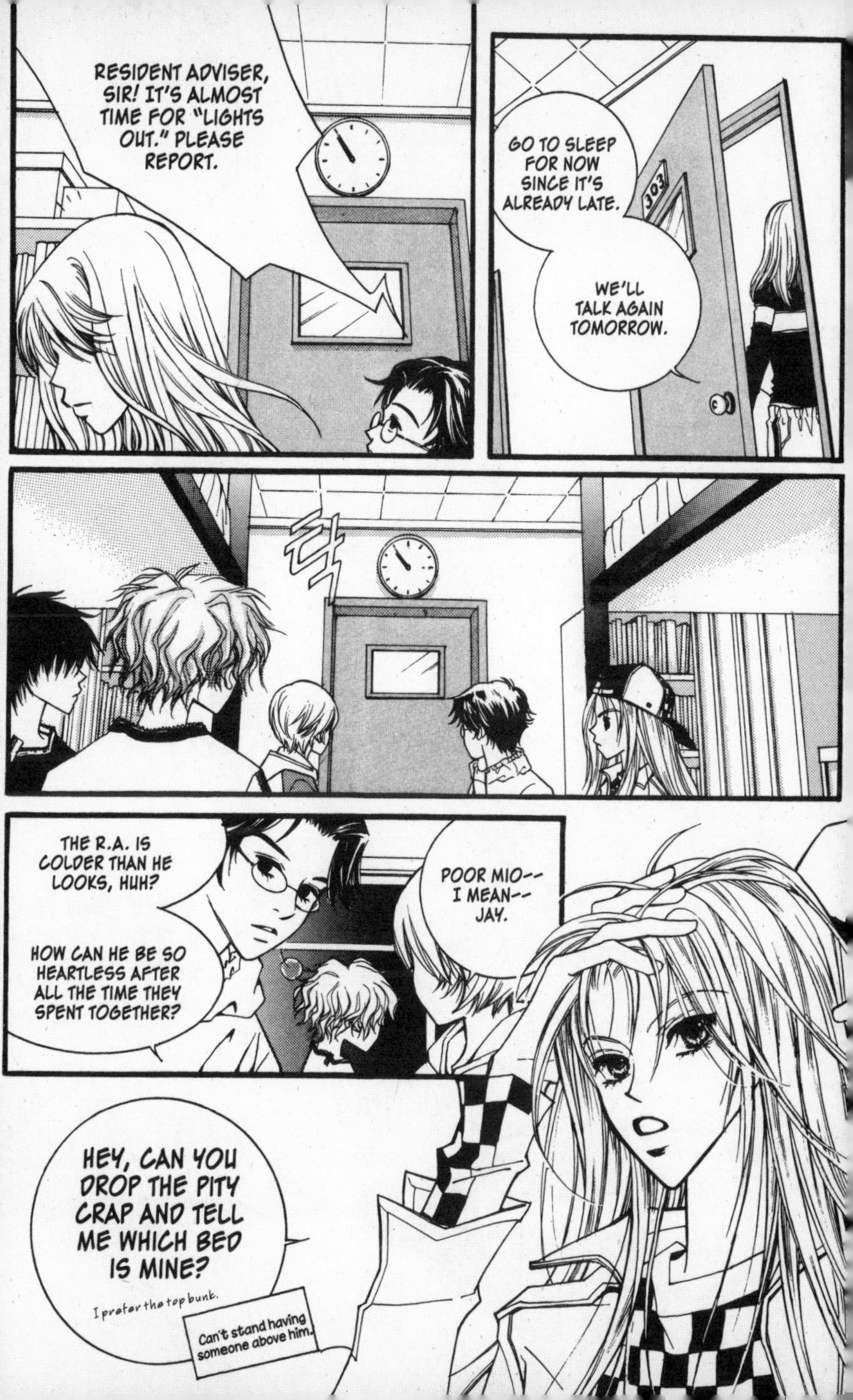

RESIDENT ADVISER, SIR! IT'S ALMOST TIME FOR "LIGHTS OUT." PLEASE REPORT.
GO TO SLEEP FOR NOW SINCE IT'S ALREADY LATE.
WE'LL TALK AGAIN TOMORROW.
303
THE R.A. IS COLDER THAN HE LOOKS, HUH?
HOW CAN HE BE SO HEARTLESS AFTER ALL THE TIME THEY SPENT TOGETHER?
POOR MIO-- I MEAN-- JAY.
HEY, CAN YOU DROP THE PITY CRAP AND TELL ME WHICH BED IS MINE?
I prefer the top bunk.
Can't stand having someone above him.

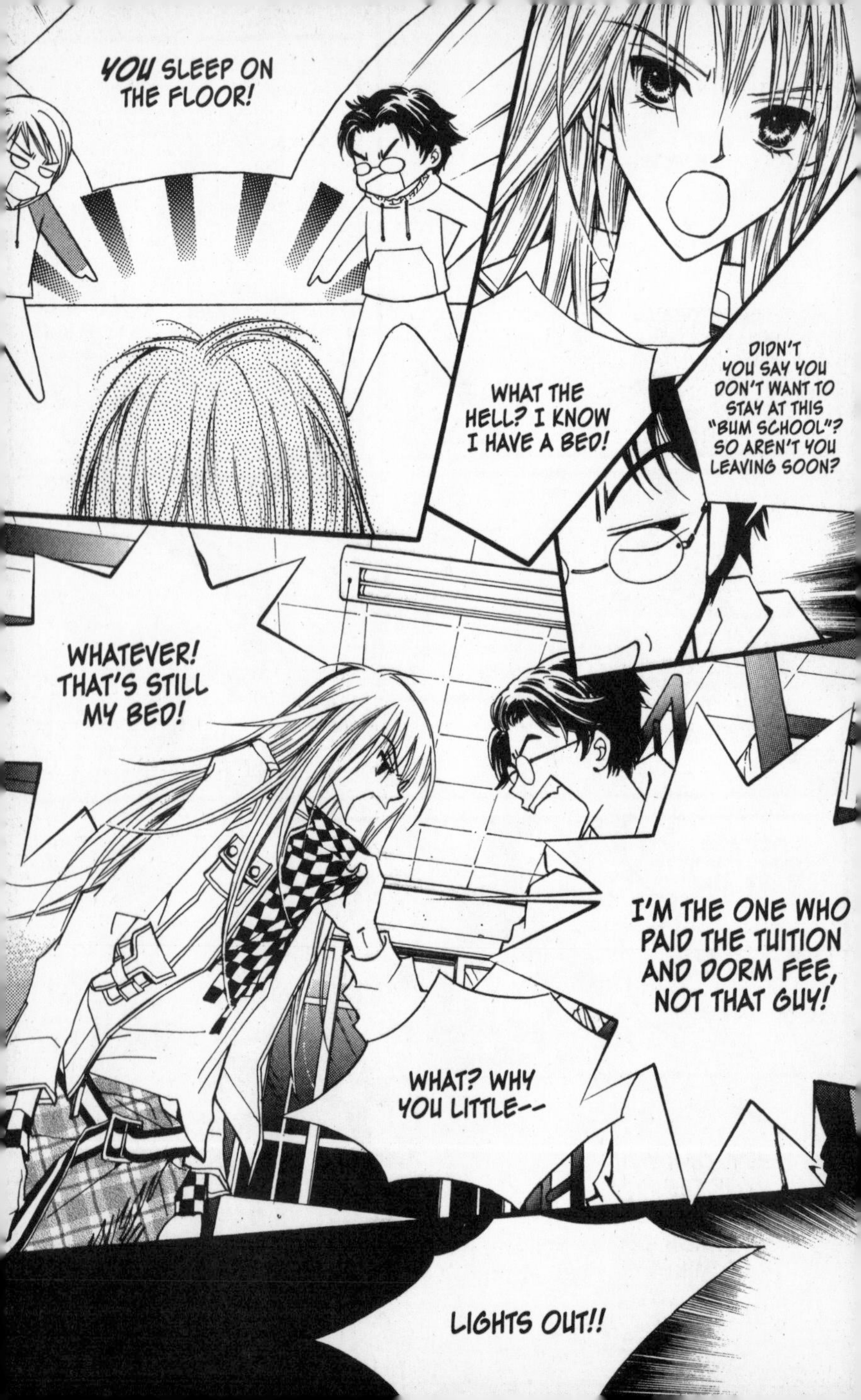
YOU SLEEP ON THE FLOOR!
WHAT THE HELL? I KNOW I HAVE A BED!
DIDN'T YOU SAY YOU DON'T WANT TO STAY AT THIS "BUM SCHOOL"? SO AREN'T YOU LEAVING SOON?
WHATEVER! THAT'S STILL MY BED!
I'M THE ONE WHO PAID THE TUITION AND DORM FEE, NOT THAT GUY!
WHAT? WHY YOU LITTLE--
LIGHTS OUT!!

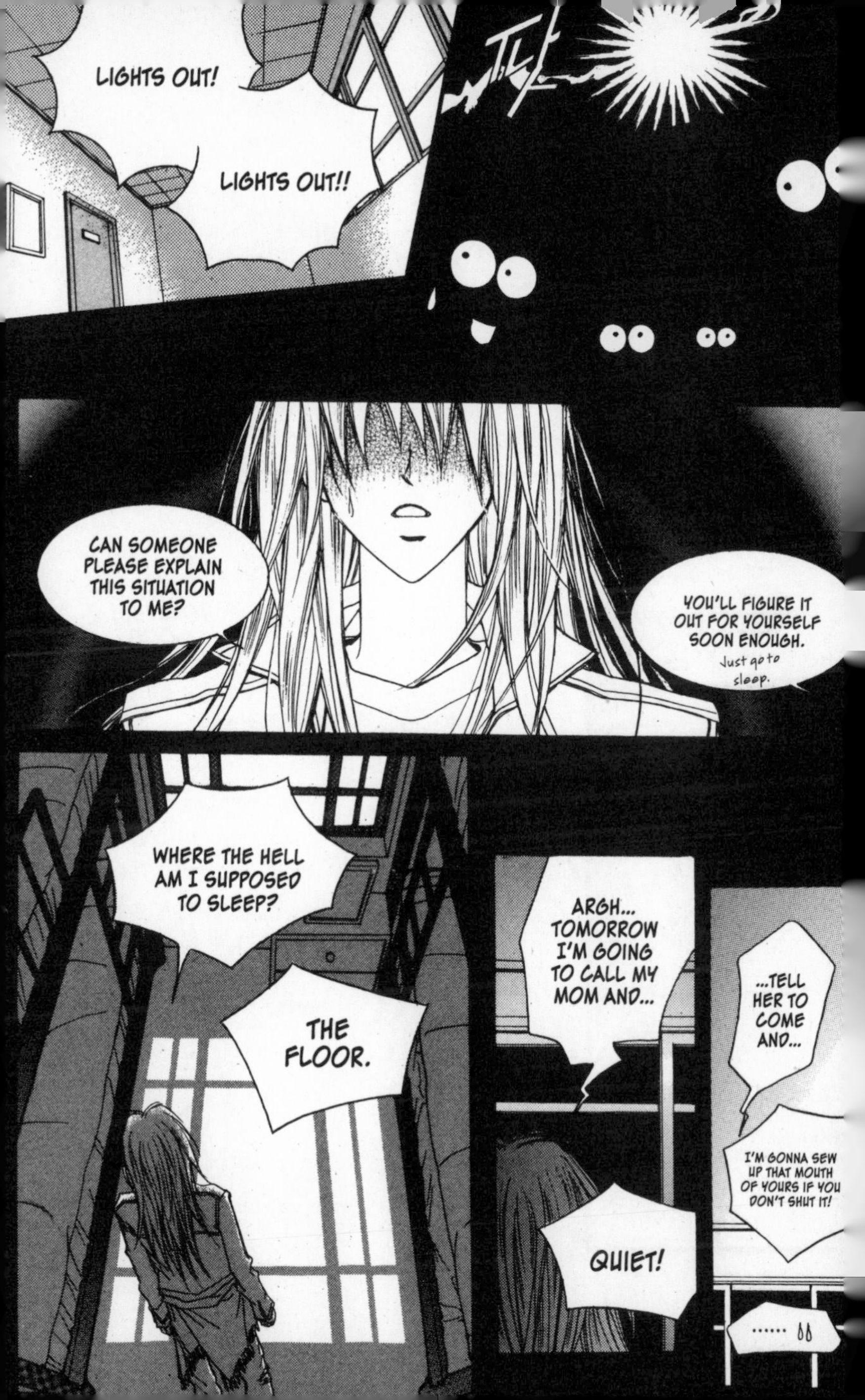
LIGHTS OUT!
LIGHTS OUT!!
CAN SOMEONE PLEASE EXPLAIN THIS SITUATION TO ME?
YOU'LL FIGURE IT OUT FOR YOURSELF SOON ENOUGH.
Just go to sleep.
WHERE THE HELL AM I SUPPOSED TO SLEEP?
THE FLOOR.
ARGH... TOMORROW I'M GOING TO CALL MY MOM AND...
...TELL HER TO COME AND...
I'M GONNA SEW UP THAT MOUTH OF YOURS IF YOU DON'T SHUT IT!
QUIET!
......

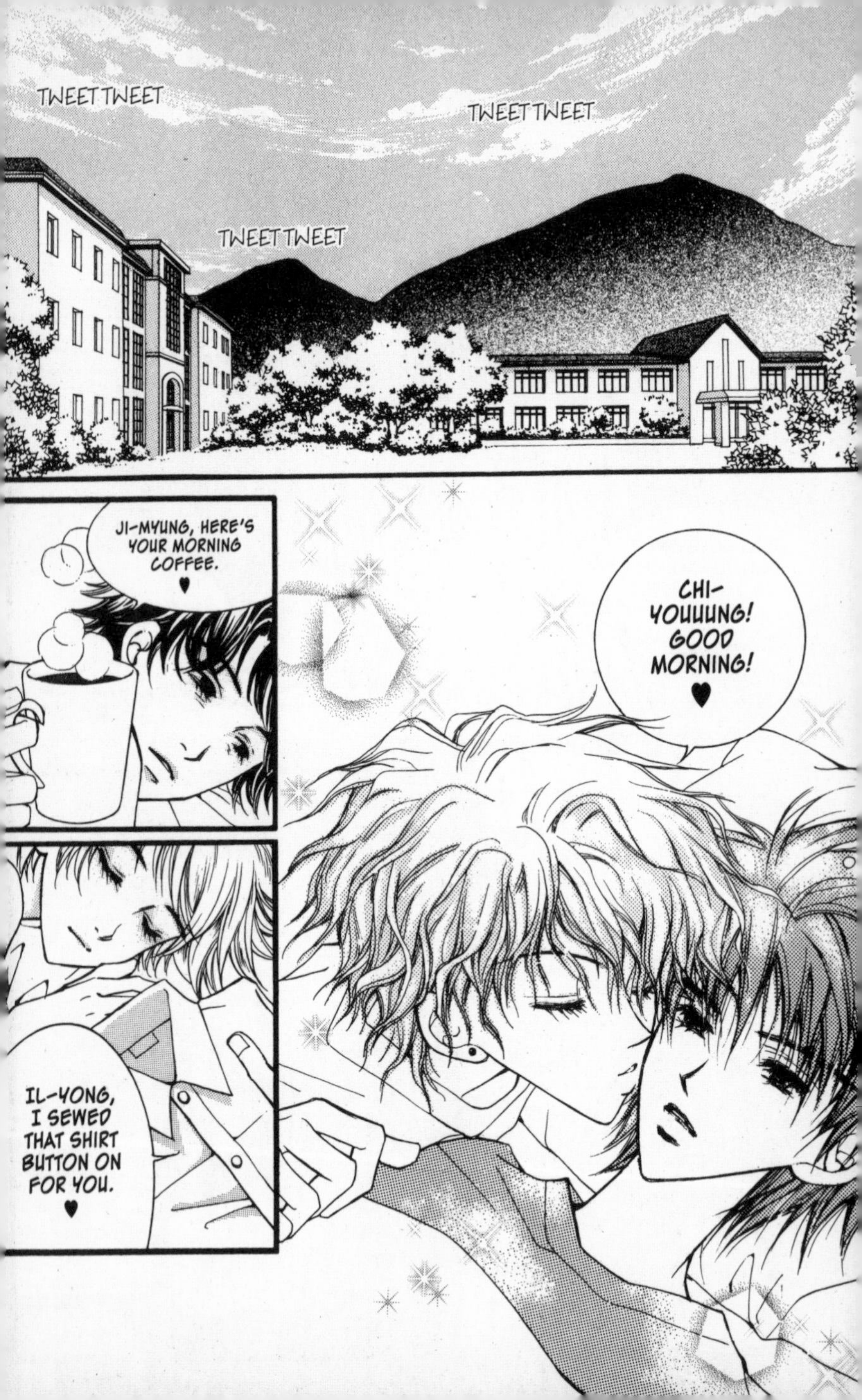
TWEET TWEET
TWEET TWEET
TWEET TWEET
JI-MYUNG, HERE'S YOUR MORNING COFFEE. ♥
IL-YONG, I SEWED THAT SHIRT BUTTON ON FOR YOU. ♥
CHI-YOUUUNG! GOOD MORNING! ♥

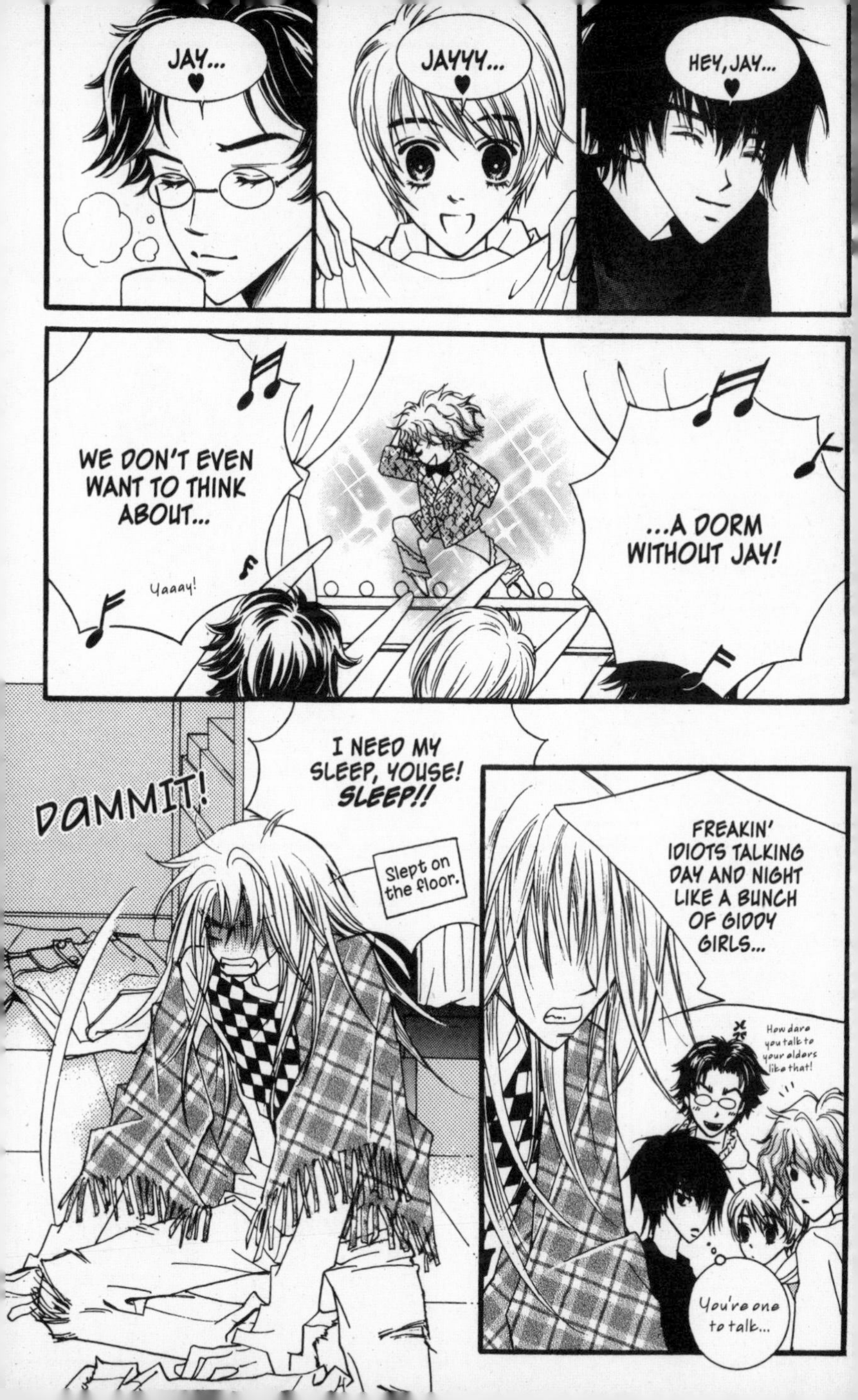

JAY...
JAYYY...
HEY, JAY...
WE DON'T EVEN WANT TO THINK ABOUT...
Yaaay!
...A DORM WITHOUT JAY!
DAMMIT!
I NEED MY SLEEP, YOUSE! SLEEP!!
Slept on the floor.
FREAKIN' IDIOTS TALKING DAY AND NIGHT LIKE A BUNCH OF GIDDY GIRLS...
How dare you talk to your elders like that!
You're one to talk...

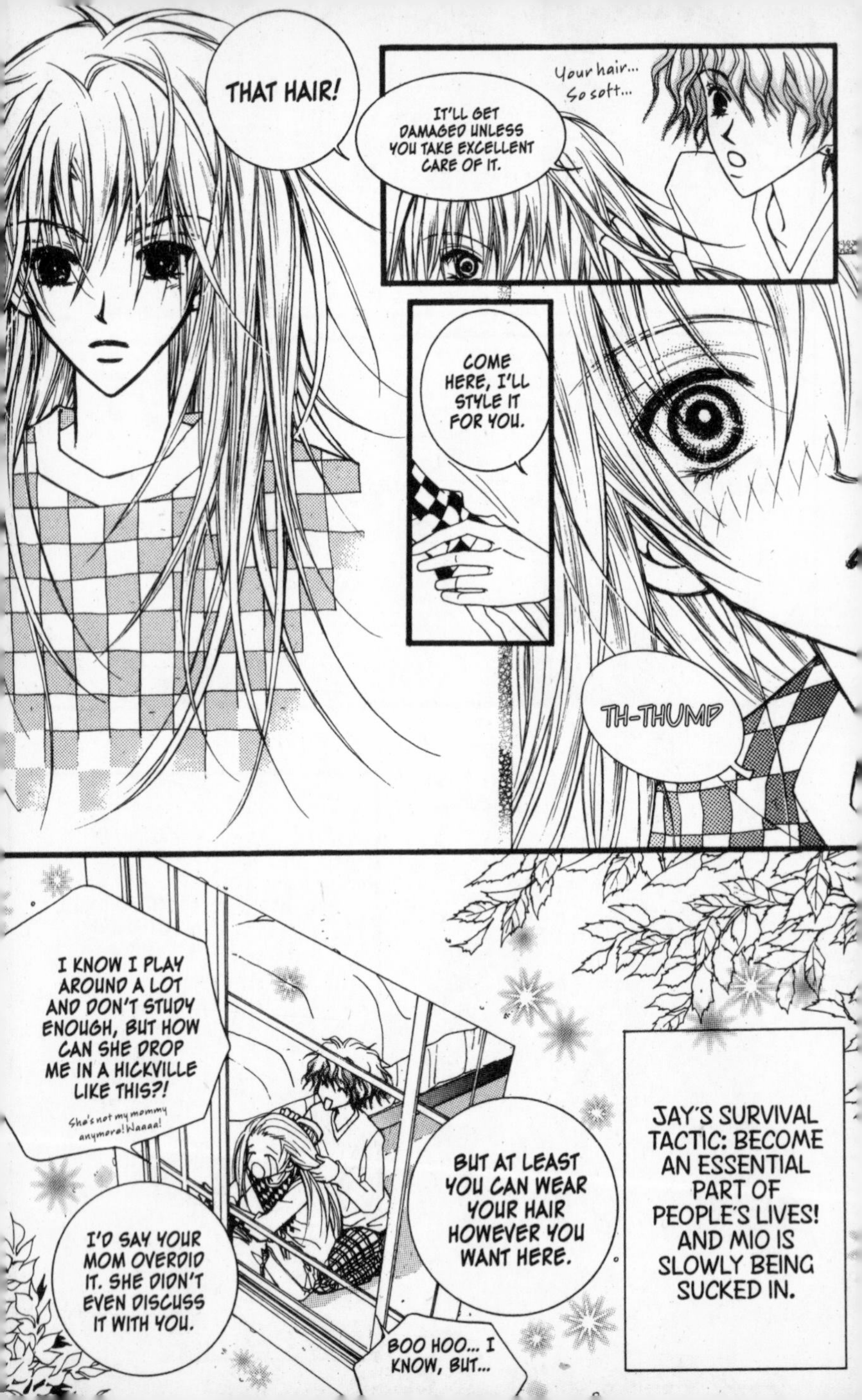
THAT HAIR!
IT'LL GET DAMAGED UNLESS YOU TAKE EXCELLENT CARE OF IT.
Your hair... So soft...
COME HERE, I'LL STYLE IT FOR YOU.
TH-THUMP
I KNOW I PLAY AROUND A LOT AND DON'T STUDY ENOUGH, BUT HOW CAN SHE DROP ME IN A HICKVILLE LIKE THIS?!
She's not my mommy anymore! Waaaa!
I'D SAY YOUR MOM OVERDID IT. SHE DIDN'T EVEN DISCUSS IT WITH YOU.
BUT AT LEAST YOU CAN WEAR YOUR HAIR HOWEVER YOU WANT HERE.
BOO HOO... I KNOW, BUT...
JAY'S SURVIVAL TACTIC: BECOME AN ESSENTIAL PART OF PEOPLE'S LIVES! AND MIO IS SLOWLY BEING SUCKED IN.

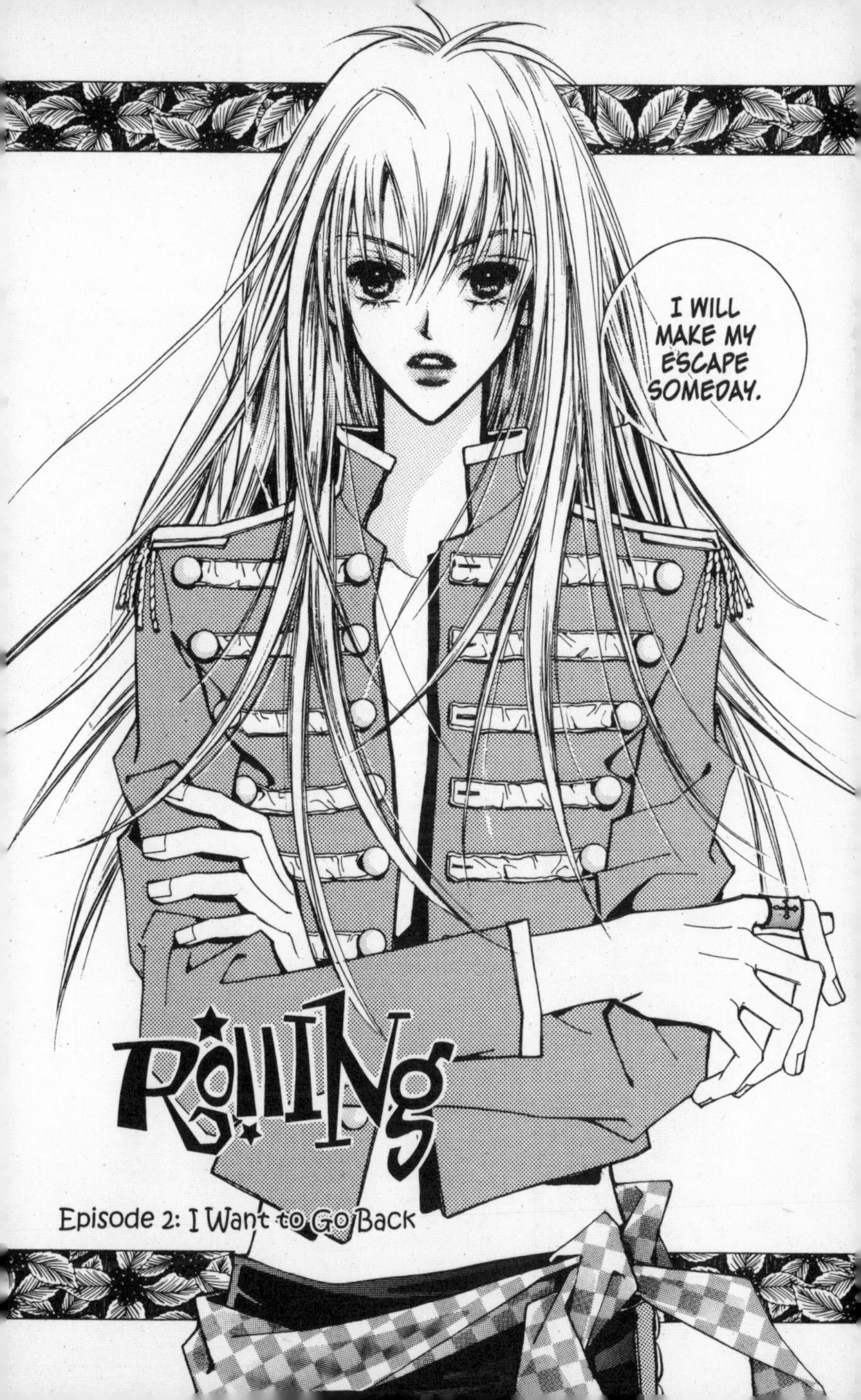
I WILL MAKE MY ESCAPE SOMEDAY.
Rolling
Episode 2: I Want to Go Back

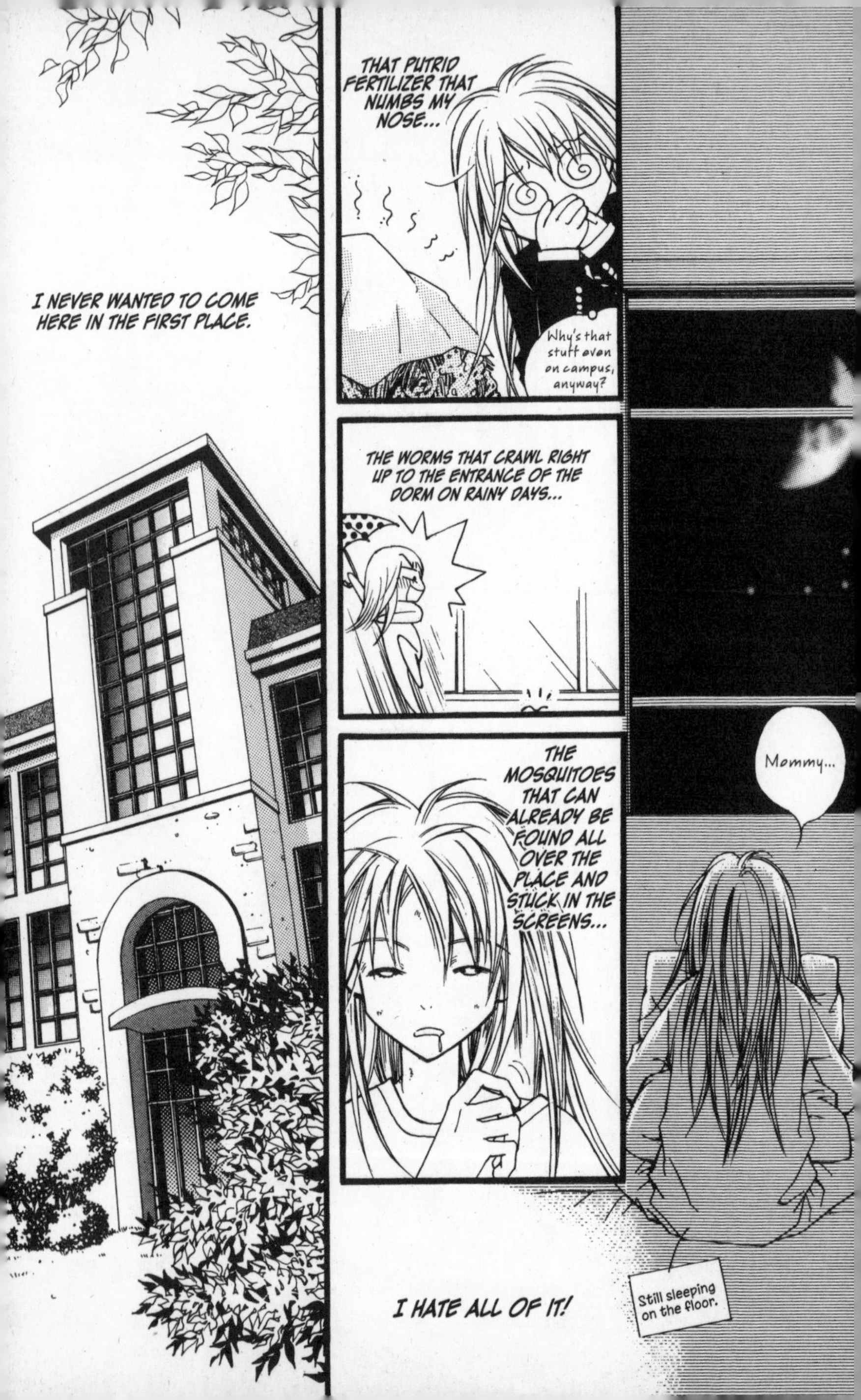
I NEVER WANTED TO COME HERE IN THE FIRST PLACE.
THAT PUTRID FERTILIZER THAT NUMBS MY NOSE...
Why's that stuff even on campus, anyway?
THE WORMS THAT CRAWL RIGHT UP TO THE ENTRANCE OF THE DORM ON RAINY DAYS...
THE MOSQUITOES THAT CAN ALREADY BE FOUND ALL OVER THE PLACE AND STUCK IN THE SCREENS...
I HATE ALL OF IT!
Mommy...
Still sleeping on the floor.

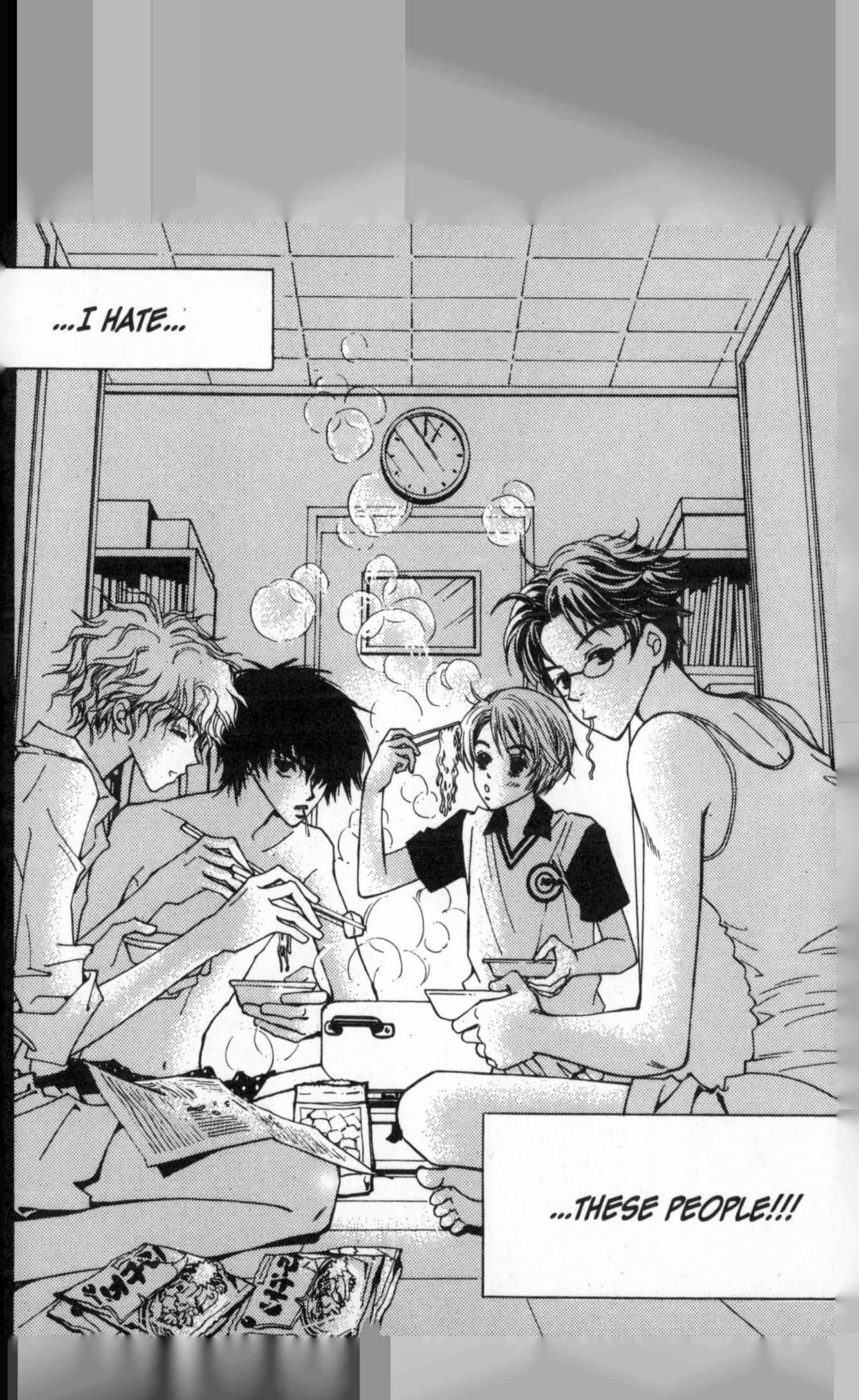
...I HATE...
...THESE PEOPLE!!!

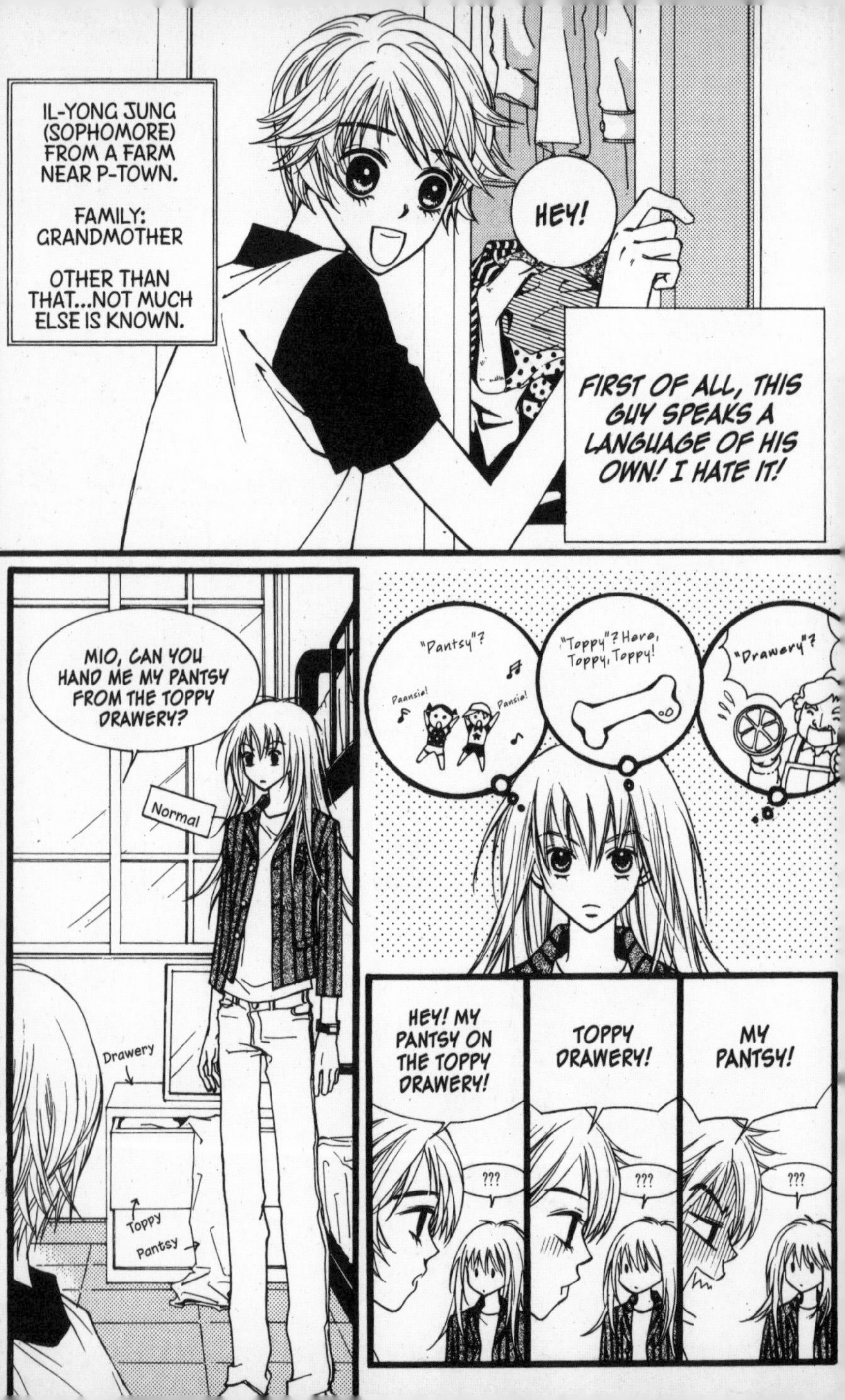
IL-YONG JUNG (SOPHOMORE) FROM A FARM NEAR P-TOWN.
FAMILY: GRANDMOTHER
OTHER THAN THAT...NOT MUCH ELSE IS KNOWN.
HEY!
FIRST OF ALL, THIS GUY SPEAKS A LANGUAGE OF HIS OWN! I HATE IT!
MIO, CAN YOU HAND ME MY PANTSY FROM THE TOPPY DRAWERY?
Normal
Drawery
Toppy
Pantsy
"Pantsy"?
Paansie!
Pansie!
"Toppy"? Here, Toppy, Toppy!
"Drawery"?
HEY! MY PANTSY ON THE TOPPY DRAWERY!
???
TOPPY DRAWERY!
???
MY PANTSY!
???

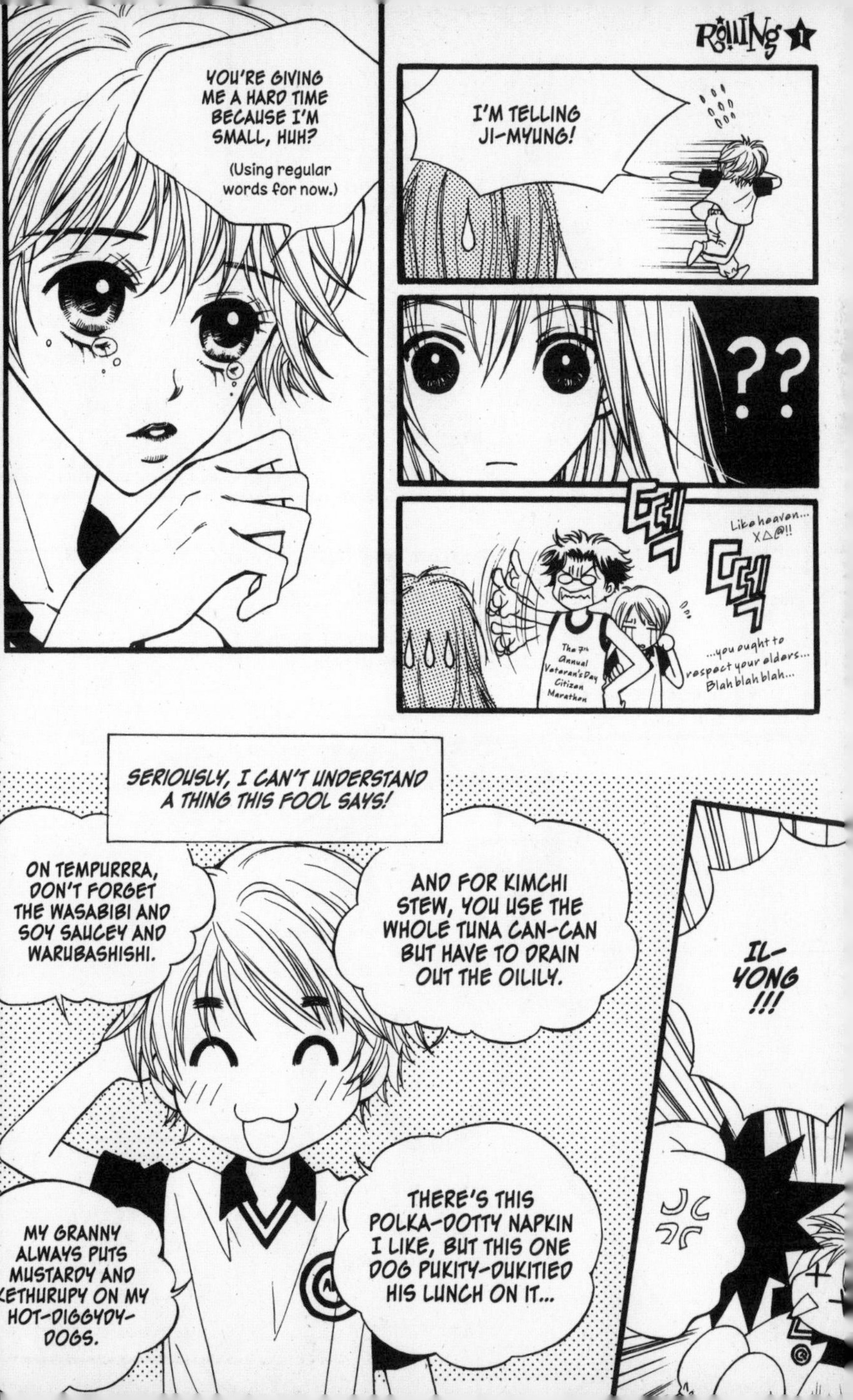
YOU'RE GIVING ME A HARD TIME BECAUSE I'M SMALL, HUH?
(Using regular words for now.)
I'M TELLING JI-MYUNG!
??
Like heaven... X△@!!
The 7th Annual Veteran's Day Citizen Marathon
...you ought to respect your elders... Blah blah blah...
SERIOUSLY, I CAN'T UNDERSTAND A THING THIS FOOL SAYS!
ON TEMPURRRA, DON'T FORGET THE WASABIBI AND SOY SAUCEY AND WARUBASHISHI.
AND FOR KIMCHI STEW, YOU USE THE WHOLE TUNA CAN-CAN BUT HAVE TO DRAIN OUT THE OILILY.
MY GRANNY ALWAYS PUTS MUSTARDY AND KETHURUPY ON MY HOT-DIGGYDY-DOGS.
THERE'S THIS POLKA-DOTTY NAPKIN I LIKE, BUT THIS ONE DOG PUKITY-DUKITIED HIS LUNCH ON IT...
IL-YONG !!!

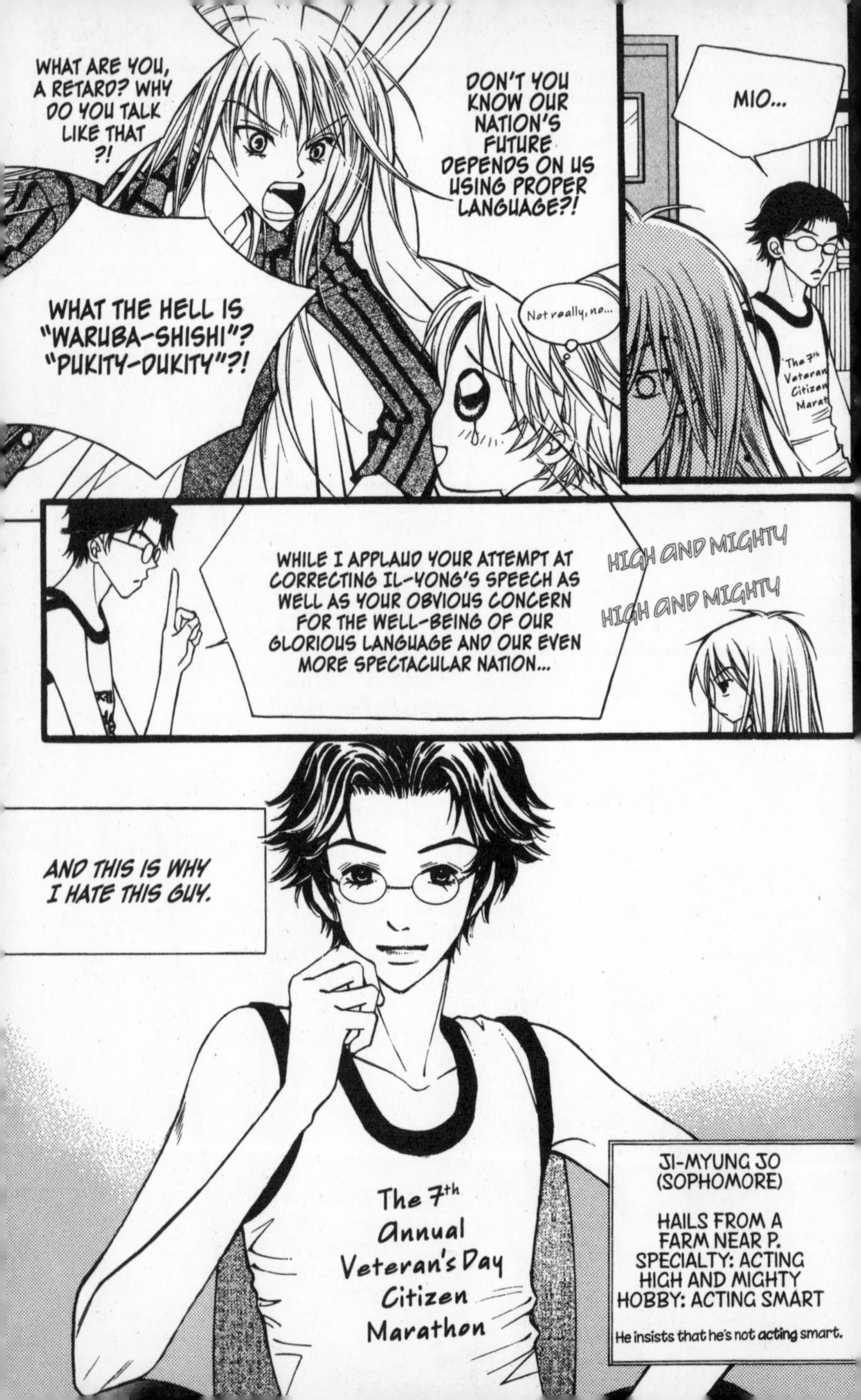

WHAT ARE YOU, A RETARD? WHY DO YOU TALK LIKE THAT ?!
DON'T YOU KNOW OUR NATION'S FUTURE DEPENDS ON US USING PROPER LANGUAGE?!
WHAT THE HELL IS "WARUBA-SHISHI"? "PUKITY-DUKITY"?!
Not really, no...
MIO...
The 7th Veteran Citizen Marat
WHILE I APPLAUD YOUR ATTEMPT AT CORRECTING IL-YONG'S SPEECH AS WELL AS YOUR OBVIOUS CONCERN FOR THE WELL-BEING OF OUR GLORIOUS LANGUAGE AND OUR EVEN MORE SPECTACULAR NATION...
HIGH AND MIGHTY
HIGH AND MIGHTY
AND THIS IS WHY I HATE THIS GUY.
The 7th Annual Veteran's Day Citizen Marathon
JI-MYUNG JO (SOPHOMORE)
HAILS FROM A FARM NEAR P.
SPECIALTY: ACTING HIGH AND MIGHTY
HOBBY: ACTING SMART
He insists that he's not acting smart.

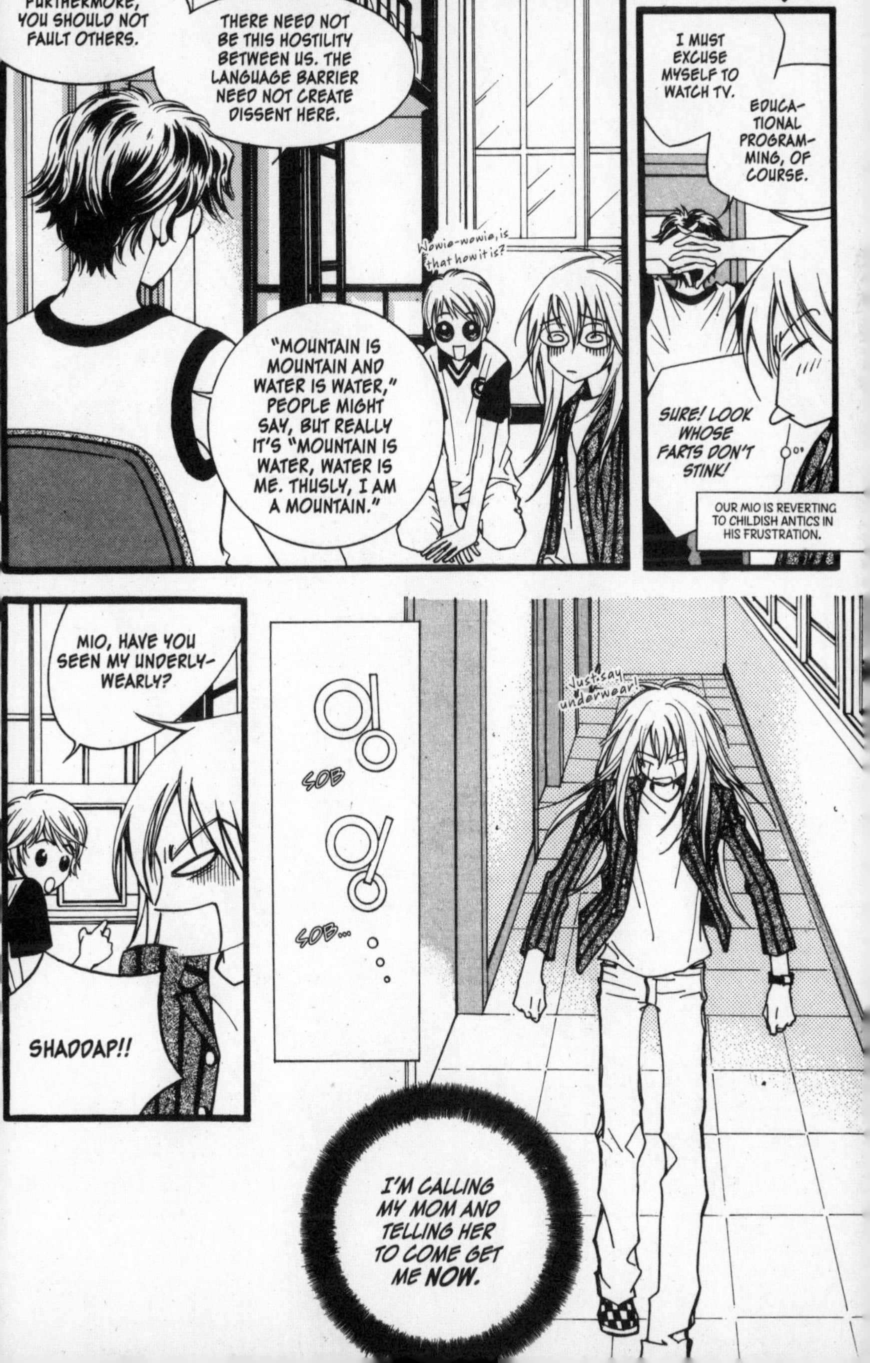
FURTHERMORE, YOU SHOULD NOT FAULT OTHERS.
THERE NEED NOT BE THIS HOSTILITY BETWEEN US. THE LANGUAGE BARRIER NEED NOT CREATE DISSENT HERE.
Wowie-wowie, is that how it is?
"MOUNTAIN IS MOUNTAIN AND WATER IS WATER," PEOPLE MIGHT SAY, BUT REALLY IT'S "MOUNTAIN IS WATER, WATER IS ME. THUSLY, I AM A MOUNTAIN."
I MUST EXCUSE MYSELF TO WATCH TV.
EDUCATIONAL PROGRAMMING, OF COURSE.
SURE! LOOK WHOSE FARTS DON'T STINK!
OUR MIO IS REVERTING TO CHILDISH ANTICS IN HIS FRUSTRATION.
MIO, HAVE YOU SEEN MY UNDERLY-WEARLY?
SHADDAP!!
SOB
SOB...
Just say underwear!
I'M CALLING MY MOM AND TELLING HER TO COME GET ME NOW.

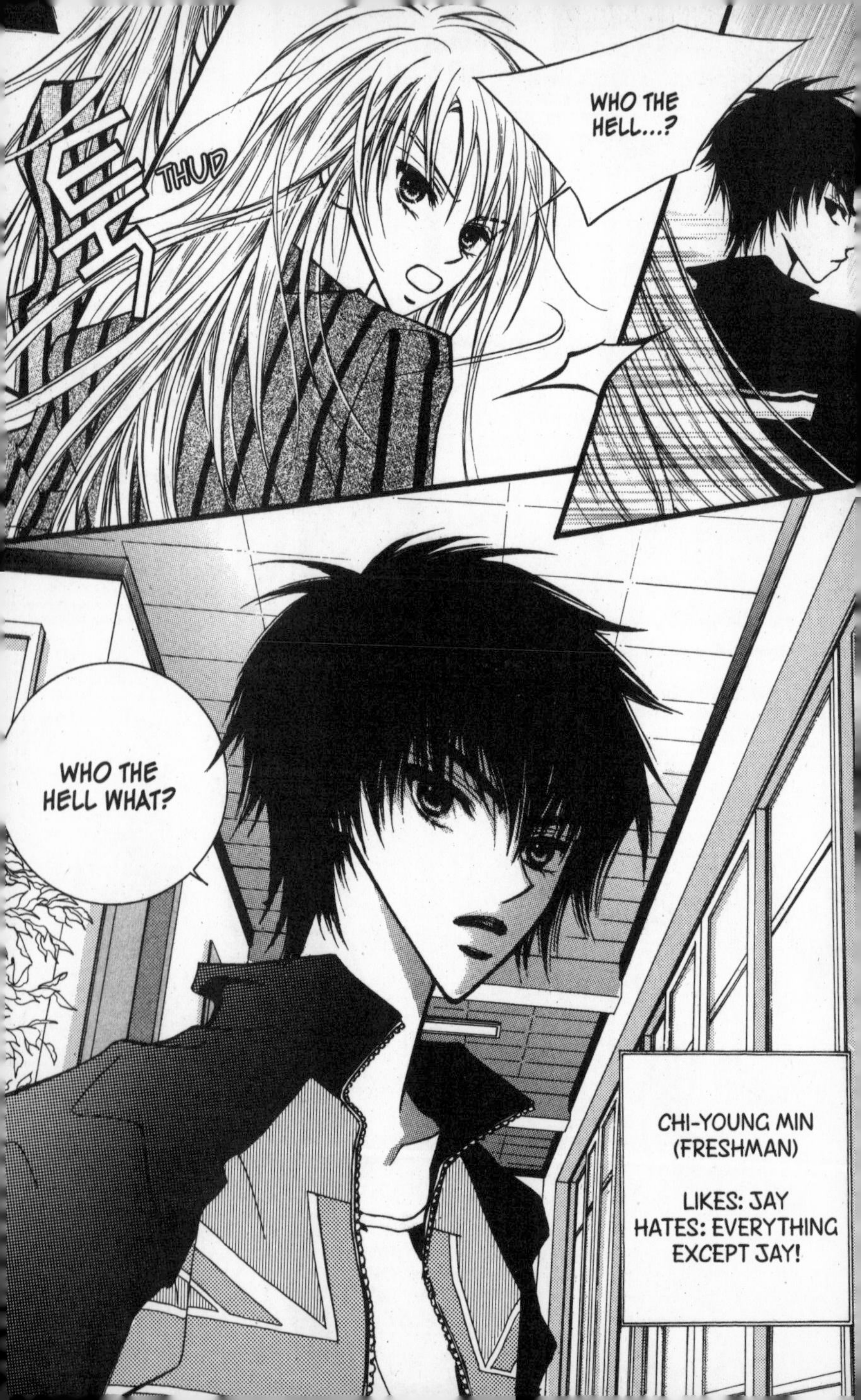
THUD
WHO THE HELL...?
WHO THE HELL WHAT?
CHI-YOUNG MIN
(FRESHMAN)
LIKES: JAY
HATES: EVERYTHING EXCEPT JAY!

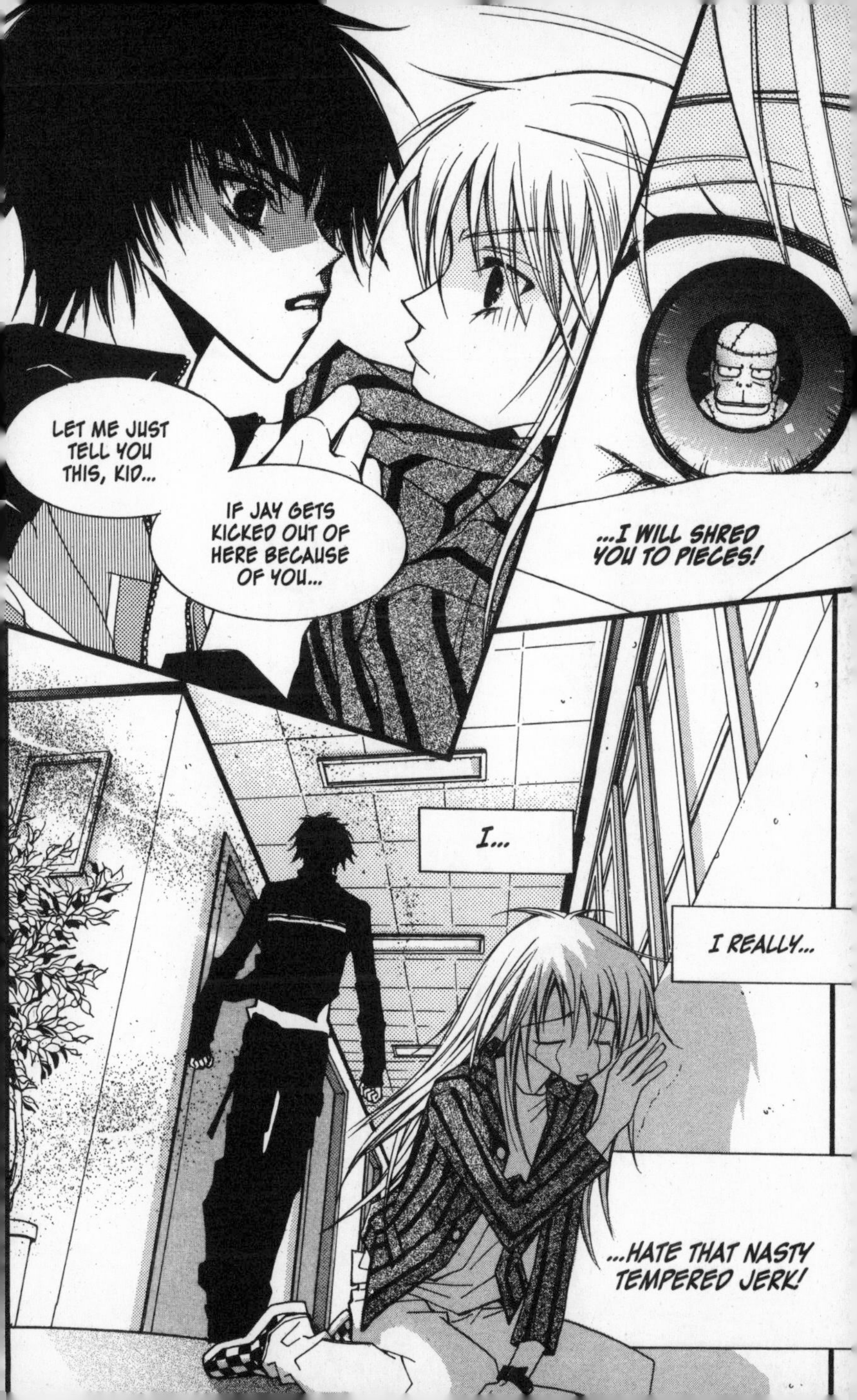
LET ME JUST TELL YOU THIS, KID...
IF JAY GETS KICKED OUT OF HERE BECAUSE OF YOU...
...I WILL SHRED YOU TO PIECES!
I...
I REALLY...
...HATE THAT NASTY TEMPERED JERK!

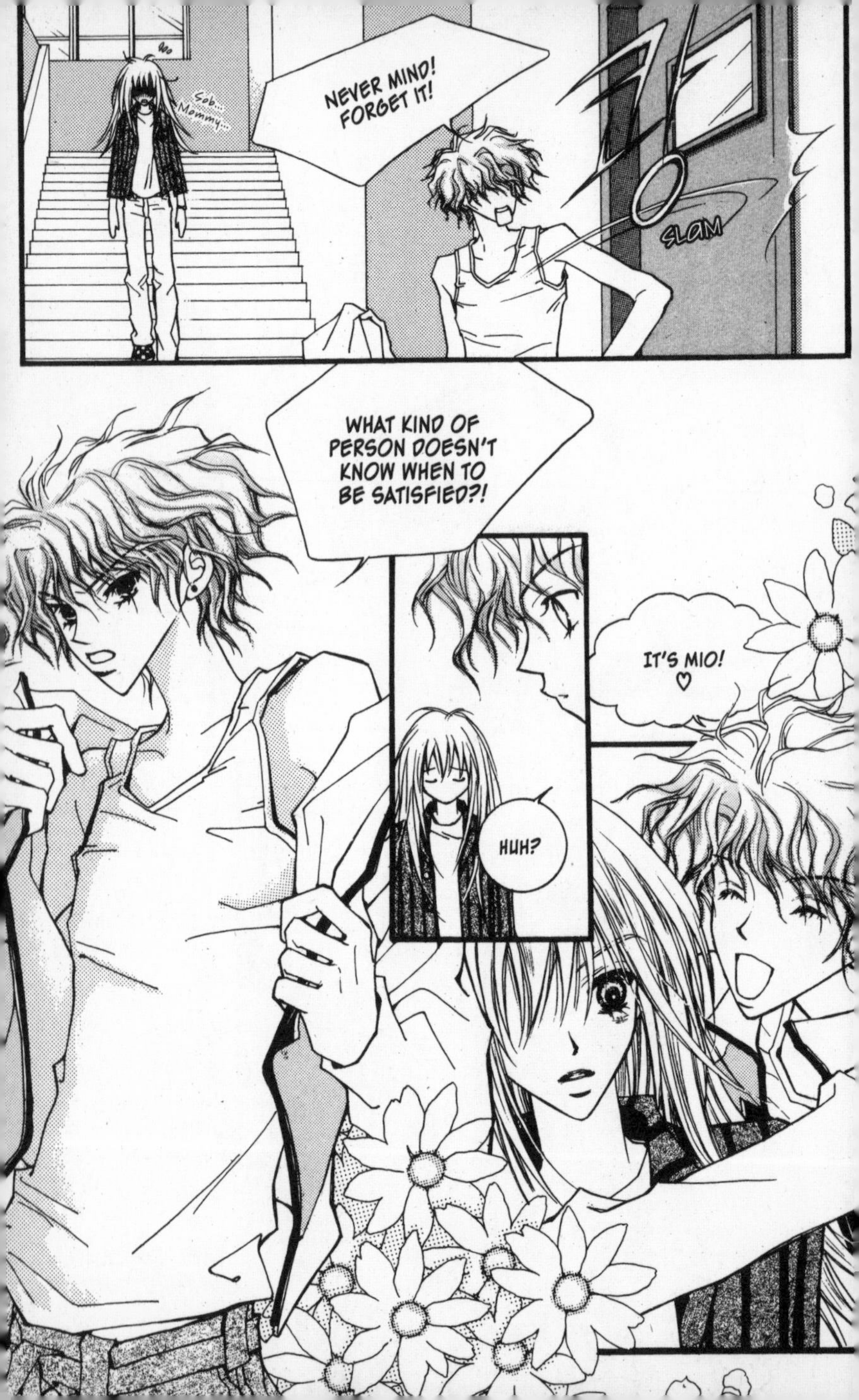
Sob... Mommy...
NEVER MIND! FORGET IT!
SLAM
WHAT KIND OF PERSON DOESN'T KNOW WHEN TO BE SATISFIED?!
HUH?
IT'S MIO! ♡

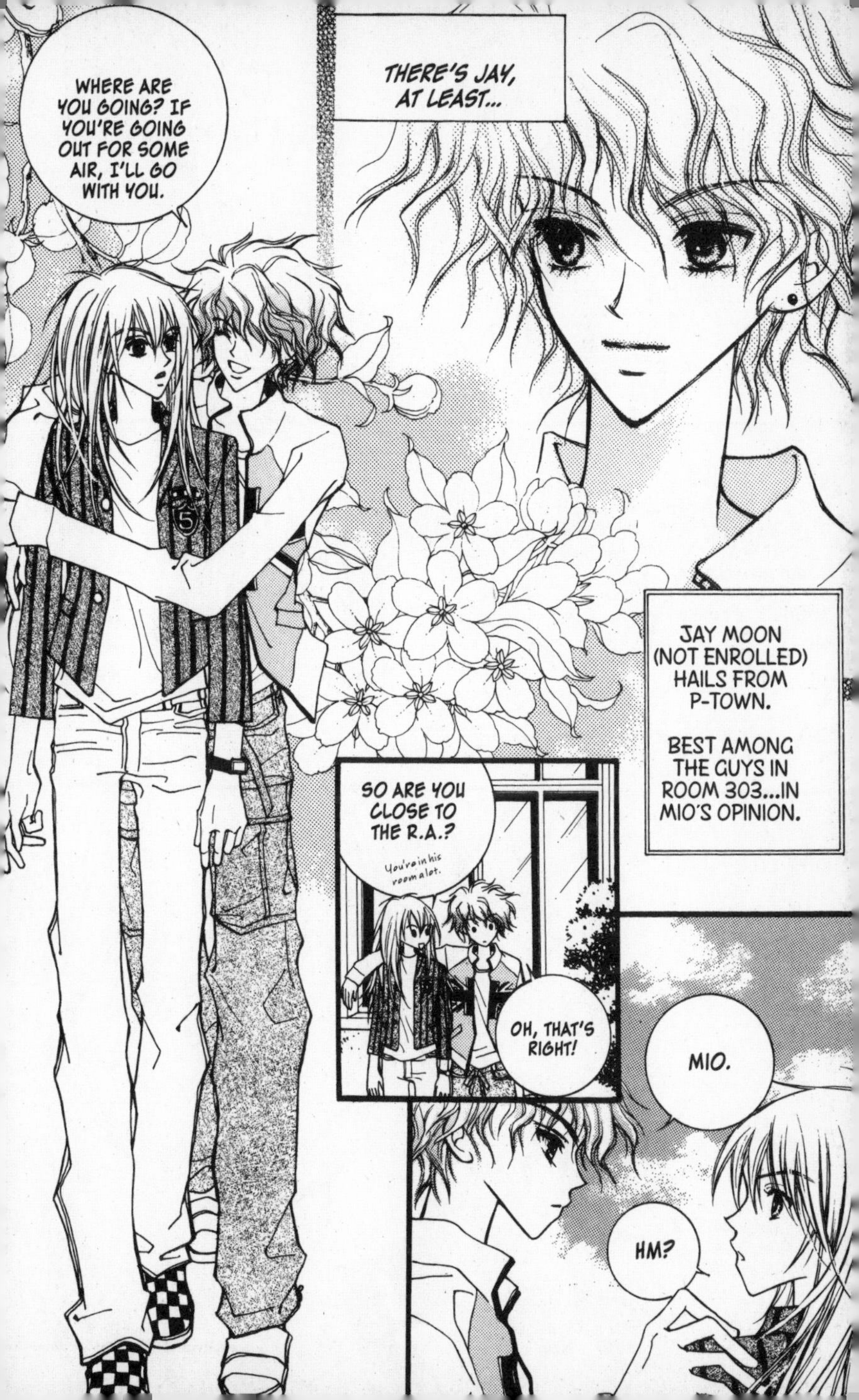
WHERE ARE YOU GOING? IF YOU'RE GOING OUT FOR SOME AIR, I'LL GO WITH YOU.
THERE'S JAY, AT LEAST...
JAY MOON (NOT ENROLLED) HAILS FROM P-TOWN.
BEST AMONG THE GUYS IN ROOM 303...IN MIO'S OPINION.
SO ARE YOU CLOSE TO THE R.A.?
You're in his room a lot.
OH, THAT'S RIGHT!
MIO.
HM?

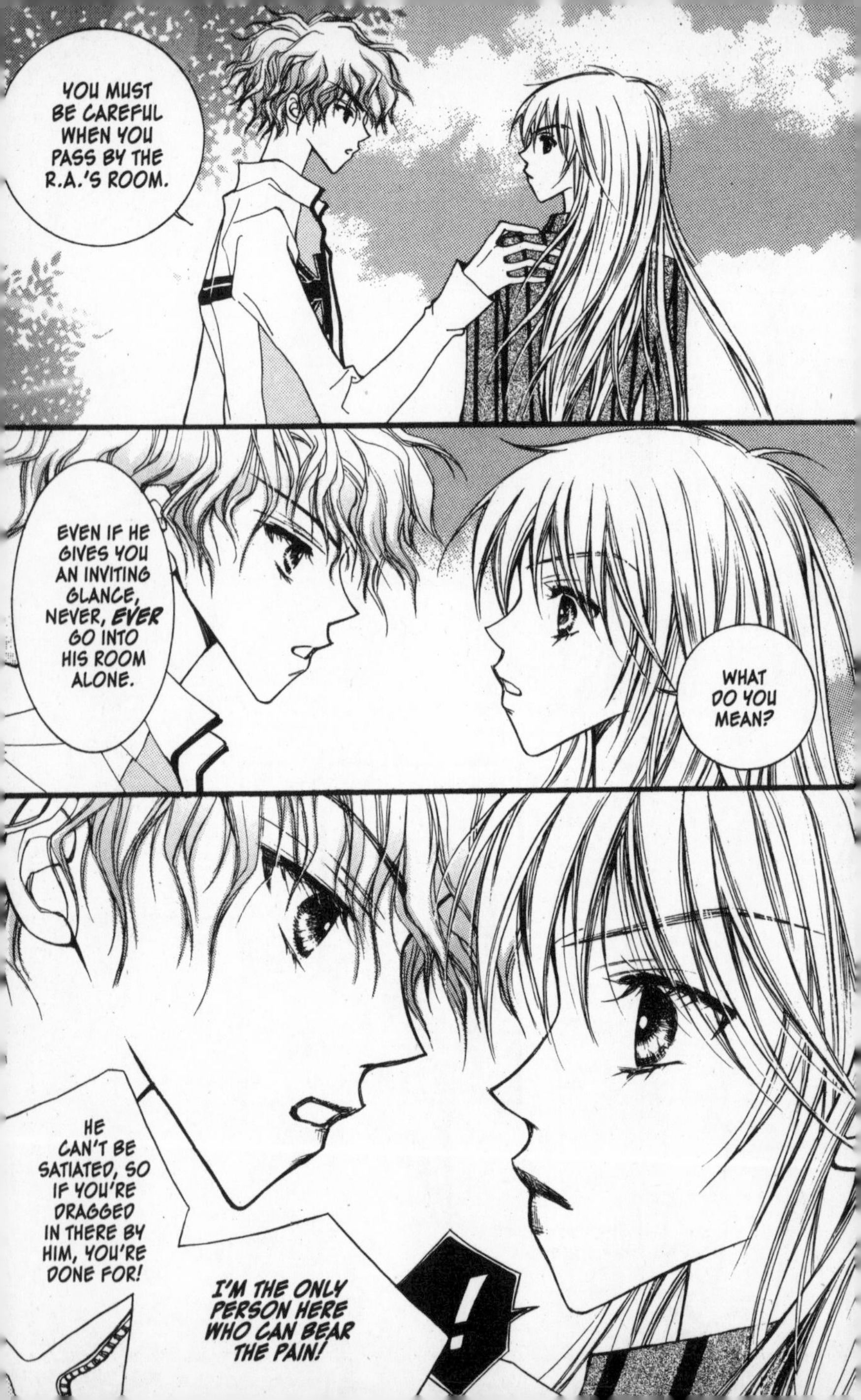
YOU MUST BE CAREFUL WHEN YOU PASS BY THE R.A.'S ROOM.
WHAT DO YOU MEAN?
EVEN IF HE GIVES YOU AN INVITING GLANCE, NEVER, *EVER* GO INTO HIS ROOM ALONE.
HE CAN'T BE SATIATED, SO IF YOU'RE DRAGGED IN THERE BY HIM, YOU'RE DONE FOR!
!
I'M THE ONLY PERSON HERE WHO CAN BEAR THE PAIN!

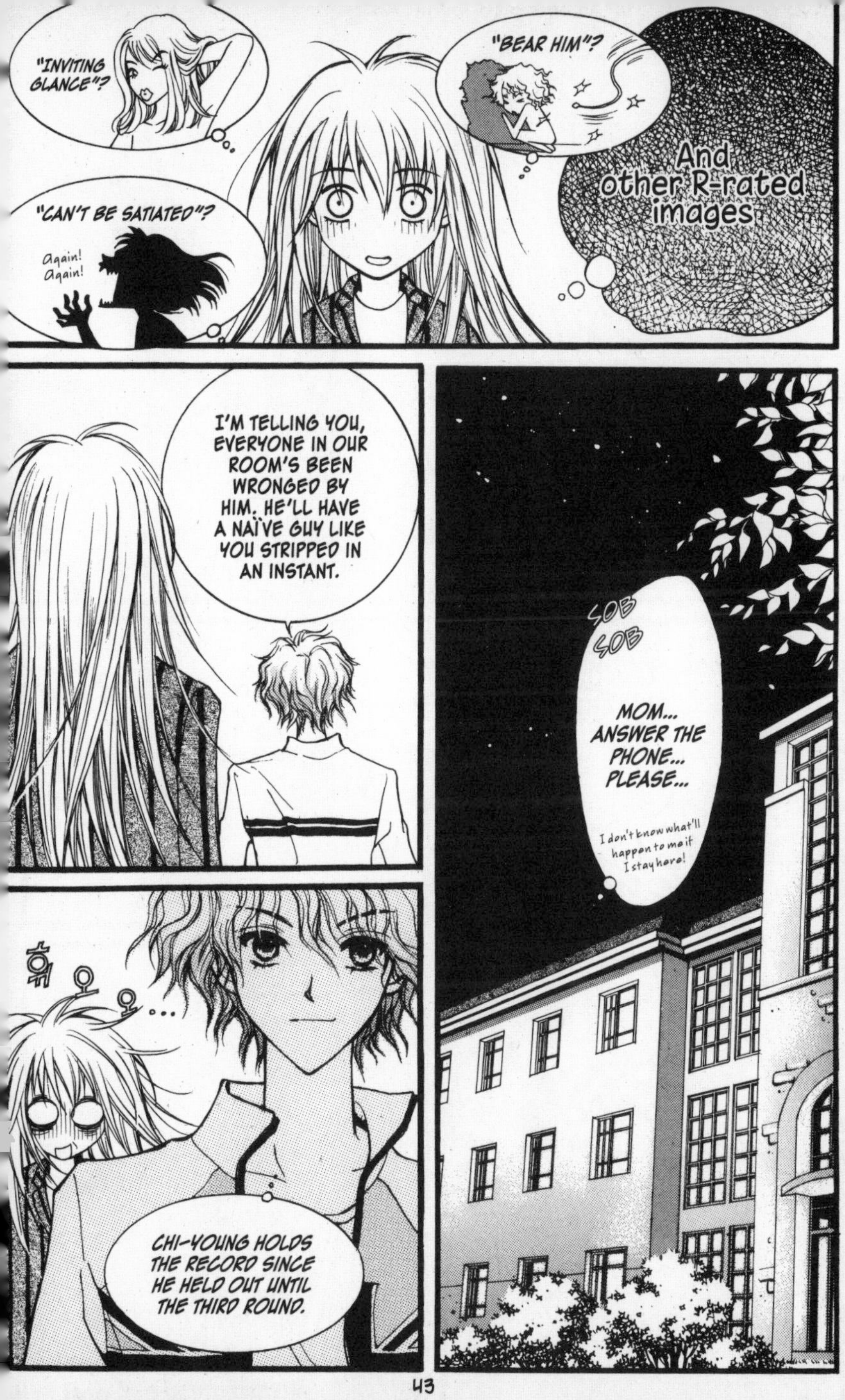
"INVITING GLANCE"?
"CAN'T BE SATIATED"?
Again! Again!
"BEAR HIM"?
And other R-rated images
I'M TELLING YOU, EVERYONE IN OUR ROOM'S BEEN WRONGED BY HIM. HE'LL HAVE A NAÏVE GUY LIKE YOU STRIPPED IN AN INSTANT.
CHI-YOUNG HOLDS THE RECORD SINCE HE HELD OUT UNTIL THE THIRD ROUND.
SOB SOB
MOM... ANSWER THE PHONE... PLEASE...
I don't know what'll happen to me if I stay here!

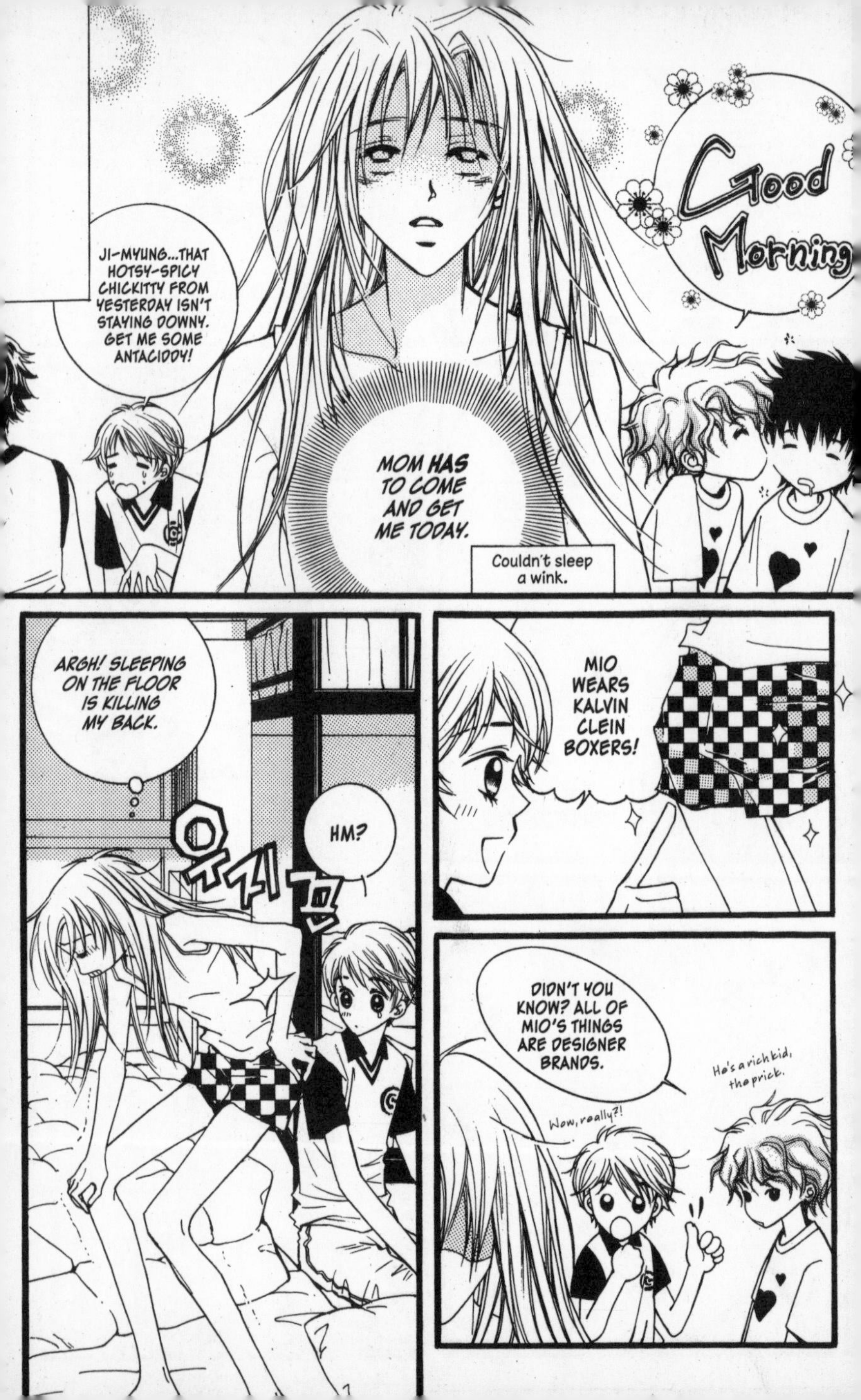
JI-MYUNG...THAT HOTSY-SPICY CHICKITTY FROM YESTERDAY ISN'T STAYING DOWNY. GET ME SOME ANTACIDDY!
Good Morning
MOM HAS TO COME AND GET ME TODAY.
Couldn't sleep a wink.
ARGH! SLEEPING ON THE FLOOR IS KILLING MY BACK.
우지끈
HM?
MIO WEARS KALVIN CLEIN BOXERS!
DIDN'T YOU KNOW? ALL OF MIO'S THINGS ARE DESIGNER BRANDS.
Wow, really?!
He's a rich kid, the prick.

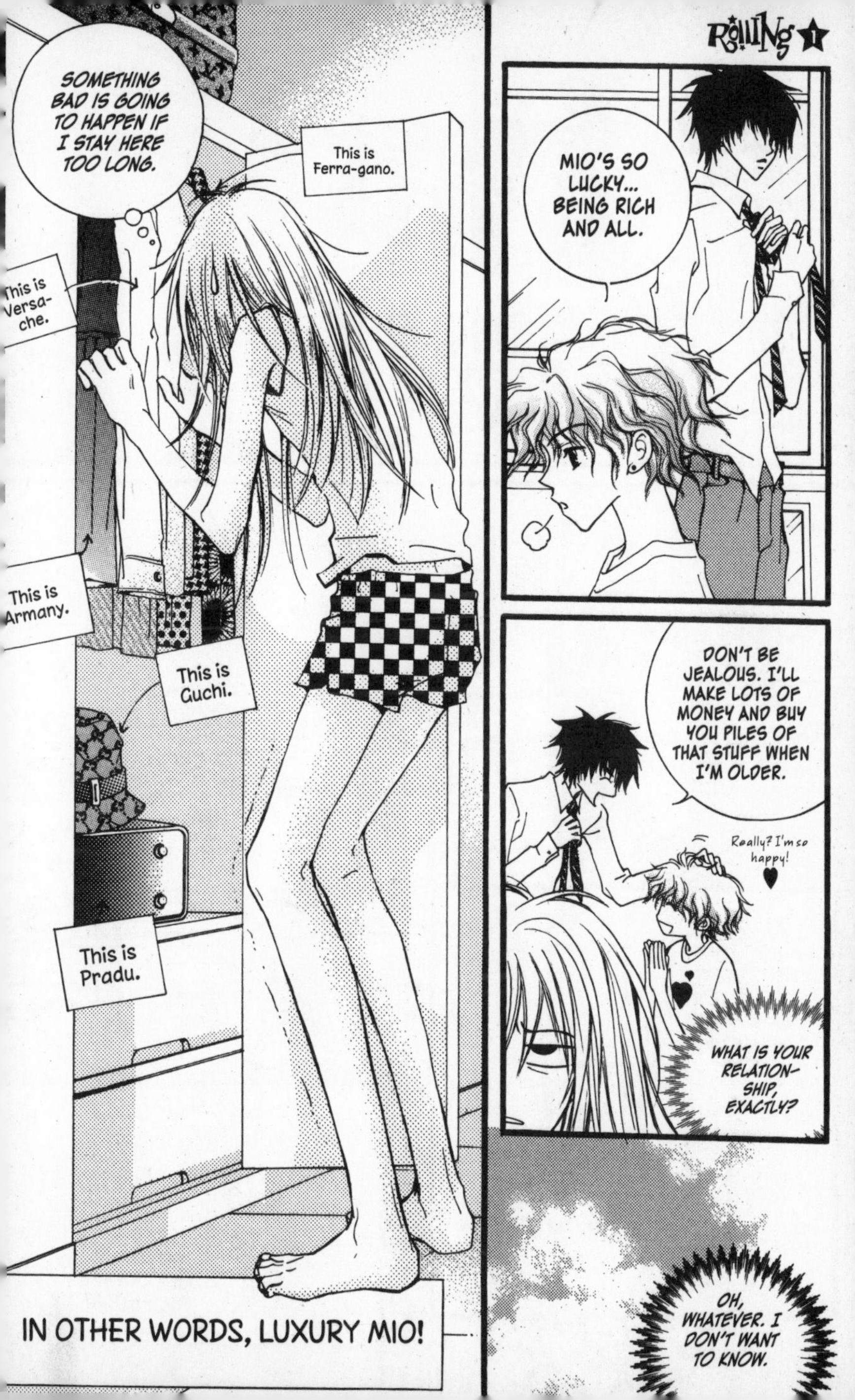
SOMETHING BAD IS GOING TO HAPPEN IF I STAY HERE TOO LONG.
This is Ferra-gano.
This is Versa-che.
This is Armany.
This is Guchi.
This is Pradu.
IN OTHER WORDS, LUXURY MIO!
MIO'S SO LUCKY... BEING RICH AND ALL.
DON'T BE JEALOUS. I'LL MAKE LOTS OF MONEY AND BUY YOU PILES OF THAT STUFF WHEN I'M OLDER.
Really? I'm so happy!
WHAT IS YOUR RELATION-SHIP, EXACTLY?
OH, WHATEVER. I DON'T WANT TO KNOW.

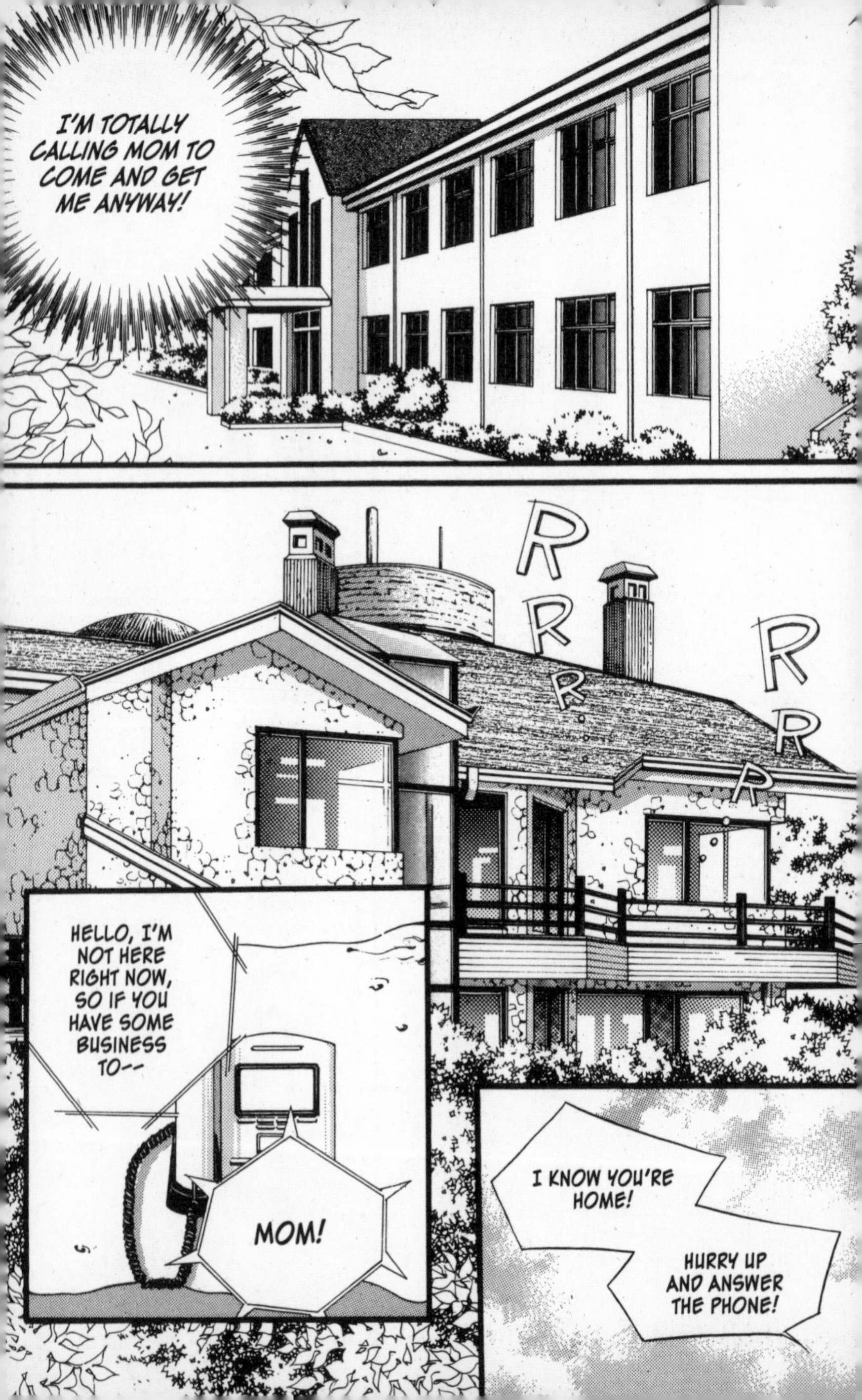
I'M TOTALLY CALLING MOM TO COME AND GET ME ANYWAY!
RRR
RRR
HELLO, I'M NOT HERE RIGHT NOW, SO IF YOU HAVE SOME BUSINESS TO--
MOM!
I KNOW YOU'RE HOME!
HURRY UP AND ANSWER THE PHONE!

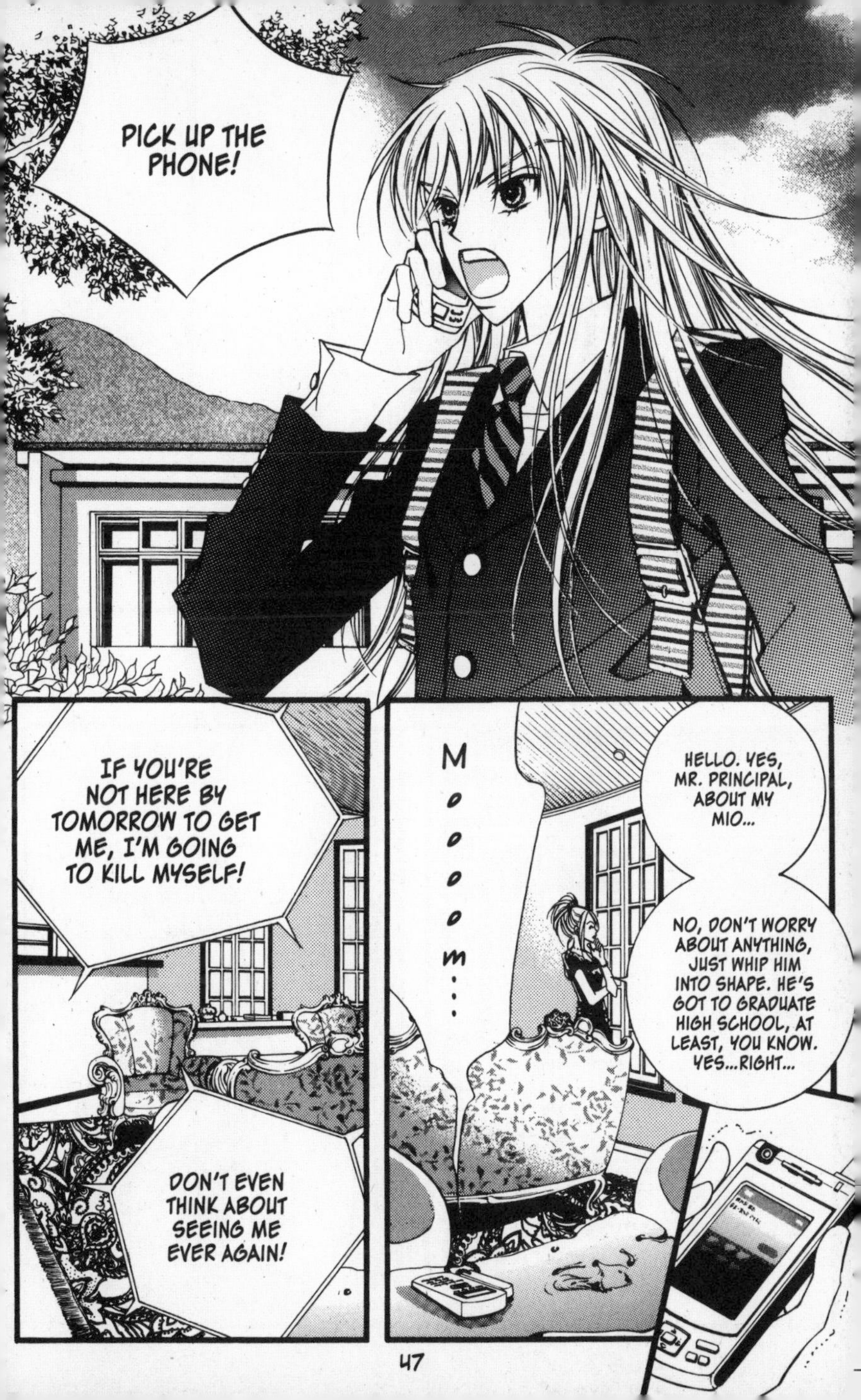
PICK UP THE PHONE!
IF YOU'RE NOT HERE BY TOMORROW TO GET ME, I'M GOING TO KILL MYSELF!
DON'T EVEN THINK ABOUT SEEING ME EVER AGAIN!
Mooooom...
HELLO. YES, MR. PRINCIPAL, ABOUT MY MIO...
NO, DON'T WORRY ABOUT ANYTHING, JUST WHIP HIM INTO SHAPE. HE'S GOT TO GRADUATE HIGH SCHOOL, AT LEAST, YOU KNOW. YES...RIGHT...

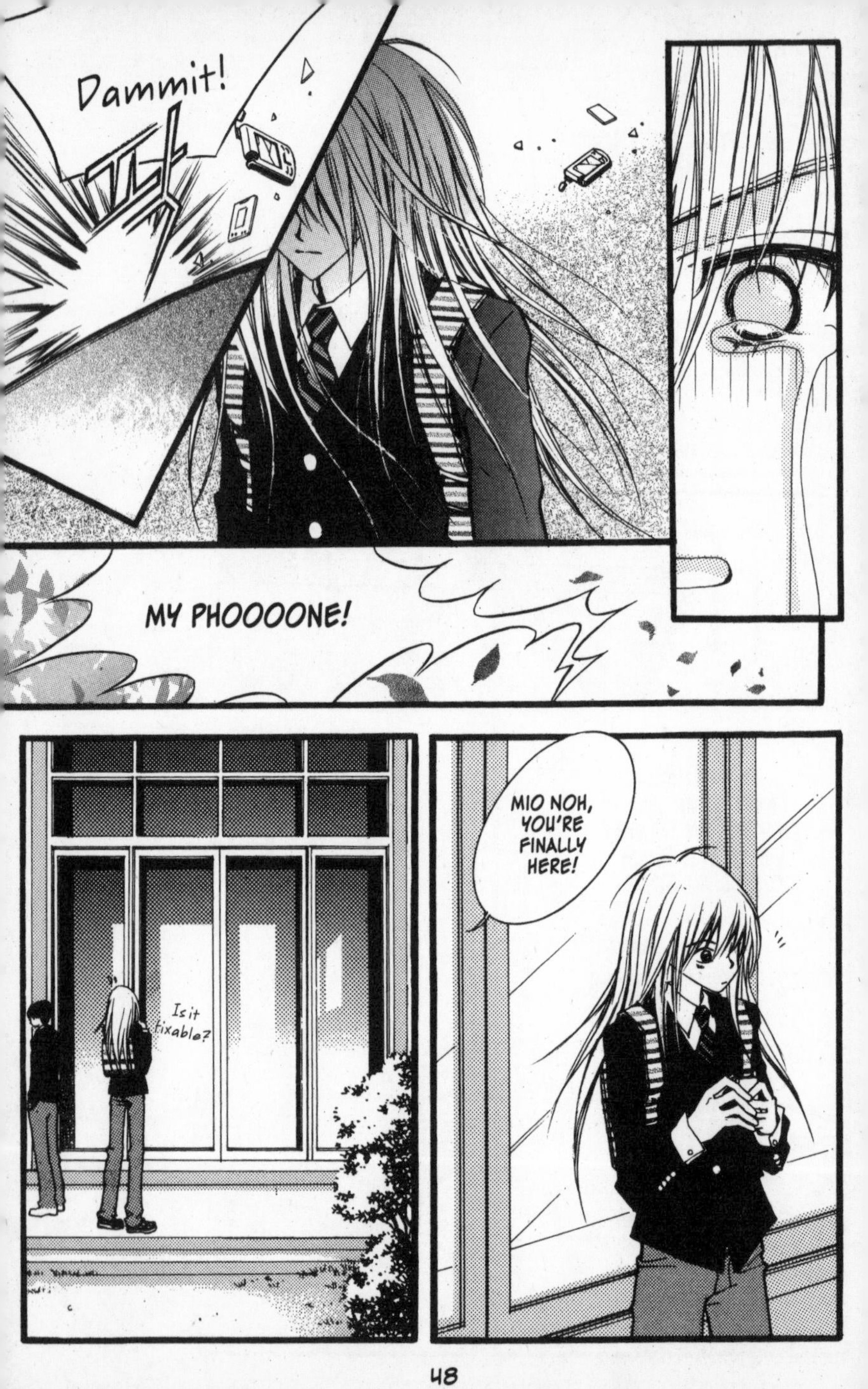
Dammit!
MY PHOOOONE!
Is it fixable?
MIO NOH, YOU'RE FINALLY HERE!

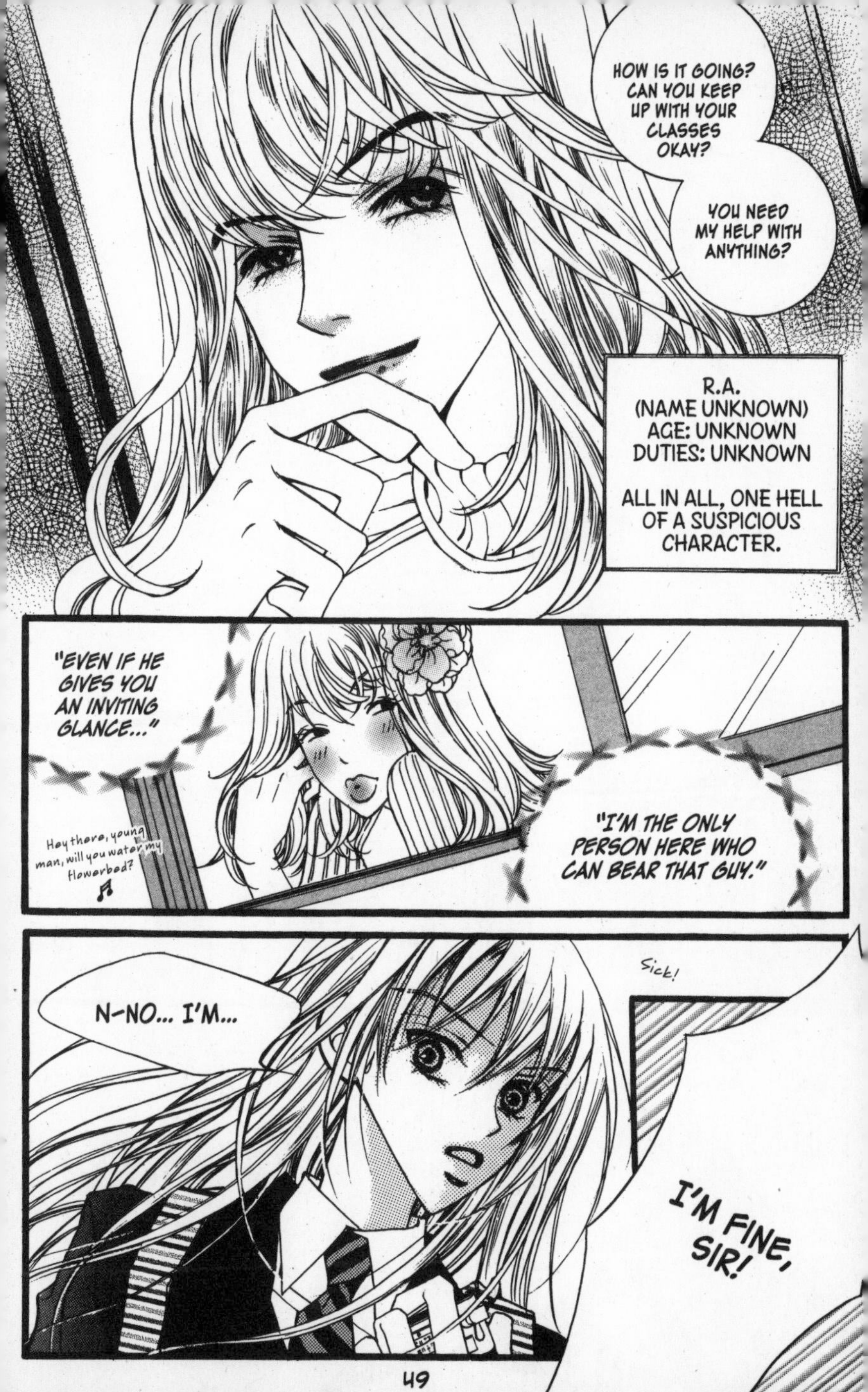
HOW IS IT GOING? CAN YOU KEEP UP WITH YOUR CLASSES OKAY?
YOU NEED MY HELP WITH ANYTHING?
R.A. (NAME UNKNOWN) AGE: UNKNOWN DUTIES: UNKNOWN
ALL IN ALL, ONE HELL OF A SUSPICIOUS CHARACTER.
"EVEN IF HE GIVES YOU AN INVITING GLANCE..."
Hey there, young man, will you water my flowerbed?
"I'M THE ONLY PERSON HERE WHO CAN BEAR THAT GUY."
N-NO... I'M...
Sick!
I'M FINE, SIR!

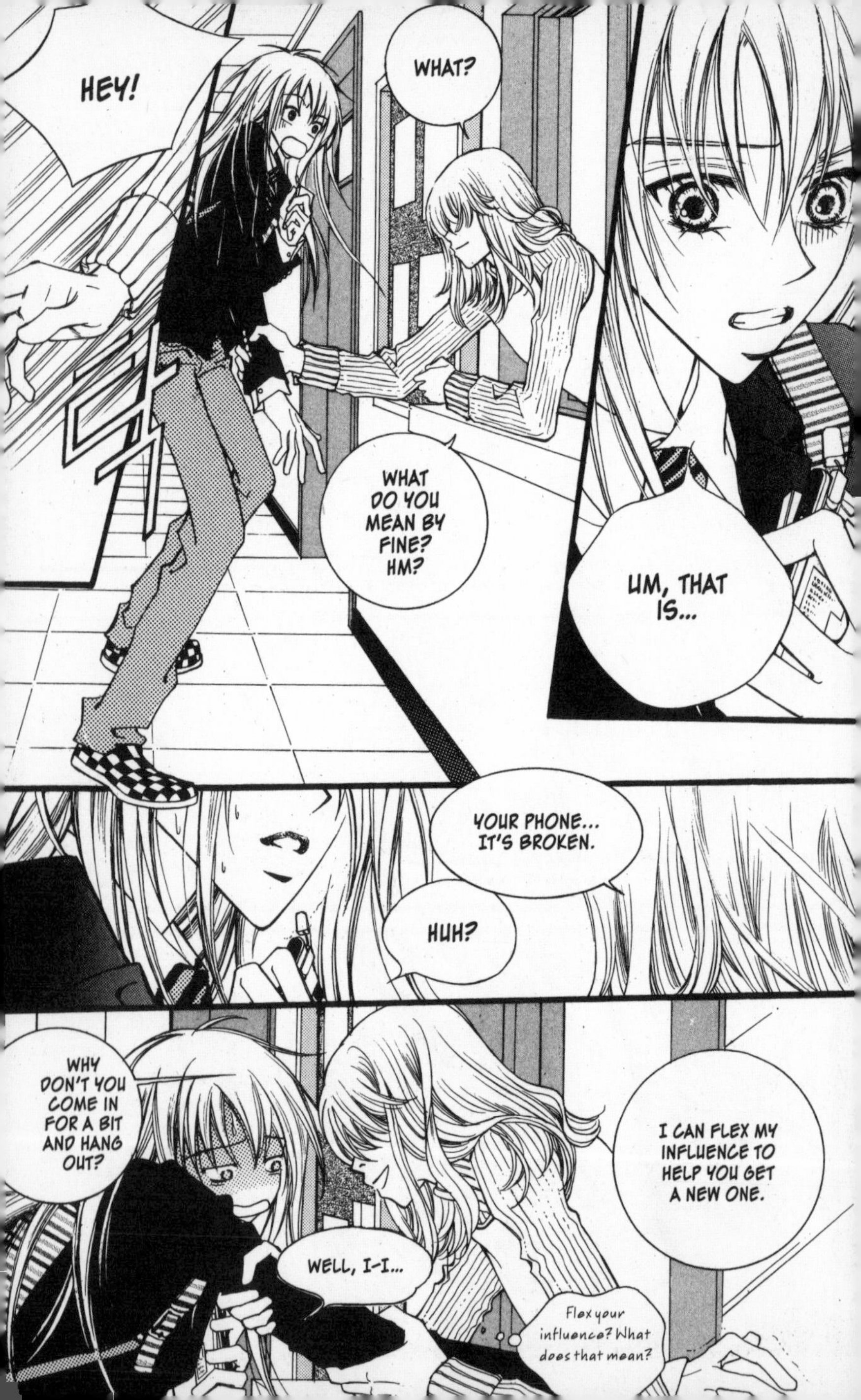
HEY!
WHAT?
WHAT DO YOU MEAN BY FINE? HM?
UM, THAT IS...
YOUR PHONE... IT'S BROKEN.
HUH?
WHY DON'T YOU COME IN FOR A BIT AND HANG OUT?
WELL, I-I...
I CAN FLEX MY INFLUENCE TO HELP YOU GET A NEW ONE.
Flex your influence? What does that mean?

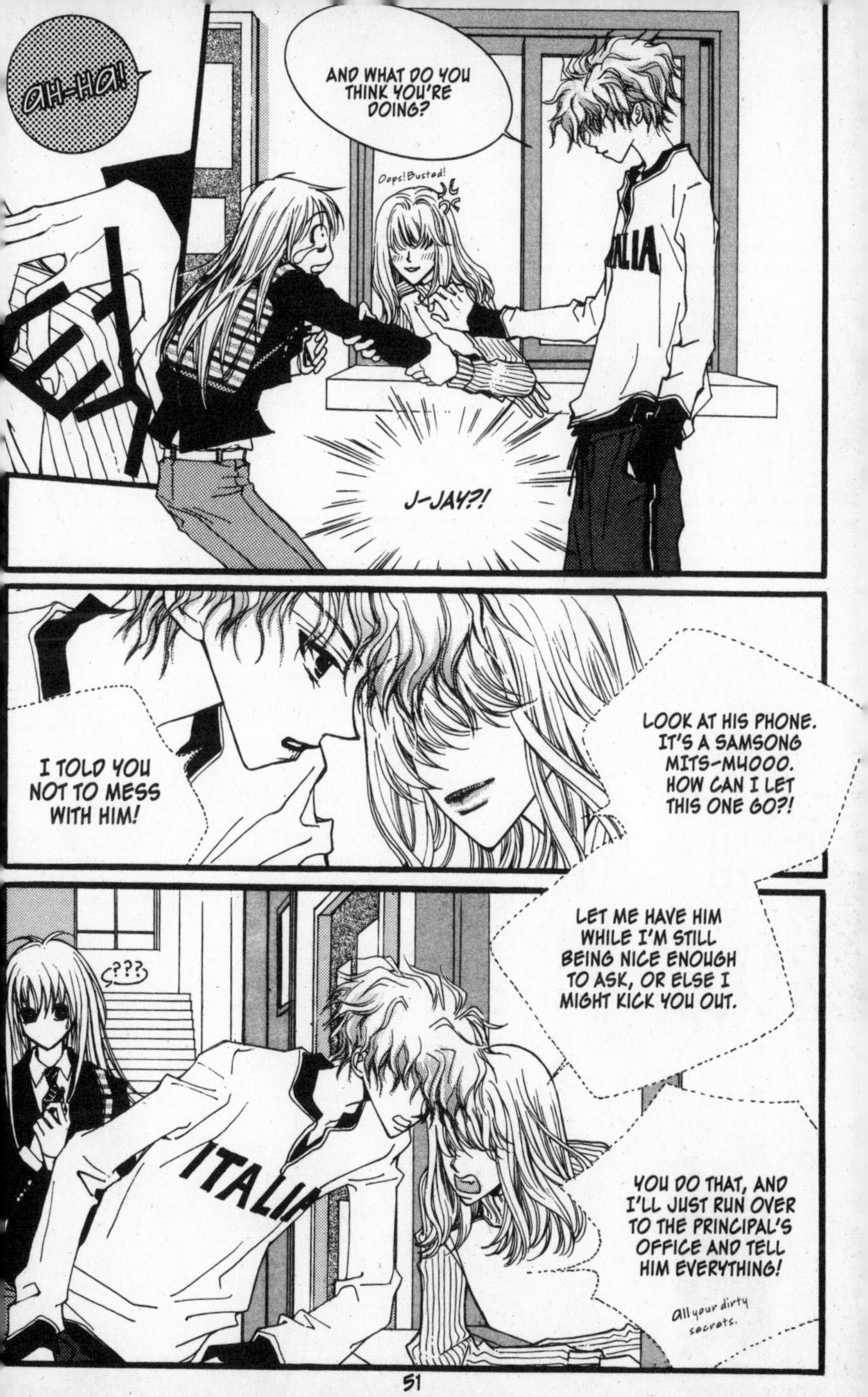
OH-HO!
AND WHAT DO YOU THINK YOU'RE DOING?
Oops! Busted!
J-JAY?!
I TOLD YOU NOT TO MESS WITH HIM!
LOOK AT HIS PHONE. IT'S A SAMSONG MITS-M4000. HOW CAN I LET THIS ONE GO?!
???
LET ME HAVE HIM WHILE I'M STILL BEING NICE ENOUGH TO ASK, OR ELSE I MIGHT KICK YOU OUT.
YOU DO THAT, AND I'LL JUST RUN OVER TO THE PRINCIPAL'S OFFICE AND TELL HIM EVERYTHING!
All your dirty secrets.

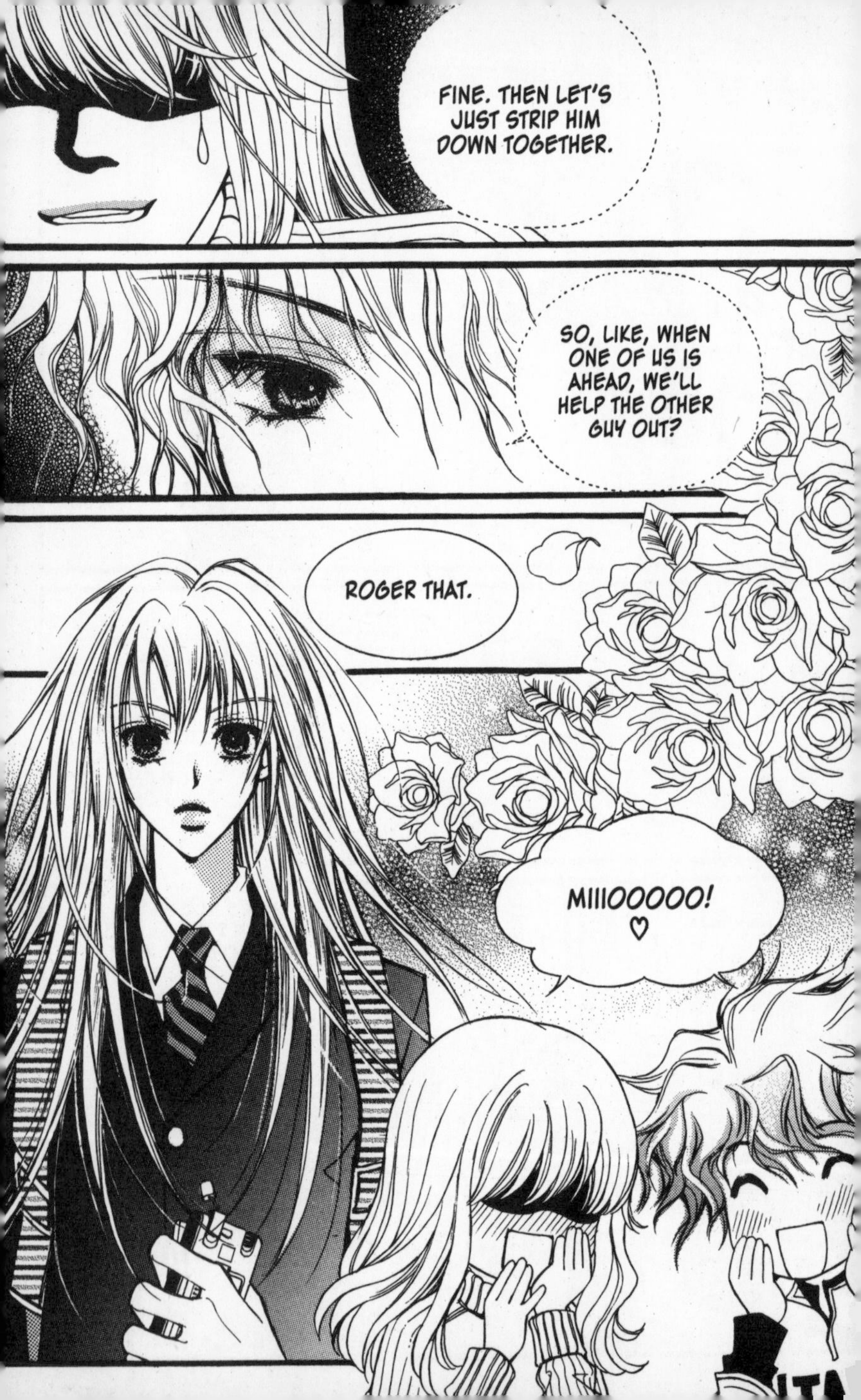
FINE. THEN LET'S JUST STRIP HIM DOWN TOGETHER.
SO, LIKE, WHEN ONE OF US IS AHEAD, WE'LL HELP THE OTHER GUY OUT?
ROGER THAT.
MIIIOOOOO! ♡

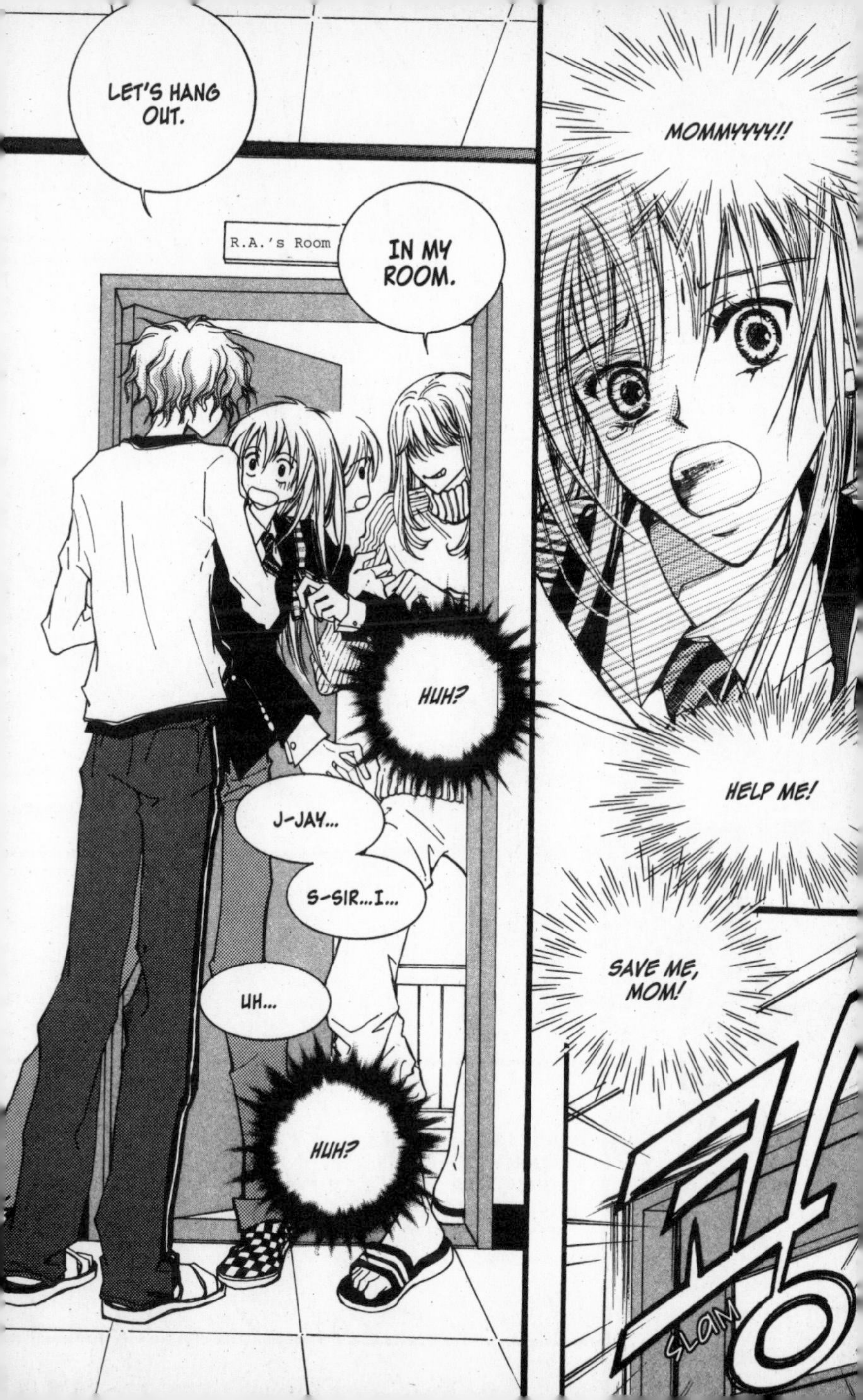

LET'S HANG OUT.
R.A.'s Room
IN MY ROOM.
HUH?
J-JAY...
S-SIR...I...
UH...
HUH?
MOMMYYYY!!
HELP ME!
SAVE ME, MOM!
SLAM

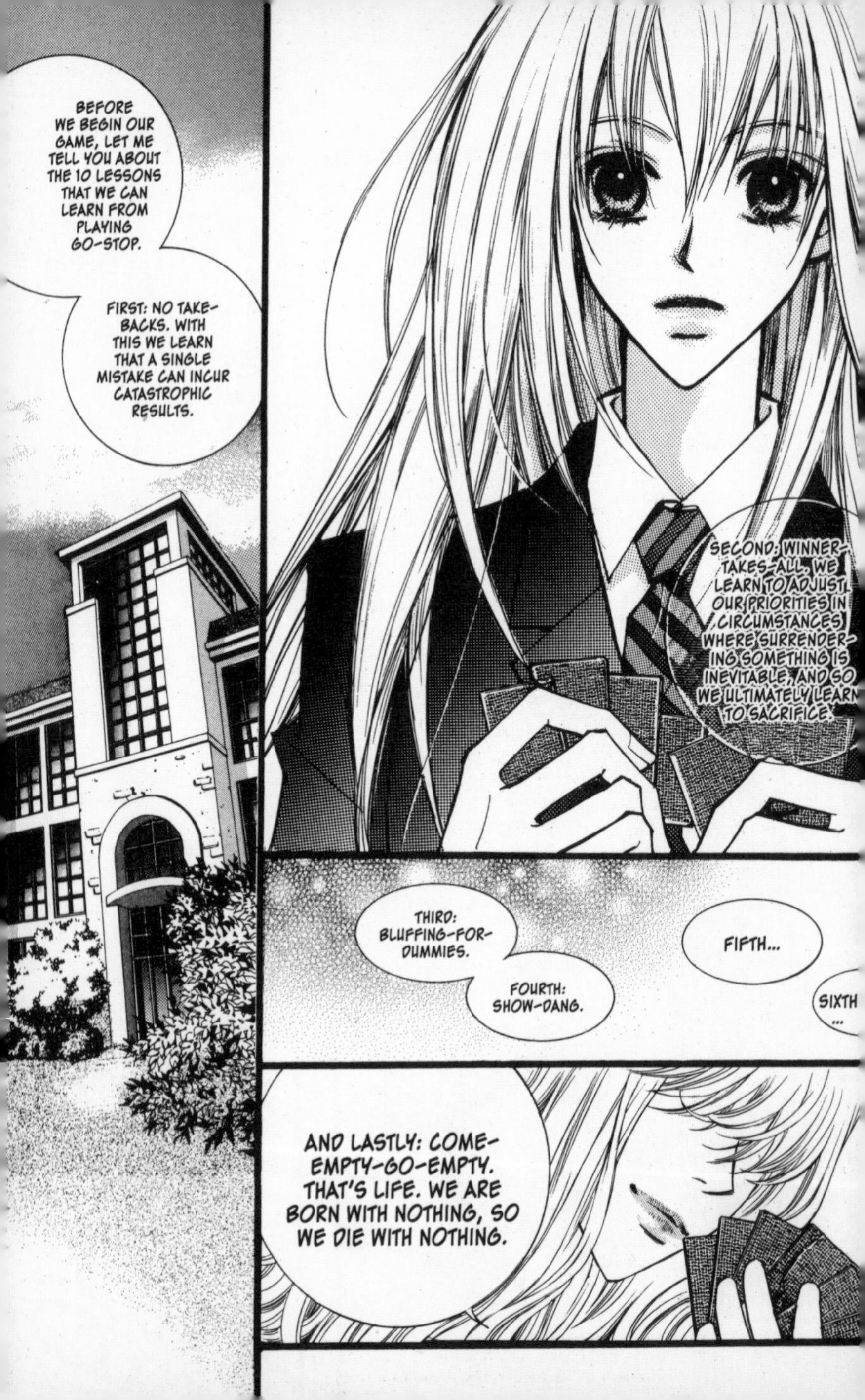
BEFORE WE BEGIN OUR GAME, LET ME TELL YOU ABOUT THE 10 LESSONS THAT WE CAN LEARN FROM PLAYING GO-STOP.
FIRST: NO TAKE-BACKS. WITH THIS WE LEARN THAT A SINGLE MISTAKE CAN INCUR CATASTROPHIC RESULTS.
SECOND: WINNER-TAKES-ALL. WE LEARN TO ADJUST OUR PRIORITIES IN CIRCUMSTANCES WHERE SURRENDER-ING SOMETHING IS INEVITABLE, AND SO WE ULTIMATELY LEARN TO SACRIFICE.
THIRD: BLUFFING-FOR-DUMMIES.
FOURTH: SHOW-DANG.
FIFTH...
SIXTH ...
AND LASTLY: COME-EMPTY-GO-EMPTY. THAT'S LIFE. WE ARE BORN WITH NOTHING, SO WE DIE WITH NOTHING.

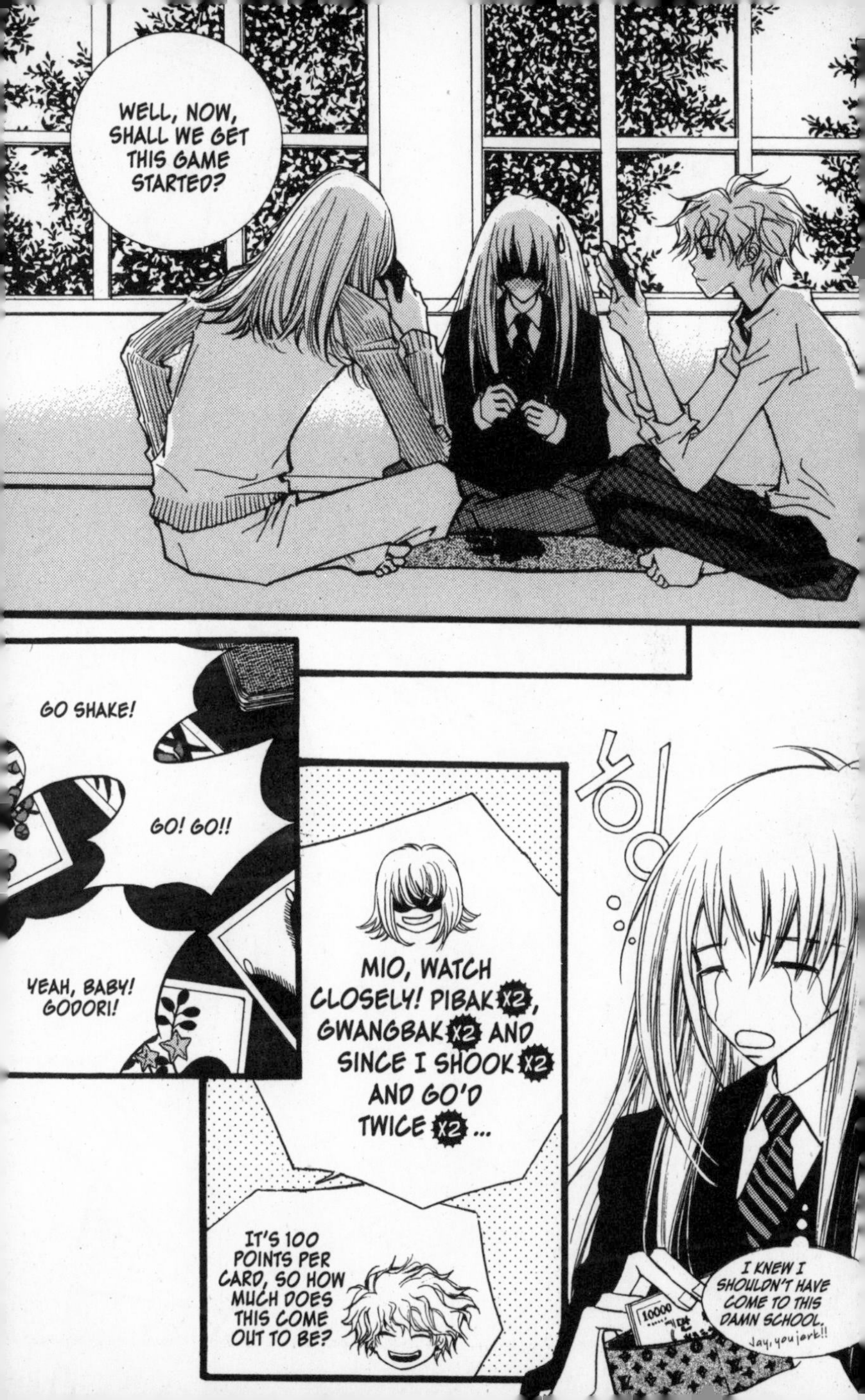
WELL, NOW, SHALL WE GET THIS GAME STARTED?
GO SHAKE!
GO! GO!!
YEAH, BABY! GODORI!
MIO, WATCH CLOSELY! PIBAK X2, GWANGBAK X2 AND SINCE I SHOOK X2 AND GO'D TWICE X2 ...
IT'S 100 POINTS PER CARD, SO HOW MUCH DOES THIS COME OUT TO BE?
I KNEW I SHOULDN'T HAVE COME TO THIS DAMN SCHOOL.
Jay, you jerk!!
10000

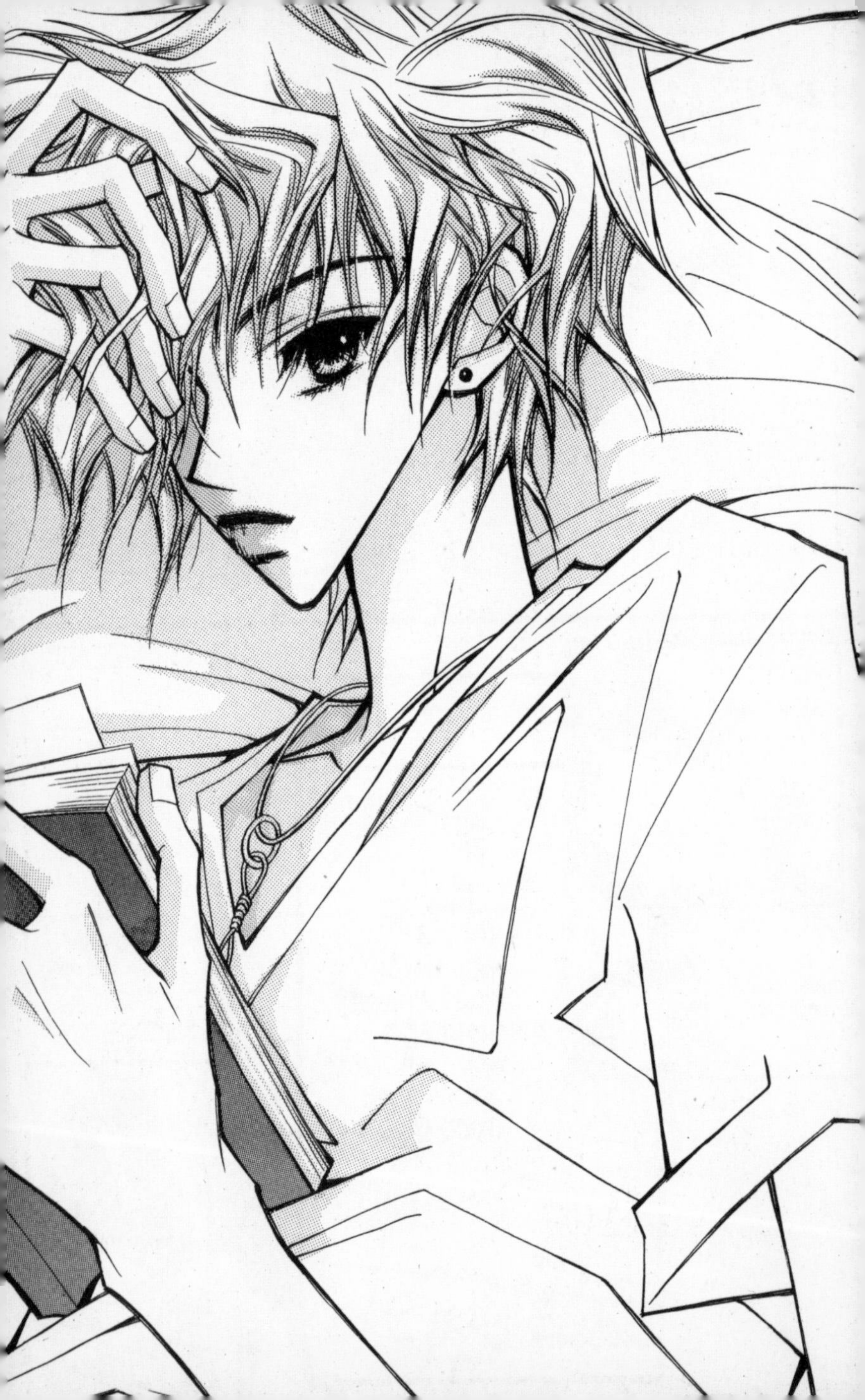

Episode 3:
The One Who
Doesn't Work

THERE ARE
MANY WAYS TO
DIFFERENTIATE
PHYSICAL BUILDS.

JAE-MA LEE'S SASANG TYPOLOGY*

* Sasang is a traditional Korean medicine, which literally translated means four body types.

TAE-YANG PERSON | TAE-EUM PERSON | SO-YANG PERSON | SO-EUM PERSON

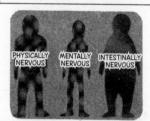

SELDEN'S GERMINAL LAYER THEORY

PHYSICALLY NERVOUS | MENTALLY NERVOUS | INTESTINALLY NERVOUS

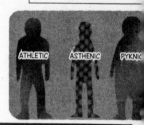

KRETSCHMER'S THREE BODY TYPES

ATHLETIC | ASTHENIC | PYKNIC

WHAT YOU MUST PAY
ATTENTION TO HERE IS THE
FACT THAT NO MATTER
WHICH METHOD YOU USE
TO DISCERN BODY TYPES,
THERE IS ALWAYS A TYPE
THAT IS NOT FIT FOR LABOR.

Shared traits: Thin and
weak-looking physique,
sensitive nerves, etc.

OTHERWISE KNOWN AS... THE HANRYANG* TYPE.

* Hanryang were men from aristocratic families who busied themselves with poetry, theatre, and the like in the old days.

Roses are red...

Violets are blue...

I wish I was on my bed...

And so do you...

IN MY
OPINION...

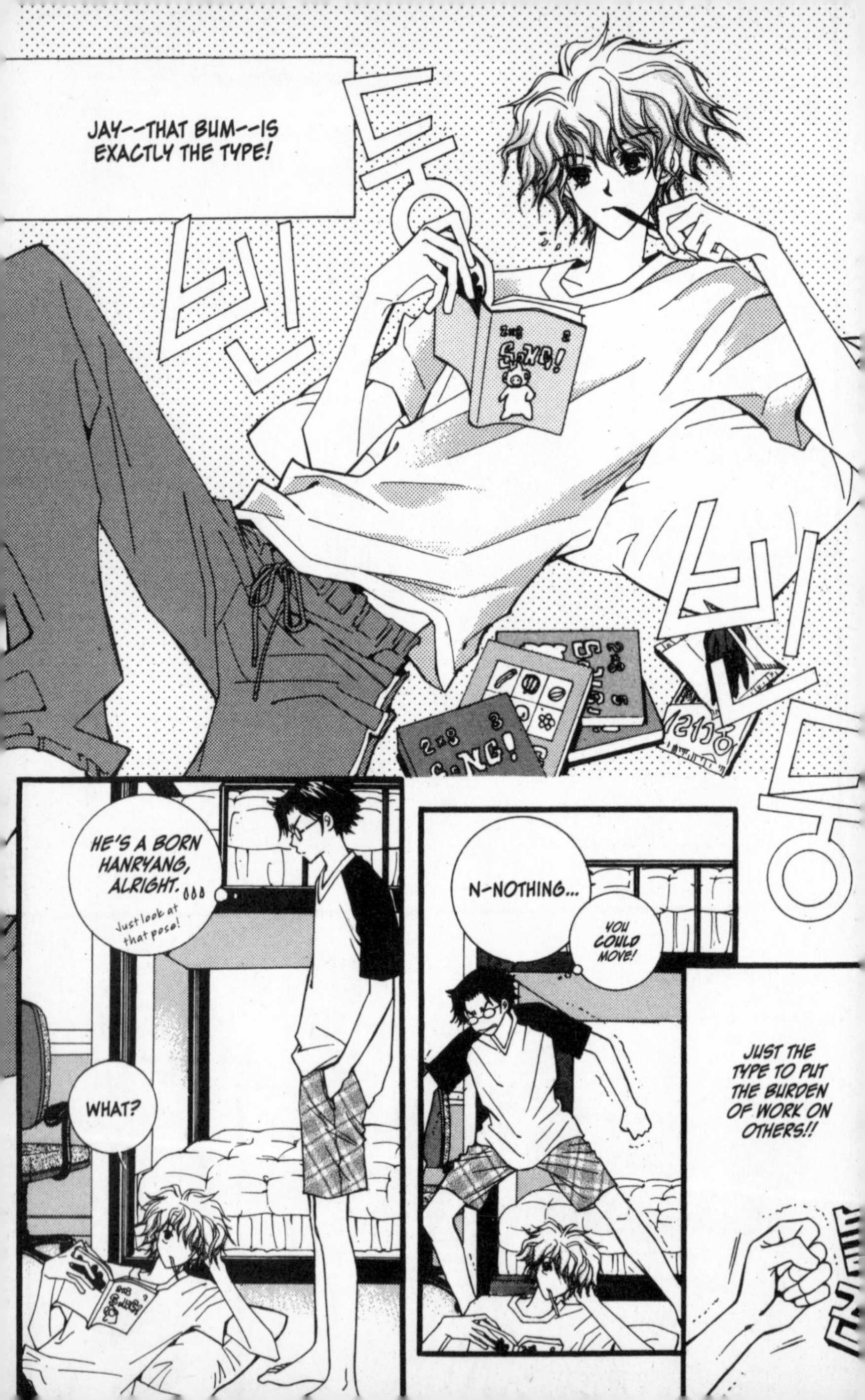
JAY--THAT BUM--IS EXACTLY THE TYPE!
HE'S A BORN HANRYANG, ALRIGHT...
Just look at that pose!
WHAT?
N-NOTHING...
YOU COULD MOVE!
JUST THE TYPE TO PUT THE BURDEN OF WORK ON OTHERS!!

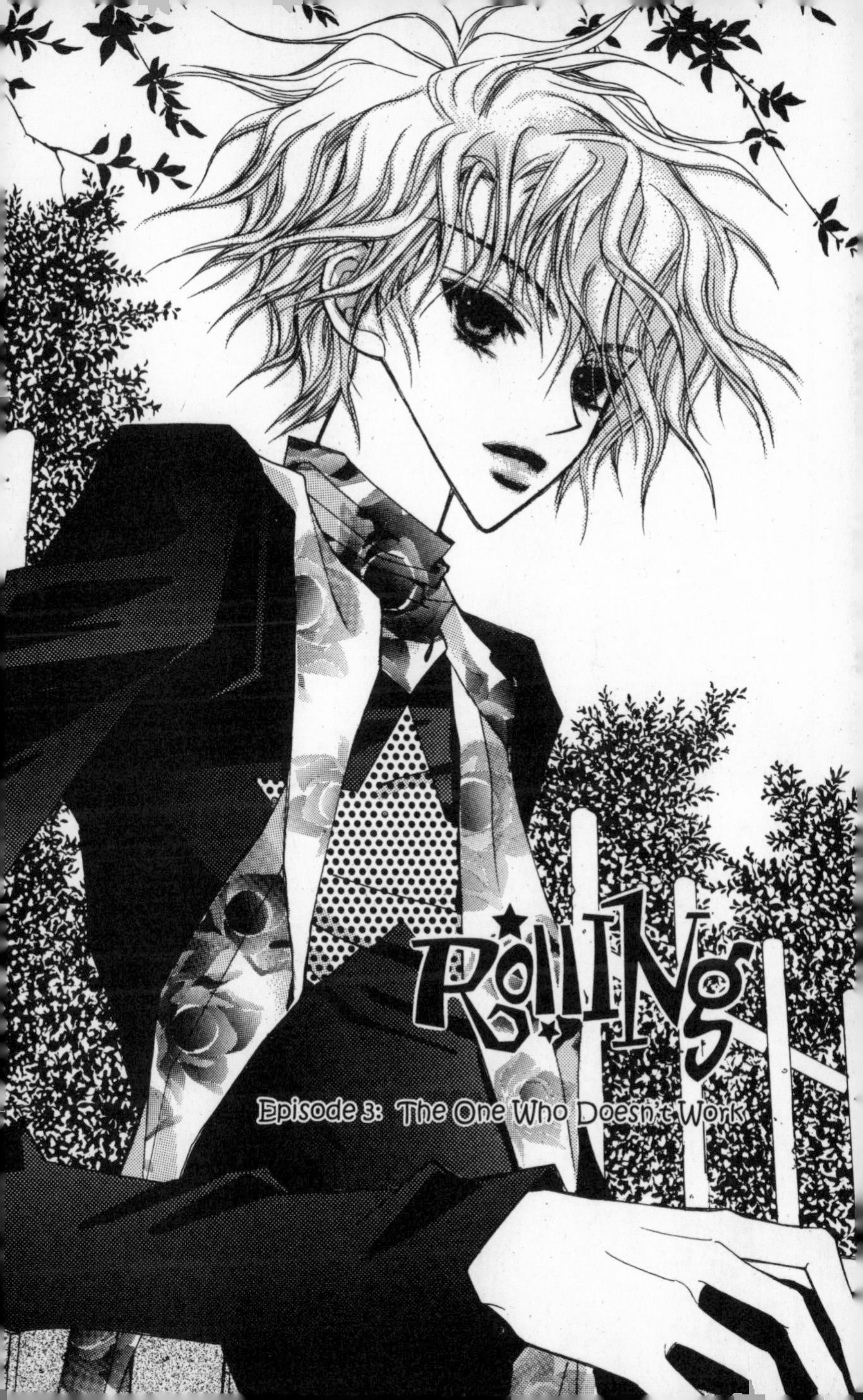
Rolling
Episode 3: The One Who Doesn't Work

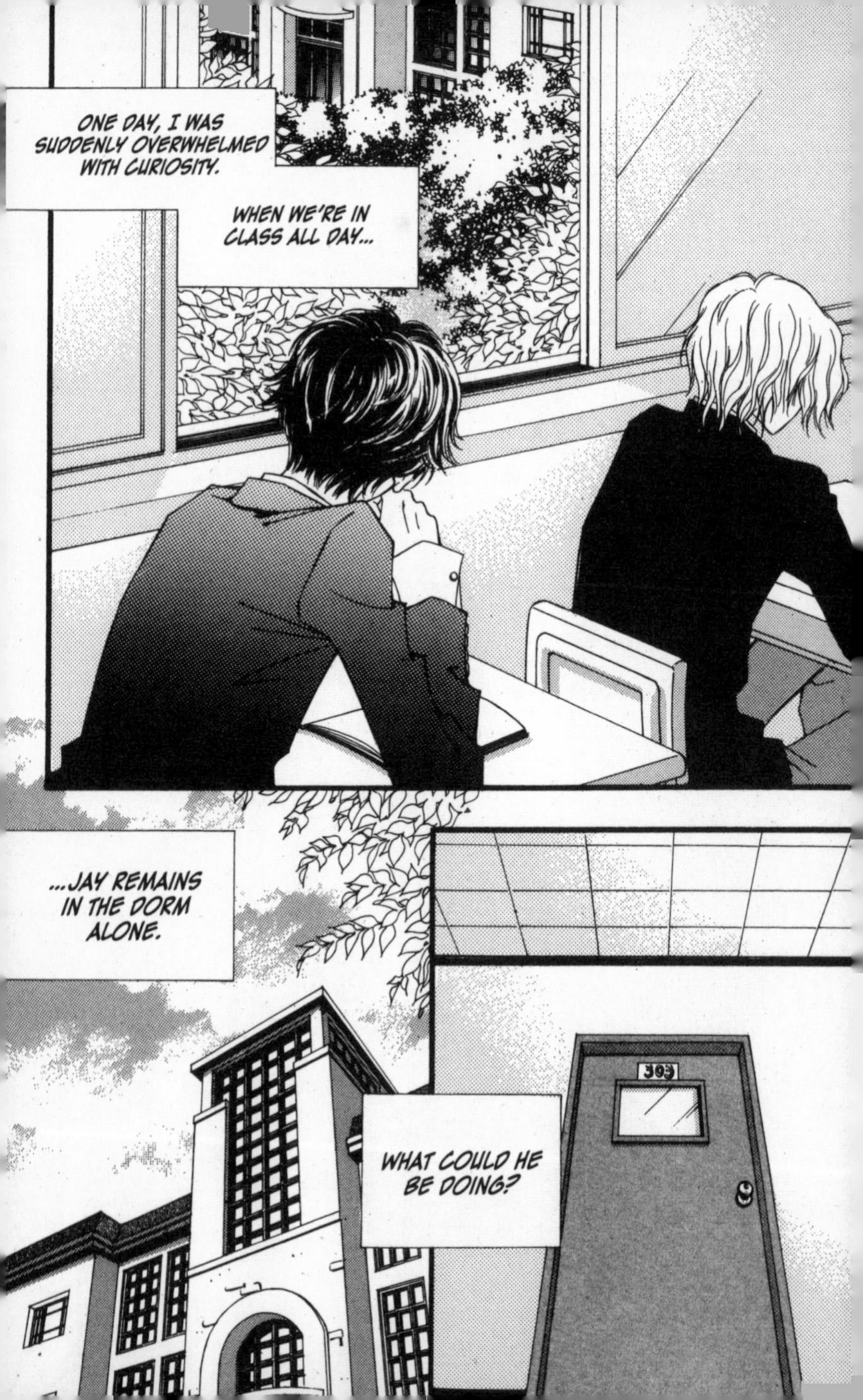

ONE DAY, I WAS SUDDENLY OVERWHELMED WITH CURIOSITY.
WHEN WE'RE IN CLASS ALL DAY...
...JAY REMAINS IN THE DORM ALONE.
WHAT COULD HE BE DOING?

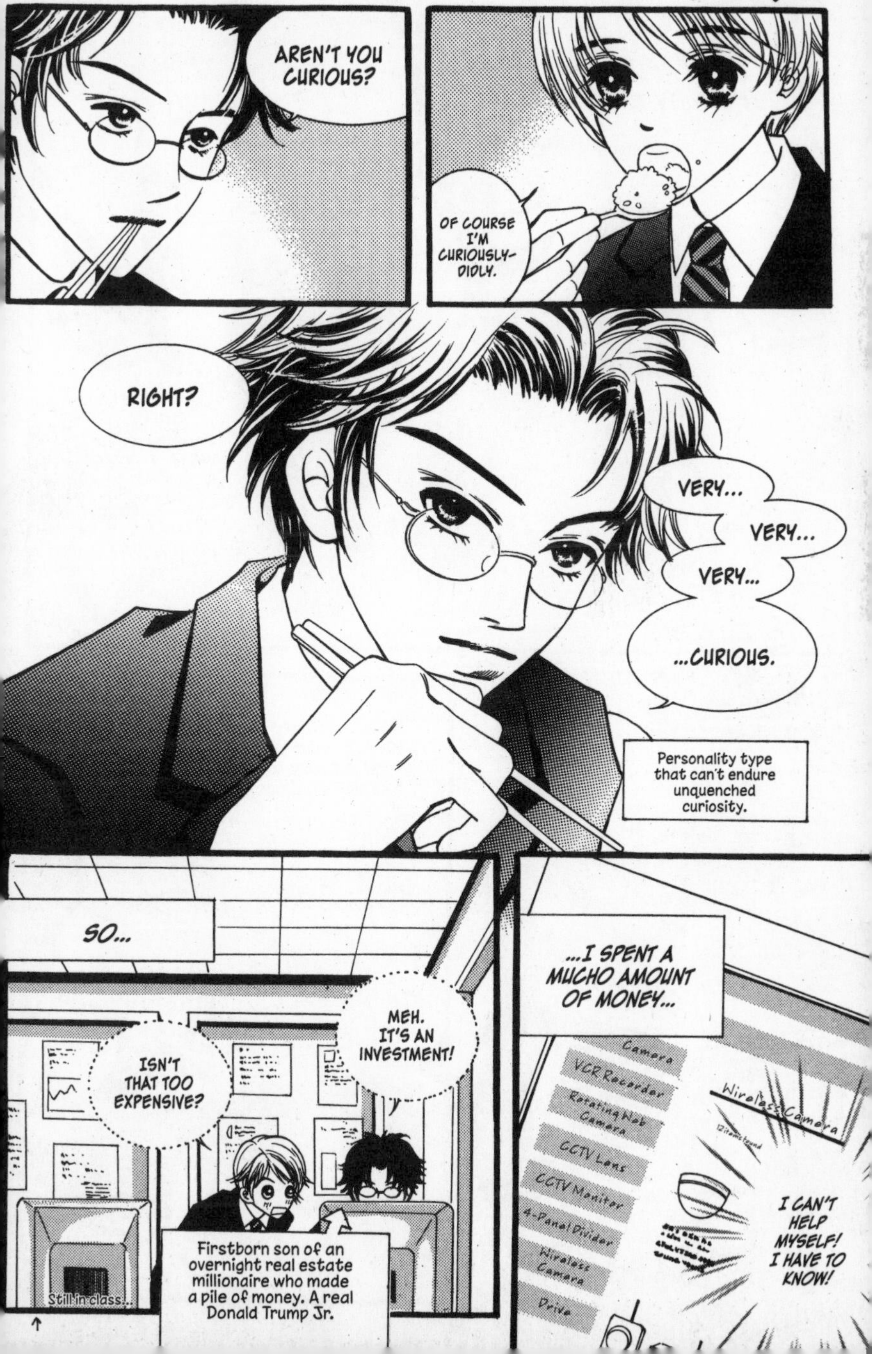
AREN'T YOU CURIOUS?
OF COURSE I'M CURIOUSLY-DIDLY.
RIGHT?
VERY...
VERY...
VERY...
...CURIOUS.
Personality type that can't endure unquenched curiosity.
SO...
ISN'T THAT TOO EXPENSIVE?
MEH. IT'S AN INVESTMENT!
Firstborn son of an overnight real estate millionaire who made a pile of money. A real Donald Trump Jr.
Still in class...
...I SPENT A MUCHO AMOUNT OF MONEY...
Camera
VCR Recorder
Rotating Web Camera
CCTV Lens
CCTV Monitor
4-Panel Divider
Wireless Camera
Drive
Wireless Camera
I CAN'T HELP MYSELF! I HAVE TO KNOW!

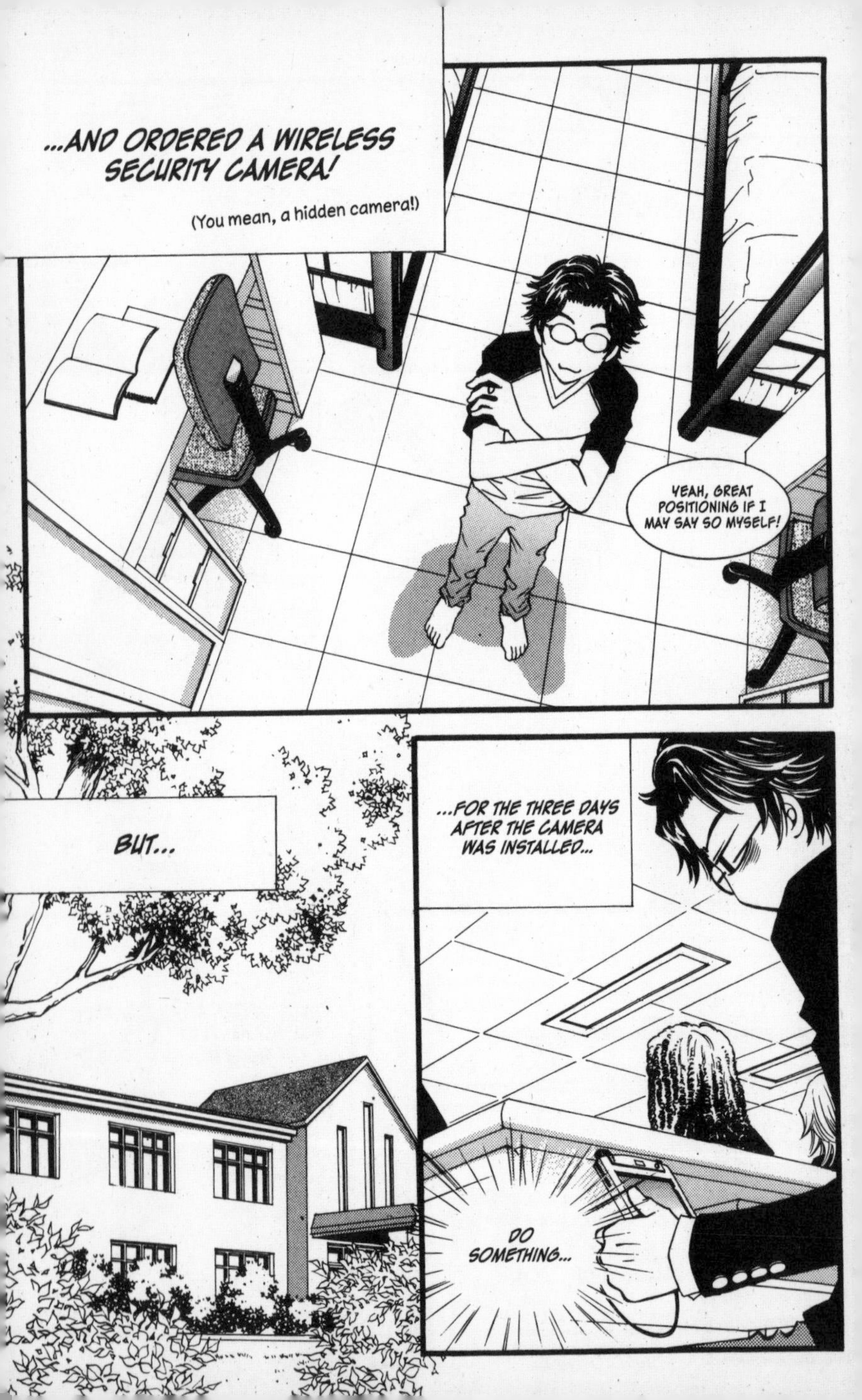
...AND ORDERED A WIRELESS SECURITY CAMERA!
(You mean, a hidden camera!)
YEAH, GREAT POSITIONING IF I MAY SAY SO MYSELF!
BUT...
...FOR THE THREE DAYS AFTER THE CAMERA WAS INSTALLED...
DO SOMETHING...

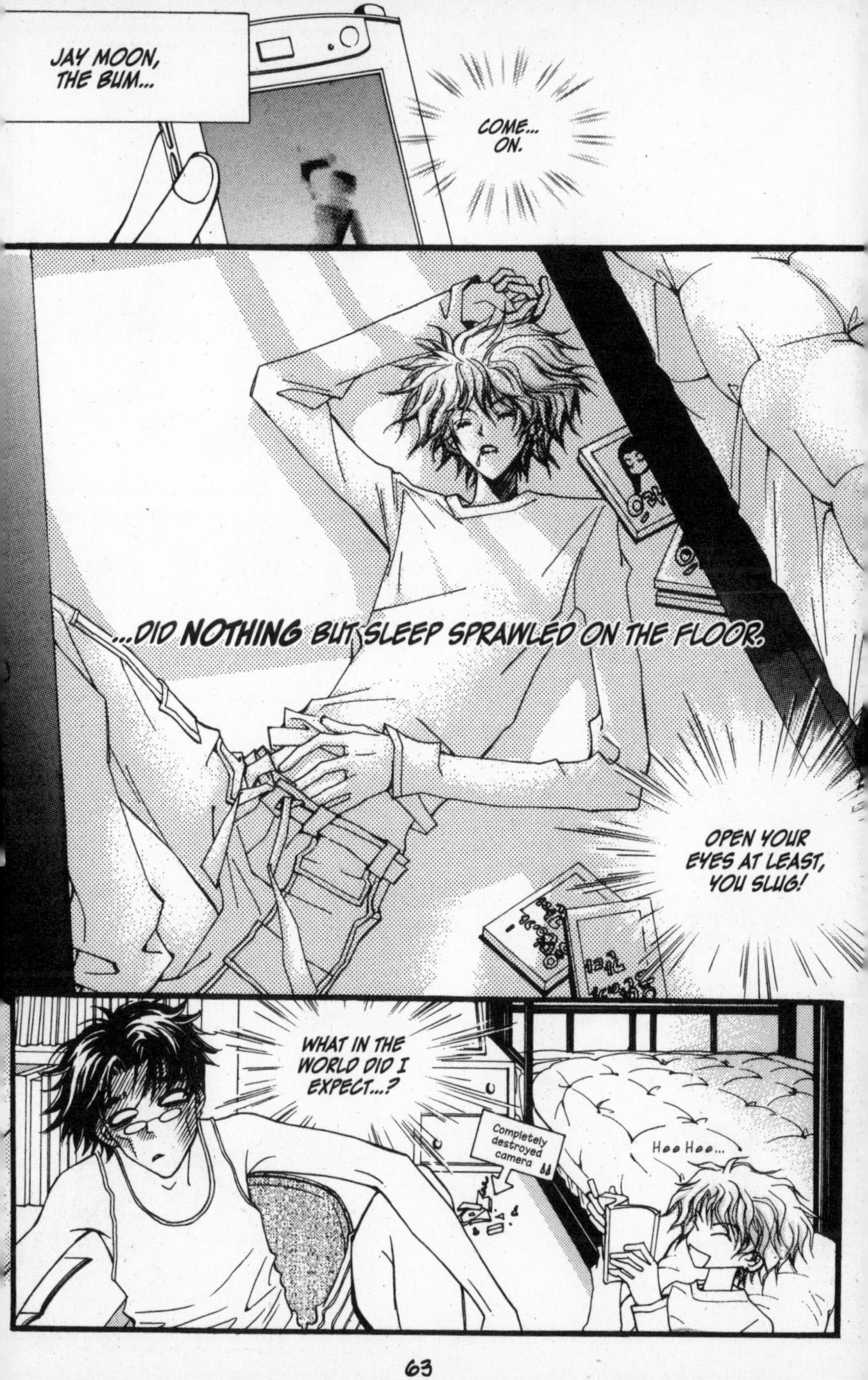
JAY MOON, THE BUM...
COME... ON.
...DID NOTHING BUT SLEEP SPRAWLED ON THE FLOOR.
OPEN YOUR EYES AT LEAST, YOU SLUG!
WHAT IN THE WORLD DID I EXPECT...?
Completely destroyed camera
Hee Hee...

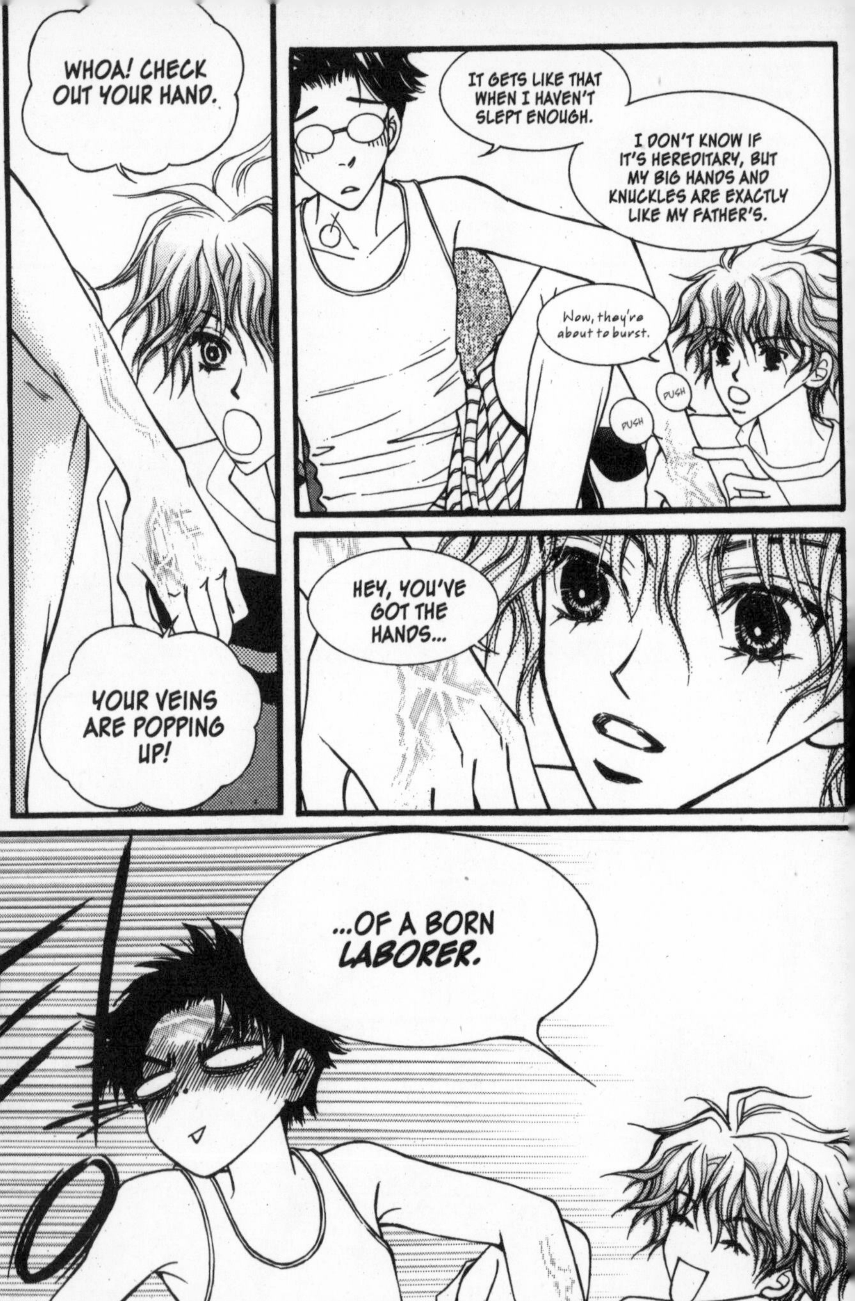
WHOA! CHECK OUT YOUR HAND.
YOUR VEINS ARE POPPING UP!
IT GETS LIKE THAT WHEN I HAVEN'T SLEPT ENOUGH.
I DON'T KNOW IF IT'S HEREDITARY, BUT MY BIG HANDS AND KNUCKLES ARE EXACTLY LIKE MY FATHER'S.
Wow, they're about to burst.
PUSH
PUSH
HEY, YOU'VE GOT THE HANDS...
...OF A BORN LABORER.

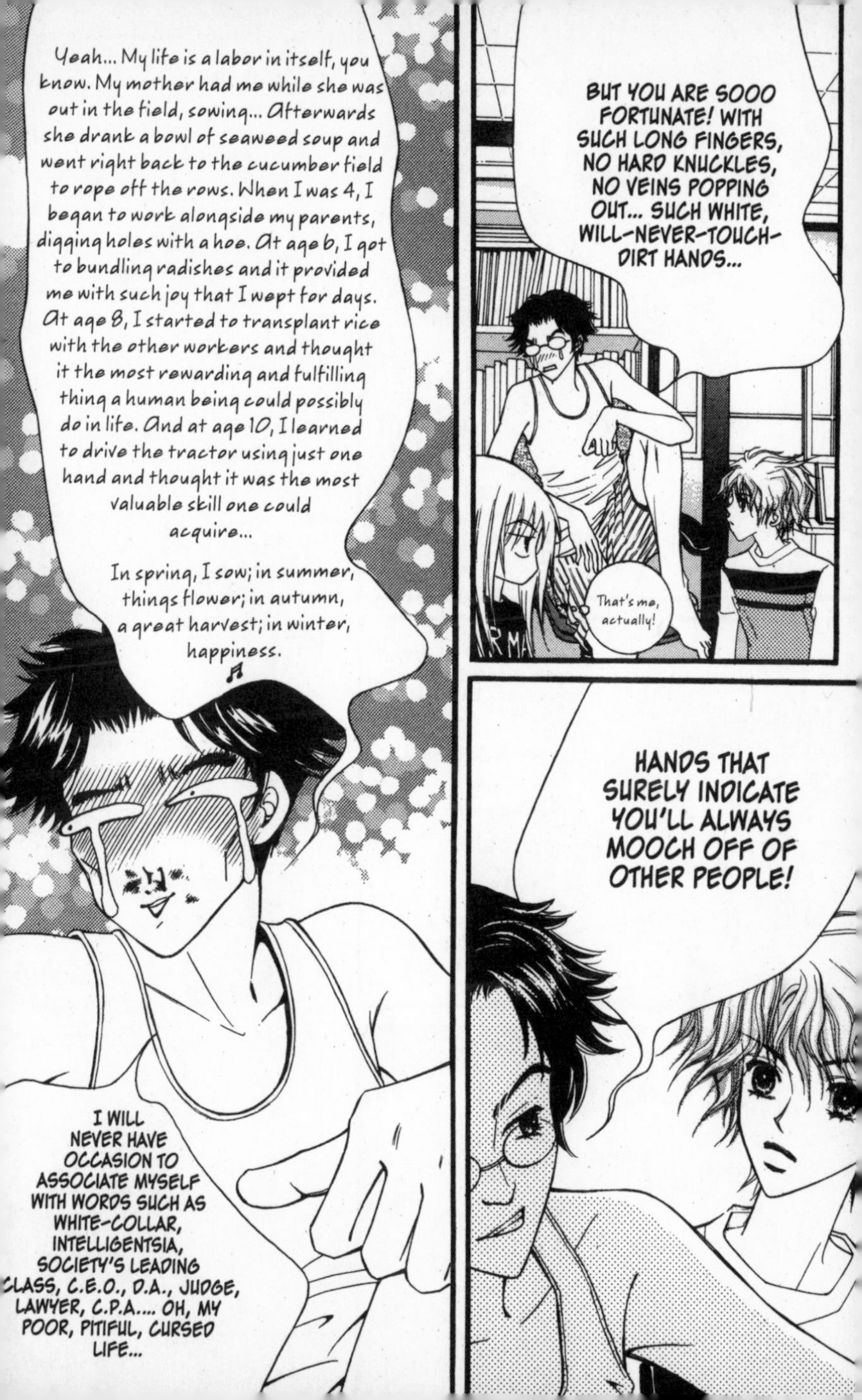
Yeah... My life is a labor in itself, you know. My mother had me while she was out in the field, sowing... Afterwards she drank a bowl of seaweed soup and went right back to the cucumber field to rope off the rows. When I was 4, I began to work alongside my parents, digging holes with a hoe. At age 6, I got to bundling radishes and it provided me with such joy that I wept for days. At age 8, I started to transplant rice with the other workers and thought it the most rewarding and fulfilling thing a human being could possibly do in life. And at age 10, I learned to drive the tractor using just one hand and thought it was the most valuable skill one could acquire...
In spring, I sow; in summer, things flower; in autumn, a great harvest; in winter, happiness.
I WILL NEVER HAVE OCCASION TO ASSOCIATE MYSELF WITH WORDS SUCH AS WHITE-COLLAR, INTELLIGENTSIA, SOCIETY'S LEADING CLASS, C.E.O., D.A., JUDGE, LAWYER, C.P.A.... OH, MY POOR, PITIFUL, CURSED LIFE...
BUT YOU ARE SOOO FORTUNATE! WITH SUCH LONG FINGERS, NO HARD KNUCKLES, NO VEINS POPPING OUT... SUCH WHITE, WILL-NEVER-TOUCH-DIRT HANDS...
That's me, actually!
HANDS THAT SURELY INDICATE YOU'LL ALWAYS MOOCH OFF OF OTHER PEOPLE!

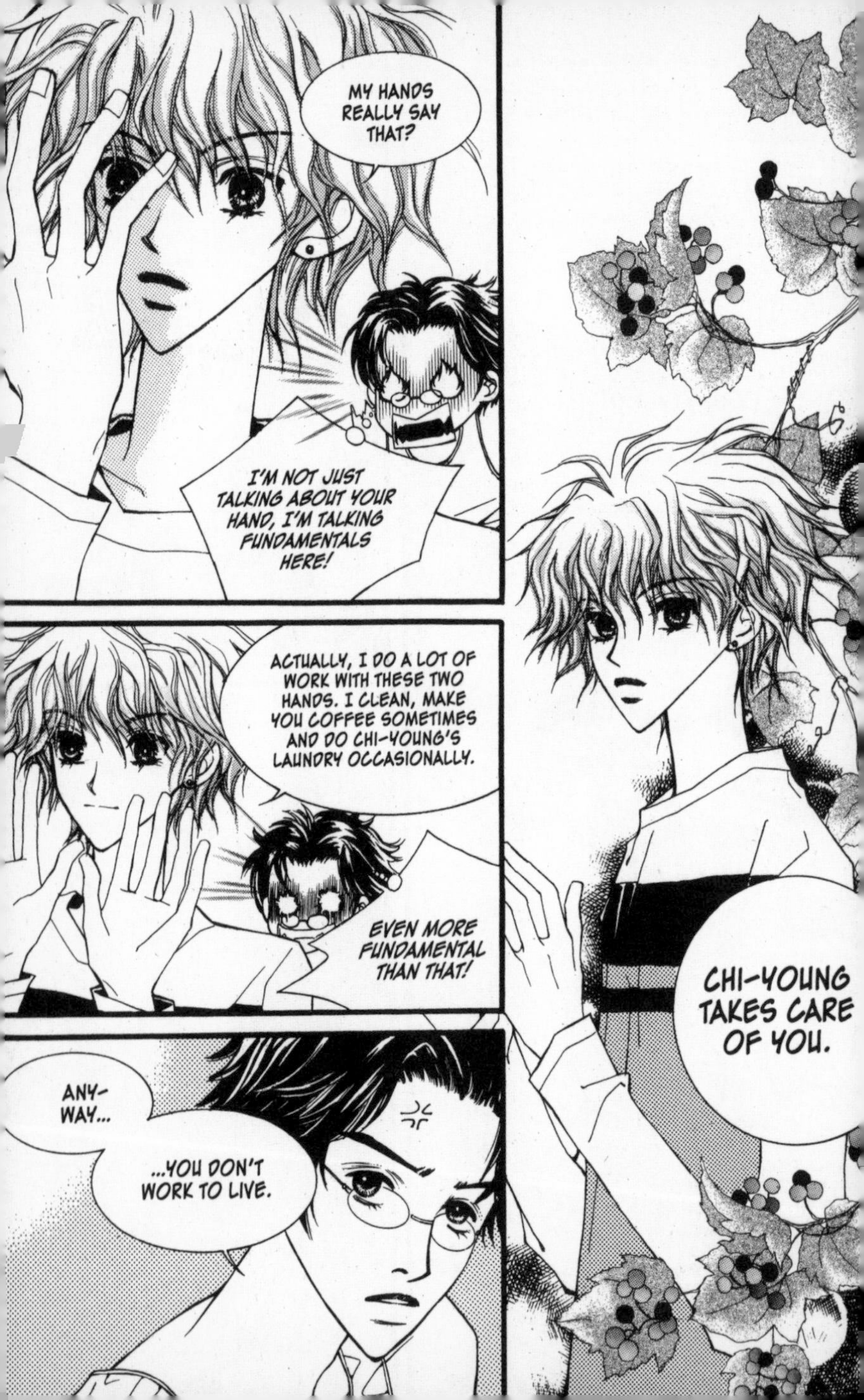
MY HANDS REALLY SAY THAT?
I'M NOT JUST TALKING ABOUT YOUR HAND, I'M TALKING FUNDAMENTALS HERE!
ACTUALLY, I DO A LOT OF WORK WITH THESE TWO HANDS. I CLEAN, MAKE YOU COFFEE SOMETIMES AND DO CHI-YOUNG'S LAUNDRY OCCASIONALLY.
EVEN MORE FUNDAMENTAL THAN THAT!
ANY-WAY...
...YOU DON'T WORK TO LIVE.
CHI-YOUNG TAKES CARE OF YOU.

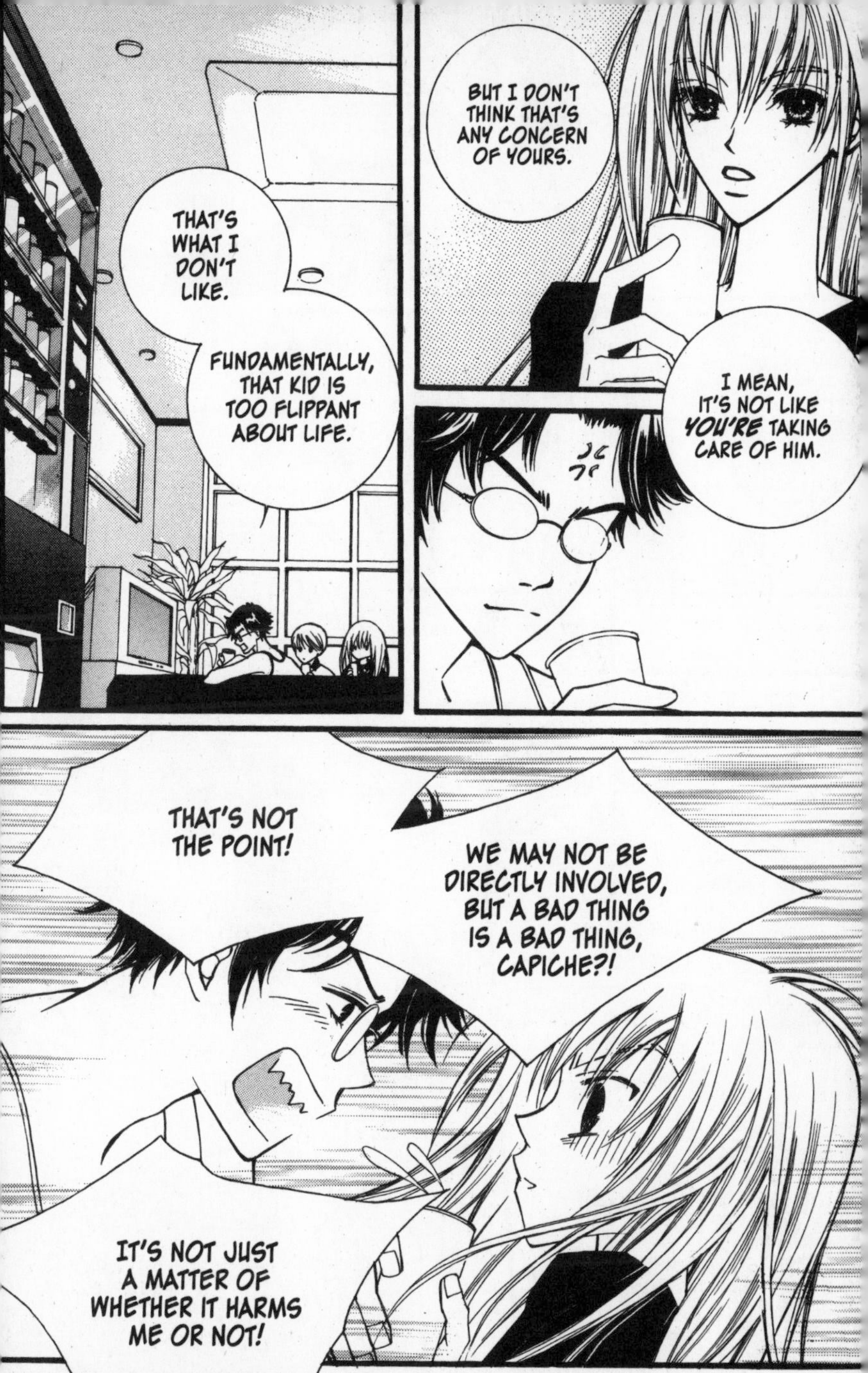
THAT'S WHAT I DON'T LIKE.
FUNDAMENTALLY, THAT KID IS TOO FLIPPANT ABOUT LIFE.
BUT I DON'T THINK THAT'S ANY CONCERN OF YOURS.
I MEAN, IT'S NOT LIKE *YOU'RE* TAKING CARE OF HIM.
THAT'S NOT THE POINT!
WE MAY NOT BE DIRECTLY INVOLVED, BUT A BAD THING IS A BAD THING, CAPICHE?!
IT'S NOT JUST A MATTER OF WHETHER IT HARMS ME OR NOT!

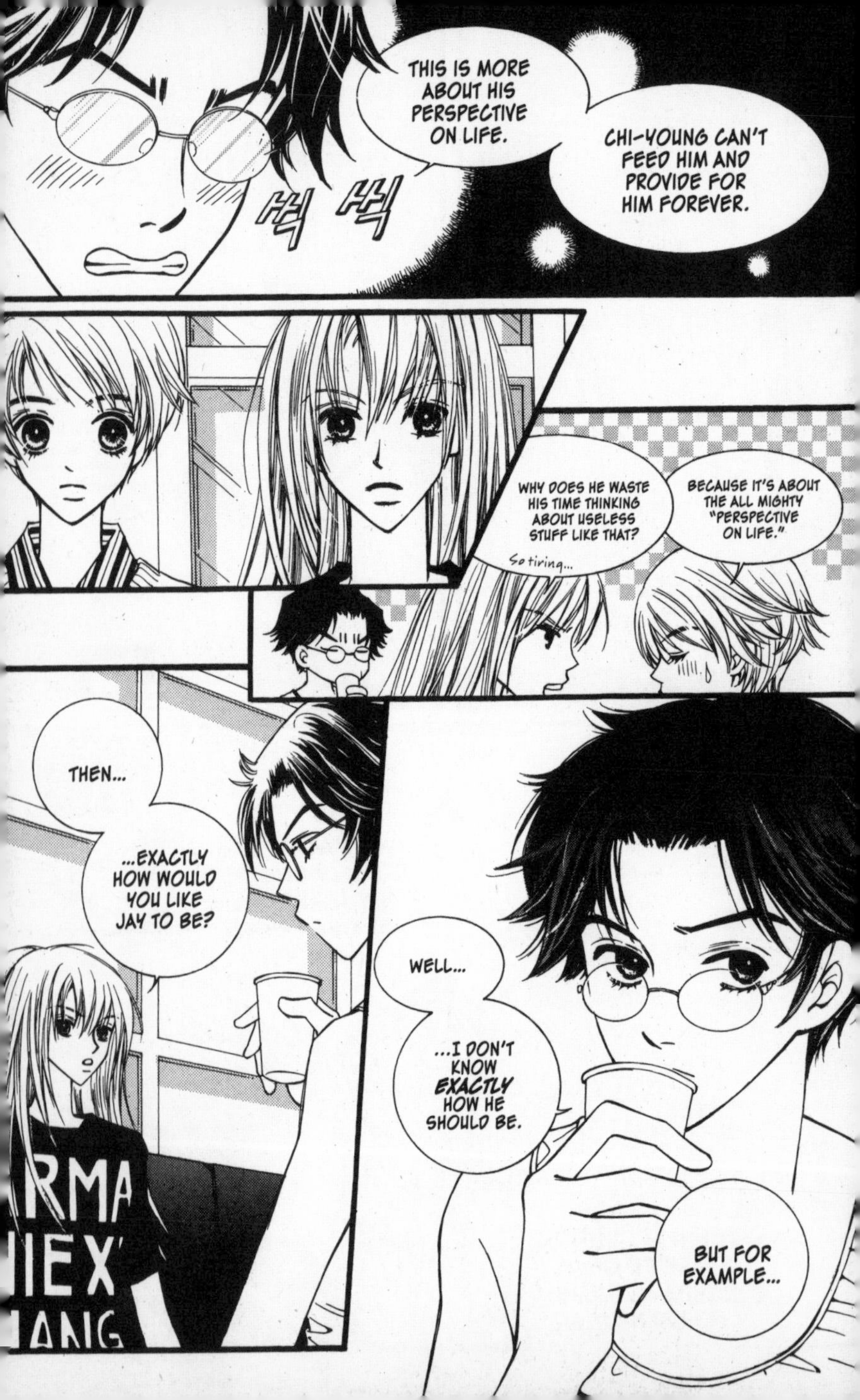
THIS IS MORE ABOUT HIS PERSPECTIVE ON LIFE.
빡 빡
CHI-YOUNG CAN'T FEED HIM AND PROVIDE FOR HIM FOREVER.
WHY DOES HE WASTE HIS TIME THINKING ABOUT USELESS STUFF LIKE THAT?
So tiring...
BECAUSE IT'S ABOUT THE ALL MIGHTY "PERSPECTIVE ON LIFE."
THEN...
...EXACTLY HOW WOULD YOU LIKE JAY TO BE?
WELL...
...I DON'T KNOW *EXACTLY* HOW HE SHOULD BE.
BUT FOR EXAMPLE...

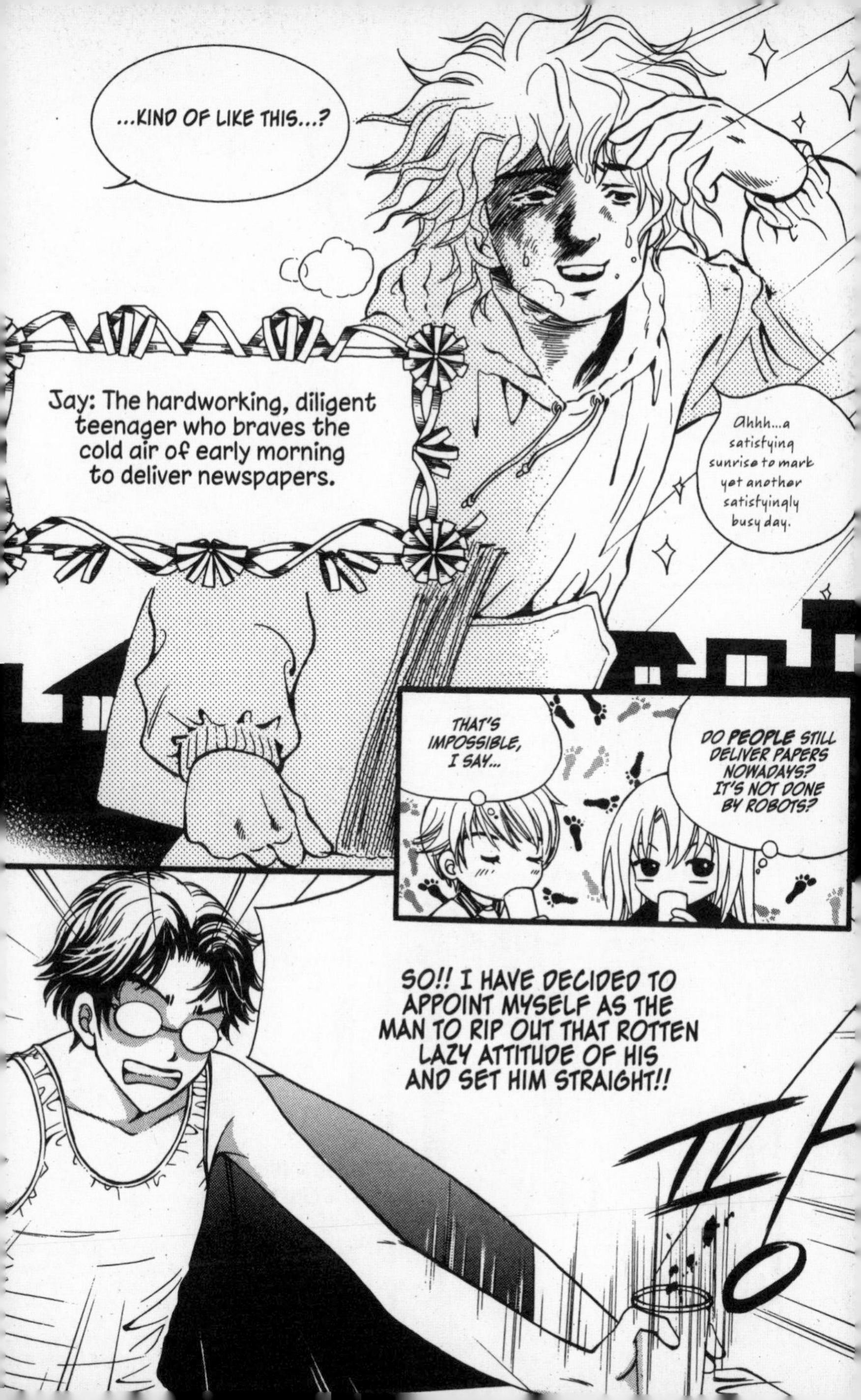
...KIND OF LIKE THIS...?
Jay: The hardworking, diligent teenager who braves the cold air of early morning to deliver newspapers.
Ahhh...a satisfying sunrise to mark yet another satisfyingly busy day.
THAT'S IMPOSSIBLE, I SAY...
DO PEOPLE STILL DELIVER PAPERS NOWADAYS? IT'S NOT DONE BY ROBOTS?
SO!! I HAVE DECIDED TO APPOINT MYSELF AS THE MAN TO RIP OUT THAT ROTTEN LAZY ATTITUDE OF HIS AND SET HIM STRAIGHT!!

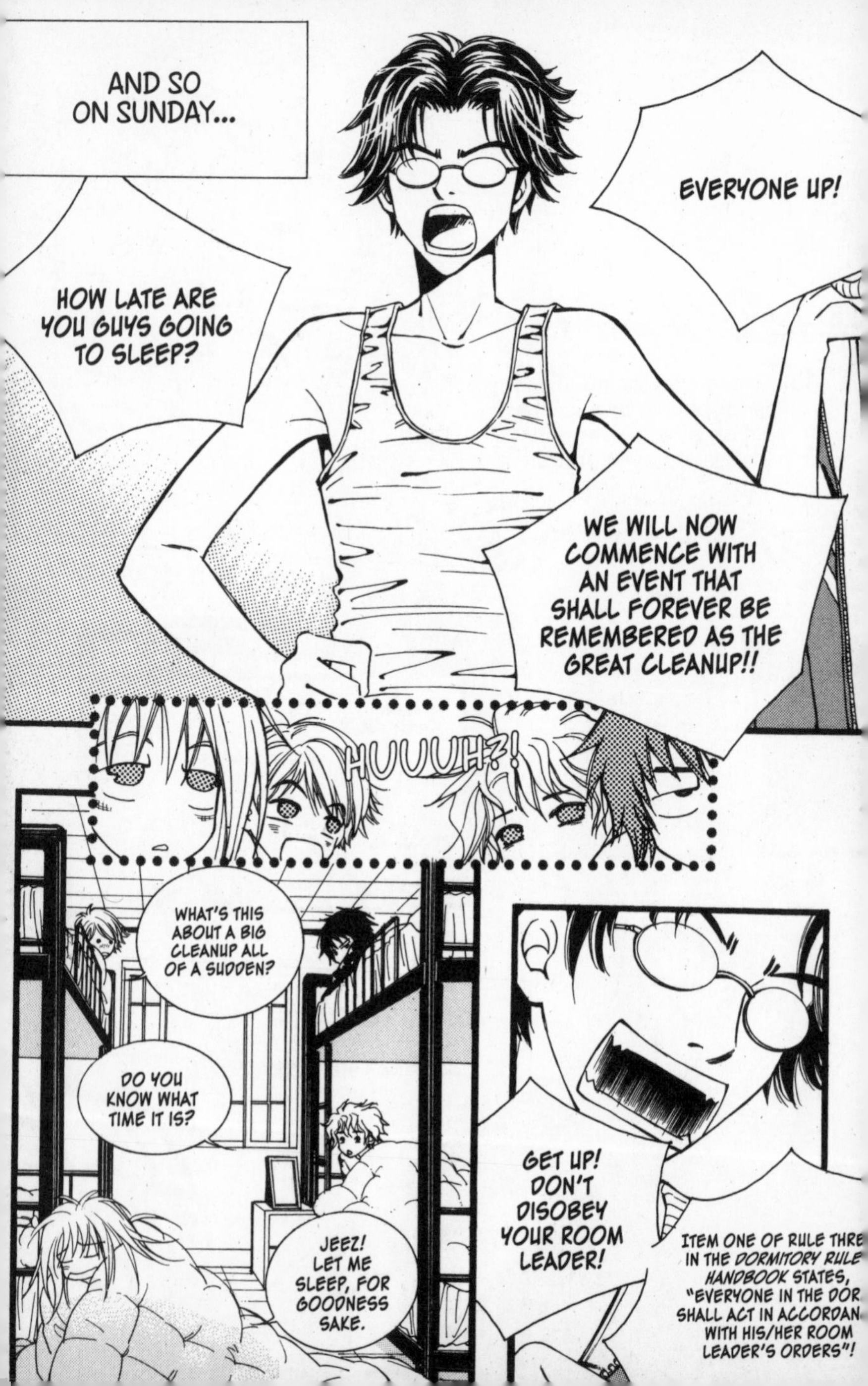

AND SO ON SUNDAY...
EVERYONE UP!
HOW LATE ARE YOU GUYS GOING TO SLEEP?
WE WILL NOW COMMENCE WITH AN EVENT THAT SHALL FOREVER BE REMEMBERED AS THE GREAT CLEANUP!!
HUUUH?!
WHAT'S THIS ABOUT A BIG CLEANUP ALL OF A SUDDEN?
DO YOU KNOW WHAT TIME IT IS?
JEEZ! LET ME SLEEP, FOR GOODNESS SAKE.
GET UP! DON'T DISOBEY YOUR ROOM LEADER!
ITEM ONE OF RULE THRE IN THE DORMITORY RULE HANDBOOK STATES, "EVERYONE IN THE DOR SHALL ACT IN ACCORDAN WITH HIS/HER ROOM LEADER'S ORDERS"!

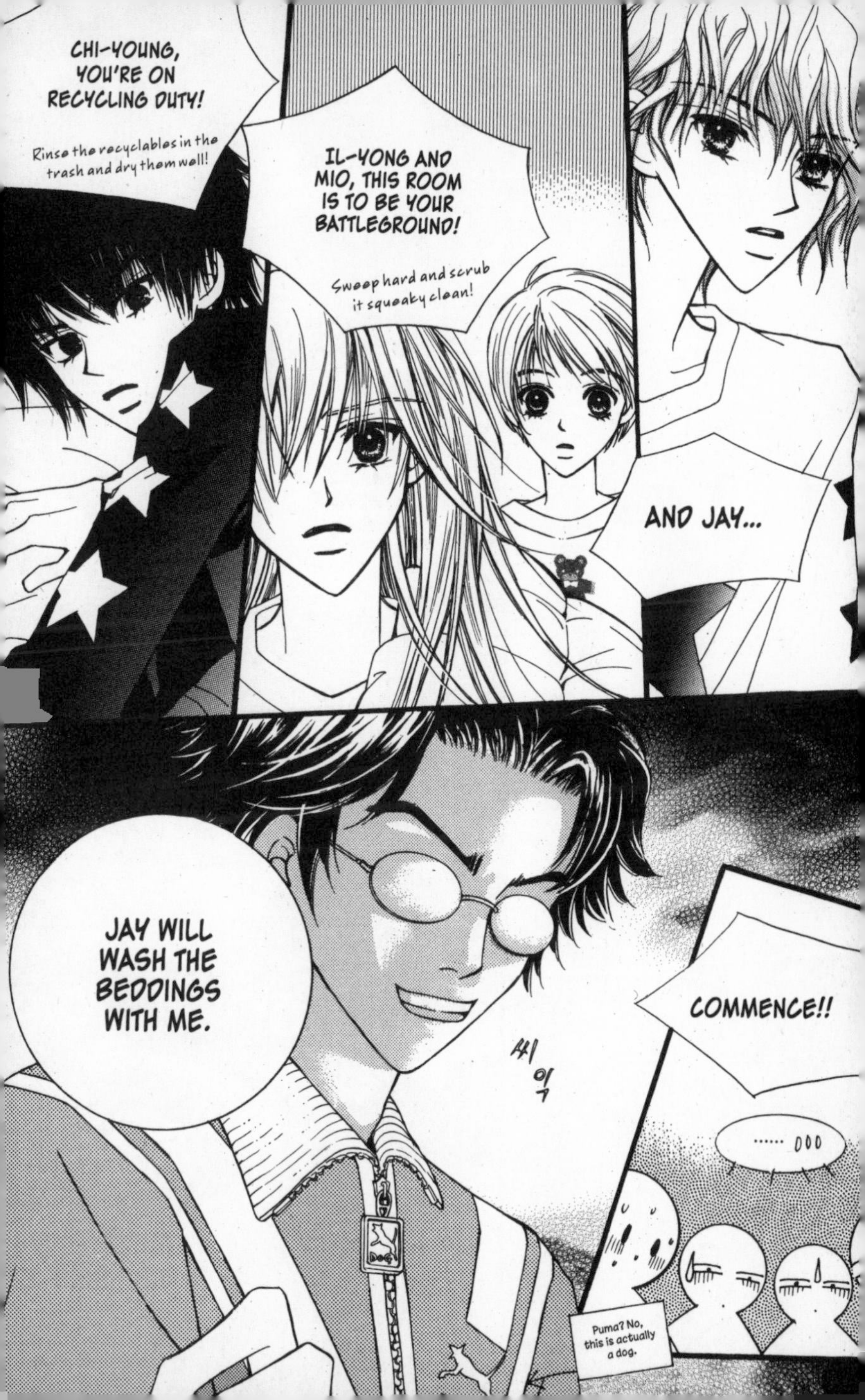

CHI-YOUNG, YOU'RE ON RECYCLING DUTY!
Rinse the recyclables in the trash and dry them well!
IL-YONG AND MIO, THIS ROOM IS TO BE YOUR BATTLEGROUND!
Sweep hard and scrub it squeaky clean!
AND JAY...
JAY WILL WASH THE BEDDINGS WITH ME.
씨익
COMMENCE!!
...... 000
Puma? No, this is actually a dog.
DOG

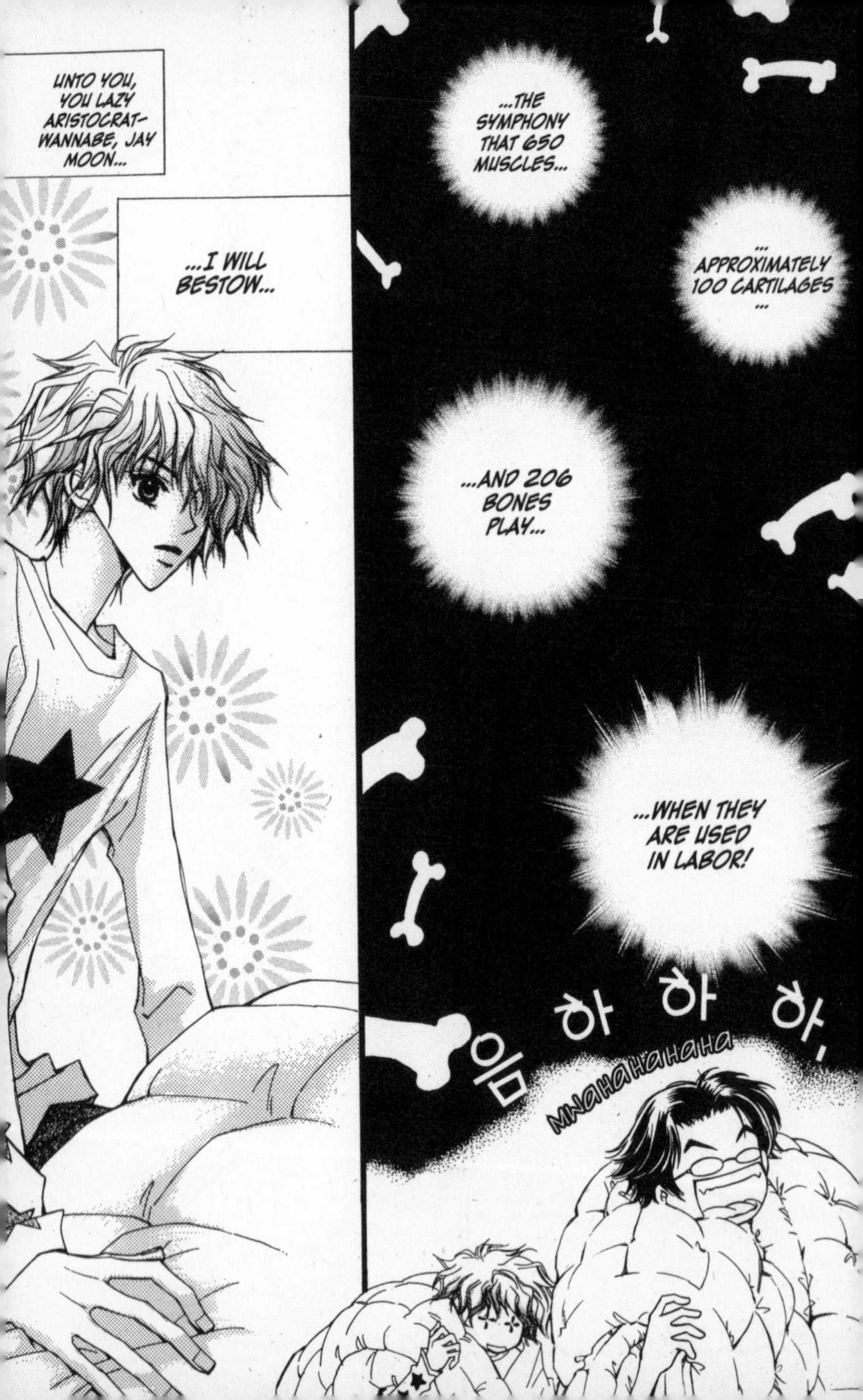
UNTO YOU, YOU LAZY ARISTOCRAT-WANNABE, JAY MOON...
...I WILL BESTOW...
...THE SYMPHONY THAT 650 MUSCLES...
...APPROXIMATELY 100 CARTILAGES...
...AND 206 BONES PLAY...
...WHEN THEY ARE USED IN LABOR!
음 하 하 하,
MWAHAHAHAHAHA

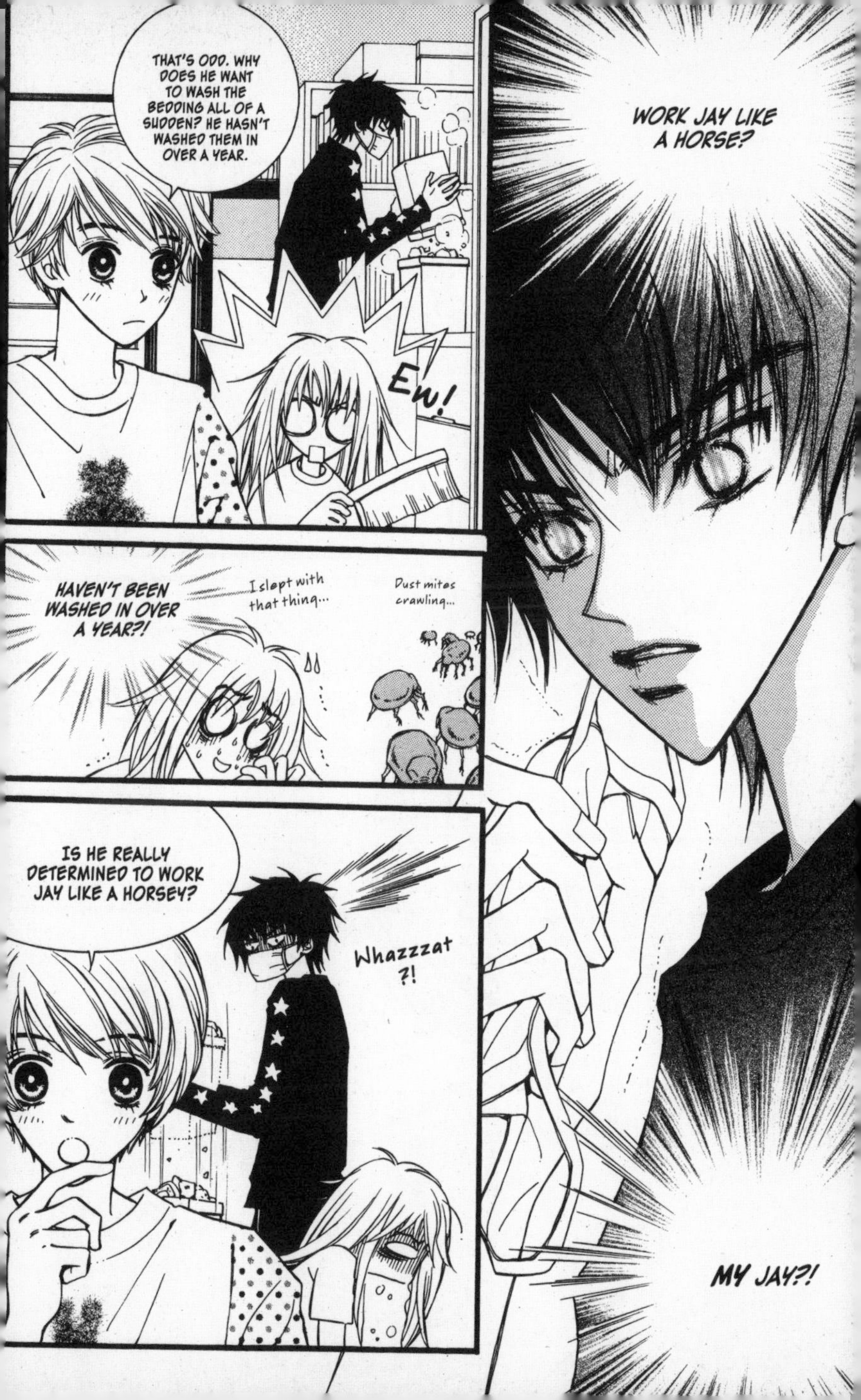
THAT'S ODD. WHY DOES HE WANT TO WASH THE BEDDING ALL OF A SUDDEN? HE HASN'T WASHED THEM IN OVER A YEAR.
Ew!
HAVEN'T BEEN WASHED IN OVER A YEAR?!
I slept with that thing...
Dust mites crawling...
IS HE REALLY DETERMINED TO WORK JAY LIKE A HORSEY?
Whazzzat ?!
WORK JAY LIKE A HORSE?
MY JAY?!

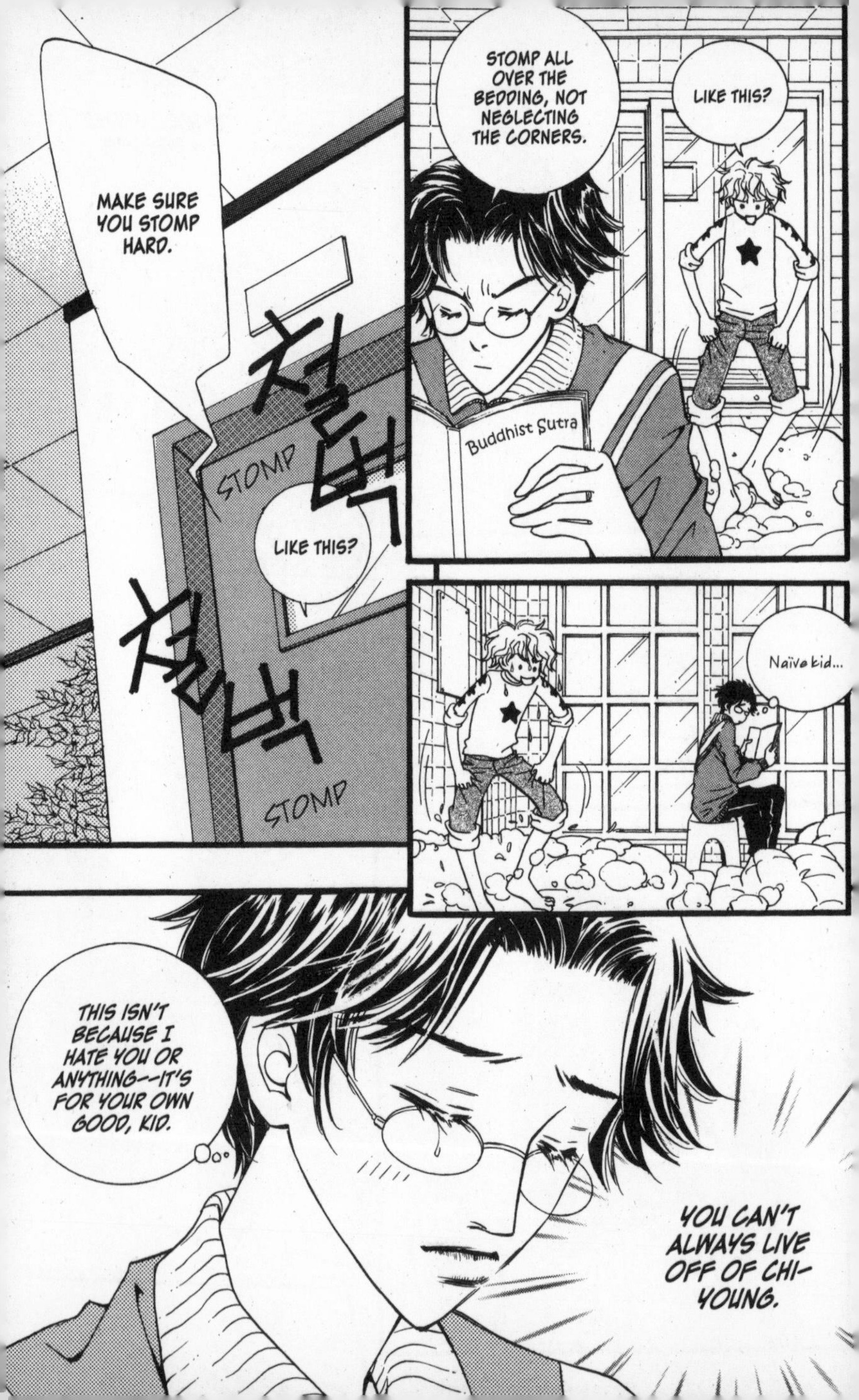
MAKE SURE YOU STOMP HARD.
STOMP
LIKE THIS?
STOMP
STOMP ALL OVER THE BEDDING, NOT NEGLECTING THE CORNERS.
LIKE THIS?
Buddhist Sutra
Naïve kid...
THIS ISN'T BECAUSE I HATE YOU OR ANYTHING--IT'S FOR YOUR OWN GOOD, KID.
YOU CAN'T ALWAYS LIVE OFF OF CHI-YOUNG.

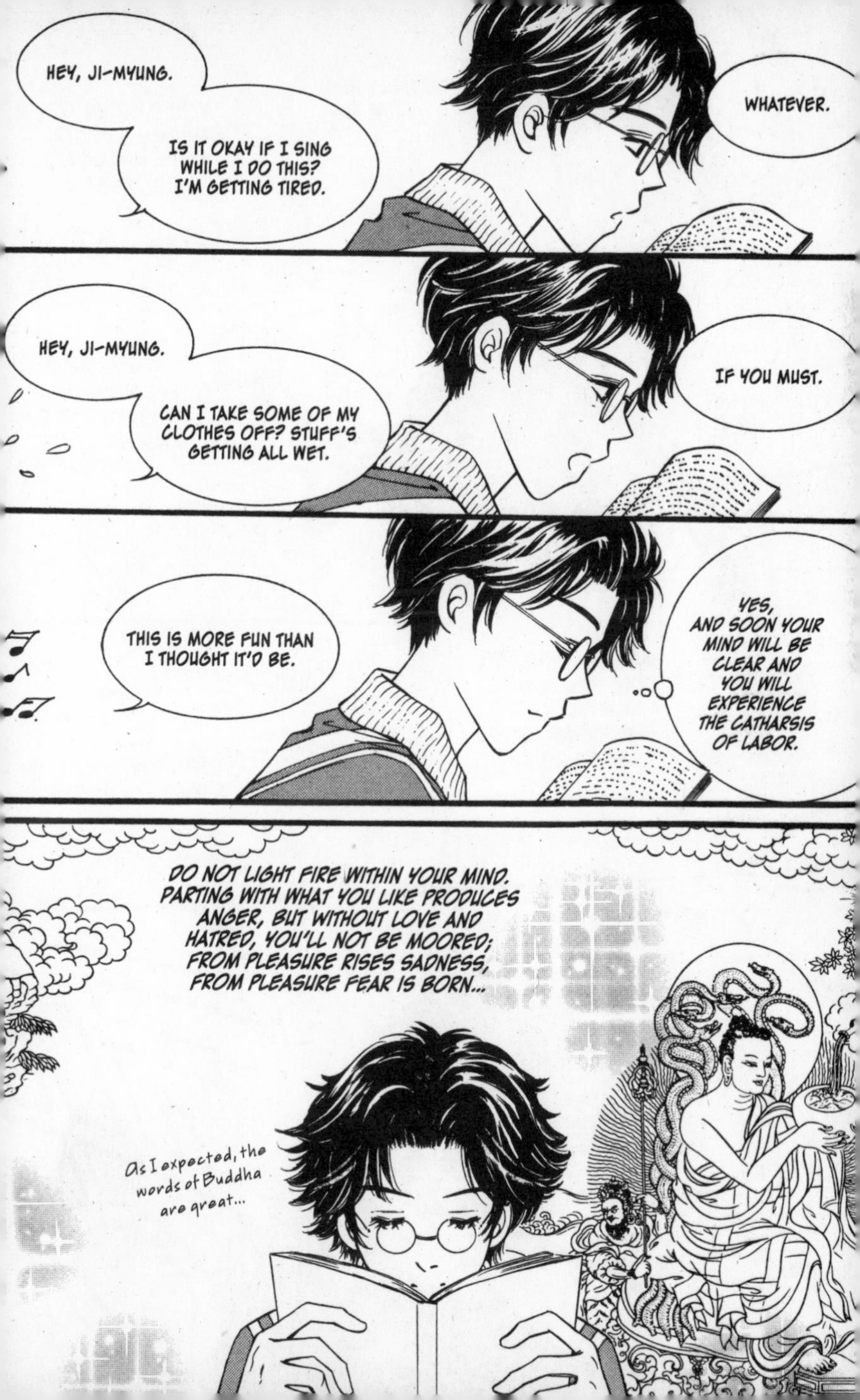
HEY, JI-MYUNG.
IS IT OKAY IF I SING WHILE I DO THIS? I'M GETTING TIRED.
WHATEVER.
HEY, JI-MYUNG.
CAN I TAKE SOME OF MY CLOTHES OFF? STUFF'S GETTING ALL WET.
IF YOU MUST.
THIS IS MORE FUN THAN I THOUGHT IT'D BE.
YES, AND SOON YOUR MIND WILL BE CLEAR AND YOU WILL EXPERIENCE THE CATHARSIS OF LABOR.
DO NOT LIGHT FIRE WITHIN YOUR MIND. PARTING WITH WHAT YOU LIKE PRODUCES ANGER, BUT WITHOUT LOVE AND HATRED, YOU'LL NOT BE MOORED; FROM PLEASURE RISES SADNESS, FROM PLEASURE FEAR IS BORN...
As I expected, the words of Buddha are great...

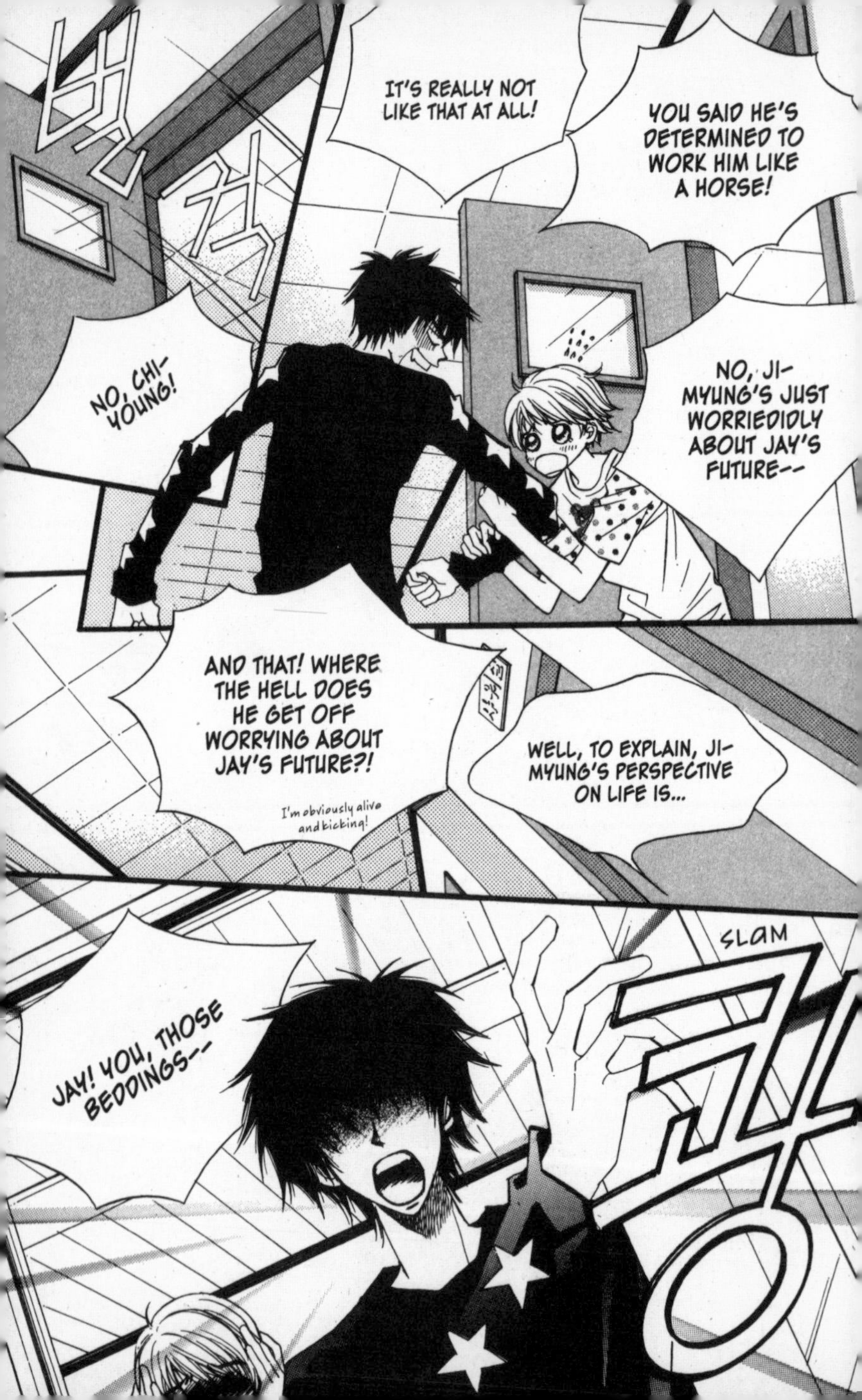
NO, CHI-YOUNG!
IT'S REALLY NOT LIKE THAT AT ALL!
YOU SAID HE'S DETERMINED TO WORK HIM LIKE A HORSE!
NO, JI-MYUNG'S JUST WORRIEDIDLY ABOUT JAY'S FUTURE--
AND THAT! WHERE THE HELL DOES HE GET OFF WORRYING ABOUT JAY'S FUTURE?!
I'm obviously alive and kicking!
WELL, TO EXPLAIN, JI-MYUNG'S PERSPECTIVE ON LIFE IS...
JAY! YOU, THOSE BEDDINGS--
SLAM

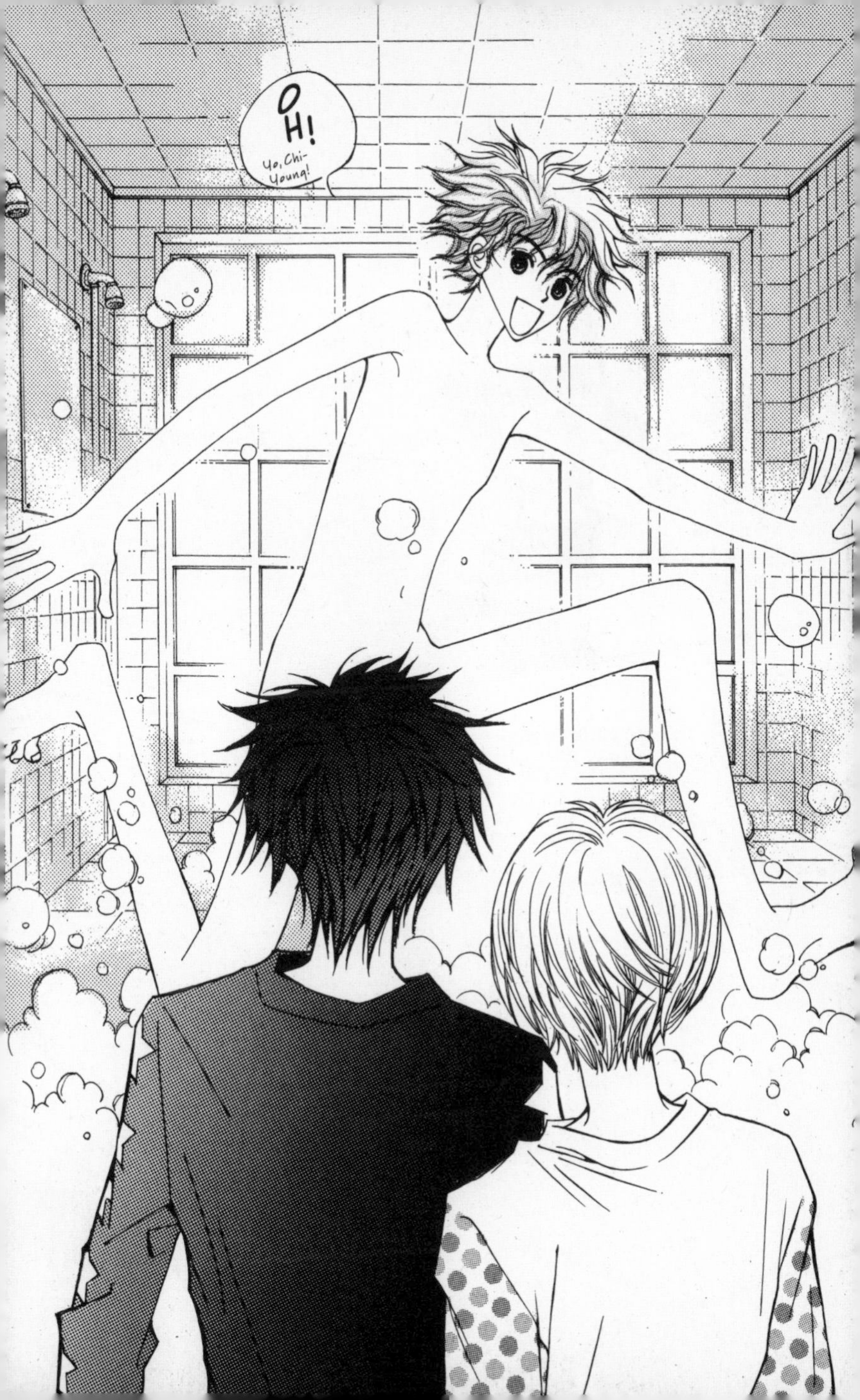

OH!
Yo, Chi-Young!

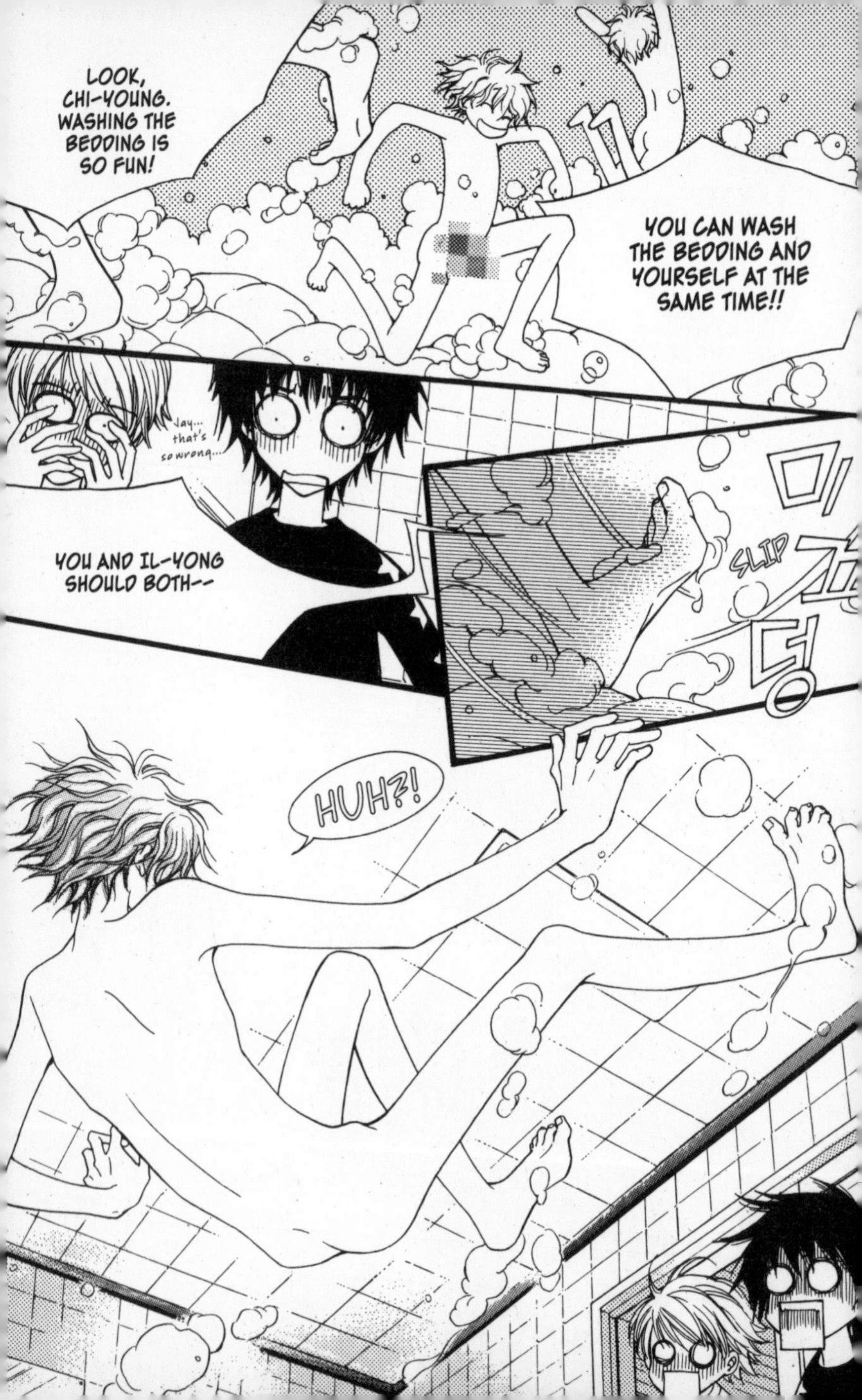
LOOK, CHI-YOUNG. WASHING THE BEDDING IS SO FUN!
YOU CAN WASH THE BEDDING AND YOURSELF AT THE SAME TIME!!
Jay... that's so wrong...
YOU AND IL-YONG SHOULD BOTH--
미끄덩
SLIP
HUH?!

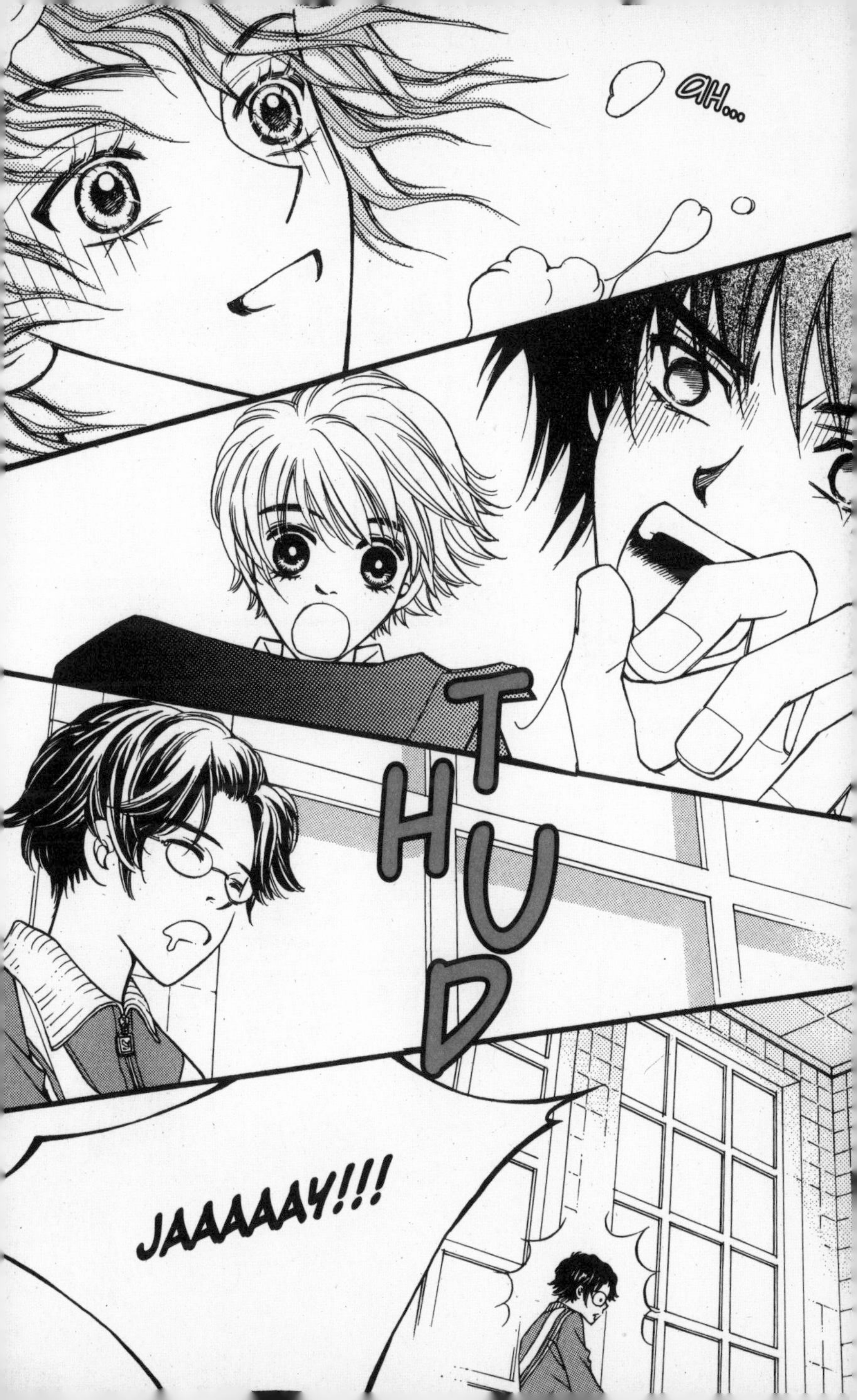
AH...
THUD
JAAAAAY!!!

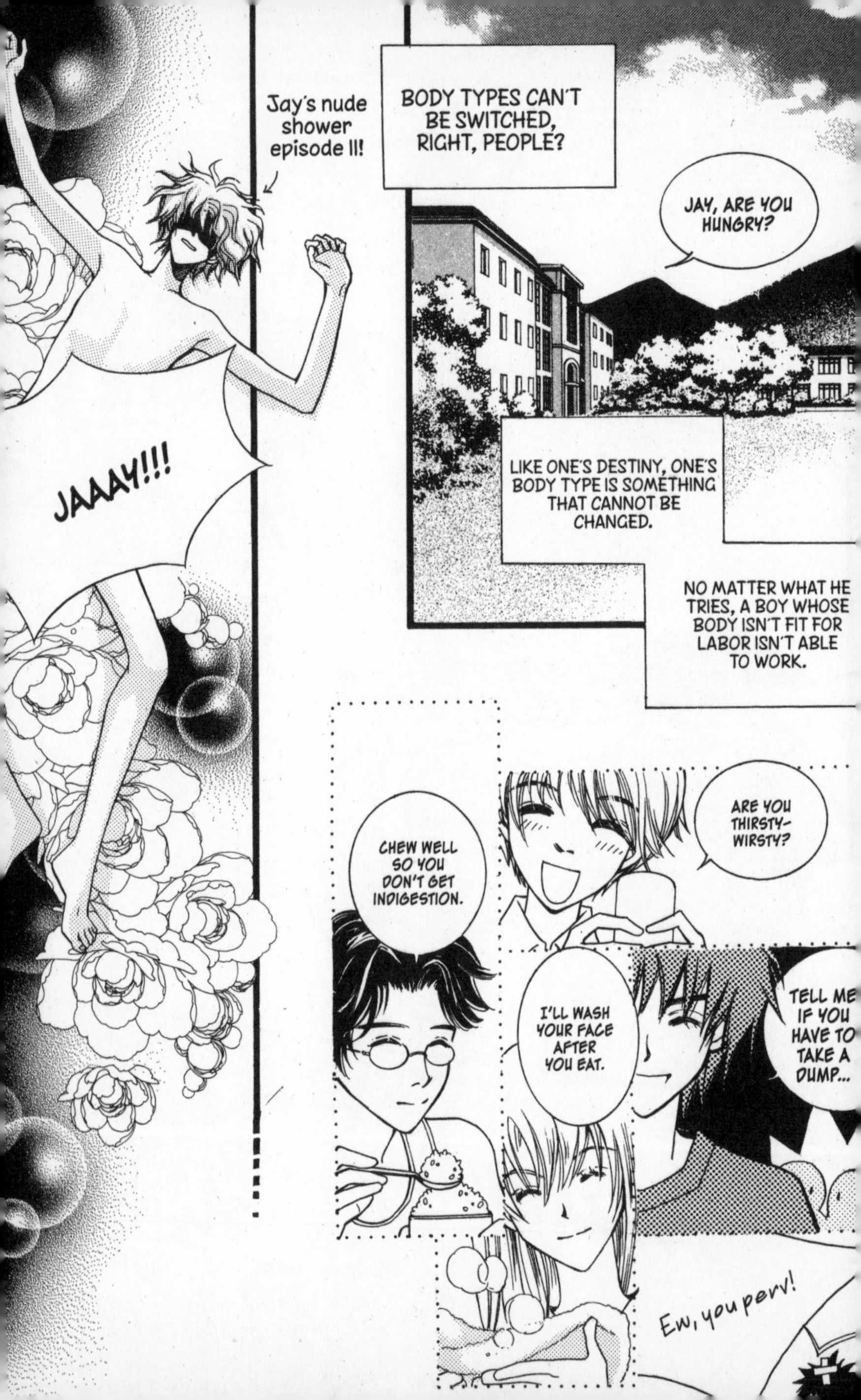
Jay's nude shower episode II!
JAAAY!!!
BODY TYPES CAN'T BE SWITCHED, RIGHT, PEOPLE?
JAY, ARE YOU HUNGRY?
LIKE ONE'S DESTINY, ONE'S BODY TYPE IS SOMETHING THAT CANNOT BE CHANGED.
NO MATTER WHAT HE TRIES, A BOY WHOSE BODY ISN'T FIT FOR LABOR ISN'T ABLE TO WORK.
CHEW WELL SO YOU DON'T GET INDIGESTION.
ARE YOU THIRSTY-WIRSTY?
I'LL WASH YOUR FACE AFTER YOU EAT.
TELL ME IF YOU HAVE TO TAKE A DUMP...
Ew, you perv!

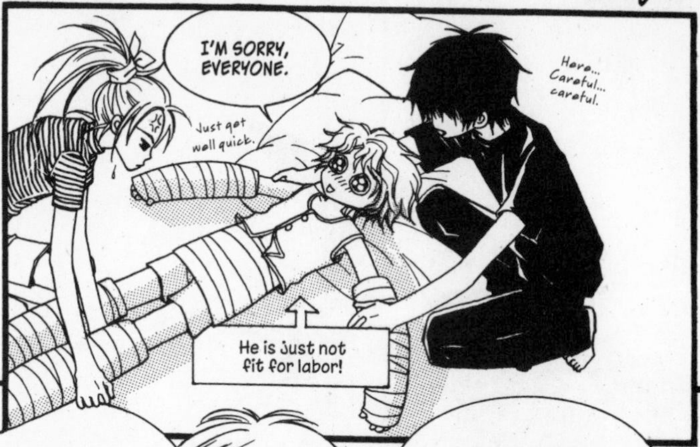
I'M SORRY, EVERYONE.
Here... Careful... careful.
Just get well quick.
He is just not fit for labor!

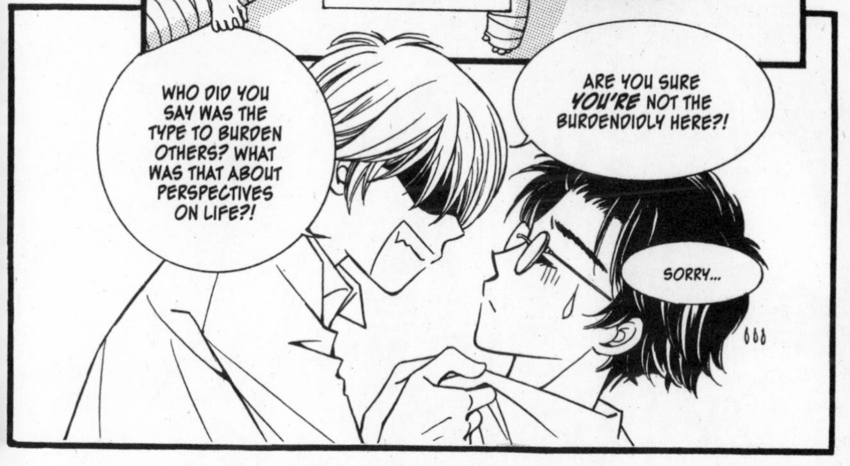
WHO DID YOU SAY WAS THE TYPE TO BURDEN OTHERS? WHAT WAS THAT ABOUT PERSPECTIVES ON LIFE?!
ARE YOU SURE ***YOU'RE*** NOT THE BURDENDIDLY HERE?!
SORRY...

...

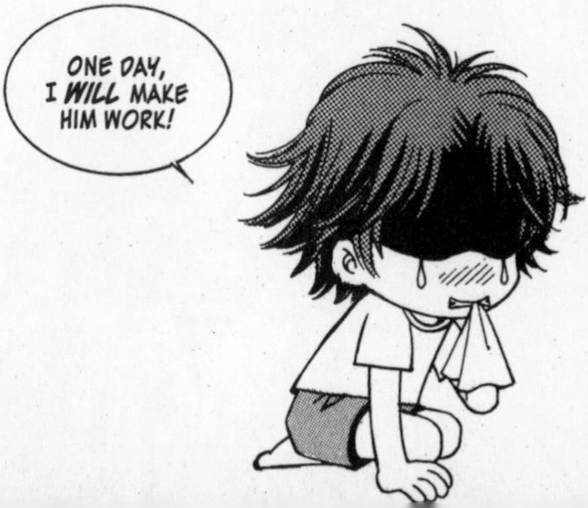
ONE DAY, I ***WILL*** MAKE HIM WORK!

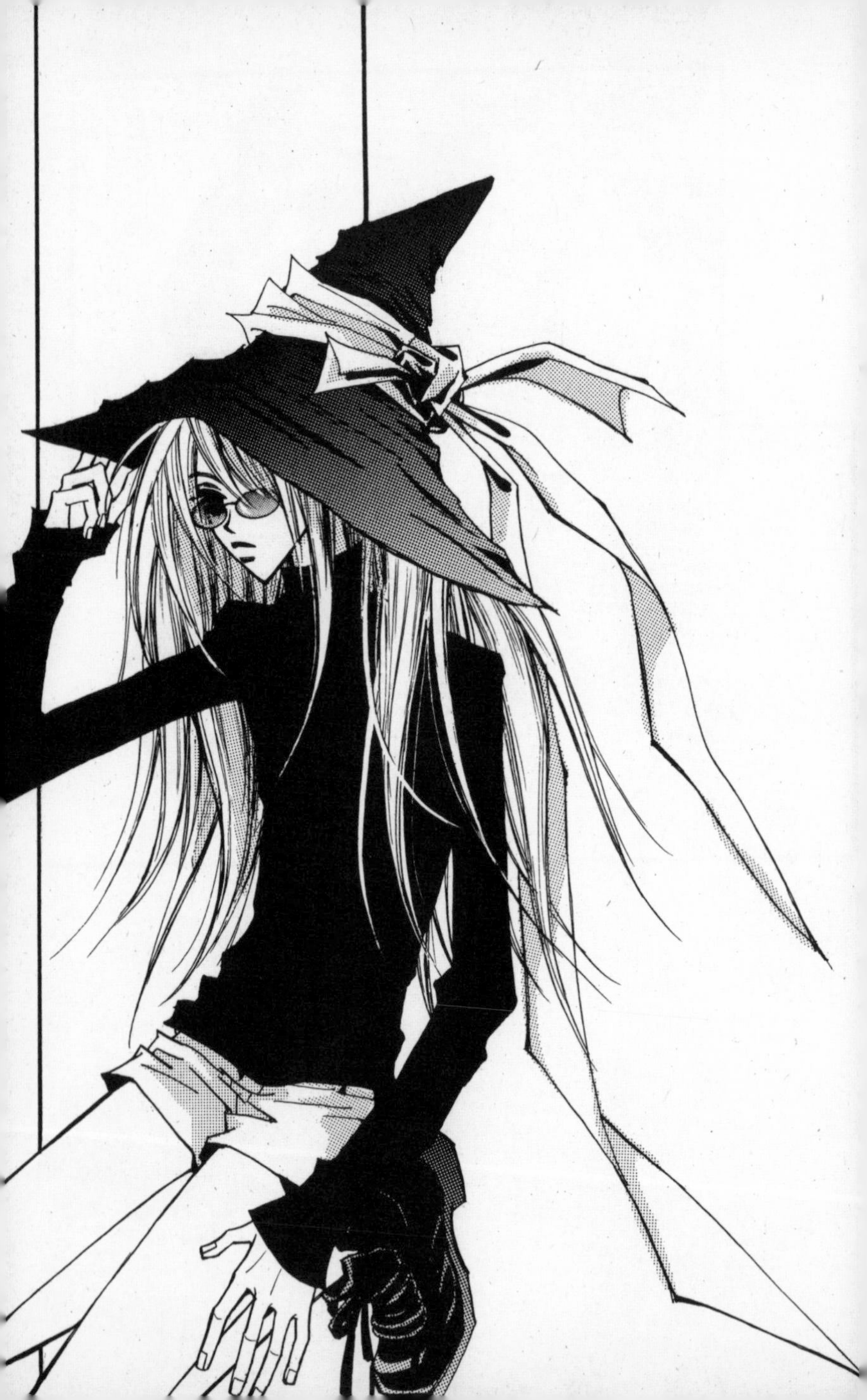

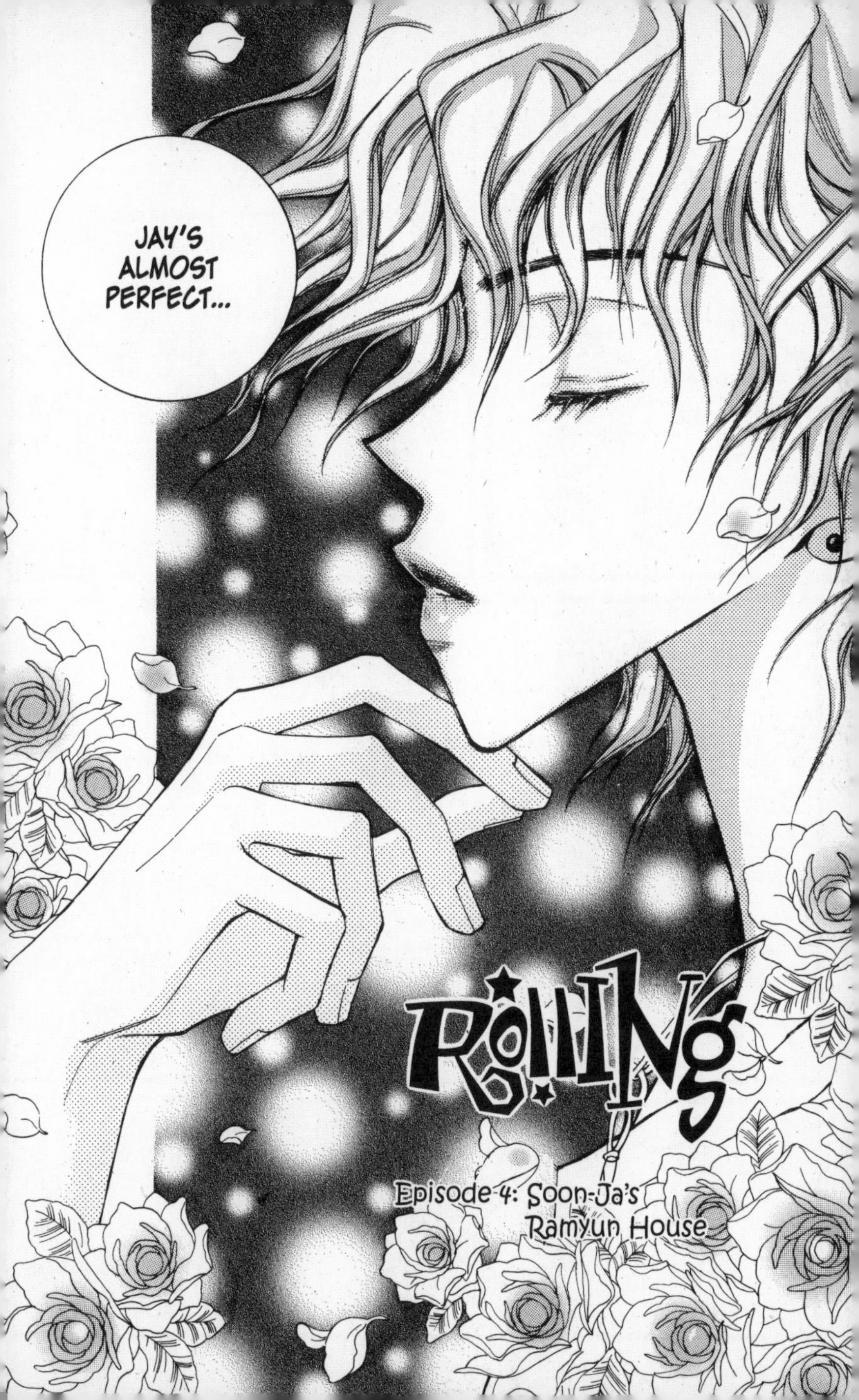
JAY'S ALMOST PERFECT...
Rolling
Episode 4: Soon-Ja's Ramyun House

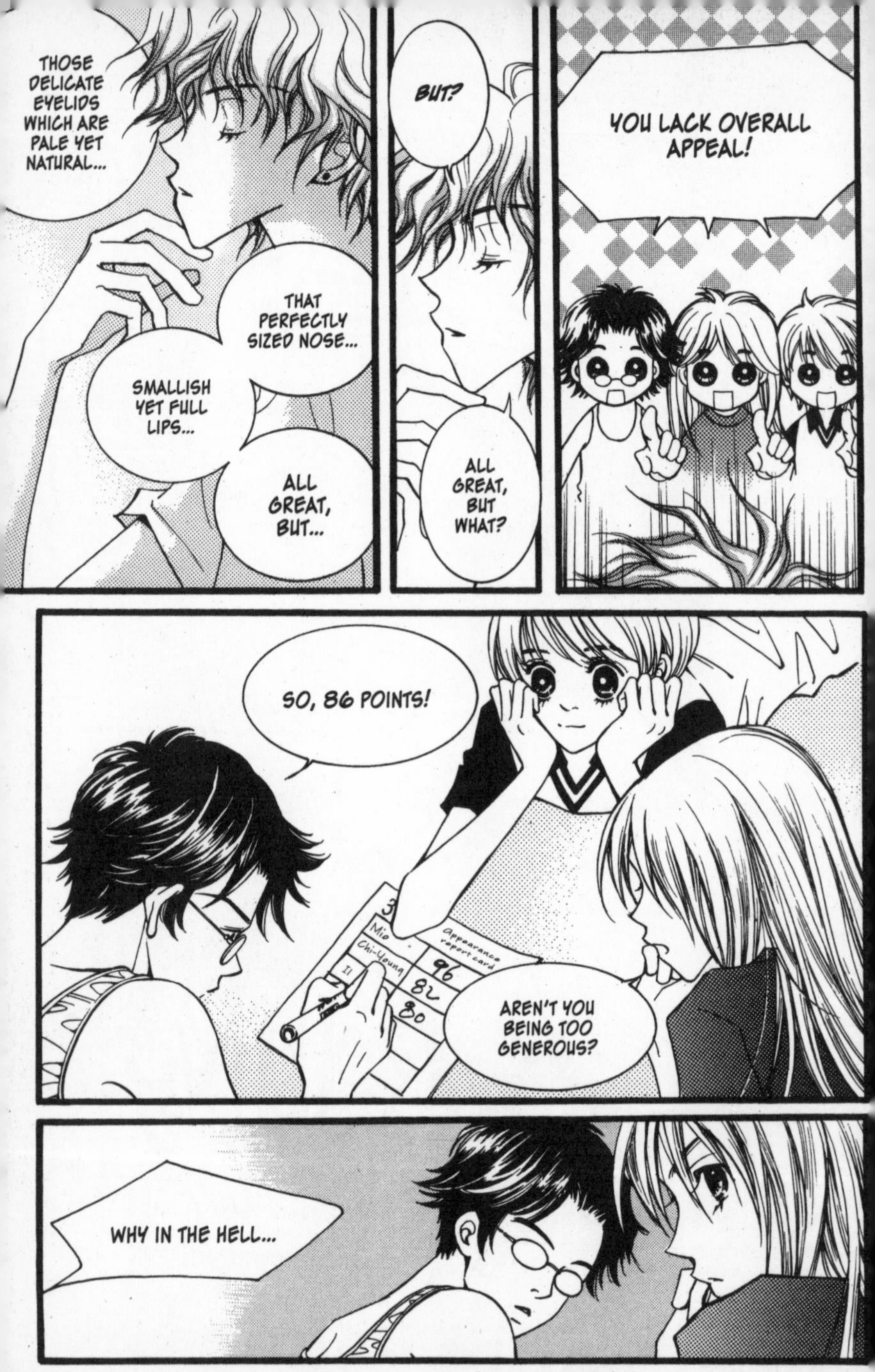
THOSE DELICATE EYELIDS WHICH ARE PALE YET NATURAL...
THAT PERFECTLY SIZED NOSE...
SMALLISH YET FULL LIPS...
ALL GREAT, BUT...
BUT?
ALL GREAT, BUT WHAT?
YOU LACK OVERALL APPEAL!
SO, 86 POINTS!
Appearance report card
Mio 96
Chi-Young 82
80
AREN'T YOU BEING TOO GENEROUS?
WHY IN THE HELL...

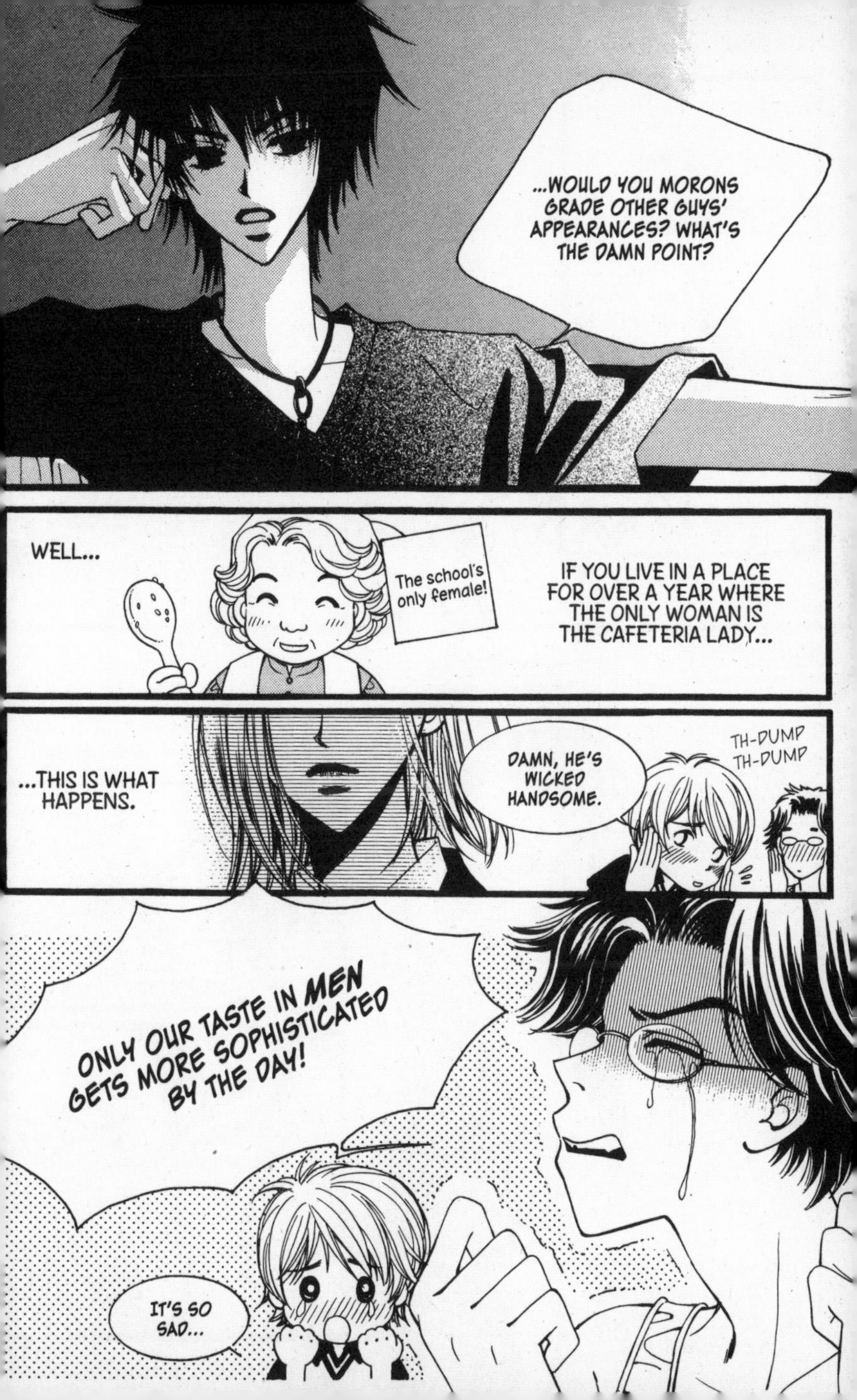
...WOULD YOU MORONS GRADE OTHER GUYS' APPEARANCES? WHAT'S THE DAMN POINT?
WELL...
The school's only female!
IF YOU LIVE IN A PLACE FOR OVER A YEAR WHERE THE ONLY WOMAN IS THE CAFETERIA LADY...
...THIS IS WHAT HAPPENS.
DAMN, HE'S WICKED HANDSOME.
TH-DUMP TH-DUMP
ONLY OUR TASTE IN MEN GETS MORE SOPHISTICATED BY THE DAY!
IT'S SO SAD...

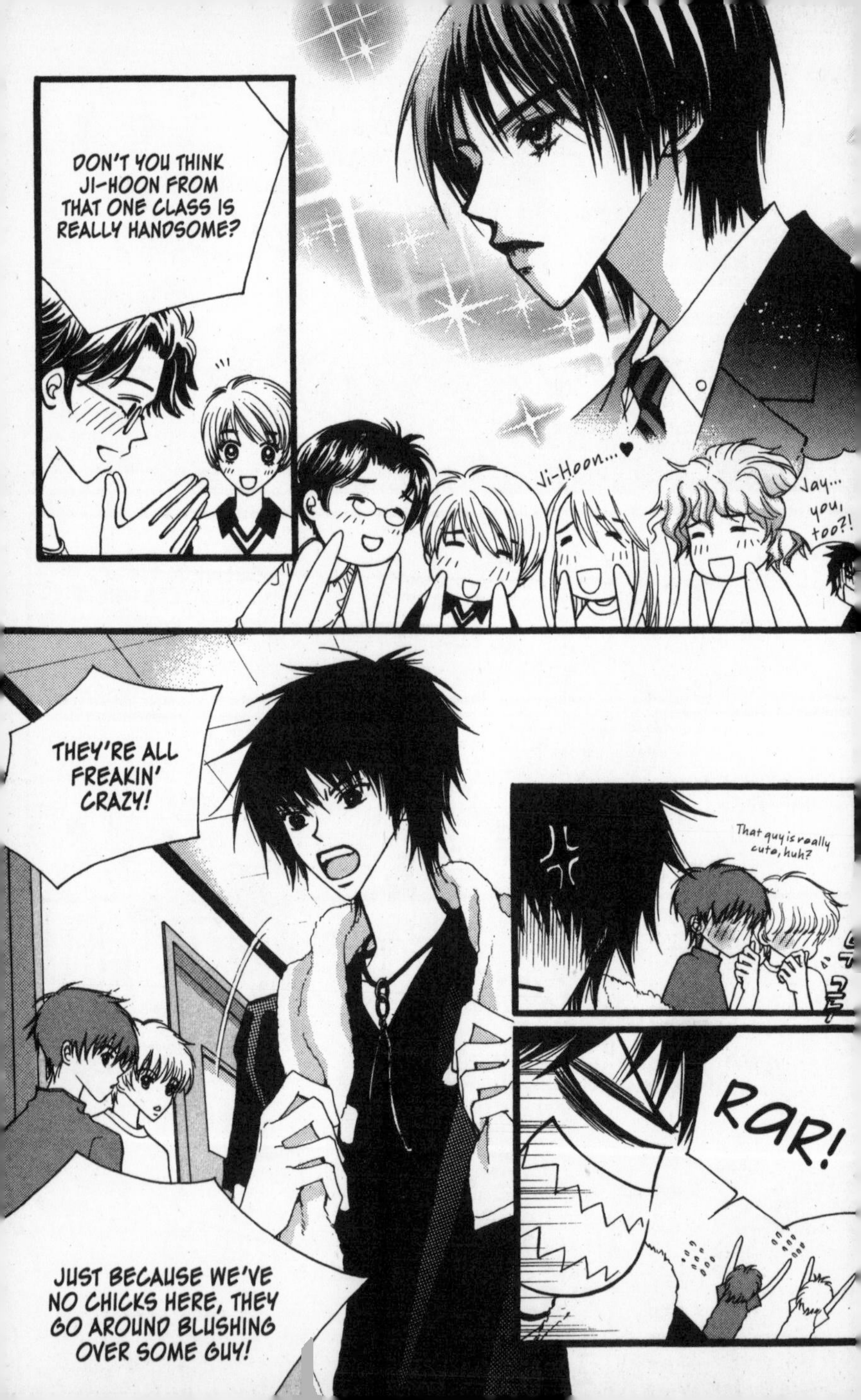
DON'T YOU THINK JI-HOON FROM THAT ONE CLASS IS REALLY HANDSOME?
Ji-Hoon...♥
Jay... you, too?!
THEY'RE ALL FREAKIN' CRAZY!
JUST BECAUSE WE'VE NO CHICKS HERE, THEY GO AROUND BLUSHING OVER SOME GUY!
That guy is really cute, huh?
RAR!

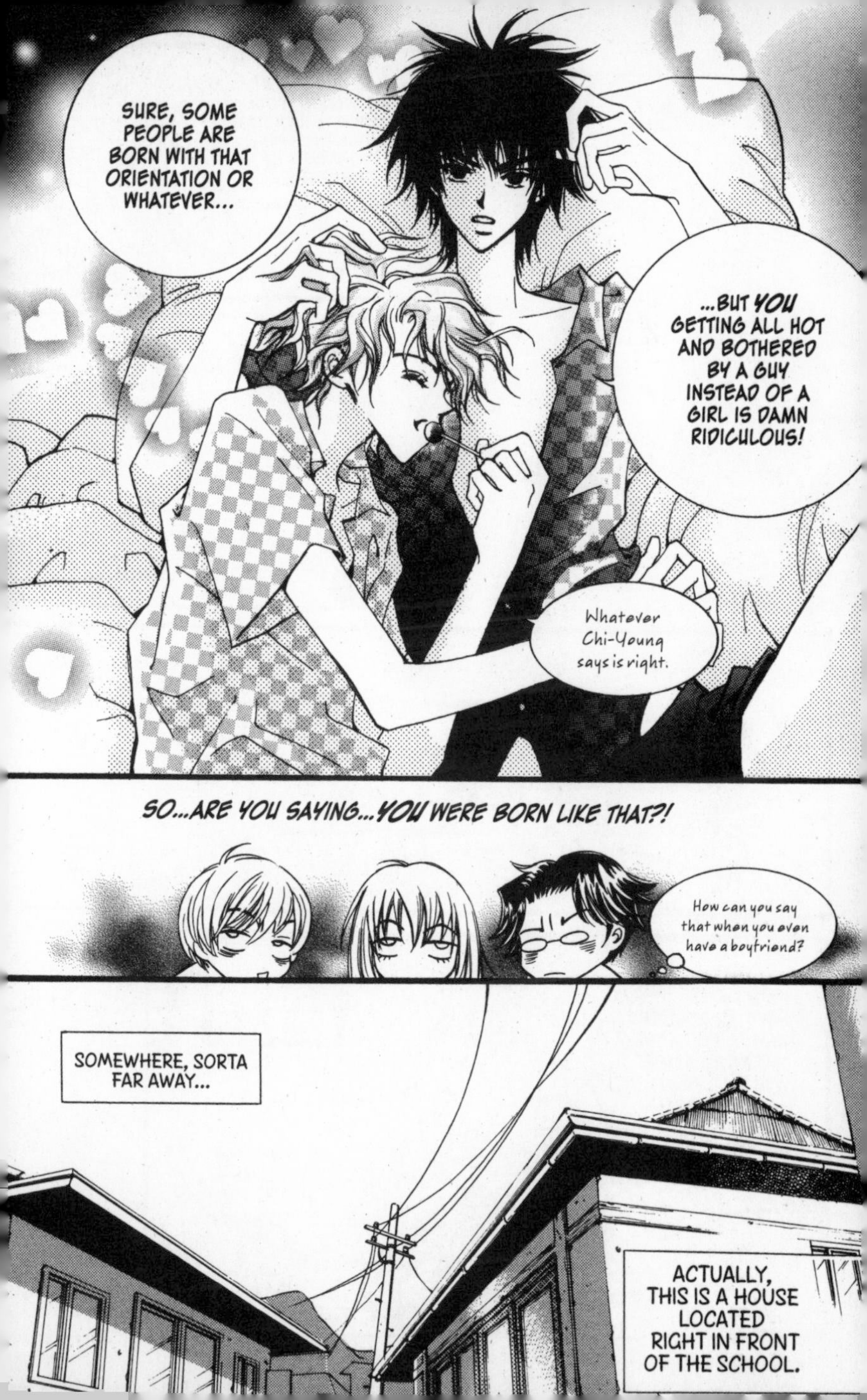
SURE, SOME PEOPLE ARE BORN WITH THAT ORIENTATION OR WHATEVER...
...BUT YOU GETTING ALL HOT AND BOTHERED BY A GUY INSTEAD OF A GIRL IS DAMN RIDICULOUS!
Whatever Chi-Young says is right.
SO...ARE YOU SAYING...YOU WERE BORN LIKE THAT?!
How can you say that when you even have a boyfriend?
SOMEWHERE, SORTA FAR AWAY...
ACTUALLY, THIS IS A HOUSE LOCATED RIGHT IN FRONT OF THE SCHOOL.

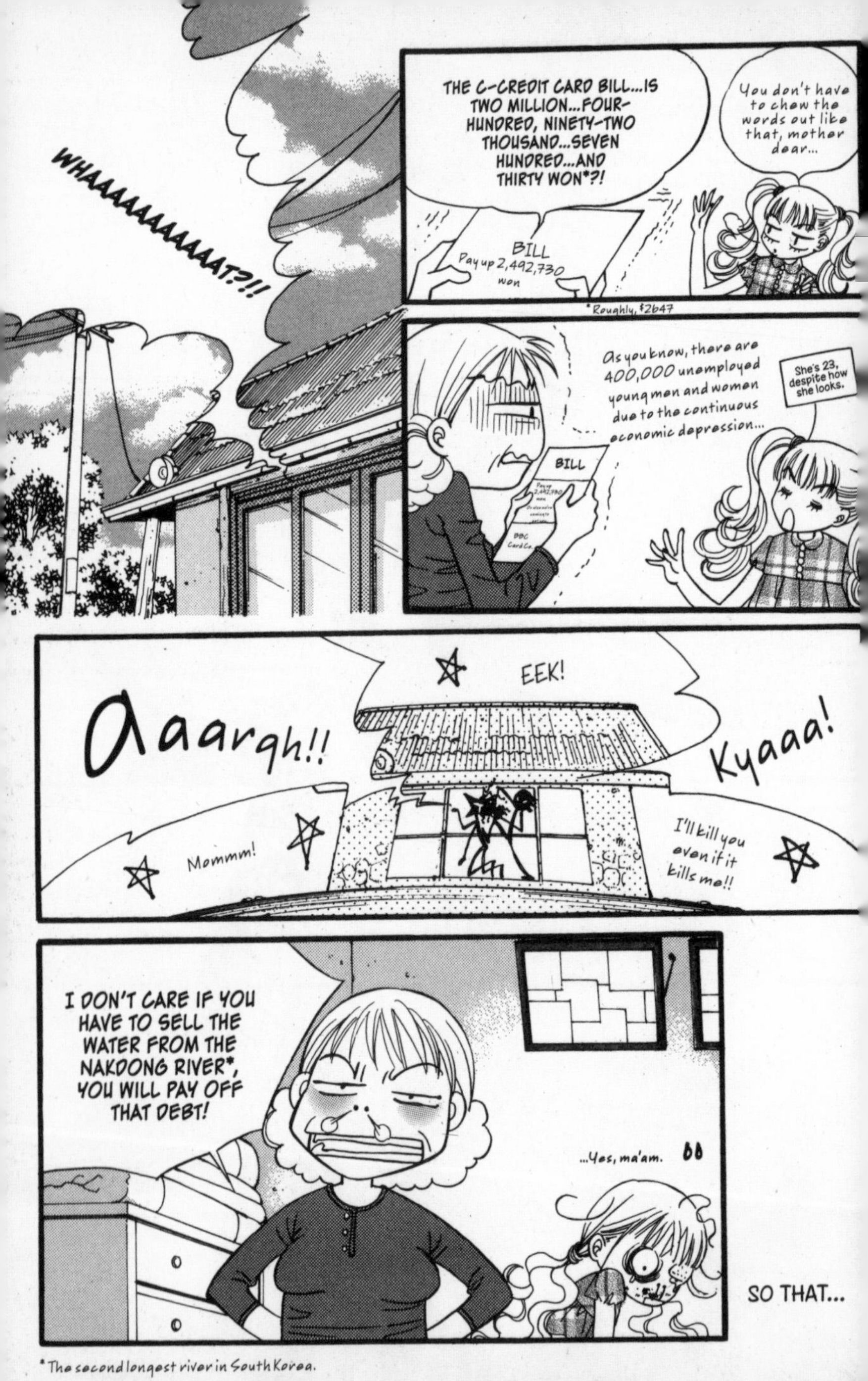
WHAAAAAAAAAAAAT?!!
THE C-CREDIT CARD BILL...IS TWO MILLION...FOUR-HUNDRED, NINETY-TWO THOUSAND...SEVEN HUNDRED...AND THIRTY WON*?!
BILL
Pay up 2,492,730 won
You don't have to chew the words out like that, mother dear...
*Roughly, $2647
BILL
As you know, there are 400,000 unemployed young men and women due to the continuous economic depression...
She's 23, despite how she looks.
EEK!
Aaargh!!
Kyaaa!
Mommm!
I'll kill you even if it kills me!!
I DON'T CARE IF YOU HAVE TO SELL THE WATER FROM THE NAKDONG RIVER*, YOU WILL PAY OFF THAT DEBT!
...Yes, ma'am.
SO THAT...

*The second longest river in South Korea.

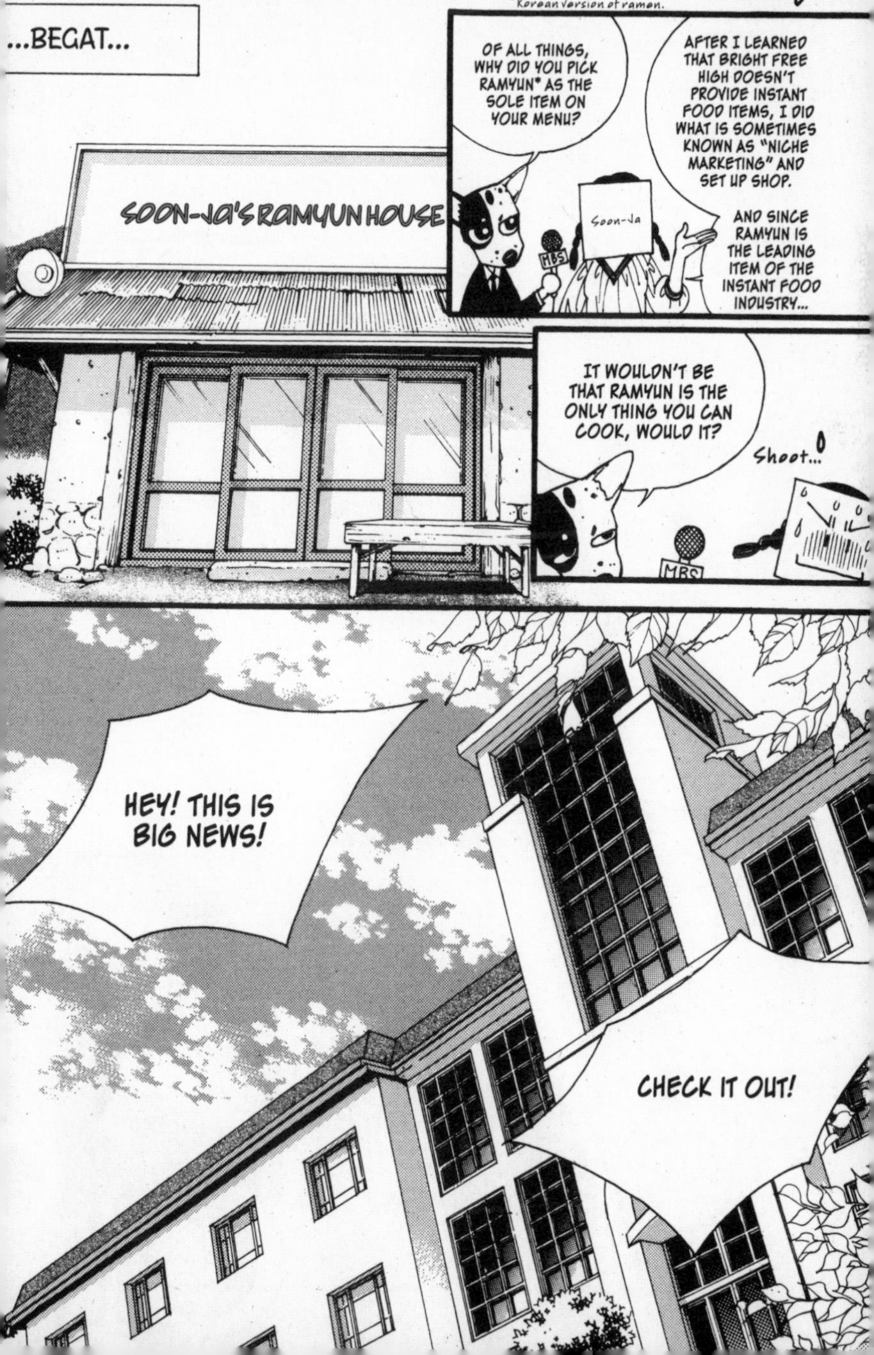
...BEGAT...
SOON-JA'S RAMYUN HOUSE
OF ALL THINGS, WHY DID YOU PICK RAMYUN* AS THE SOLE ITEM ON YOUR MENU?
AFTER I LEARNED THAT BRIGHT FREE HIGH DOESN'T PROVIDE INSTANT FOOD ITEMS, I DID WHAT IS SOMETIMES KNOWN AS "NICHE MARKETING" AND SET UP SHOP.
AND SINCE RAMYUN IS THE LEADING ITEM OF THE INSTANT FOOD INDUSTRY...
MBS
Soon-Ja
IT WOULDN'T BE THAT RAMYUN IS THE ONLY THING YOU CAN COOK, WOULD IT?
Shoot...
MBS
HEY! THIS IS BIG NEWS!
CHECK IT OUT!

*Korean version of ramen.

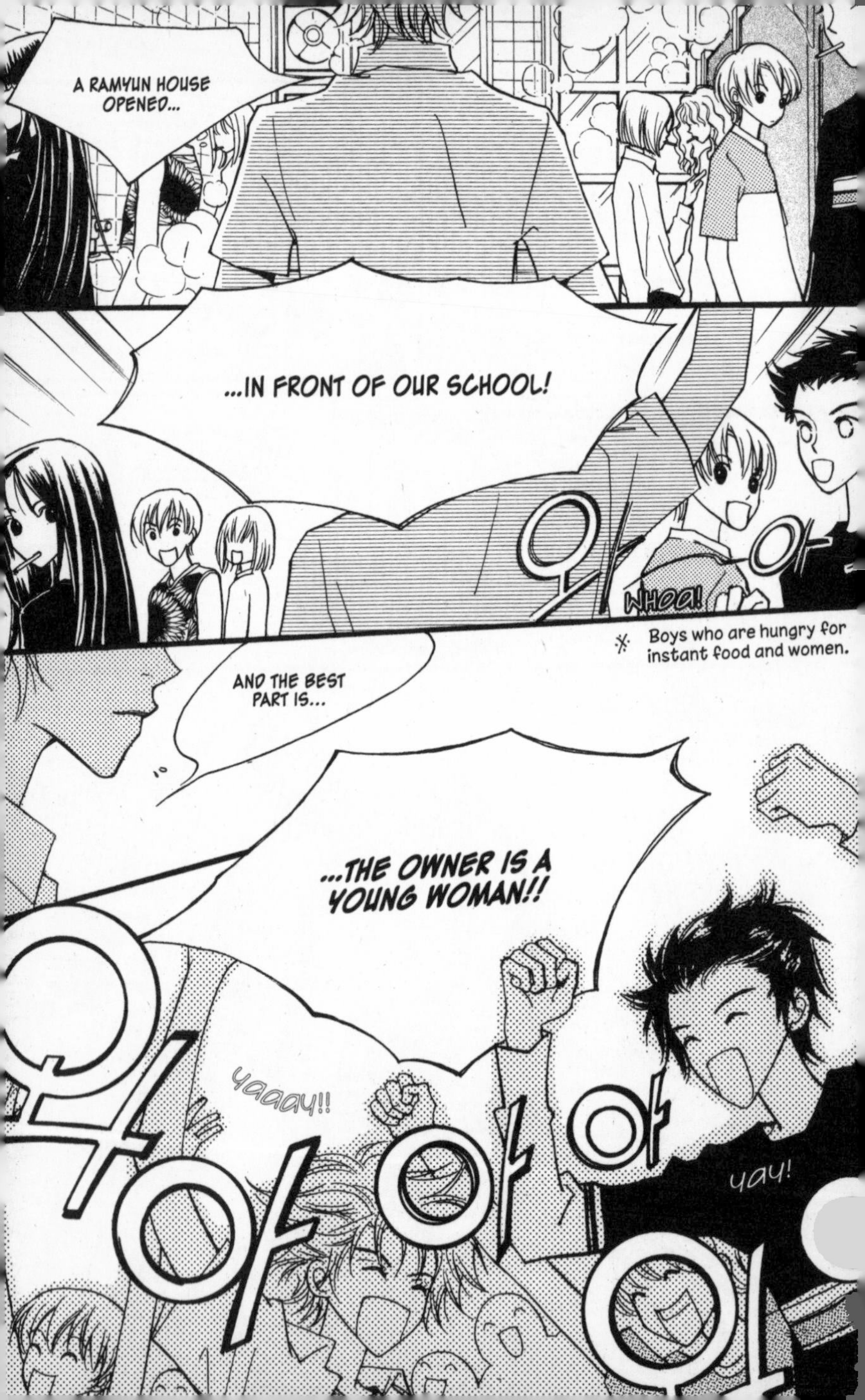
A RAMYUN HOUSE OPENED...
...IN FRONT OF OUR SCHOOL!
WHOA!
※ Boys who are hungry for instant food and women.
AND THE BEST PART IS...
...THE OWNER IS A YOUNG WOMAN!!
yaaay!!
yay!

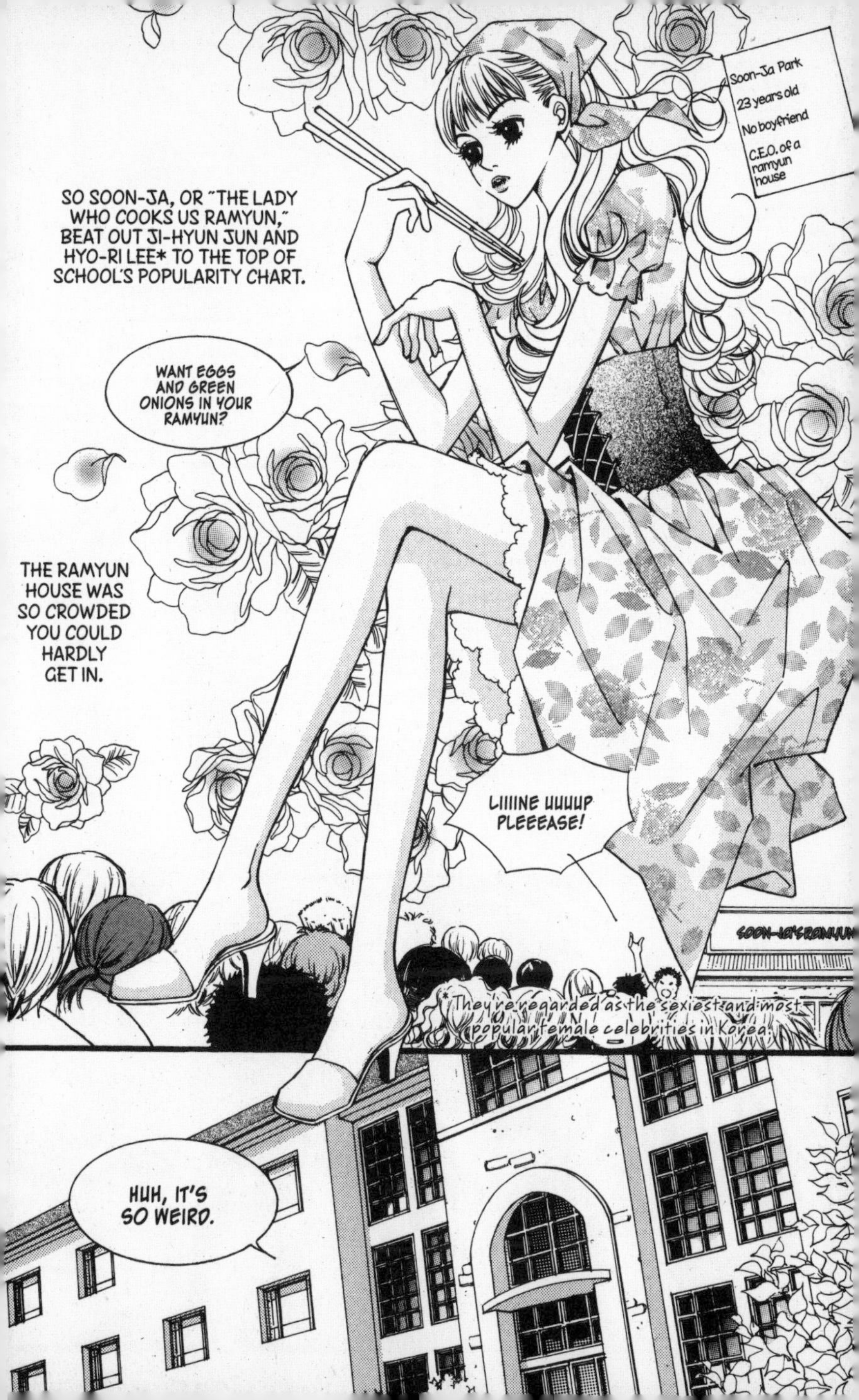
SO SOON-JA, OR "THE LADY WHO COOKS US RAMYUN," BEAT OUT JI-HYUN JUN AND HYO-RI LEE* TO THE TOP OF SCHOOL'S POPULARITY CHART.
Soon-Ja Park
23 years old
No boyfriend
C.E.O. of a ramyun house
WANT EGGS AND GREEN ONIONS IN YOUR RAMYUN?
THE RAMYUN HOUSE WAS SO CROWDED YOU COULD HARDLY GET IN.
LIIIINE UUUUP PLEEEASE!
*They're regarded as the sexiest and most popular female celebrities in Korea.
HUH, IT'S SO WEIRD.

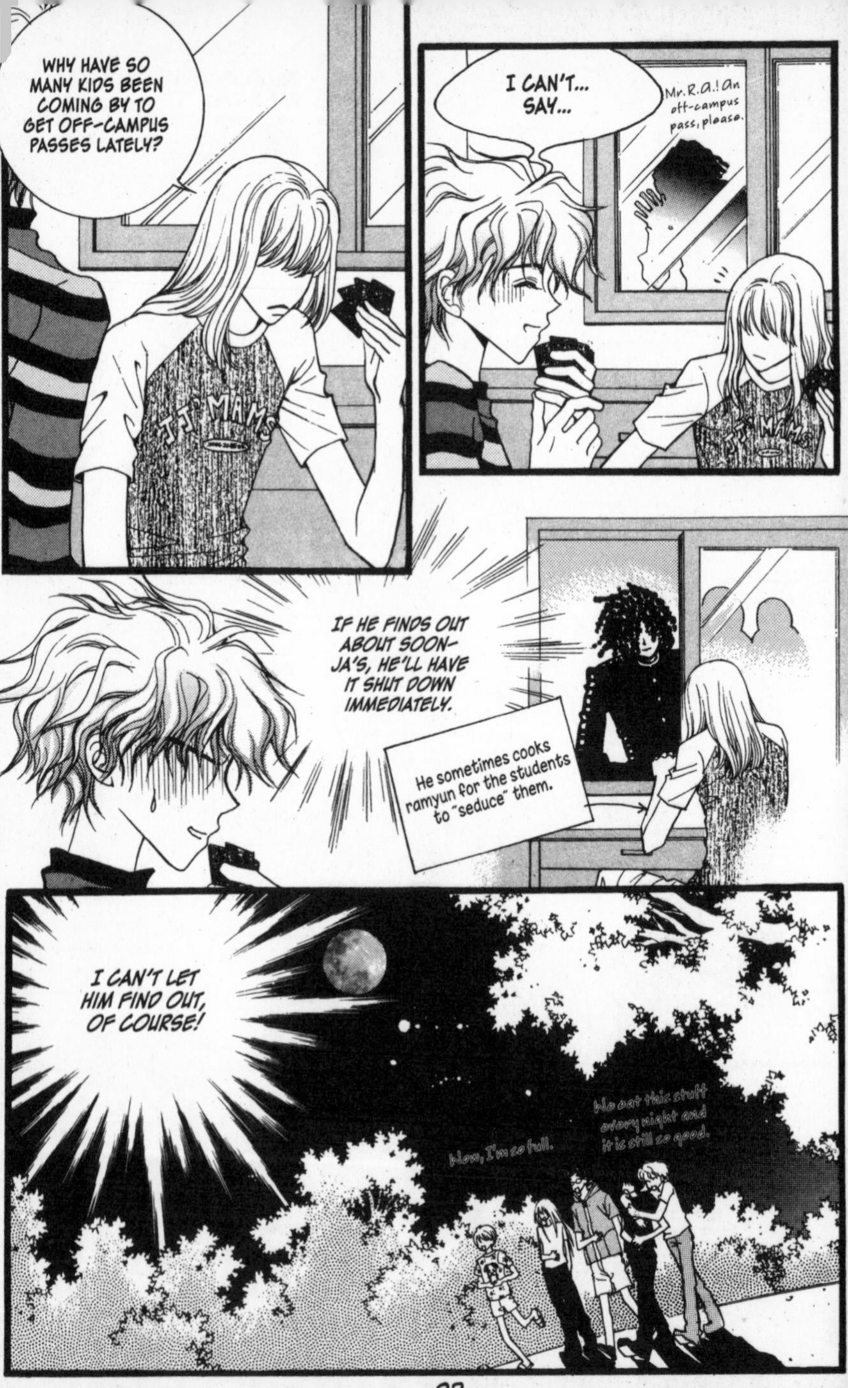
WHY HAVE SO MANY KIDS BEEN COMING BY TO GET OFF-CAMPUS PASSES LATELY?
I CAN'T... SAY...
Mr. R.A.! An off-campus pass, please.
IF HE FINDS OUT ABOUT SOON-JA'S, HE'LL HAVE IT SHUT DOWN IMMEDIATELY.
He sometimes cooks ramyun for the students to "seduce" them.
I CAN'T LET HIM FIND OUT, OF COURSE!
Wow, I'm so full.
We eat this stuff every night and it is still so good.

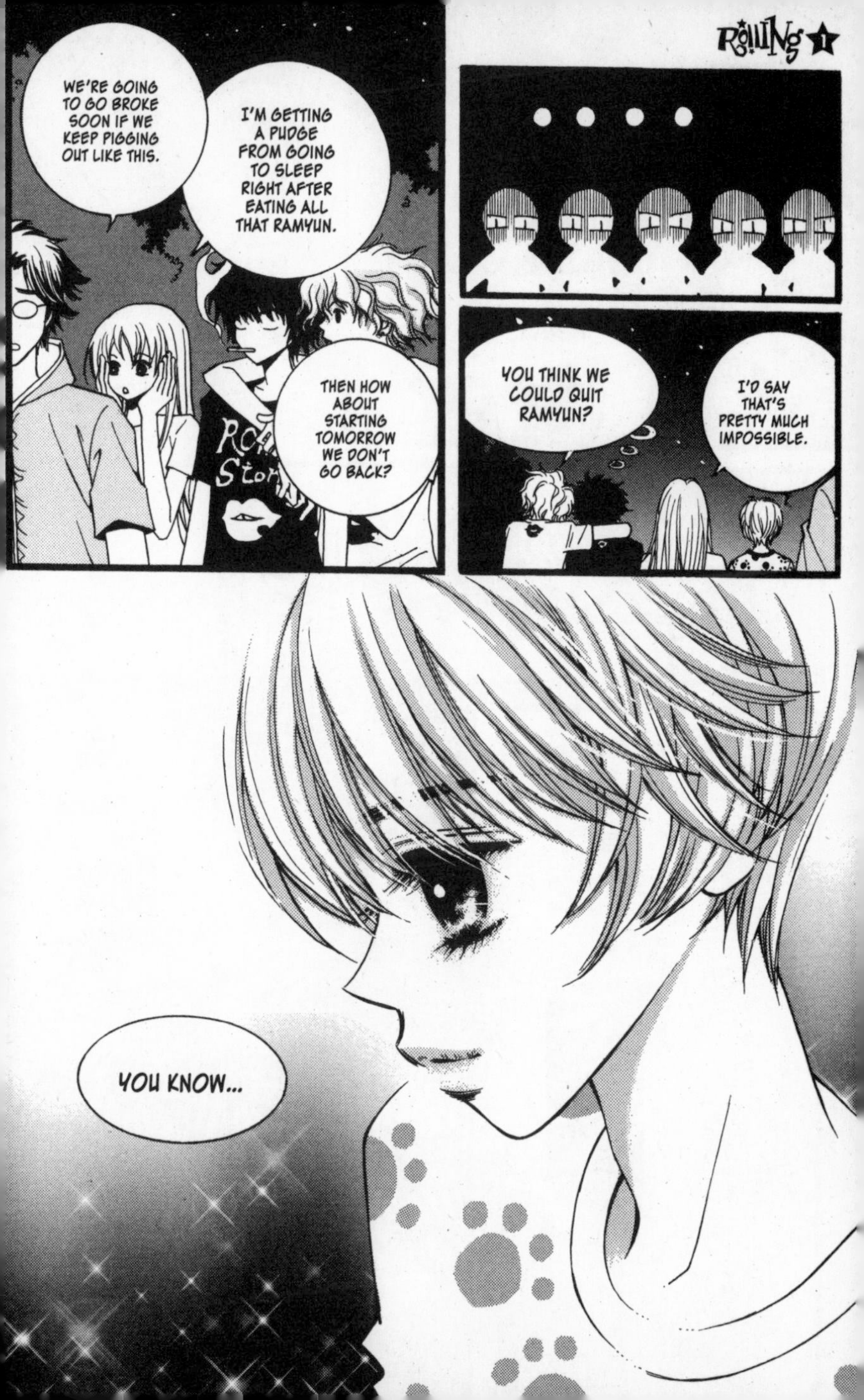
WE'RE GOING TO GO BROKE SOON IF WE KEEP PIGGING OUT LIKE THIS.
I'M GETTING A PUDGE FROM GOING TO SLEEP RIGHT AFTER EATING ALL THAT RAMYUN.
THEN HOW ABOUT STARTING TOMORROW WE DON'T GO BACK?
....
YOU THINK WE COULD QUIT RAMYUN?
I'D SAY THAT'S PRETTY MUCH IMPOSSIBLE.
YOU KNOW...

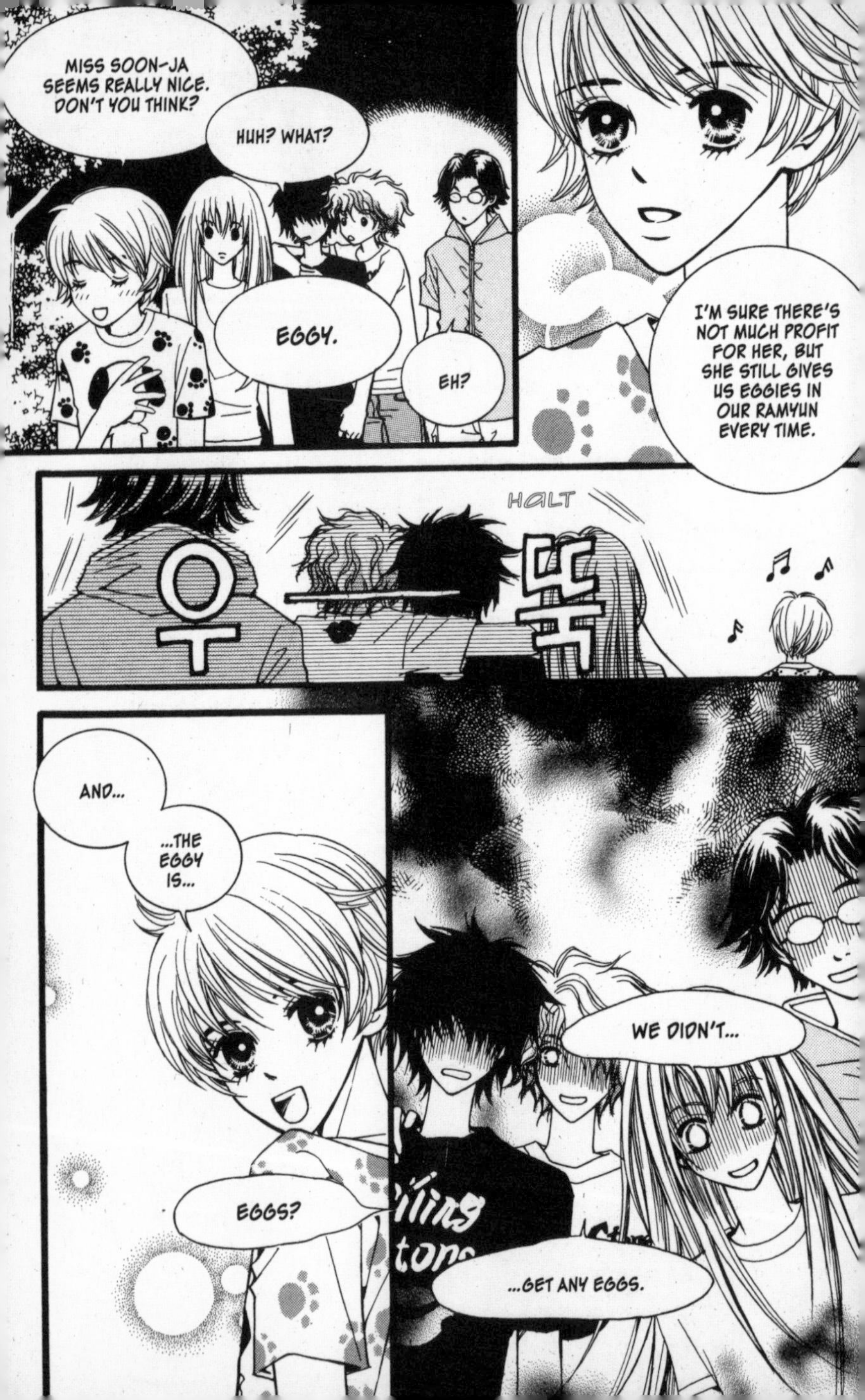
MISS SOON-JA SEEMS REALLY NICE. DON'T YOU THINK?
HUH? WHAT?
EGGY.
EH?
I'M SURE THERE'S NOT MUCH PROFIT FOR HER, BUT SHE STILL GIVES US EGGIES IN OUR RAMYUN EVERY TIME.
우뚝
HALT
AND...
...THE EGGY IS...
EGGS?
WE DIDN'T...
...GET ANY EGGS.

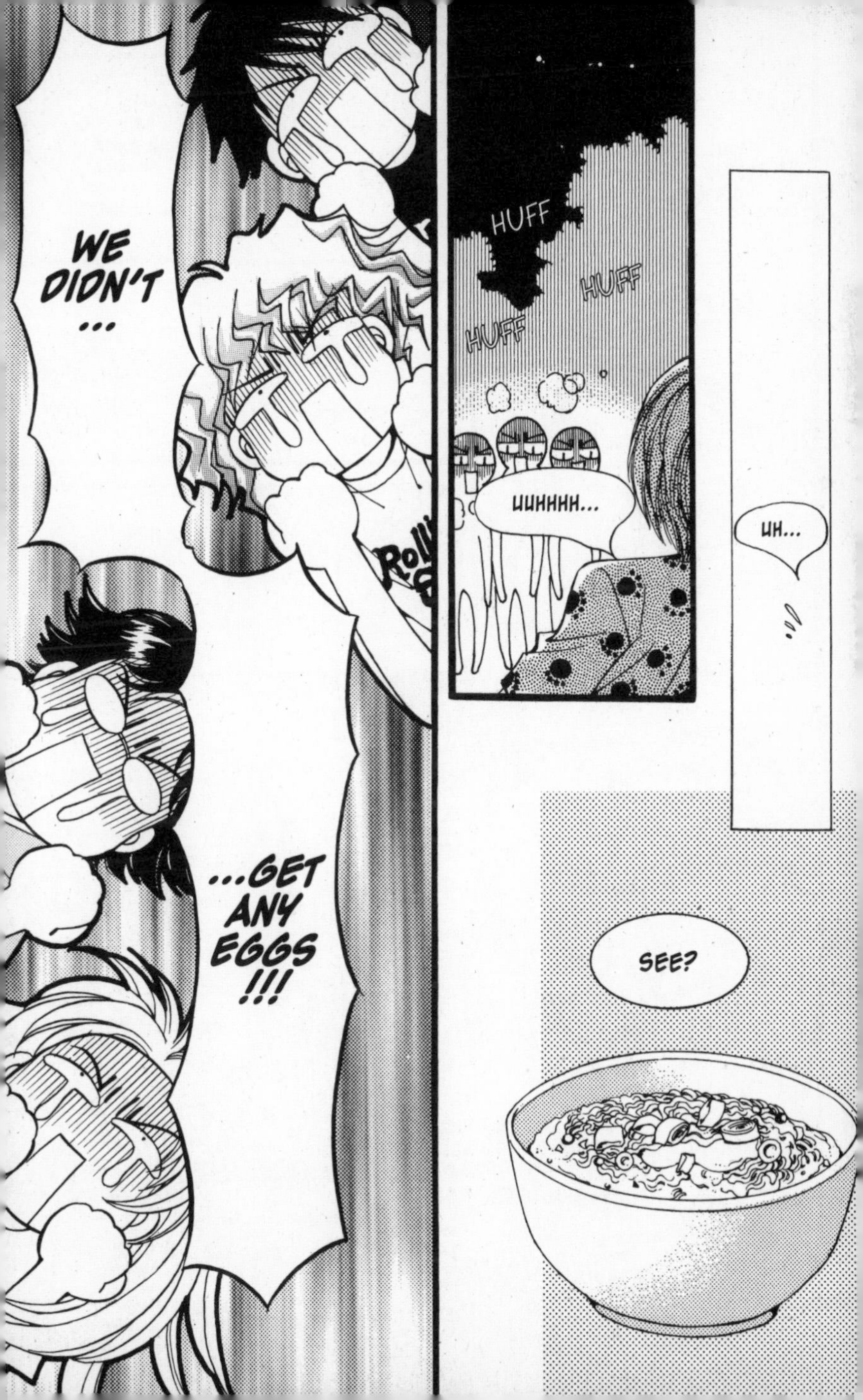
WE DIDN'T ...
...GET ANY EGGS !!!
HUFF
HUFF
HUFF
UUHHHH...
UH...
SEE?

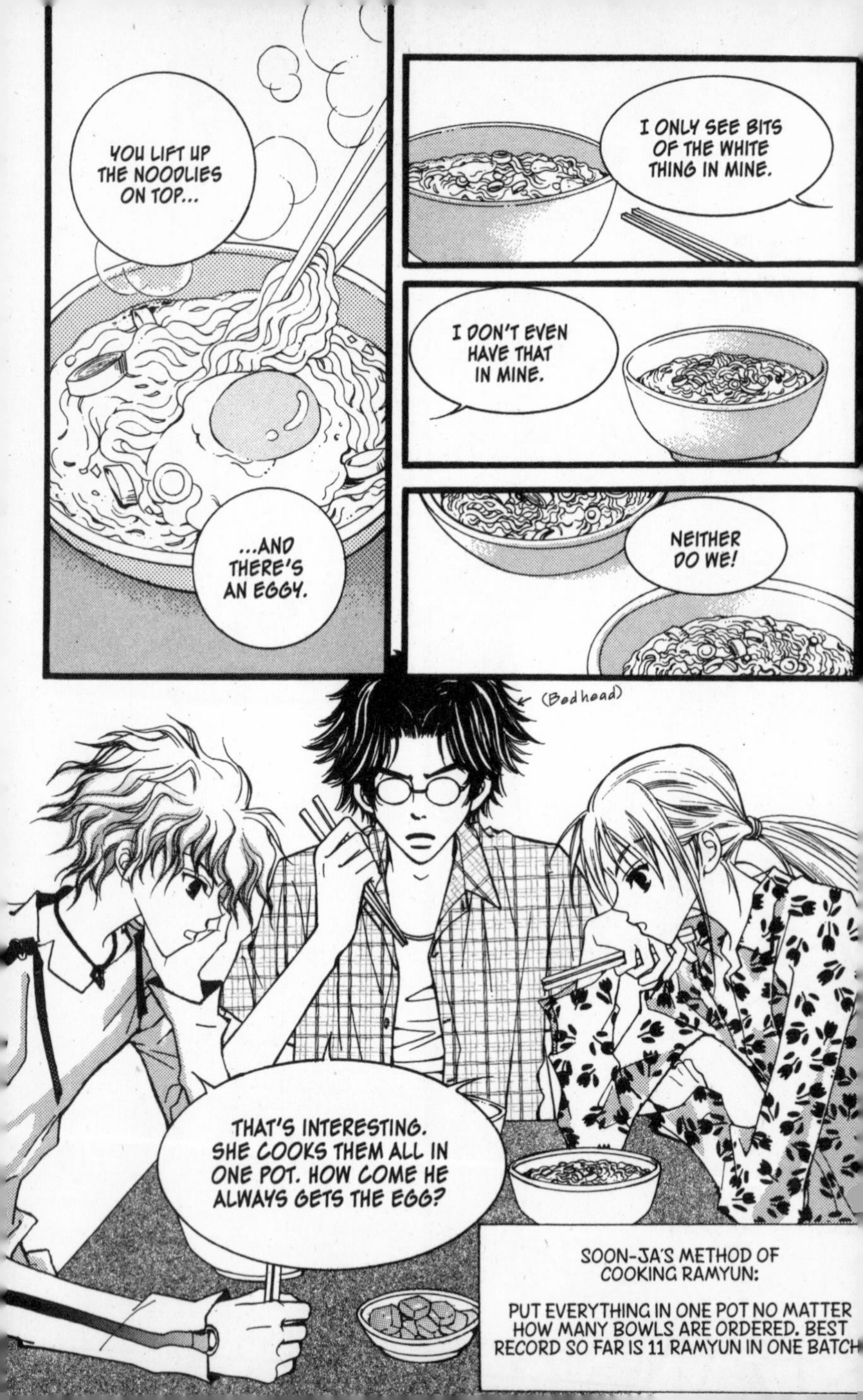
YOU LIFT UP THE NOODLIES ON TOP...
...AND THERE'S AN EGGY.
I ONLY SEE BITS OF THE WHITE THING IN MINE.
I DON'T EVEN HAVE THAT IN MINE.
NEITHER DO WE!
(Bedhead)
THAT'S INTERESTING. SHE COOKS THEM ALL IN ONE POT. HOW COME HE ALWAYS GETS THE EGG?
SOON-JA'S METHOD OF COOKING RAMYUN:
PUT EVERYTHING IN ONE POT NO MATTER HOW MANY BOWLS ARE ORDERED. BEST RECORD SO FAR IS 11 RAMYUN IN ONE BATCH

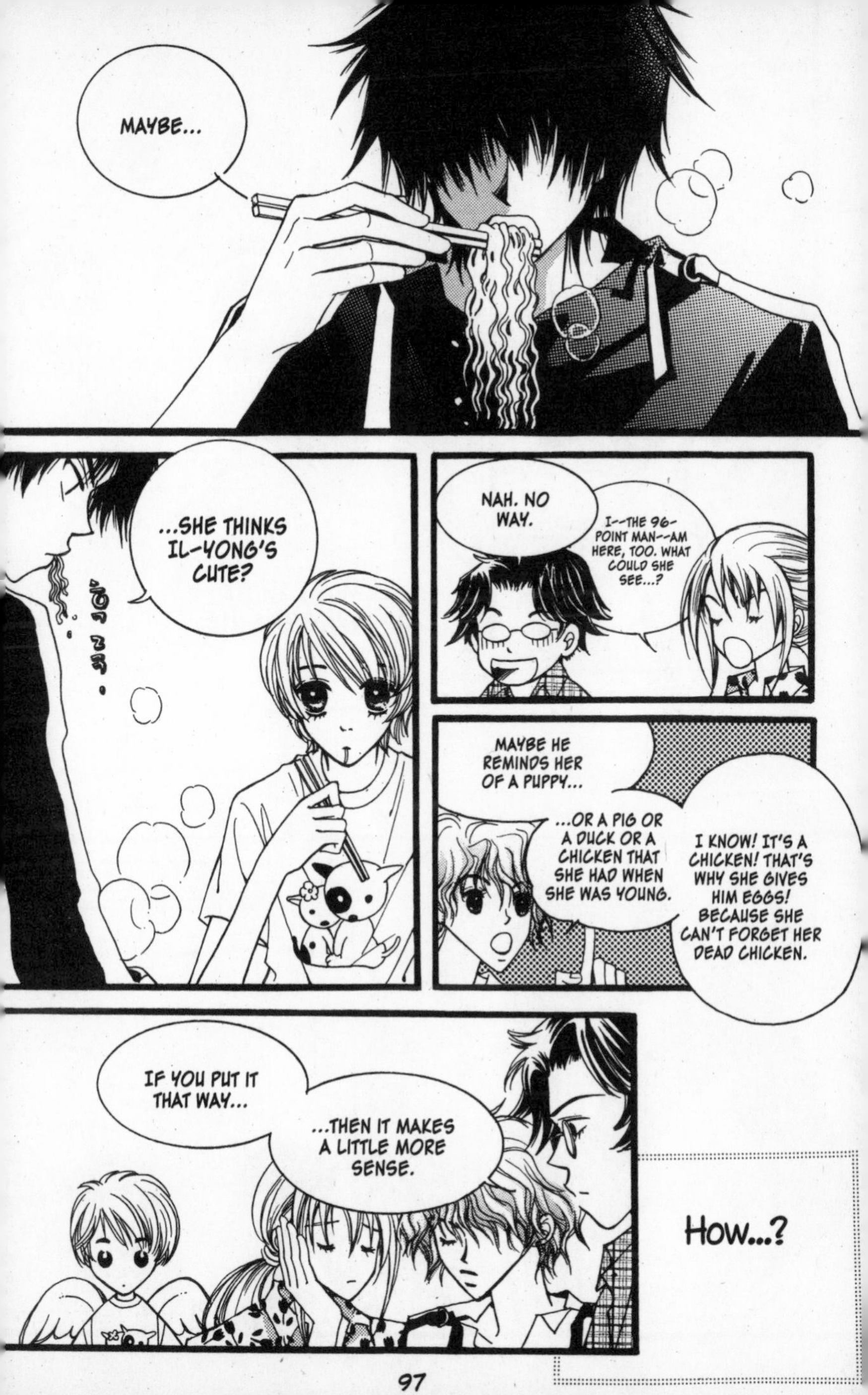
MAYBE...
...SHE THINKS IL-YONG'S CUTE?
NAH. NO WAY.
I--THE 96-POINT MAN--AM HERE, TOO. WHAT COULD SHE SEE...?
MAYBE HE REMINDS HER OF A PUPPY...
...OR A PIG OR A DUCK OR A CHICKEN THAT SHE HAD WHEN SHE WAS YOUNG.
I KNOW! IT'S A CHICKEN! THAT'S WHY SHE GIVES HIM EGGS! BECAUSE SHE CAN'T FORGET HER DEAD CHICKEN.
IF YOU PUT IT THAT WAY...
...THEN IT MAKES A LITTLE MORE SENSE.
How...?

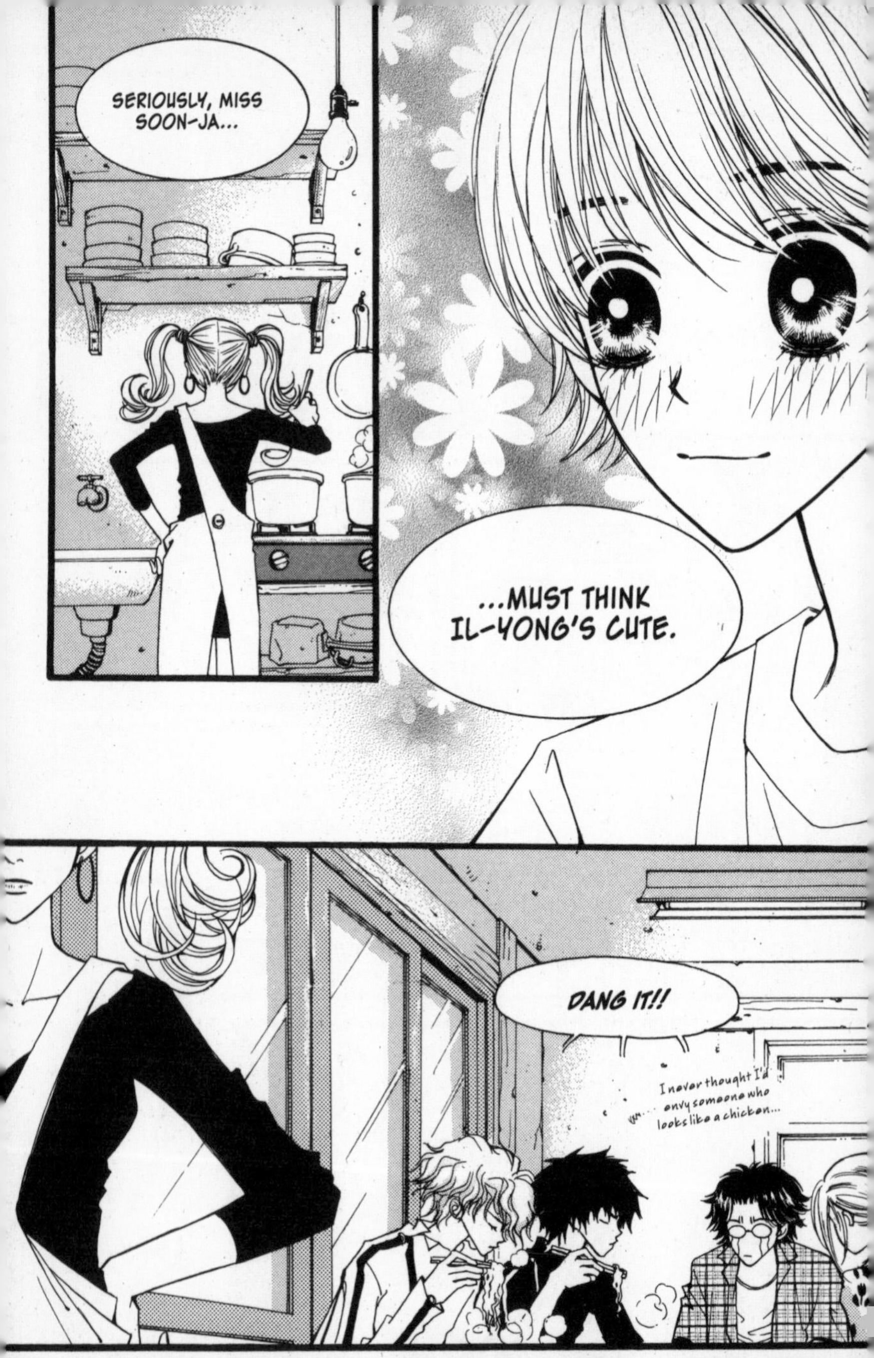
SERIOUSLY, MISS SOON-JA...
...MUST THINK IL-YONG'S CUTE.
DANG IT!!
I never thought I'd envy someone who looks like a chicken...

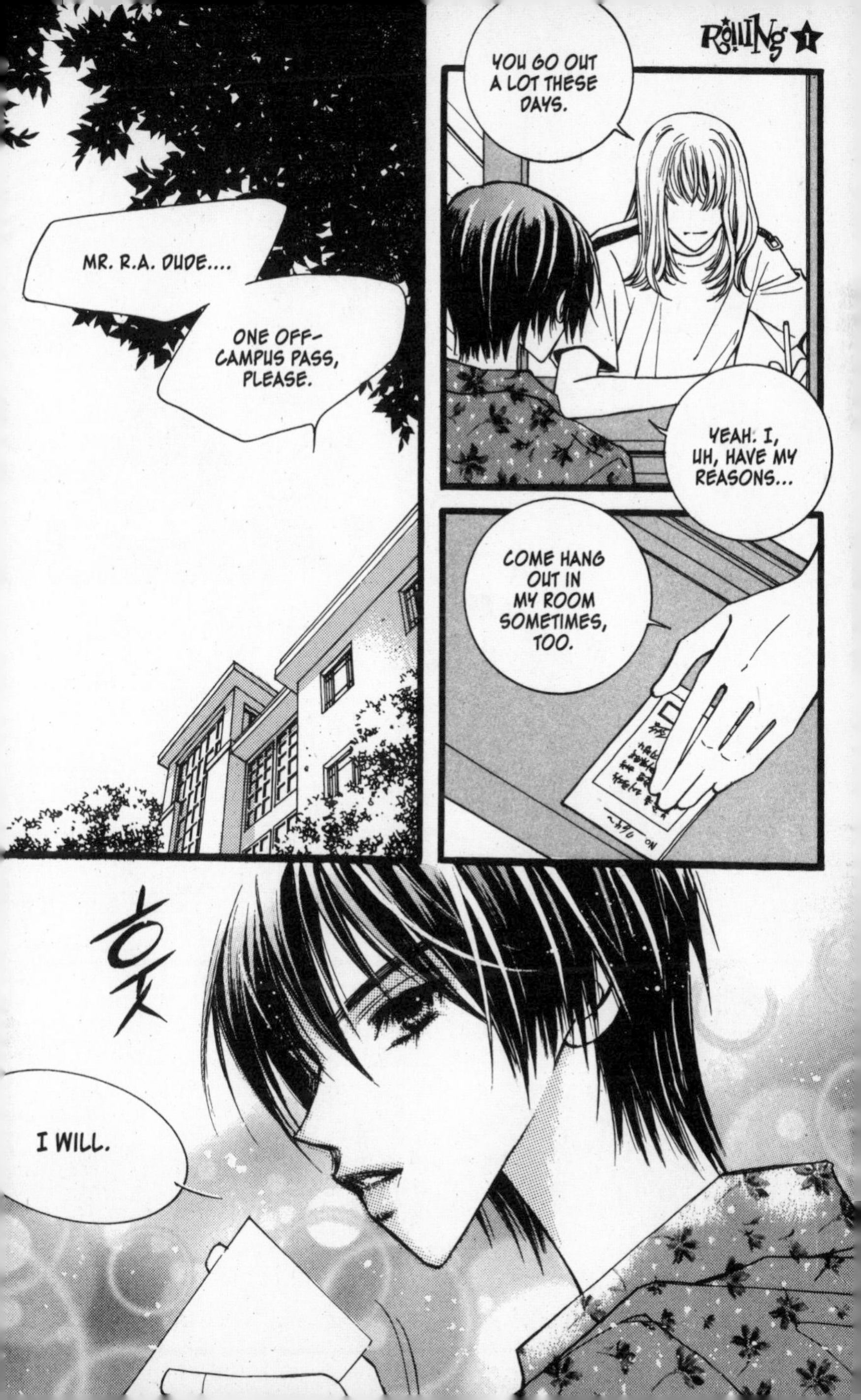
MR. R.A. DUDE....
ONE OFF-CAMPUS PASS, PLEASE.
YOU GO OUT A LOT THESE DAYS.
YEAH. I, UH, HAVE MY REASONS...
COME HANG OUT IN MY ROOM SOMETIMES, TOO.
I WILL.

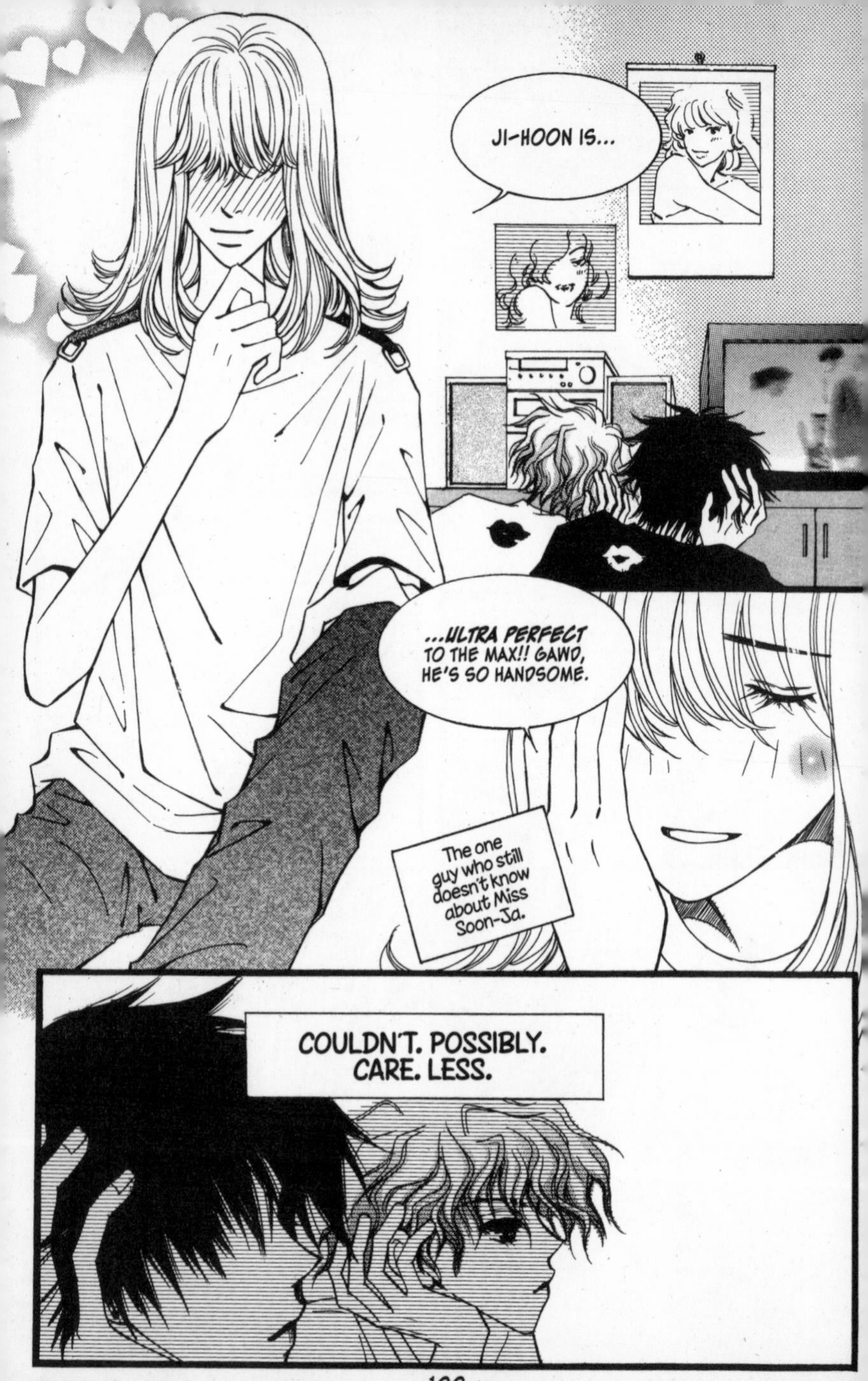
JI-HOON IS...
...ULTRA PERFECT TO THE MAX!! GAWD, HE'S SO HANDSOME.
The one guy who still doesn't know about Miss Soon-Ja.
COULDN'T. POSSIBLY. CARE. LESS.

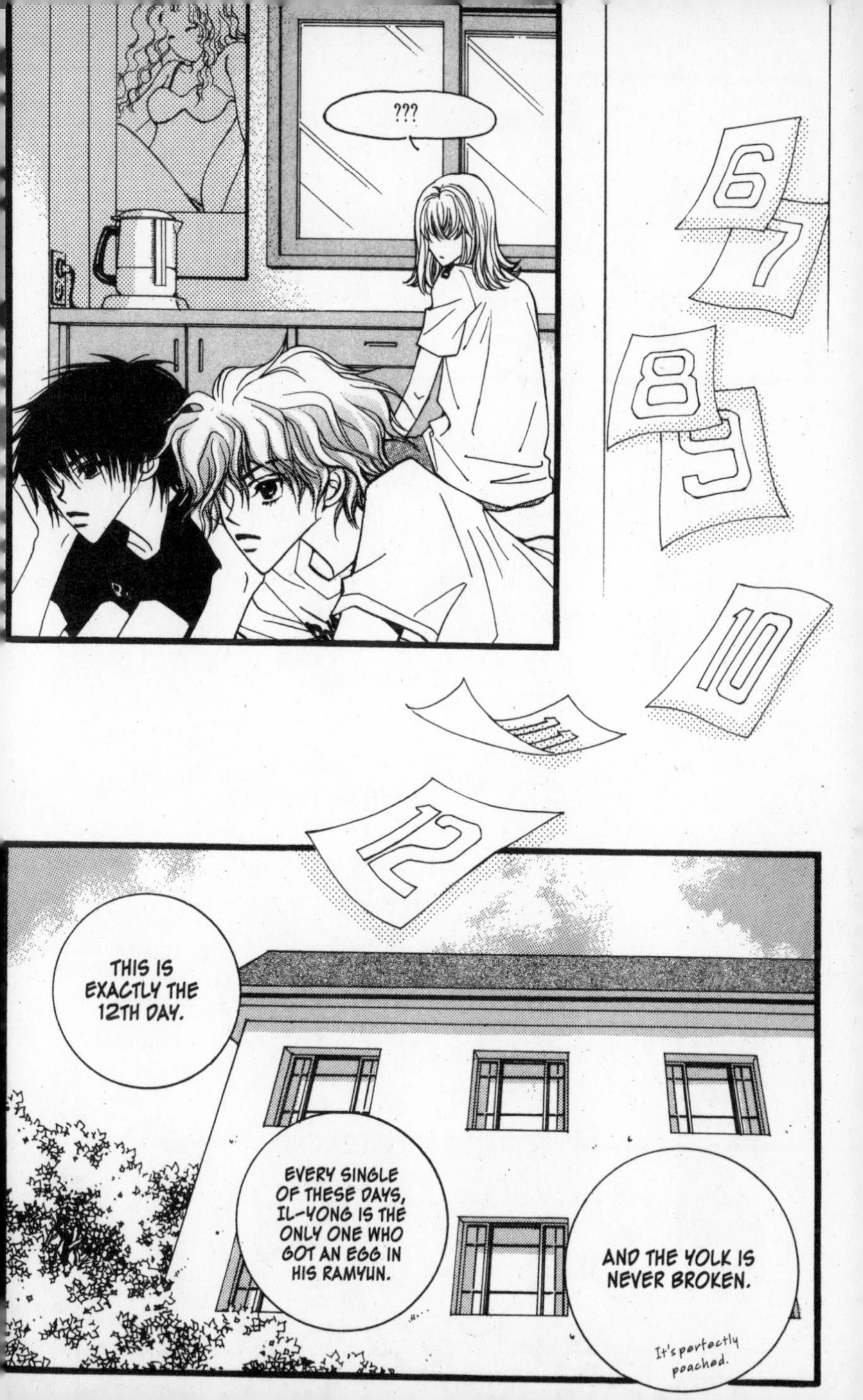
???
6
7
8
9
10
12
THIS IS EXACTLY THE 12TH DAY.
EVERY SINGLE OF THESE DAYS, IL-YONG IS THE ONLY ONE WHO GOT AN EGG IN HIS RAMYUN.
AND THE YOLK IS NEVER BROKEN.
It's perfectly poached.

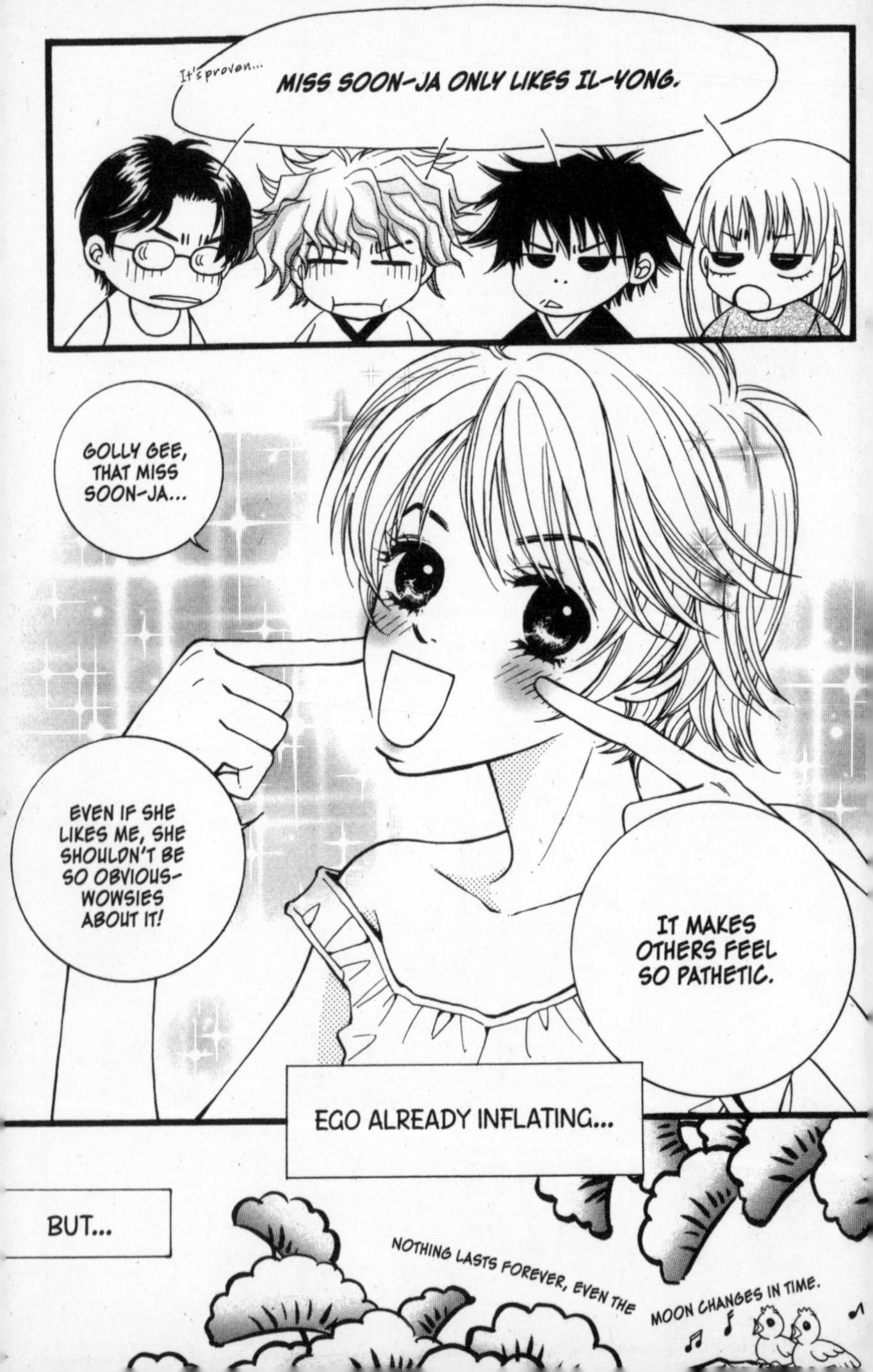
It's proven...
MISS SOON-JA ONLY LIKES IL-YONG.
GOLLY GEE, THAT MISS SOON-JA...
EVEN IF SHE LIKES ME, SHE SHOULDN'T BE SO OBVIOUS-WOWSIES ABOUT IT!
IT MAKES OTHERS FEEL SO PATHETIC.
EGO ALREADY INFLATING...
BUT...
NOTHING LASTS FOREVER, EVEN THE MOON CHANGES IN TIME.

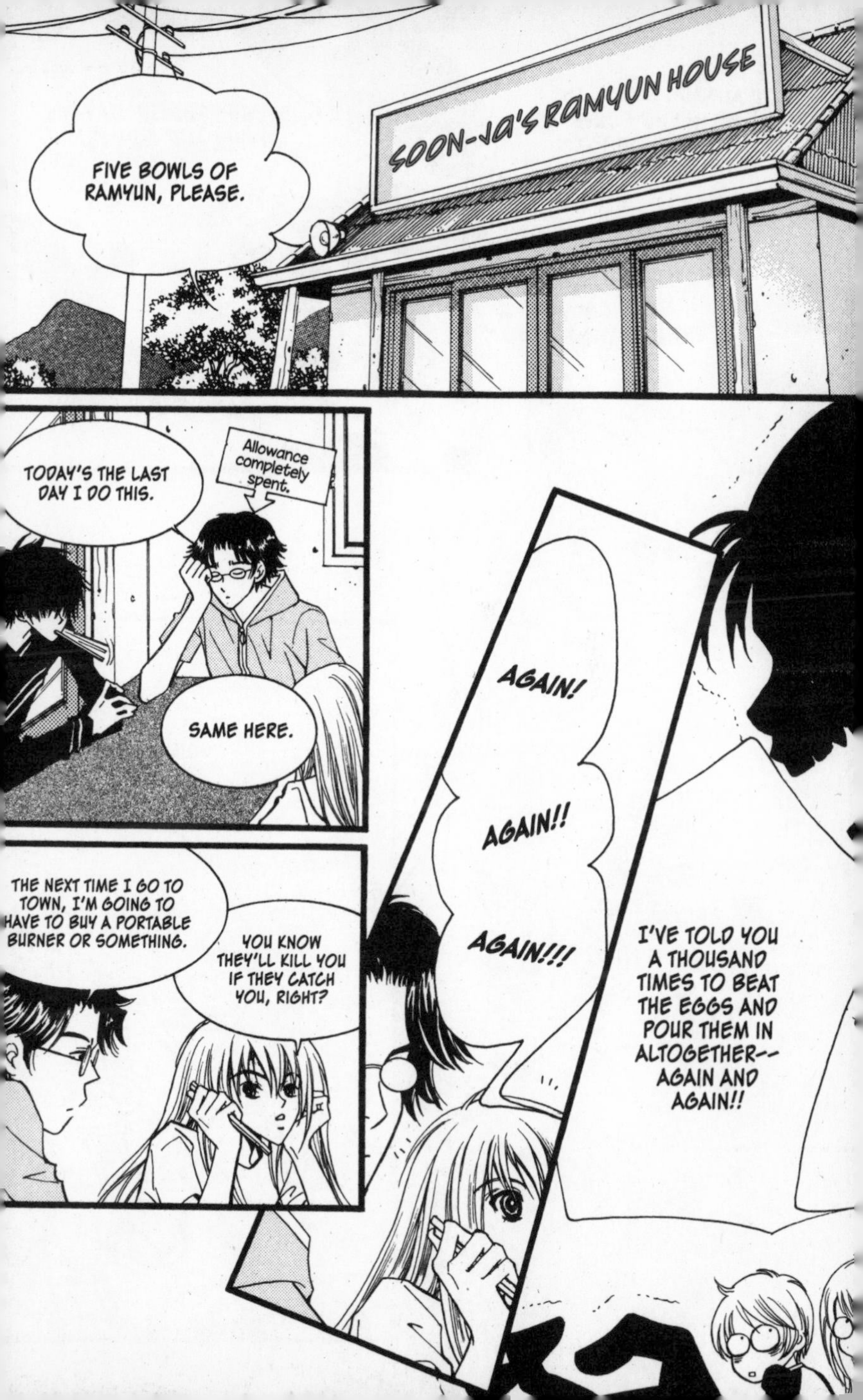

FIVE BOWLS OF RAMYUN, PLEASE.
SOON-JA'S RAMYUN HOUSE
TODAY'S THE LAST DAY I DO THIS.
Allowance completely spent.
SAME HERE.
THE NEXT TIME I GO TO TOWN, I'M GOING TO HAVE TO BUY A PORTABLE BURNER OR SOMETHING.
YOU KNOW THEY'LL KILL YOU IF THEY CATCH YOU, RIGHT?
AGAIN!
AGAIN!!
AGAIN!!!
I'VE TOLD YOU A THOUSAND TIMES TO BEAT THE EGGS AND POUR THEM IN ALTOGETHER--AGAIN AND AGAIN!!

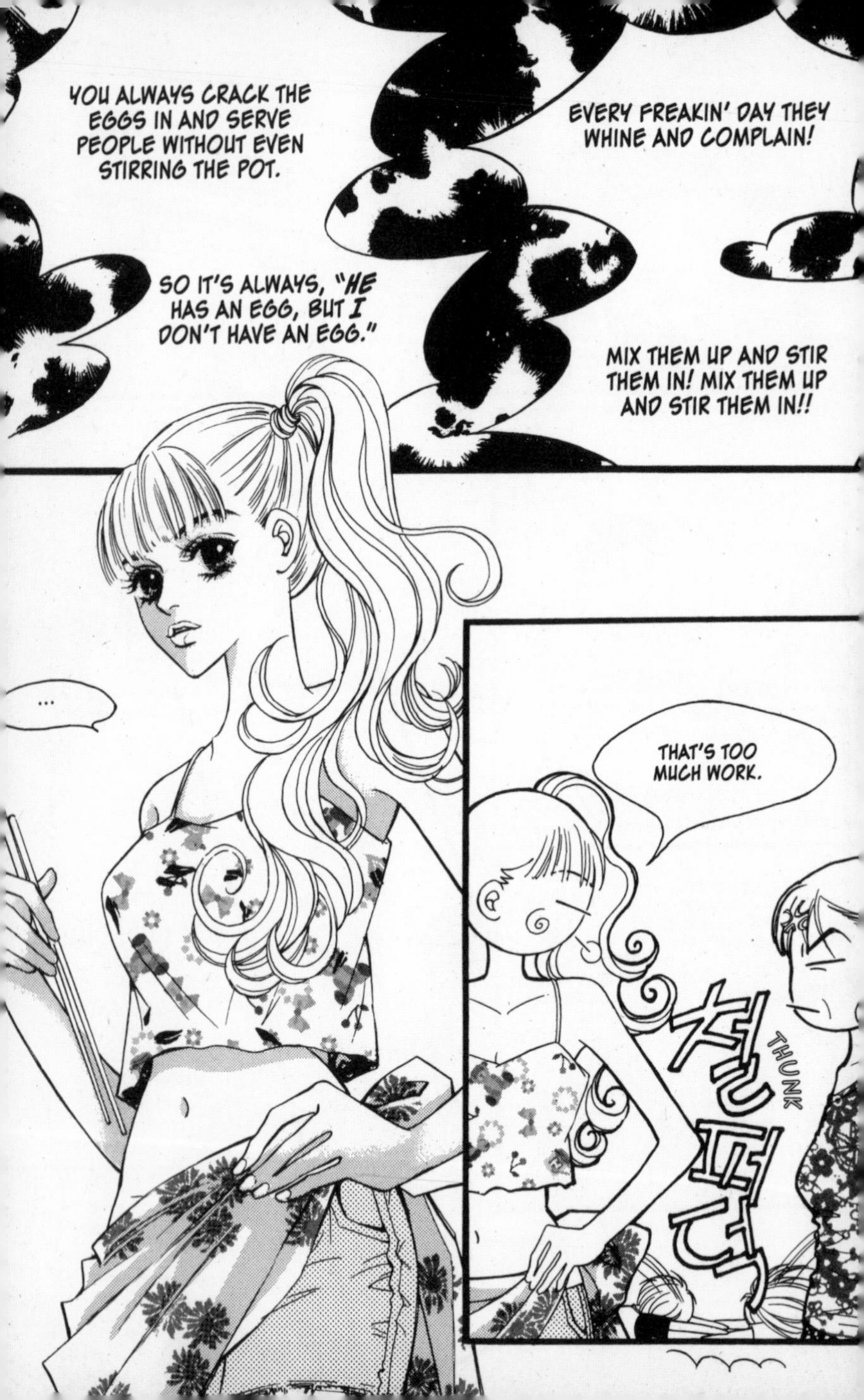
YOU ALWAYS CRACK THE EGGS IN AND SERVE PEOPLE WITHOUT EVEN STIRRING THE POT.
EVERY FREAKIN' DAY THEY WHINE AND COMPLAIN!
SO IT'S ALWAYS, "*HE* HAS AN EGG, BUT *I* DON'T HAVE AN EGG."
MIX THEM UP AND STIR THEM IN! MIX THEM UP AND STIR THEM IN!!
...
THAT'S TOO MUCH WORK.
THUNK

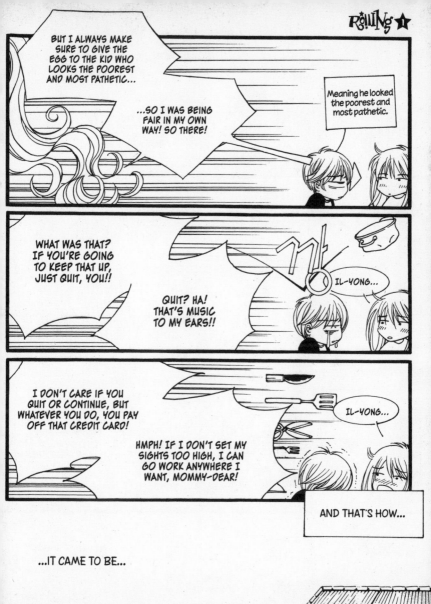

BUT I ALWAYS MAKE SURE TO GIVE THE EGG TO THE KID WHO LOOKS THE POOREST AND MOST PATHETIC...

...SO I WAS BEING FAIR IN MY OWN WAY! SO THERE!

Meaning he looked the poorest and most pathetic.

WHAT WAS THAT? IF YOU'RE GOING TO KEEP THAT UP, JUST QUIT, YOU!!

QUIT? HA! THAT'S MUSIC TO MY EARS!!

IL-YONG...

I DON'T CARE IF YOU QUIT OR CONTINUE, BUT WHATEVER YOU DO, YOU PAY OFF THAT CREDIT CARD!

HMPH! IF I DON'T SET MY SIGHTS TOO HIGH, I CAN GO WORK ANYWHERE I WANT, MOMMY-DEAR!

IL-YONG...

AND THAT'S HOW...

...IT CAME TO BE...

THAT'S HOW THEIR BELOVED LADY WENT AND LEFT THEM.

It's closed.

RAMYUN HOUSE

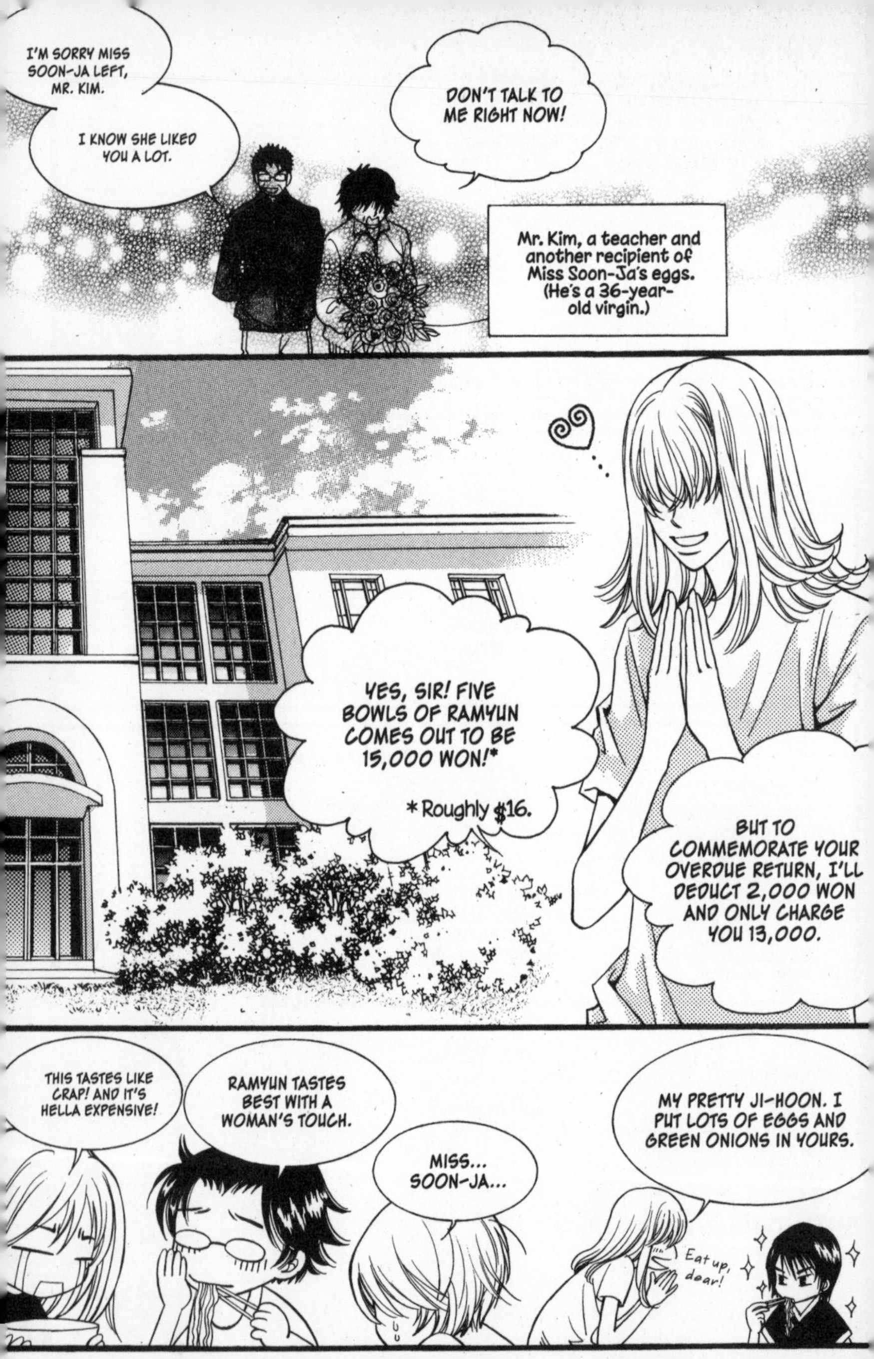
I'M SORRY MISS SOON-JA LEFT, MR. KIM.
I KNOW SHE LIKED YOU A LOT.
DON'T TALK TO ME RIGHT NOW!
Mr. Kim, a teacher and another recipient of Miss Soon-Ja's eggs. (He's a 36-year-old virgin.)
YES, SIR! FIVE BOWLS OF RAMYUN COMES OUT TO BE 15,000 WON!*
* Roughly $16.
BUT TO COMMEMORATE YOUR OVERDUE RETURN, I'LL DEDUCT 2,000 WON AND ONLY CHARGE YOU 13,000.
THIS TASTES LIKE CRAP! AND IT'S HELLA EXPENSIVE!
RAMYUN TASTES BEST WITH A WOMAN'S TOUCH.
MISS... SOON-JA...
MY PRETTY JI-HOON. I PUT LOTS OF EGGS AND GREEN ONIONS IN YOURS.
Eat up, dear!

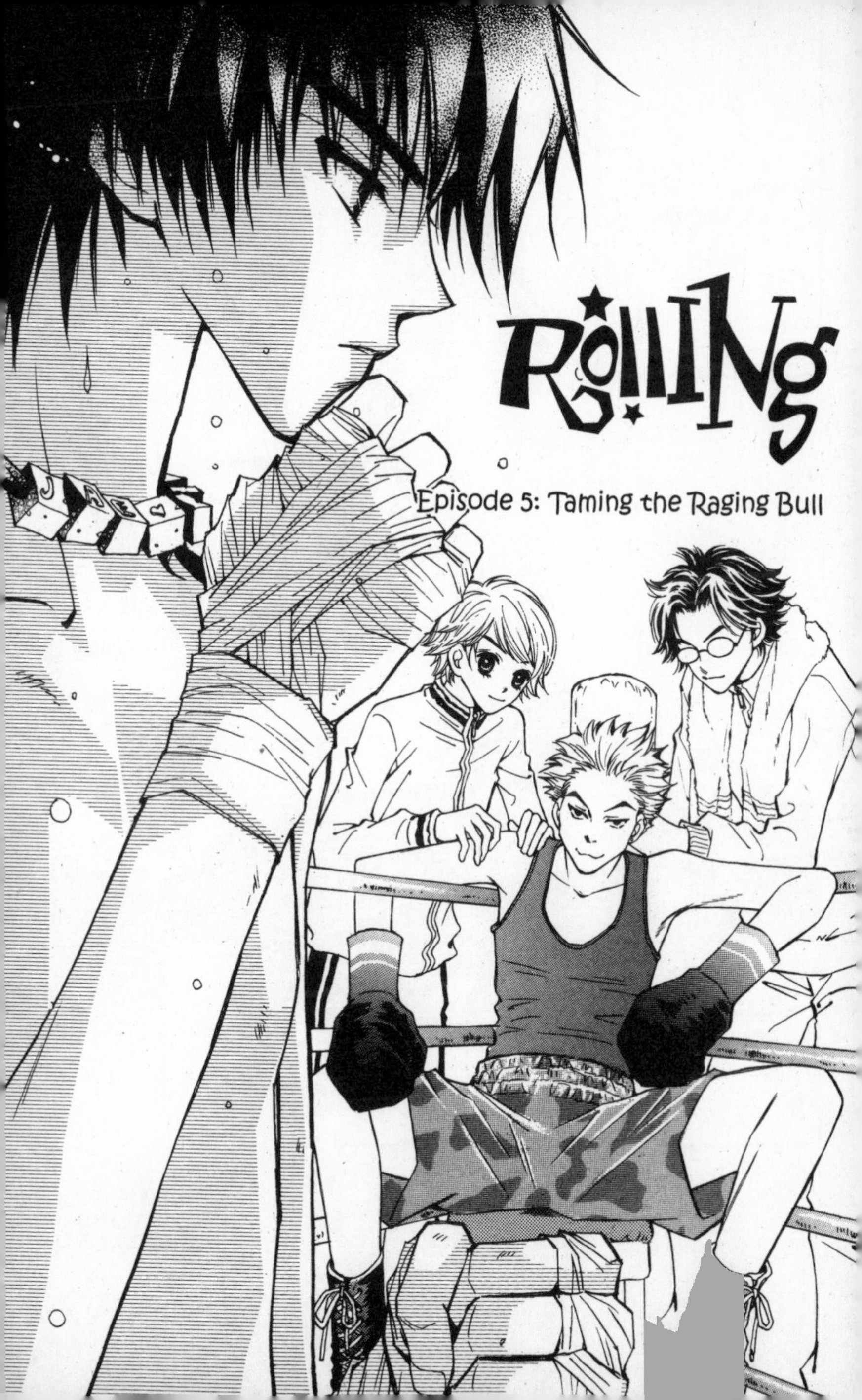
Rolling
Episode 5: Taming the Raging Bull

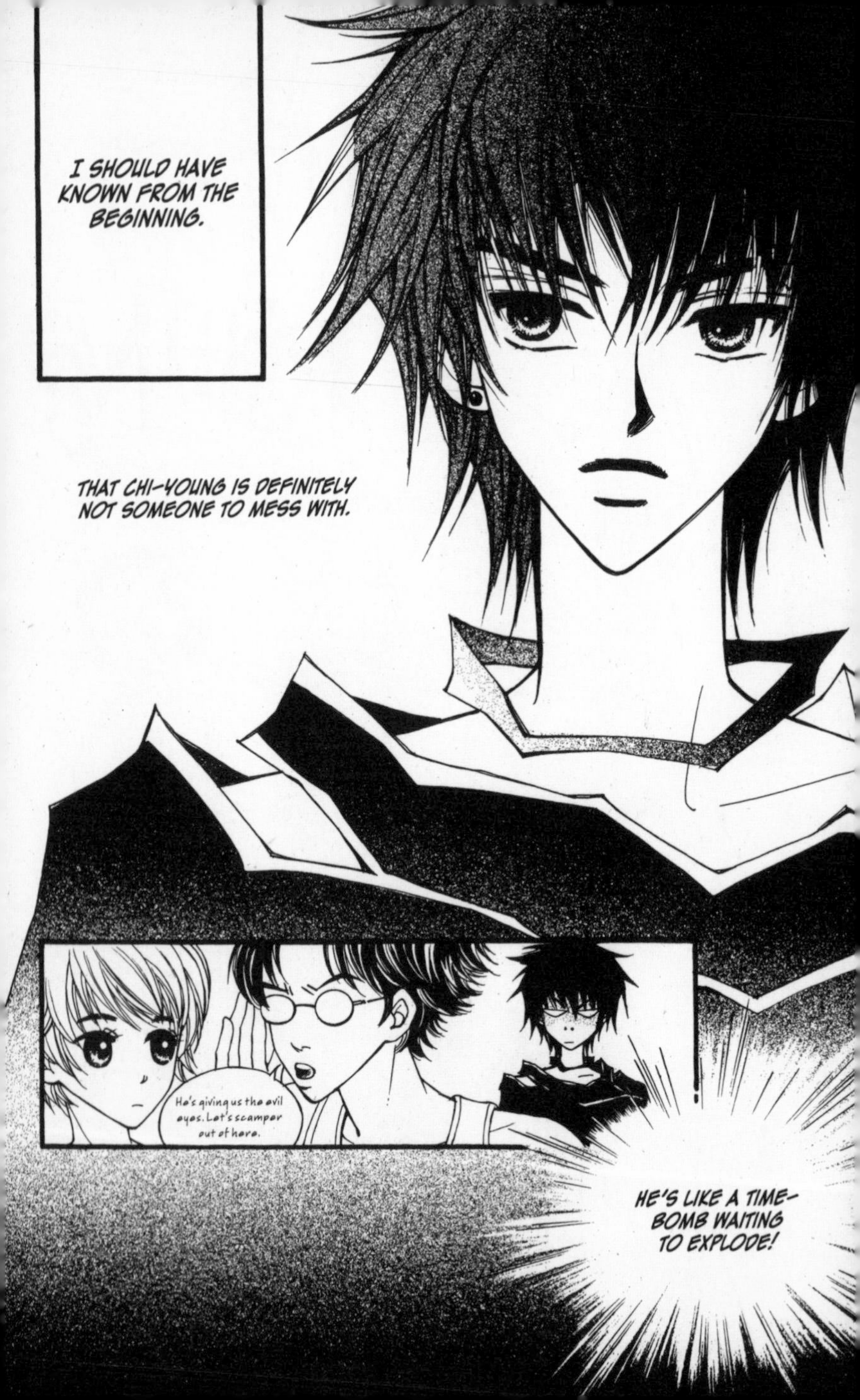
I SHOULD HAVE KNOWN FROM THE BEGINNING.
THAT CHI-YOUNG IS DEFINITELY NOT SOMEONE TO MESS WITH.
He's giving us the evil eyes. Let's scamper out of here.
HE'S LIKE A TIME-BOMB WAITING TO EXPLODE!

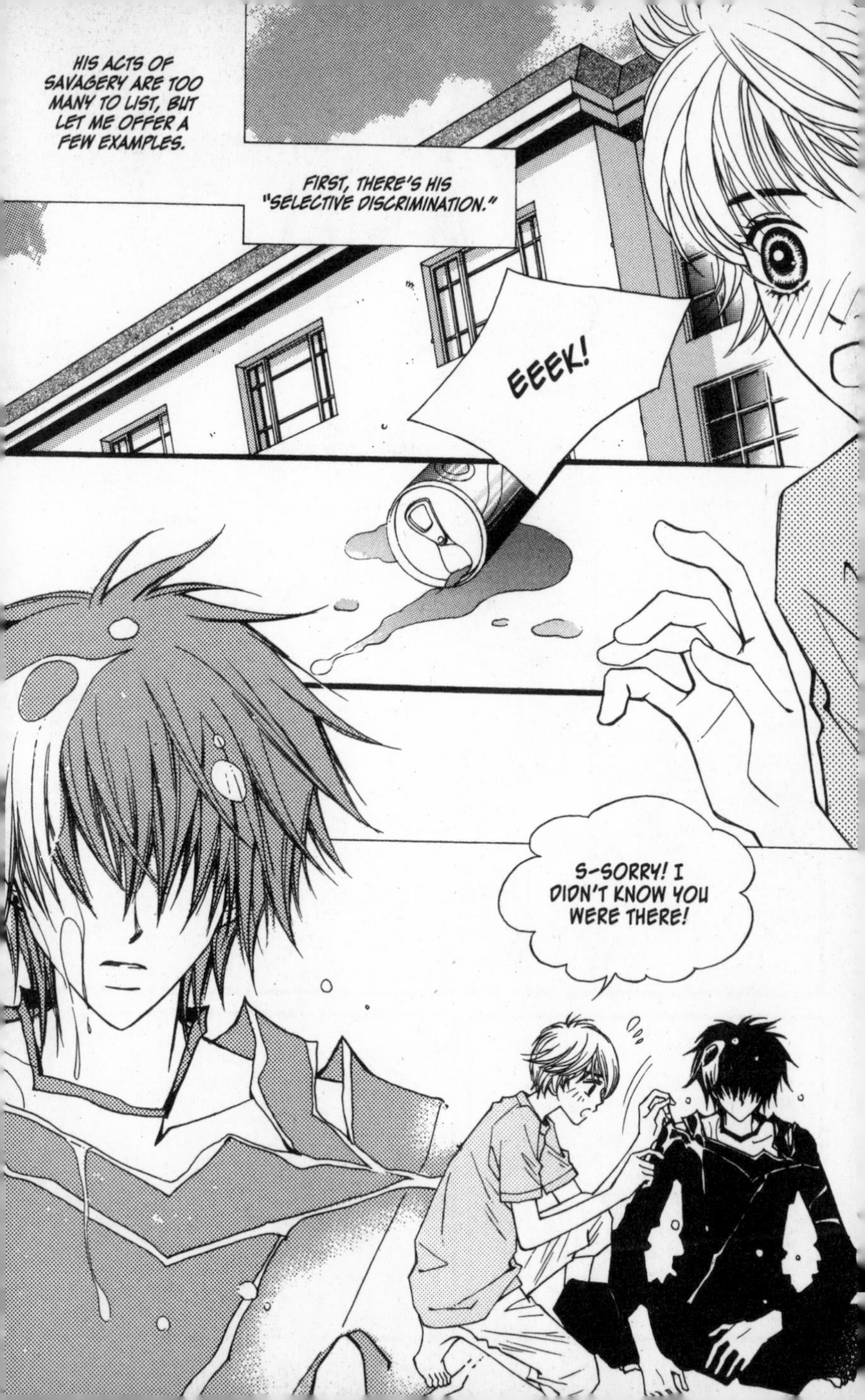
HIS ACTS OF SAVAGERY ARE TOO MANY TO LIST, BUT LET ME OFFER A FEW EXAMPLES.
FIRST, THERE'S HIS "SELECTIVE DISCRIMINATION."
EEEK!
S-SORRY! I DIDN'T KNOW YOU WERE THERE!

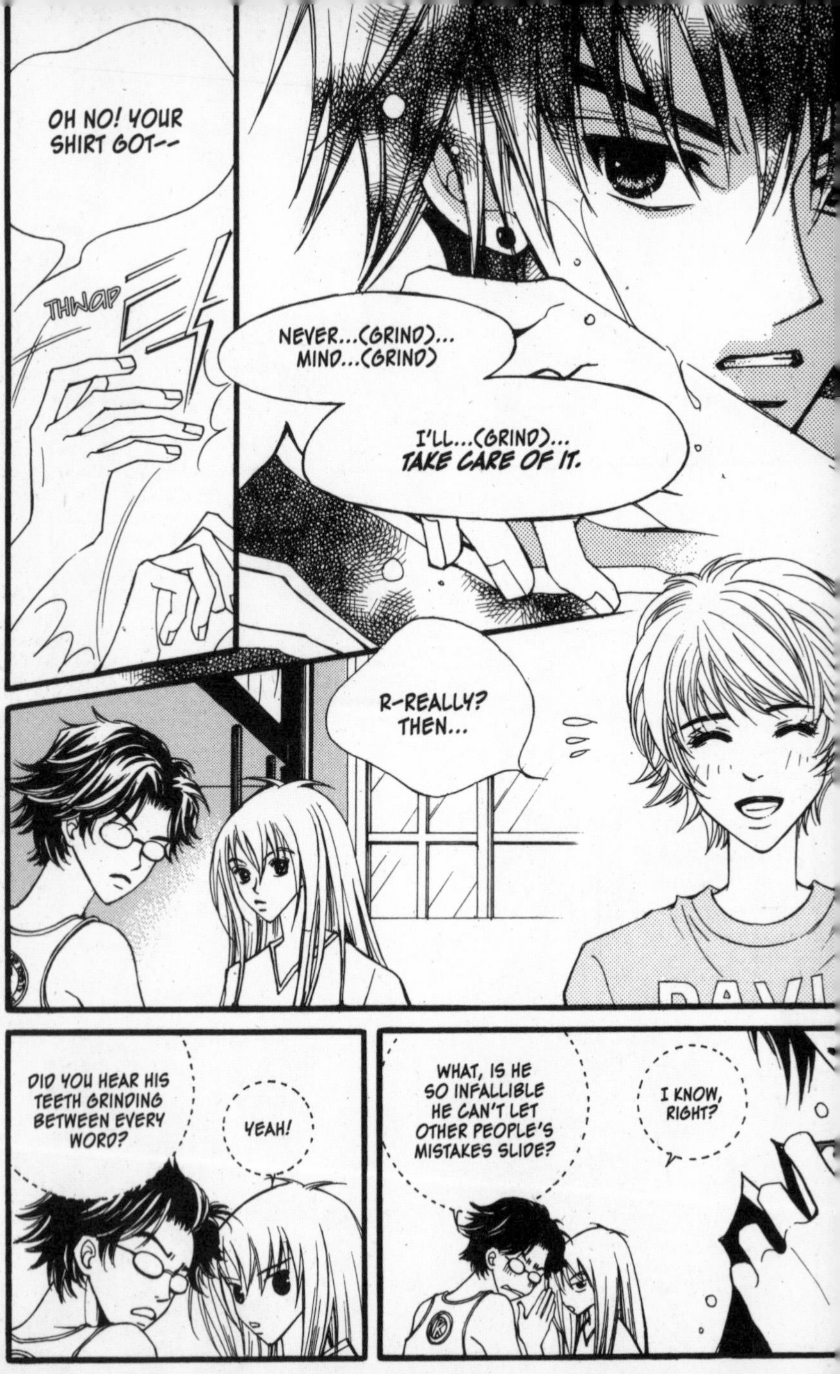
OH NO! YOUR SHIRT GOT--
THWAP
NEVER...(GRIND)... MIND...(GRIND)
I'LL...(GRIND)... TAKE CARE OF IT.
R-REALLY? THEN...
DID YOU HEAR HIS TEETH GRINDING BETWEEN EVERY WORD?
YEAH!
WHAT, IS HE SO INFALLIBLE HE CAN'T LET OTHER PEOPLE'S MISTAKES SLIDE?
I KNOW, RIGHT?

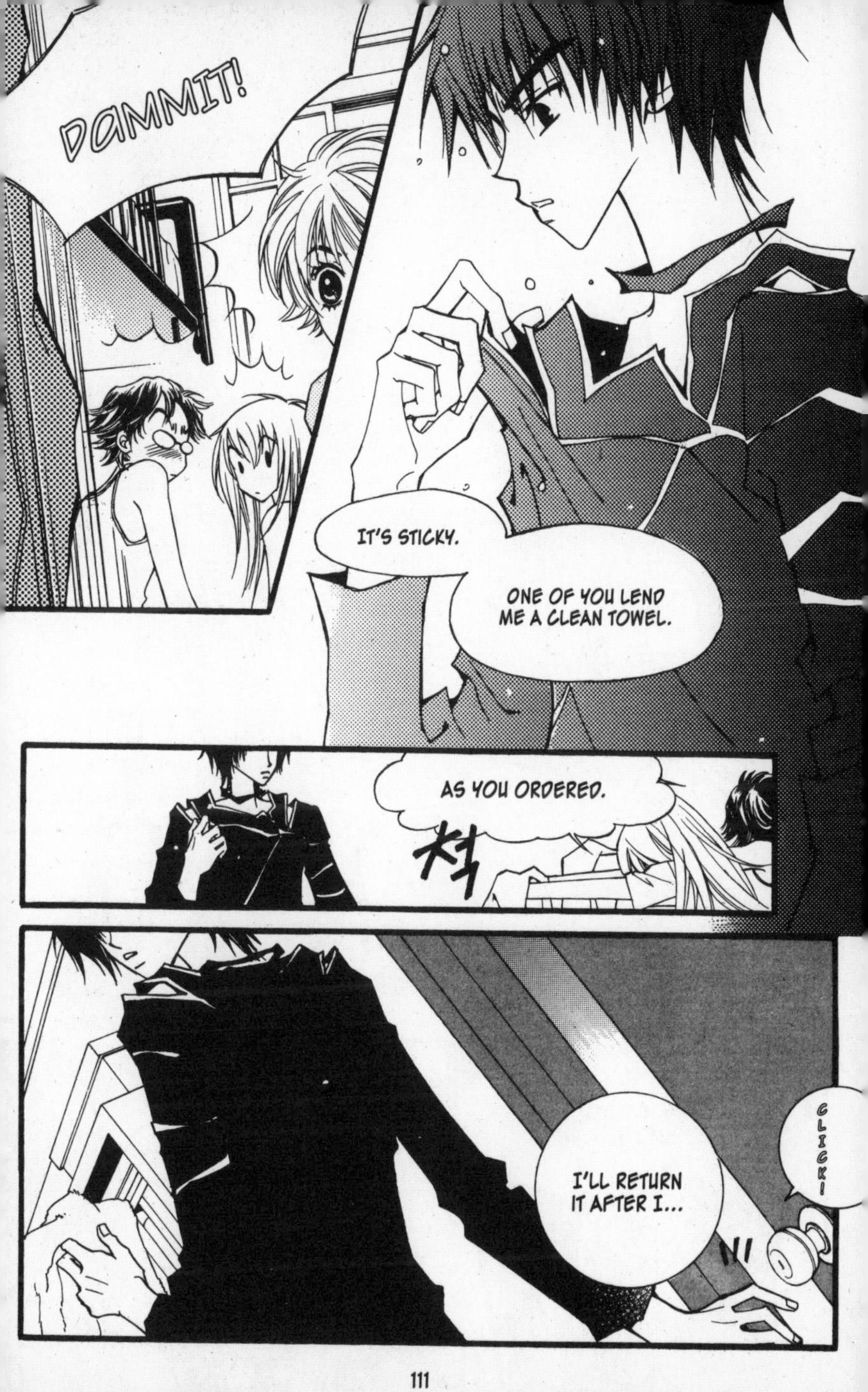
DAMMIT!
IT'S STICKY.
ONE OF YOU LEND ME A CLEAN TOWEL.
AS YOU ORDERED.
I'LL RETURN IT AFTER I...
CLICK!

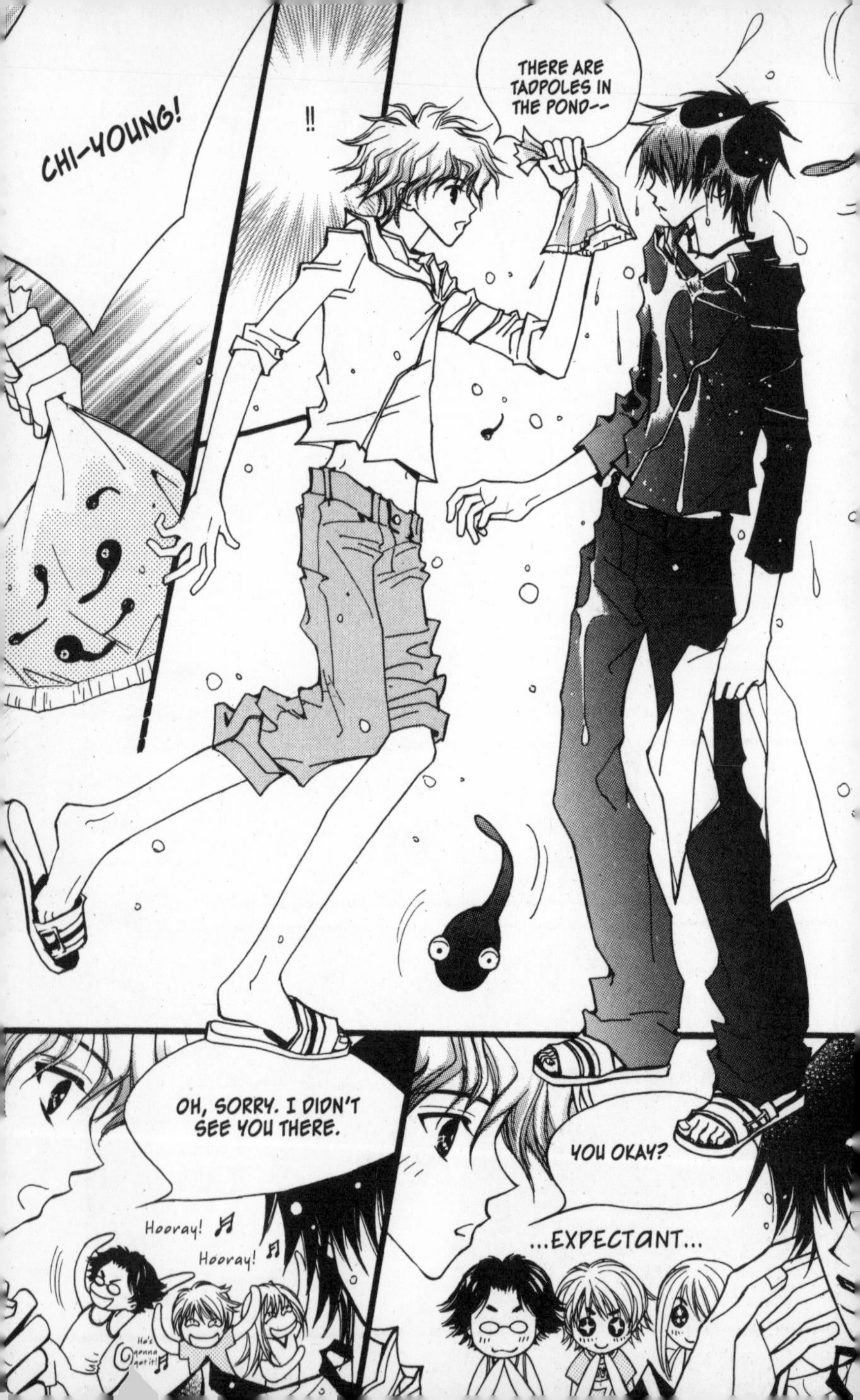
CHI-YOUNG!
!!
THERE ARE TADPOLES IN THE POND--
OH, SORRY. I DIDN'T SEE YOU THERE.
Hooray!
Hooray!
He's gonna get it!
YOU OKAY?
...EXPECTANT...

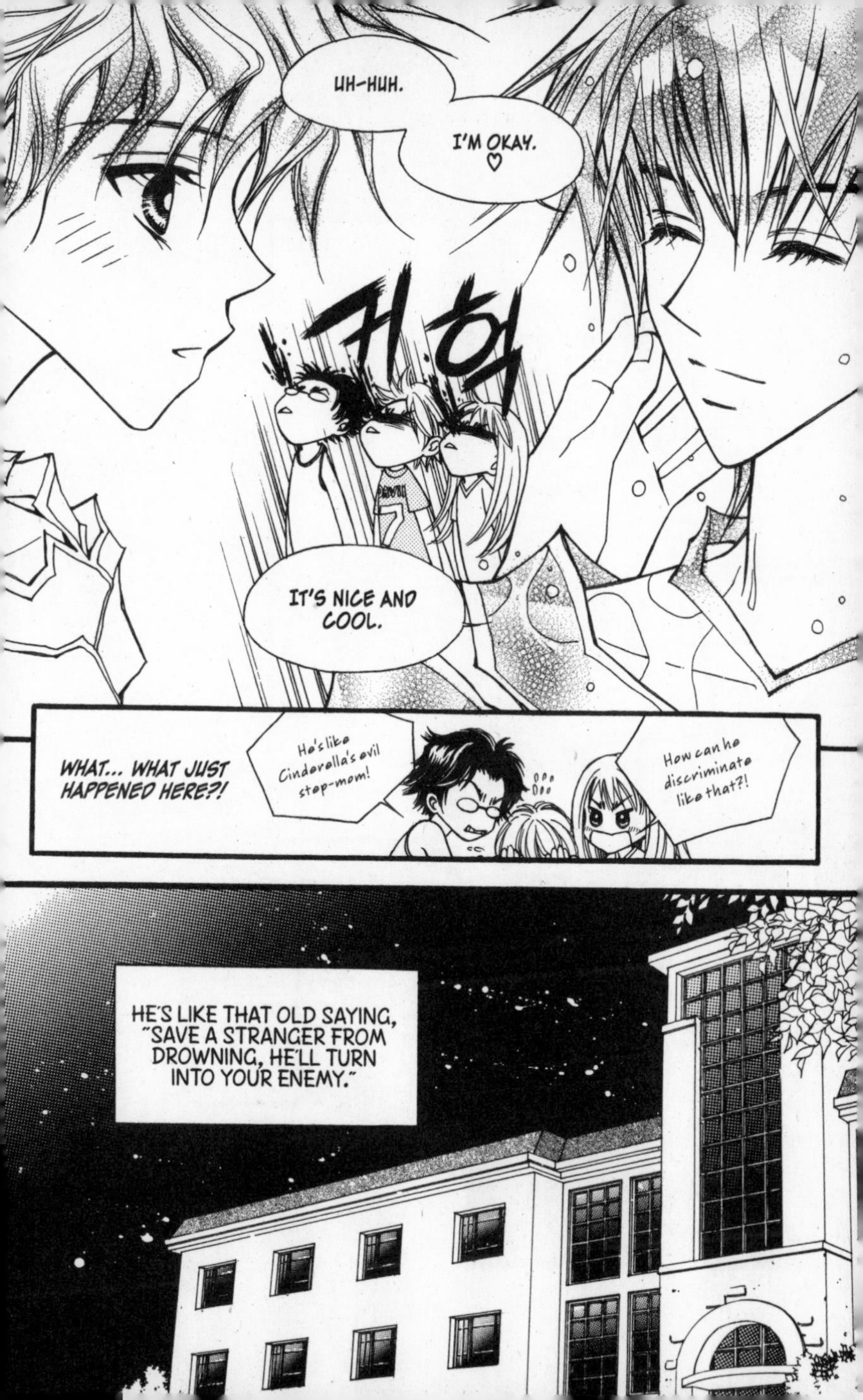
UH-HUH.
I'M OKAY. ♡
커헉
IT'S NICE AND COOL.
WHAT... WHAT JUST HAPPENED HERE?!
He's like Cinderella's evil step-mom!
How can he discriminate like that?!
HE'S LIKE THAT OLD SAYING, "SAVE A STRANGER FROM DROWNING, HE'LL TURN INTO YOUR ENEMY."

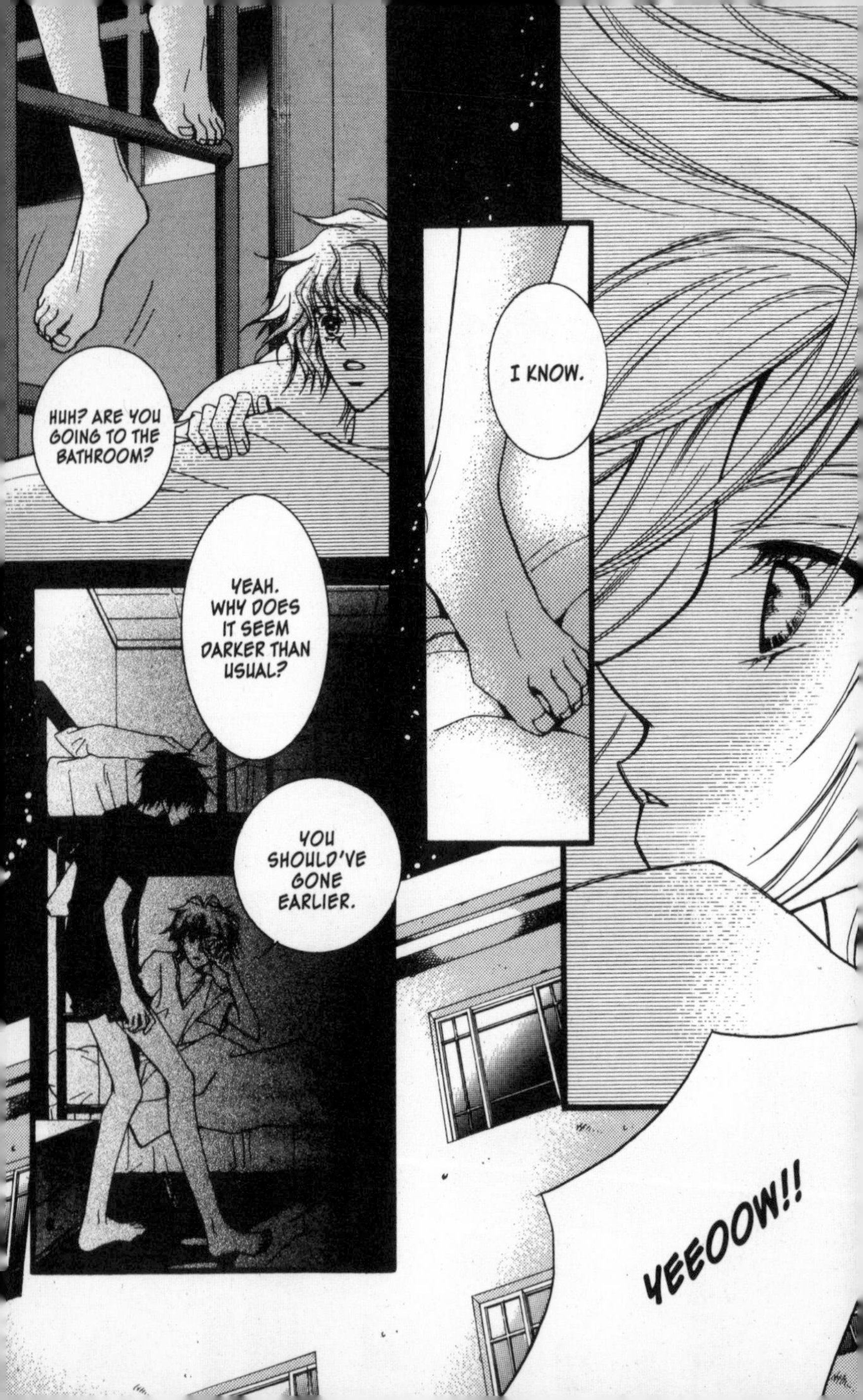
HUH? ARE YOU GOING TO THE BATHROOM?
I KNOW.
YEAH. WHY DOES IT SEEM DARKER THAN USUAL?
YOU SHOULD'VE GONE EARLIER.
YEEOOW!!

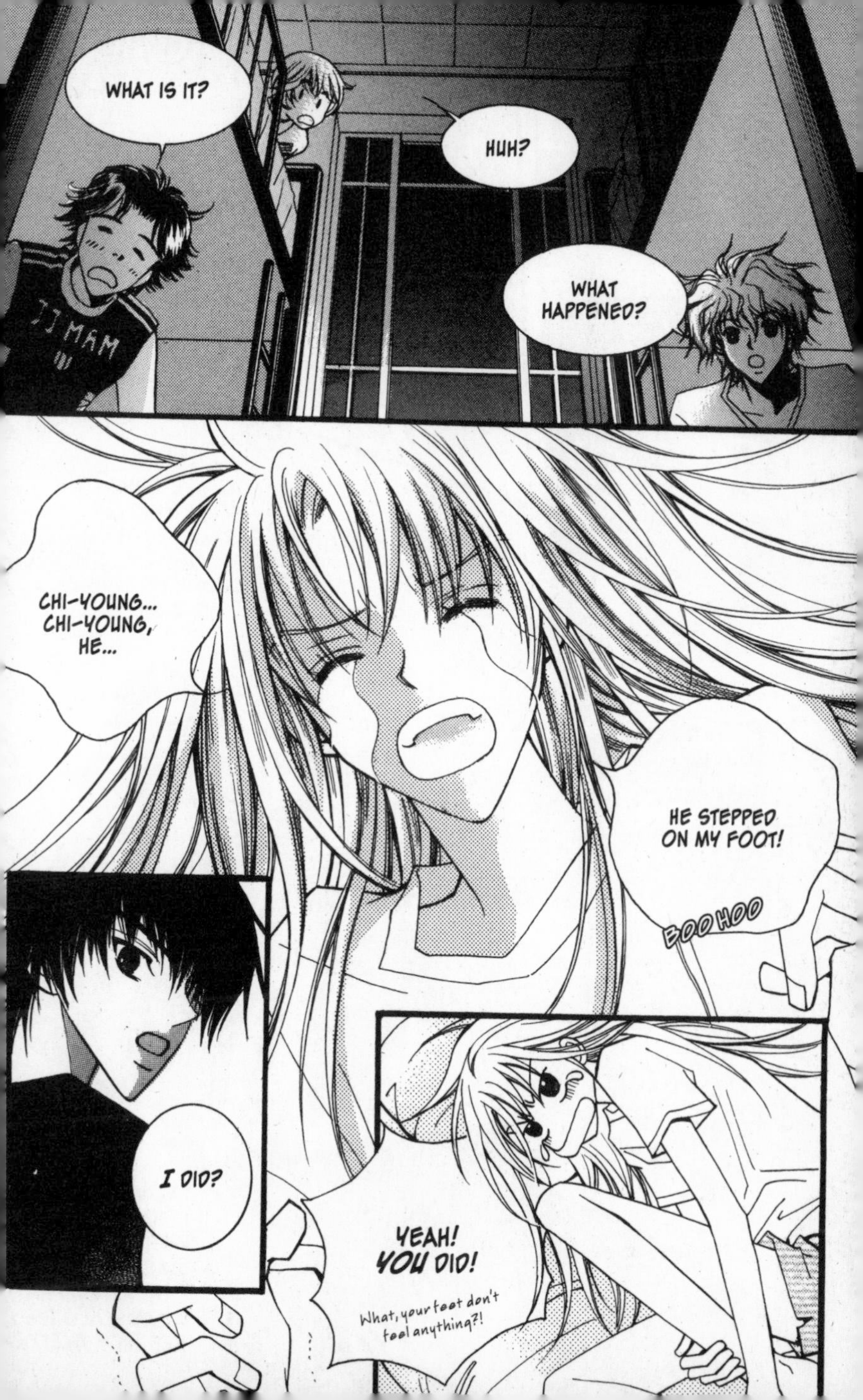
WHAT IS IT?
HUH?
WHAT HAPPENED?
CHI-YOUNG... CHI-YOUNG, HE...
HE STEPPED ON MY FOOT!
BOO HOO
I DID?
YEAH! YOU DID!
What, your feet don't feel anything?!

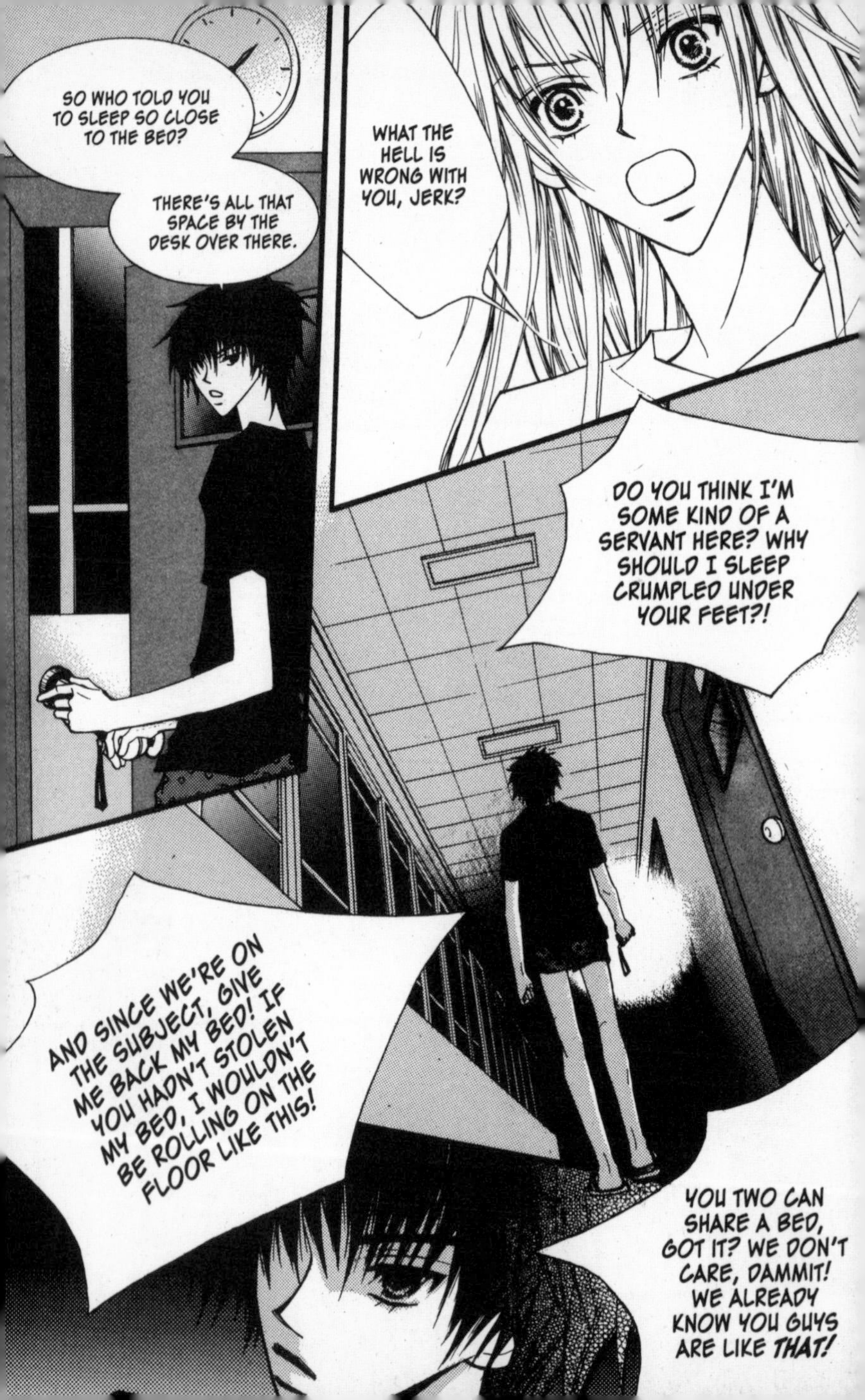
SO WHO TOLD YOU TO SLEEP SO CLOSE TO THE BED?
THERE'S ALL THAT SPACE BY THE DESK OVER THERE.
WHAT THE HELL IS WRONG WITH YOU, JERK?
DO YOU THINK I'M SOME KIND OF A SERVANT HERE? WHY SHOULD I SLEEP CRUMPLED UNDER YOUR FEET?!
AND SINCE WE'RE ON THE SUBJECT, GIVE ME BACK MY BED! IF YOU HADN'T STOLEN MY BED, I WOULDN'T BE ROLLING ON THE FLOOR LIKE THIS!
YOU TWO CAN SHARE A BED, GOT IT? WE DON'T CARE, DAMMIT! WE ALREADY KNOW YOU GUYS ARE LIKE *THAT!*

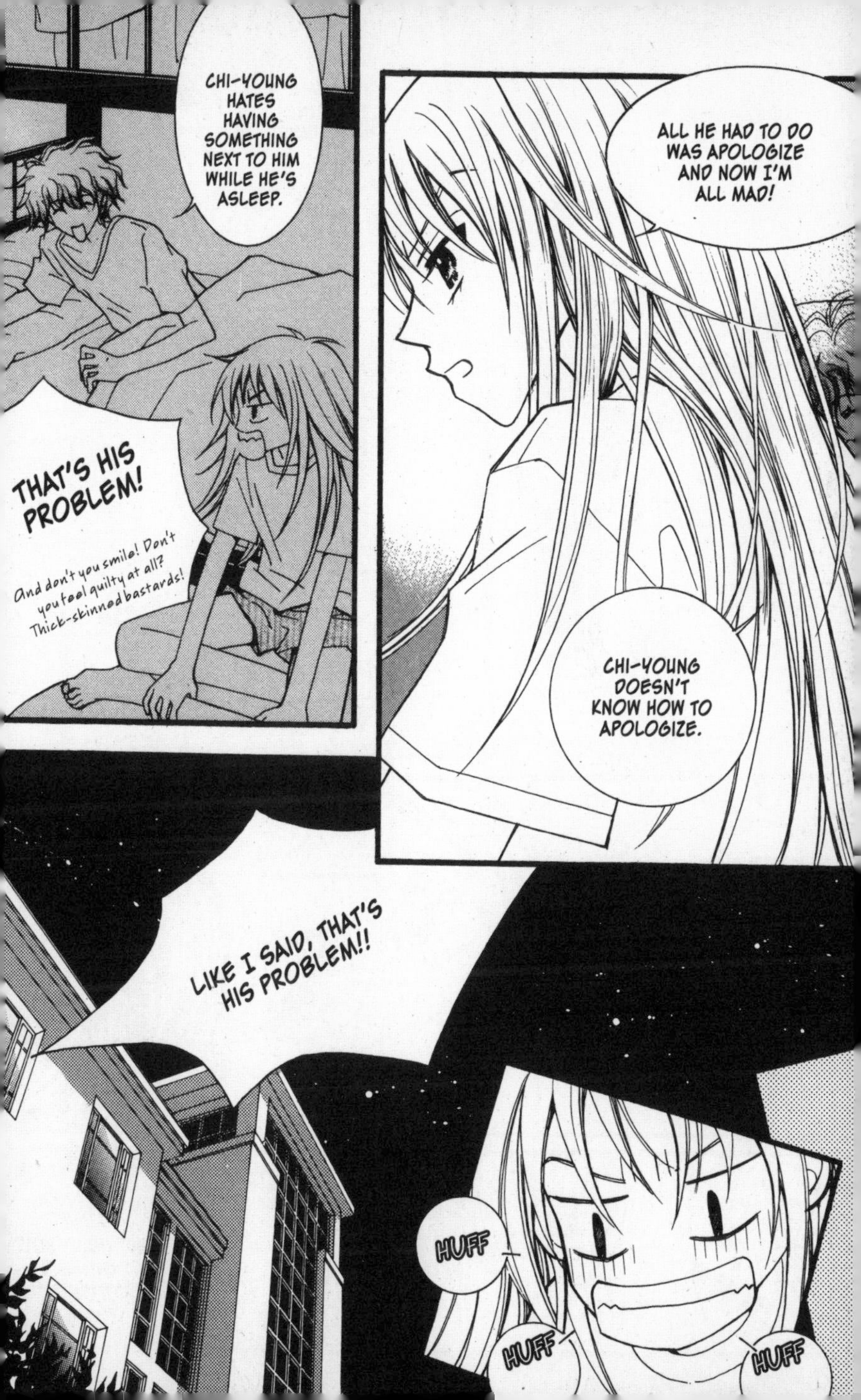
CHI-YOUNG HATES HAVING SOMETHING NEXT TO HIM WHILE HE'S ASLEEP.
THAT'S HIS PROBLEM!
And don't you smile! Don't you feel guilty at all? Thick-skinned bastards!
ALL HE HAD TO DO WAS APOLOGIZE AND NOW I'M ALL MAD!
CHI-YOUNG DOESN'T KNOW HOW TO APOLOGIZE.
LIKE I SAID, THAT'S HIS PROBLEM!!
HUFF
HUFF
HUFF

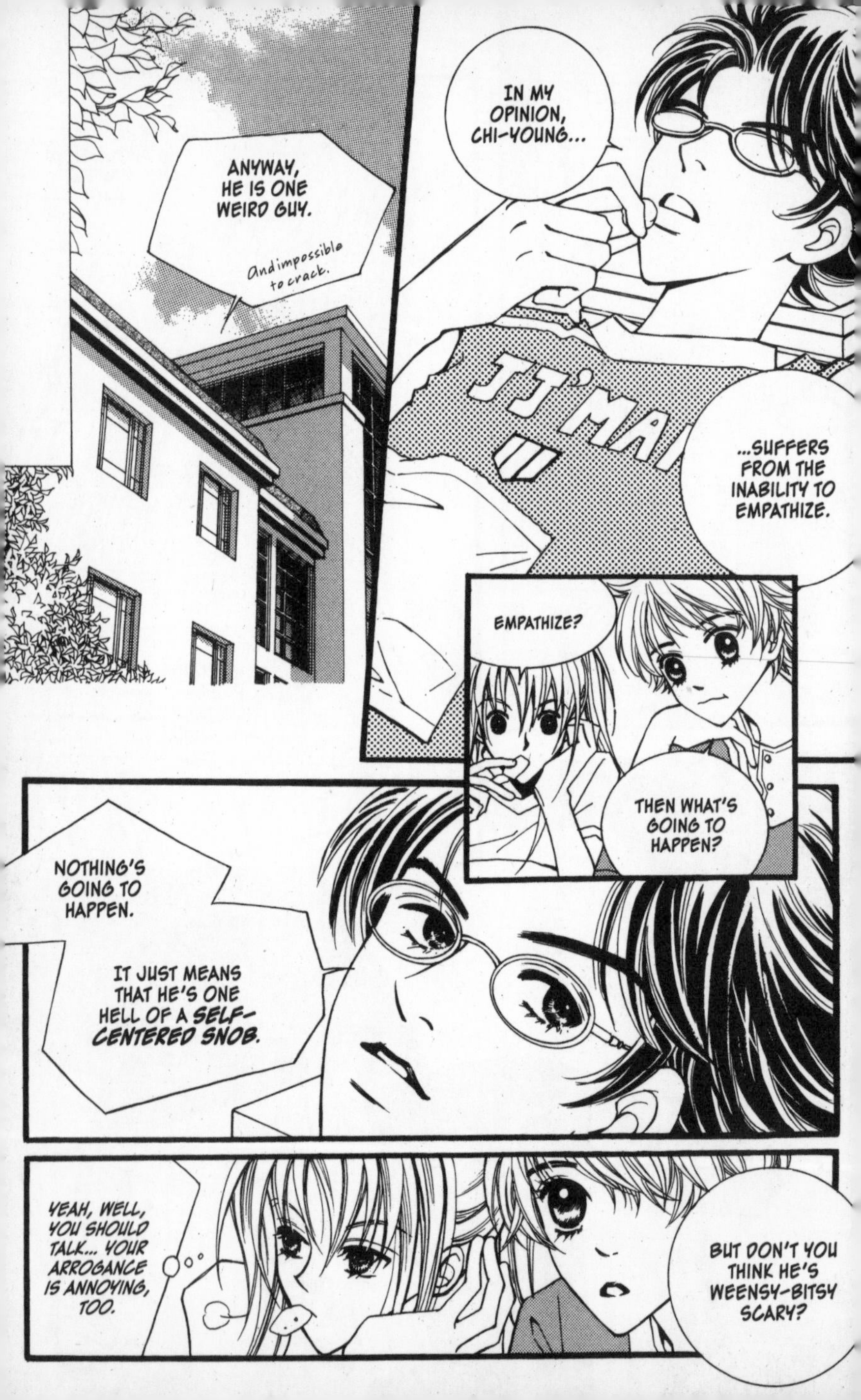
ANYWAY, HE IS ONE WEIRD GUY.
And impossible to crack.
IN MY OPINION, CHI-YOUNG...
...SUFFERS FROM THE INABILITY TO EMPATHIZE.
EMPATHIZE?
THEN WHAT'S GOING TO HAPPEN?
NOTHING'S GOING TO HAPPEN.
IT JUST MEANS THAT HE'S ONE HELL OF A SELF-CENTERED SNOB.
YEAH, WELL, YOU SHOULD TALK... YOUR ARROGANCE IS ANNOYING, TOO.
BUT DON'T YOU THINK HE'S WEENSY-BITSY SCARY?

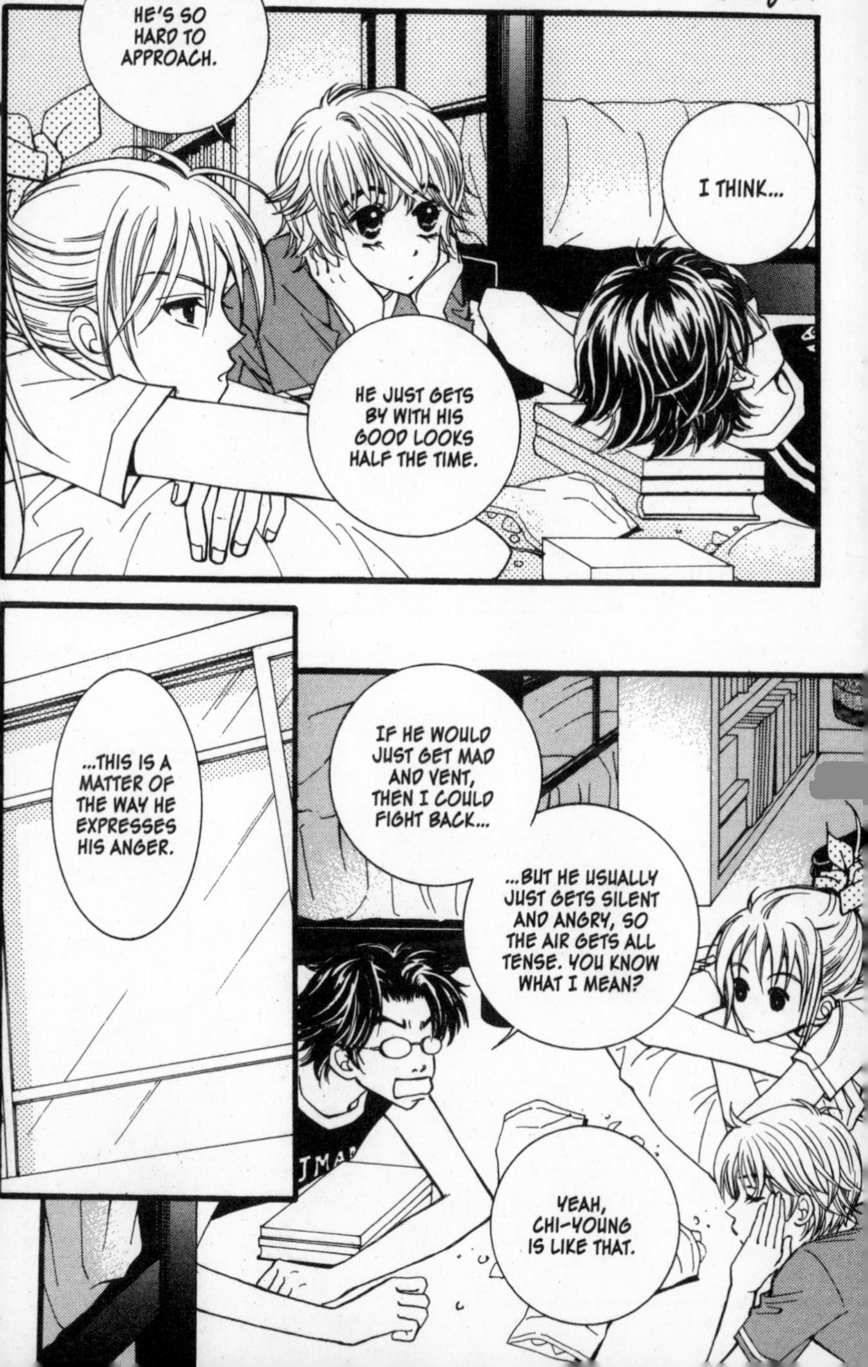
HE'S SO HARD TO APPROACH.
HE JUST GETS BY WITH HIS GOOD LOOKS HALF THE TIME.
I THINK...
...THIS IS A MATTER OF THE WAY HE EXPRESSES HIS ANGER.
IF HE WOULD JUST GET MAD AND VENT, THEN I COULD FIGHT BACK...
...BUT HE USUALLY JUST GETS SILENT AND ANGRY, SO THE AIR GETS ALL TENSE. YOU KNOW WHAT I MEAN?
YEAH, CHI-YOUNG IS LIKE THAT.

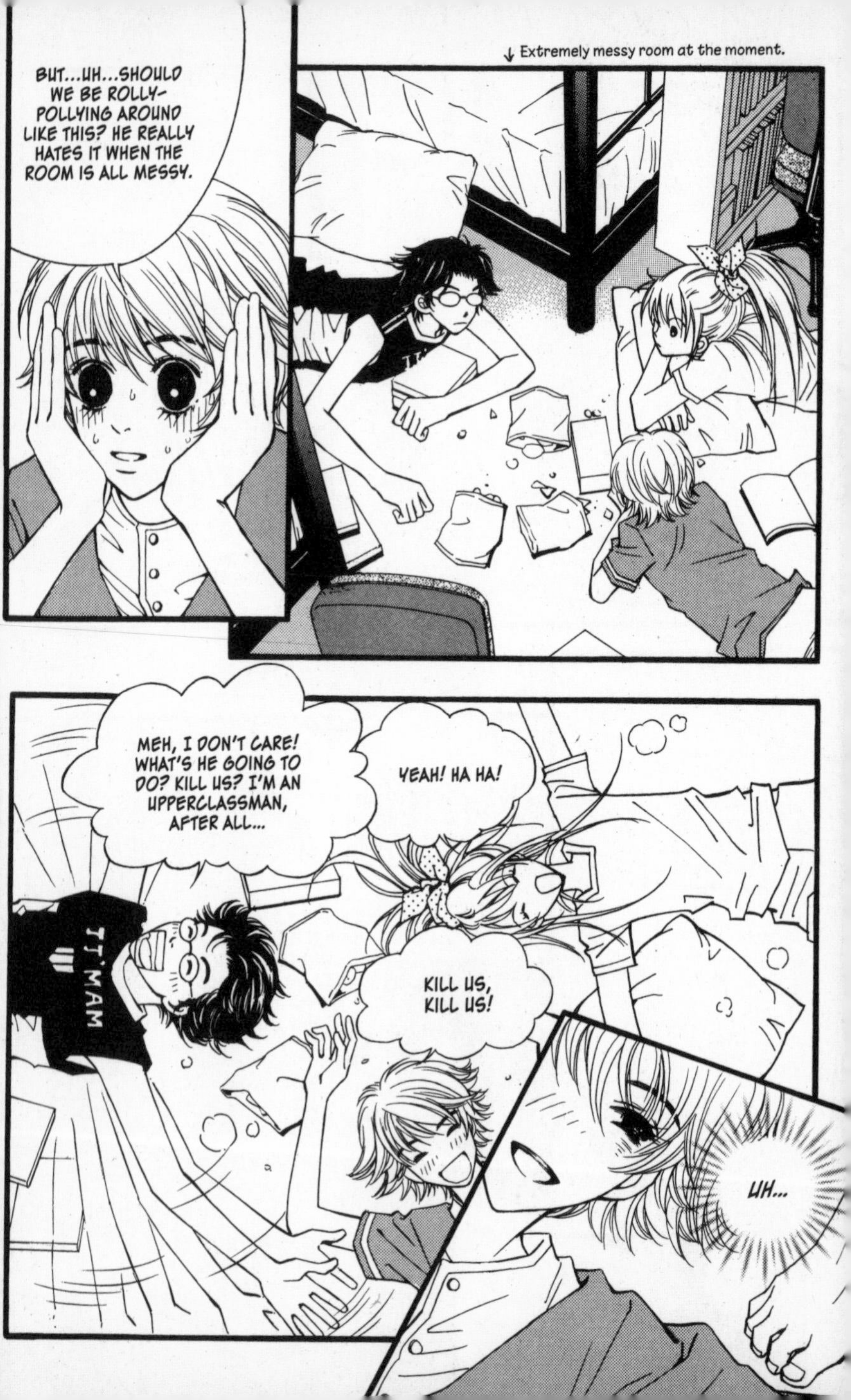
BUT...UH...SHOULD WE BE ROLLY-POLLYING AROUND LIKE THIS? HE REALLY HATES IT WHEN THE ROOM IS ALL MESSY.
↓ Extremely messy room at the moment.
MEH, I DON'T CARE! WHAT'S HE GOING TO DO? KILL US? I'M AN UPPERCLASSMAN, AFTER ALL...
YEAH! HA HA!
KILL US, KILL US!
UH...

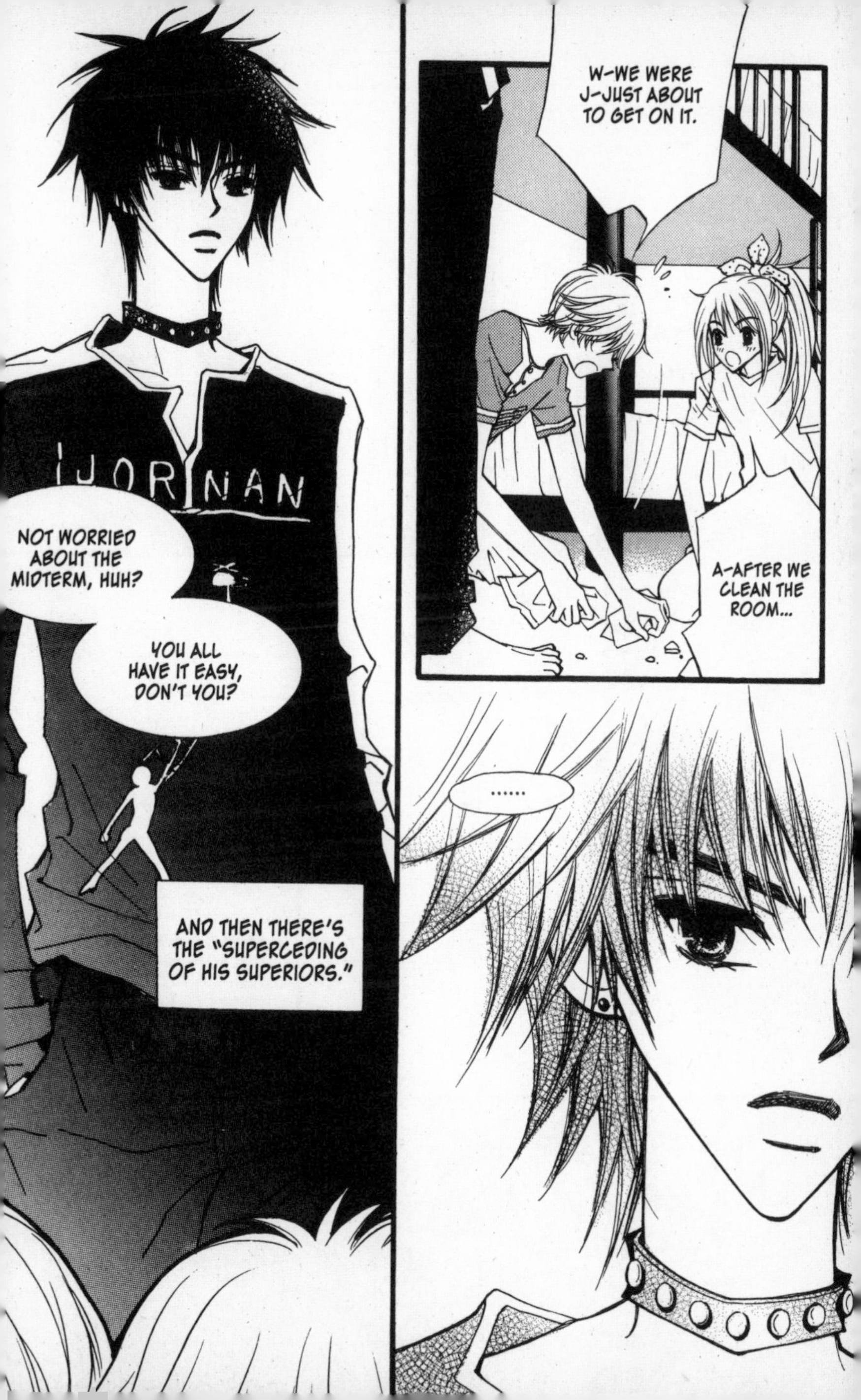
NOT WORRIED ABOUT THE MIDTERM, HUH?
YOU ALL HAVE IT EASY, DON'T YOU?
AND THEN THERE'S THE "SUPERCEDING OF HIS SUPERIORS."
W-WE WERE J-JUST ABOUT TO GET ON IT.
A-AFTER WE CLEAN THE ROOM...
......

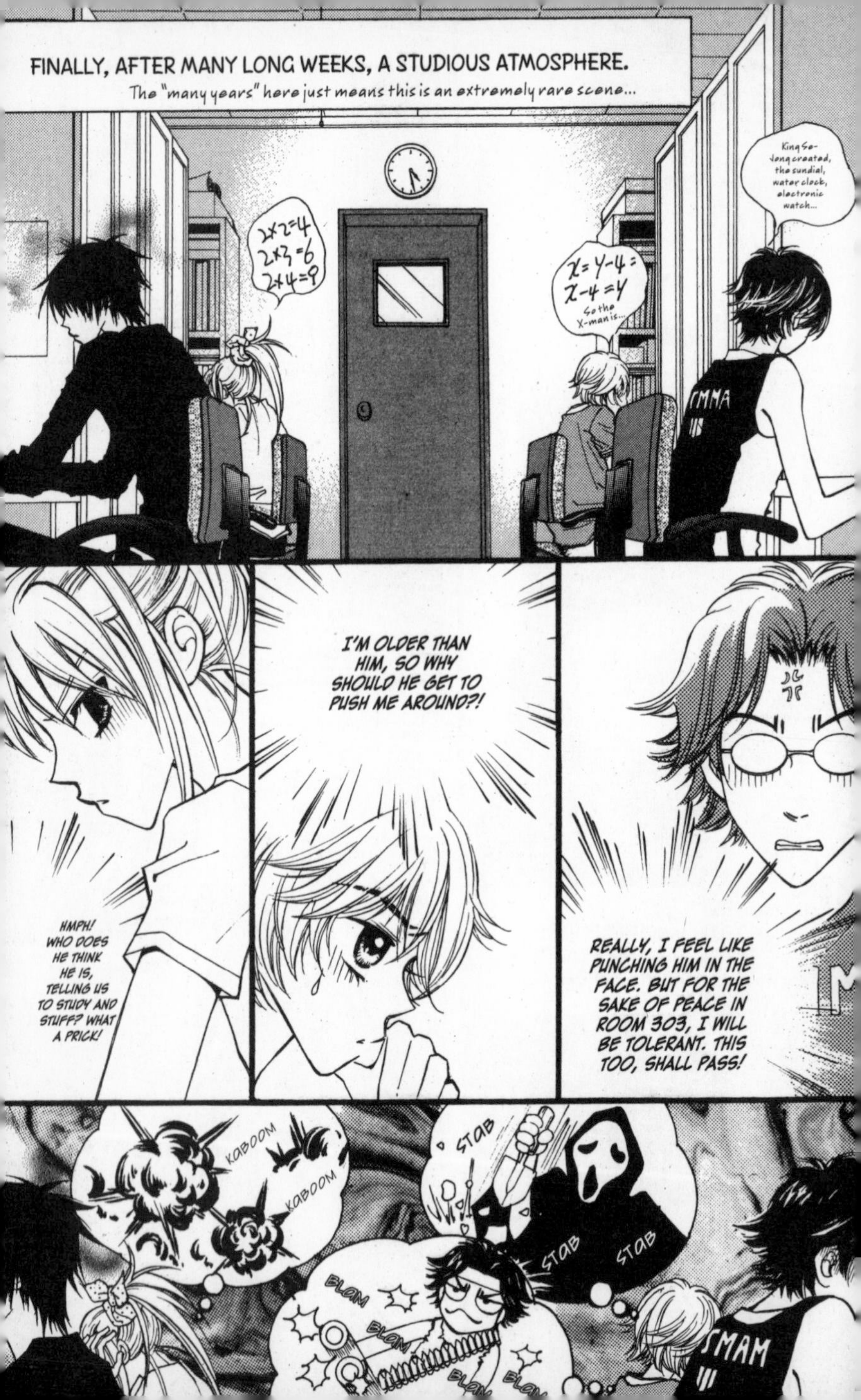
FINALLY, AFTER MANY LONG WEEKS, A STUDIOUS ATMOSPHERE.
The "many years" here just means this is an extremely rare scene...
2×2=4 2×3=6 2×4=9
x=y-4= x-4=y So the X-man is...
King Se-Jong created, the sundial, water clock, electronic watch...
HMPH! WHO DOES HE THINK HE IS, TELLING US TO STUDY AND STUFF? WHAT A PRICK!
I'M OLDER THAN HIM, SO WHY SHOULD HE GET TO PUSH ME AROUND?!
REALLY, I FEEL LIKE PUNCHING HIM IN THE FACE. BUT FOR THE SAKE OF PEACE IN ROOM 303, I WILL BE TOLERANT. THIS TOO, SHALL PASS!
KABOOM
KABOOM
STAB
STAB
STAB
BLAM
BLAM
BLAM
BLAM
BLAM

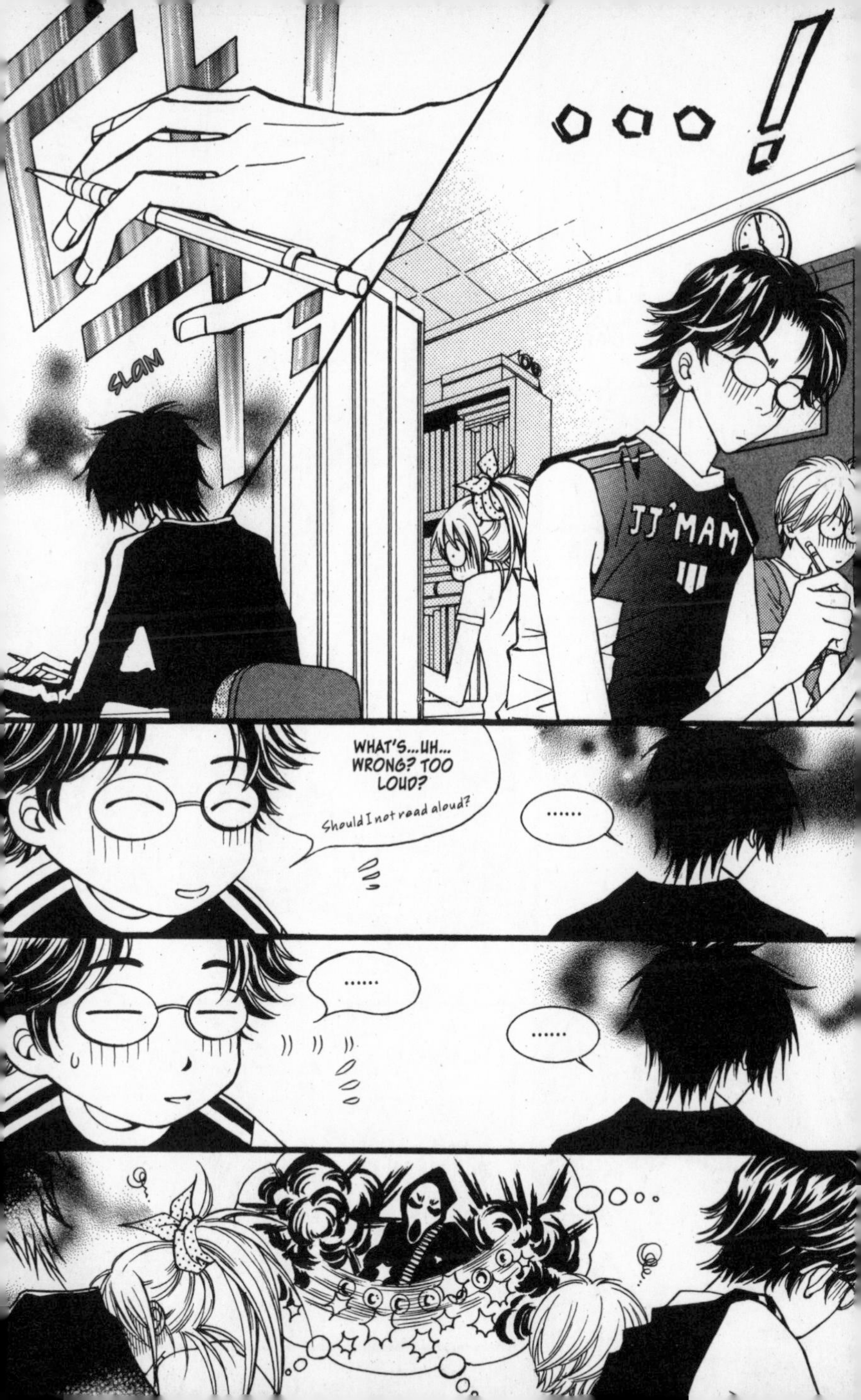

SLAM
JJ'MAM
WHAT'S...UH... WRONG? TOO LOUD?
Should I not read aloud?
......
......
......

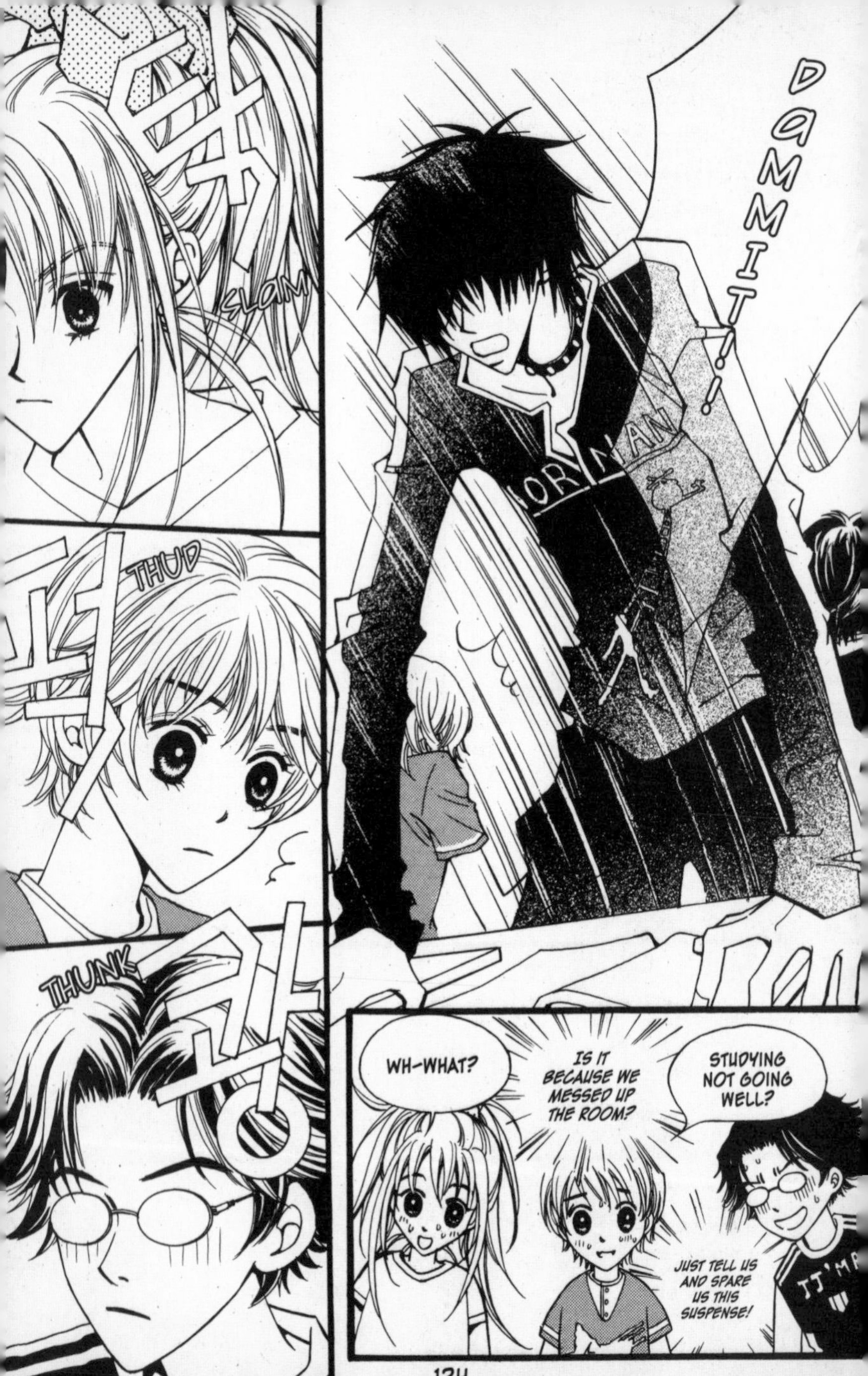
SLAM
THUD
THUNK
DAMMIT!!
WH-WHAT?
IS IT BECAUSE WE MESSED UP THE ROOM?
STUDYING NOT GOING WELL?
JUST TELL US AND SPARE US THIS SUSPENSE!

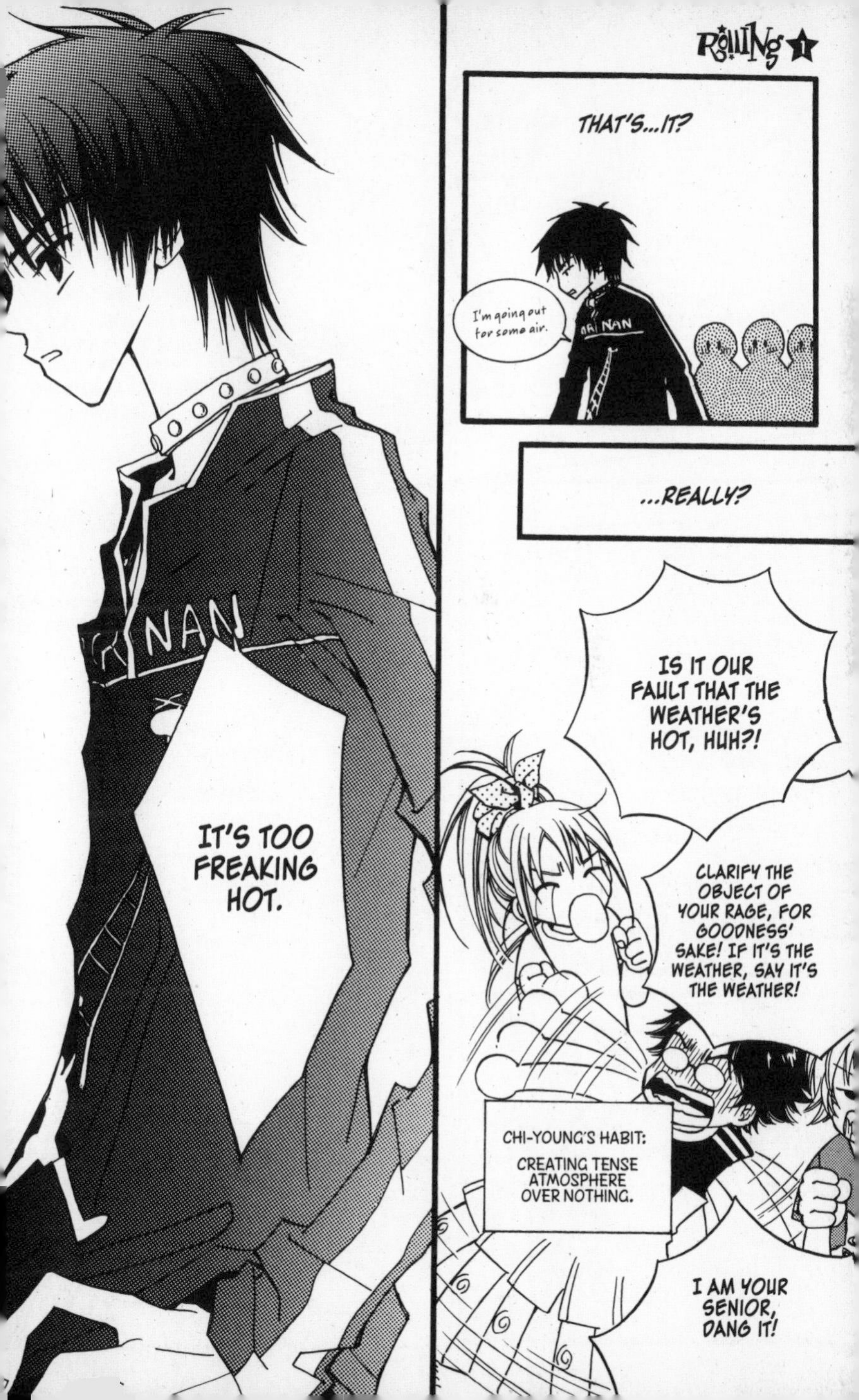
IT'S TOO FREAKING HOT.
THAT'S...IT?
I'm going out for some air.
...REALLY?
IS IT OUR FAULT THAT THE WEATHER'S HOT, HUH?!
CLARIFY THE OBJECT OF YOUR RAGE, FOR GOODNESS' SAKE! IF IT'S THE WEATHER, SAY IT'S THE WEATHER!
CHI-YOUNG'S HABIT: CREATING TENSE ATMOSPHERE OVER NOTHING.
I AM YOUR SENIOR, DANG IT!

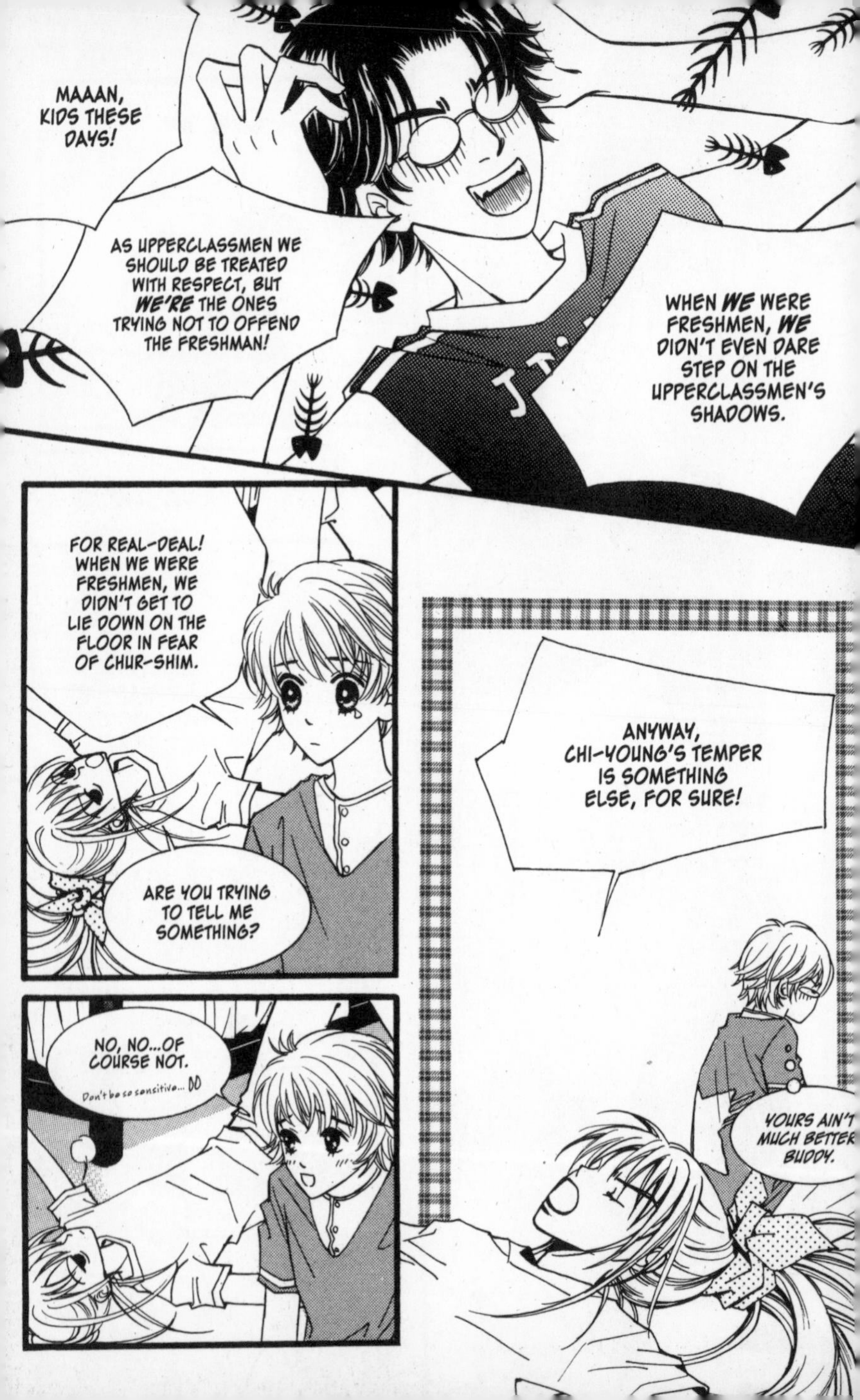
MAAAN, KIDS THESE DAYS!
AS UPPERCLASSMEN WE SHOULD BE TREATED WITH RESPECT, BUT *WE'RE* THE ONES TRYING NOT TO OFFEND THE FRESHMAN!
WHEN *WE* WERE FRESHMEN, *WE* DIDN'T EVEN DARE STEP ON THE UPPERCLASSMEN'S SHADOWS.
FOR REAL-DEAL! WHEN WE WERE FRESHMEN, WE DIDN'T GET TO LIE DOWN ON THE FLOOR IN FEAR OF CHUR-SHIM.
ARE YOU TRYING TO TELL ME SOMETHING?
NO, NO...OF COURSE NOT.
Don't be so sensitive...
ANYWAY, CHI-YOUNG'S TEMPER IS SOMETHING ELSE, FOR SURE!
YOURS AIN'T MUCH BETTER BUDDY.

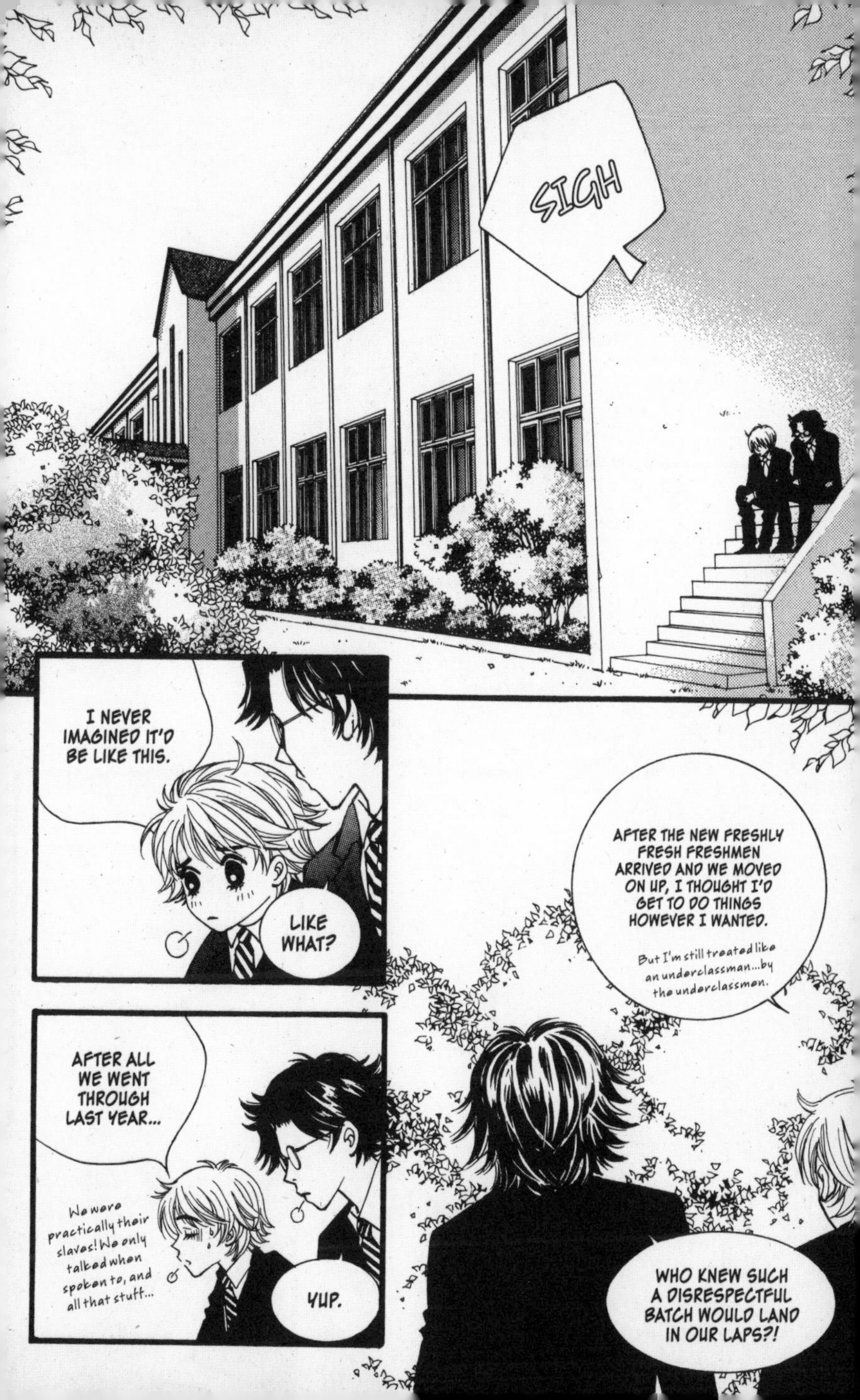
SIGH
I NEVER IMAGINED IT'D BE LIKE THIS.
LIKE WHAT?
AFTER ALL WE WENT THROUGH LAST YEAR...
We were practically their slaves! We only talked when spoken to, and all that stuff...
YUP.
AFTER THE NEW FRESHLY FRESH FRESHMEN ARRIVED AND WE MOVED ON UP, I THOUGHT I'D GET TO DO THINGS HOWEVER I WANTED.
But I'm still treated like an underclassman...by the underclassmen.
WHO KNEW SUCH A DISRESPECTFUL BATCH WOULD LAND IN OUR LAPS?!

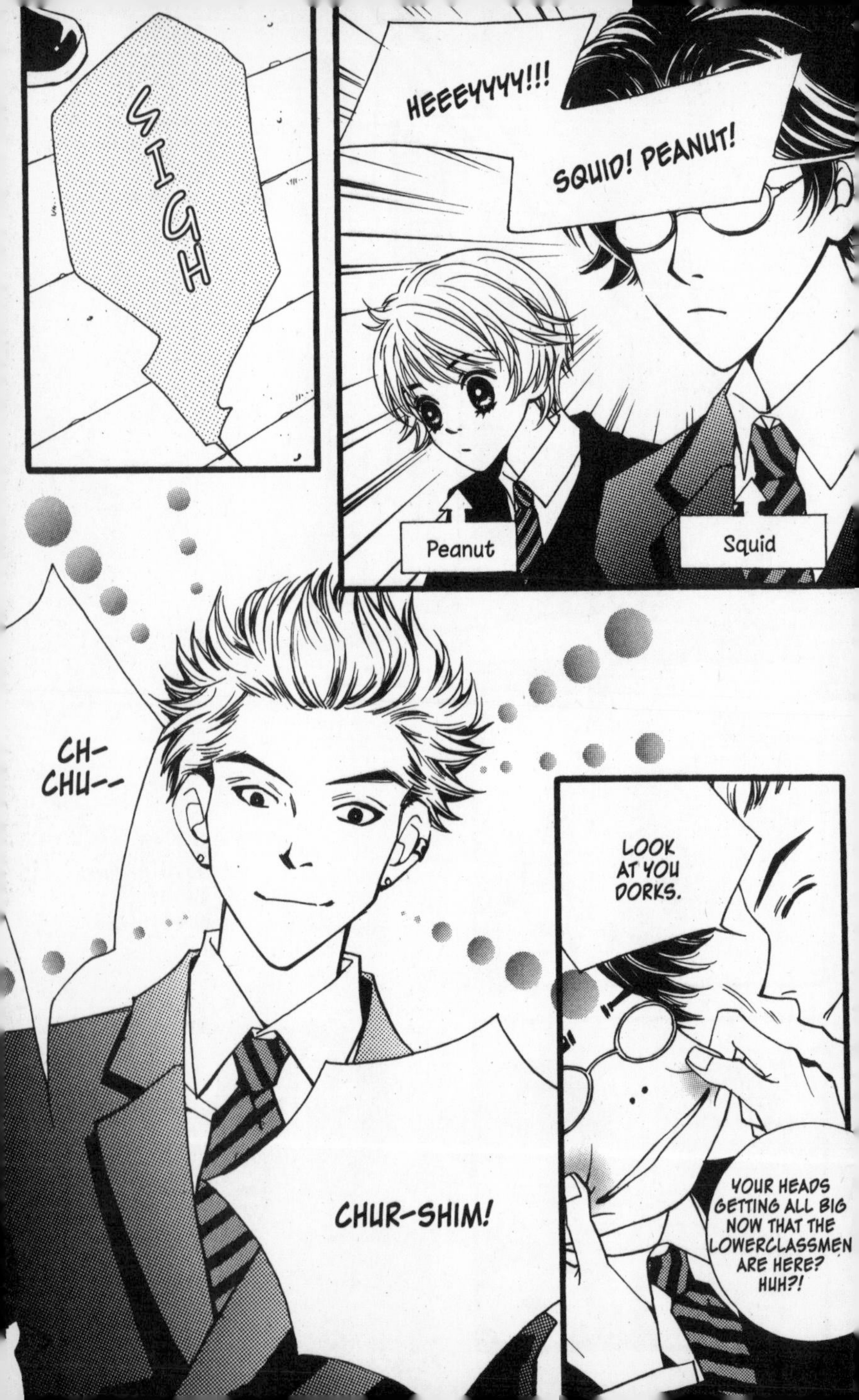
SIGH
HEEEYYYY!!!!
SQUID! PEANUT!
Peanut
Squid
CH-
CHU--
CHUR-SHIM!
LOOK AT YOU DORKS.
YOUR HEADS GETTING ALL BIG NOW THAT THE LOWERCLASSMEN ARE HERE? HUH?!

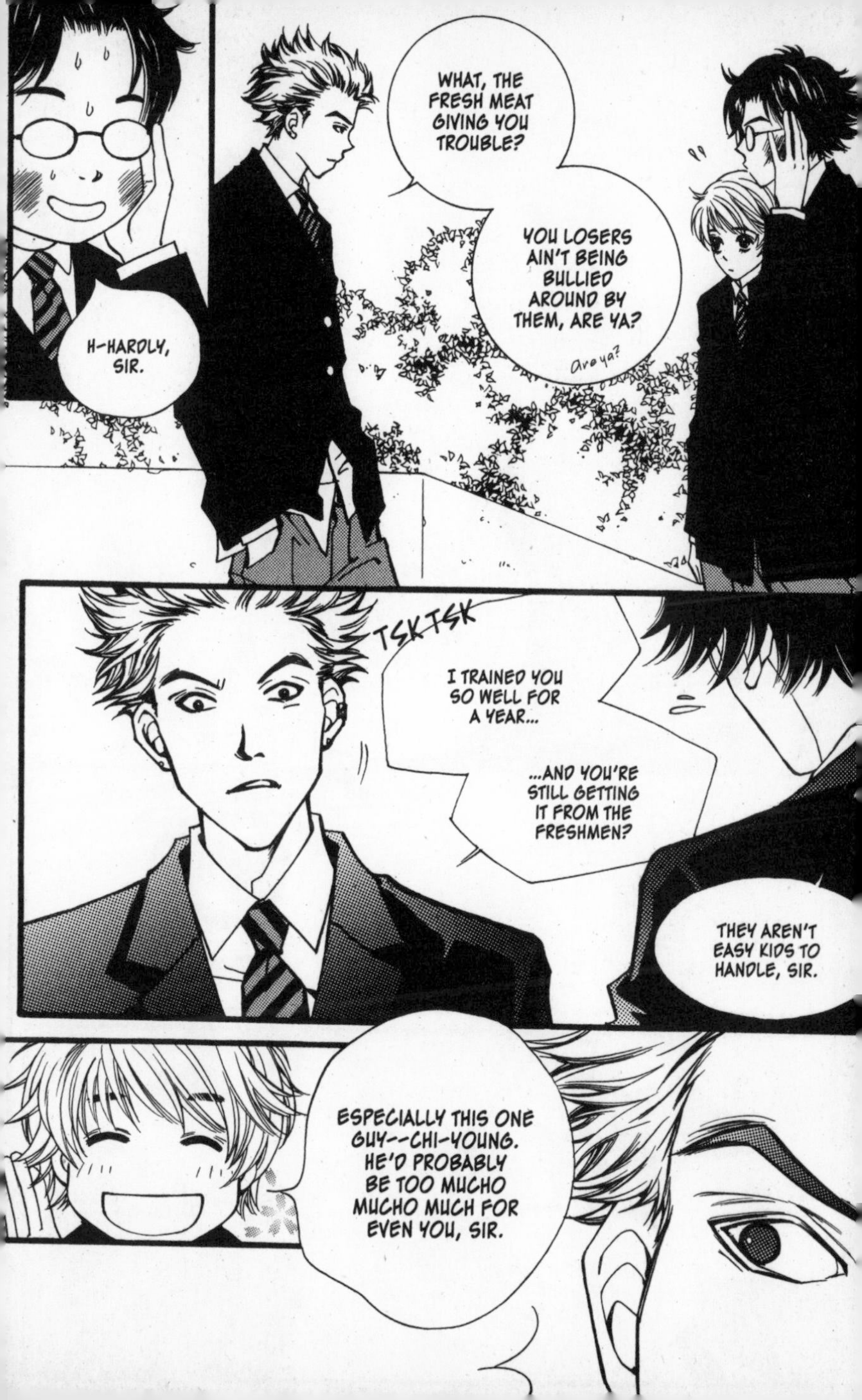

H-HARDLY, SIR.
WHAT, THE FRESH MEAT GIVING YOU TROUBLE?
YOU LOSERS AIN'T BEING BULLIED AROUND BY THEM, ARE YA?
are ya?
TSK TSK
I TRAINED YOU SO WELL FOR A YEAR...
...AND YOU'RE STILL GETTING IT FROM THE FRESHMEN?
THEY AREN'T EASY KIDS TO HANDLE, SIR.
ESPECIALLY THIS ONE GUY--CHI-YOUNG. HE'D PROBABLY BE TOO MUCHO MUCHO MUCH FOR EVEN YOU, SIR.

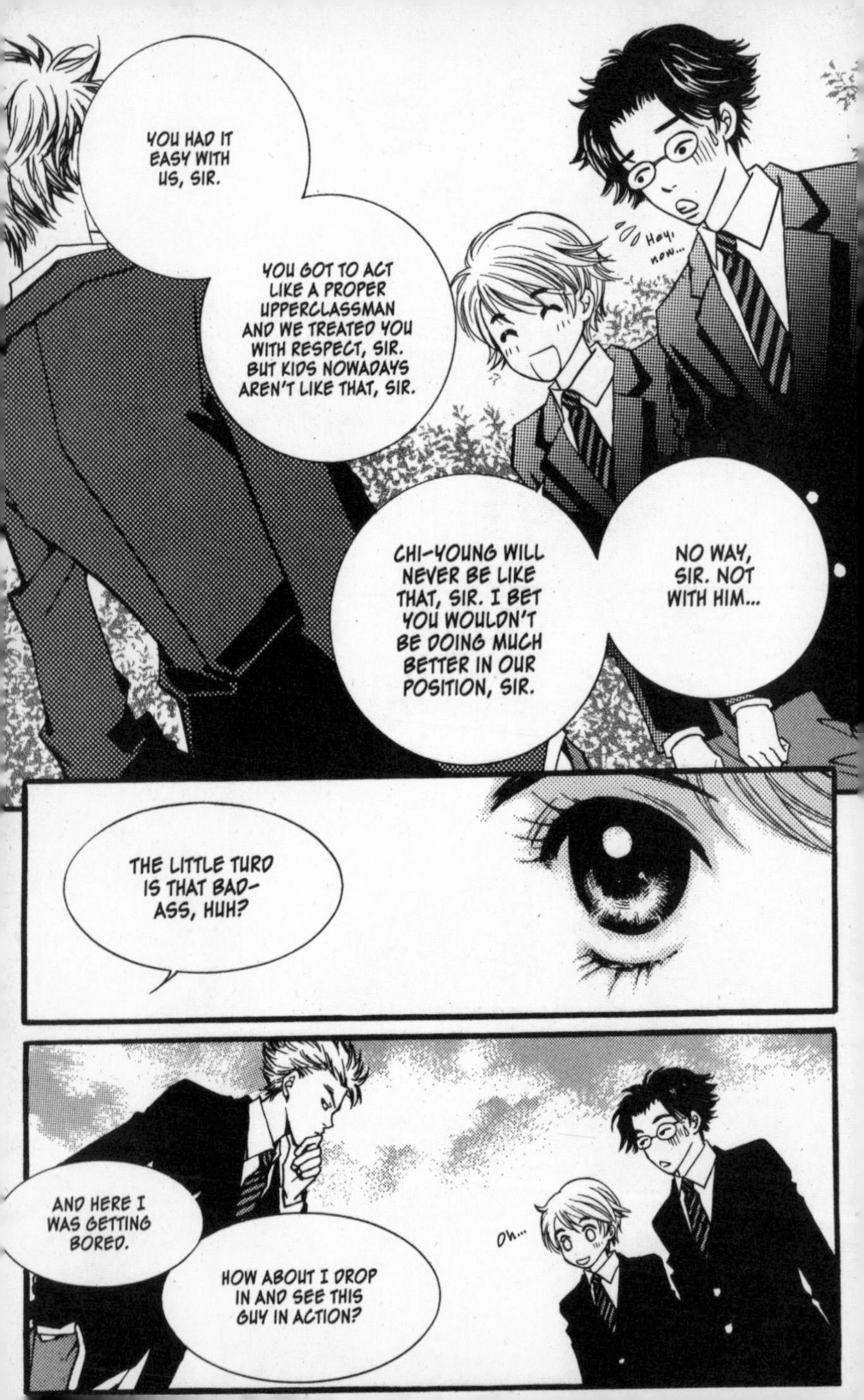
YOU HAD IT EASY WITH US, SIR.
YOU GOT TO ACT LIKE A PROPER UPPERCLASSMAN AND WE TREATED YOU WITH RESPECT, SIR. BUT KIDS NOWADAYS AREN'T LIKE THAT, SIR.
Hey, now...
CHI-YOUNG WILL NEVER BE LIKE THAT, SIR. I BET YOU WOULDN'T BE DOING MUCH BETTER IN OUR POSITION, SIR.
NO WAY, SIR. NOT WITH HIM...
THE LITTLE TURD IS THAT BAD-ASS, HUH?
AND HERE I WAS GETTING BORED.
HOW ABOUT I DROP IN AND SEE THIS GUY IN ACTION?
Oh...

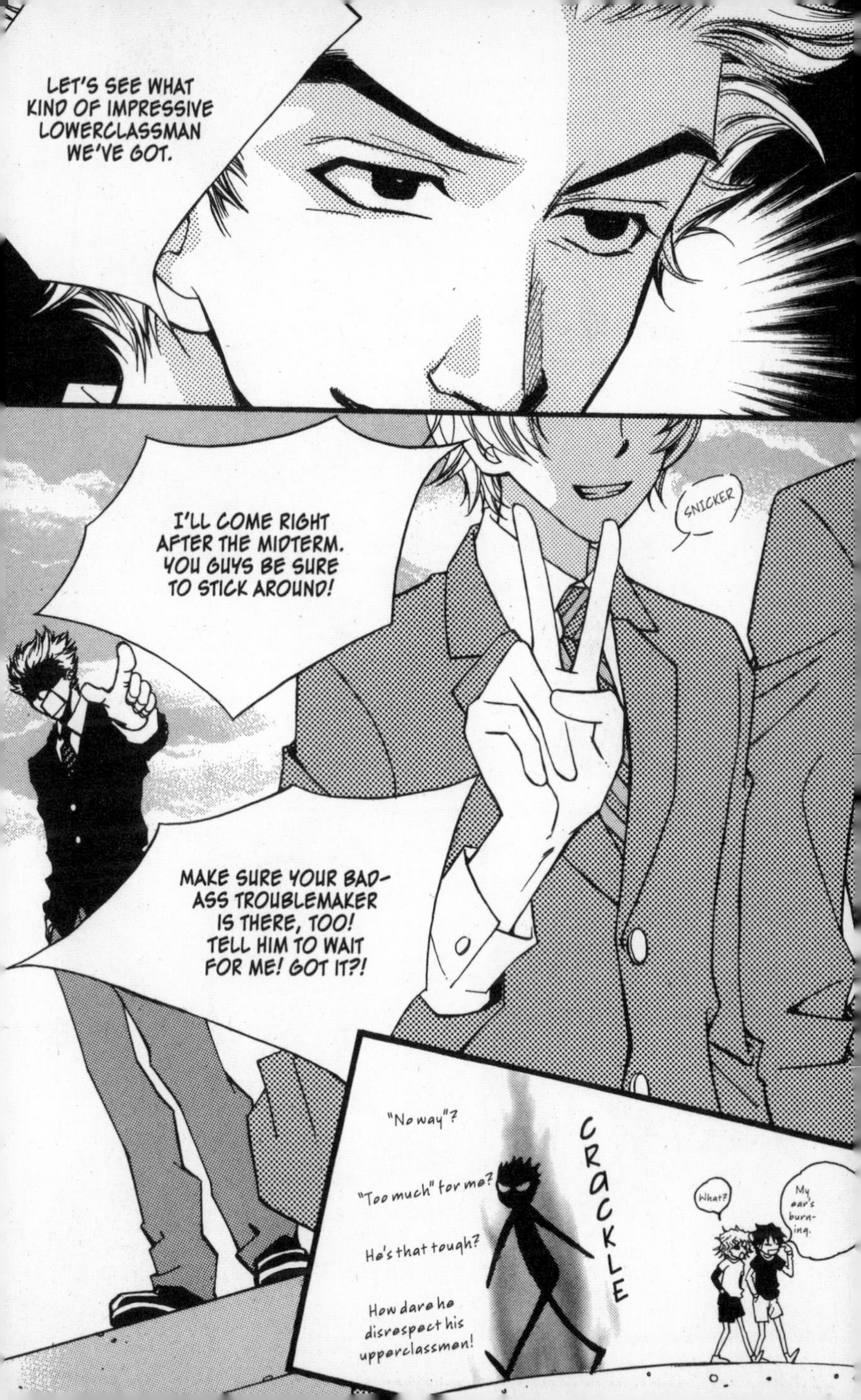
LET'S SEE WHAT KIND OF IMPRESSIVE LOWERCLASSMAN WE'VE GOT.
I'LL COME RIGHT AFTER THE MIDTERM. YOU GUYS BE SURE TO STICK AROUND!
SNICKER
MAKE SURE YOUR BAD-ASS TROUBLEMAKER IS THERE, TOO! TELL HIM TO WAIT FOR ME! GOT IT?!
"No way"?
"Too much" for me?
He's that tough?
How dare he disrespect his upperclassmen!
CRACKLE
What?
My ear's burning.

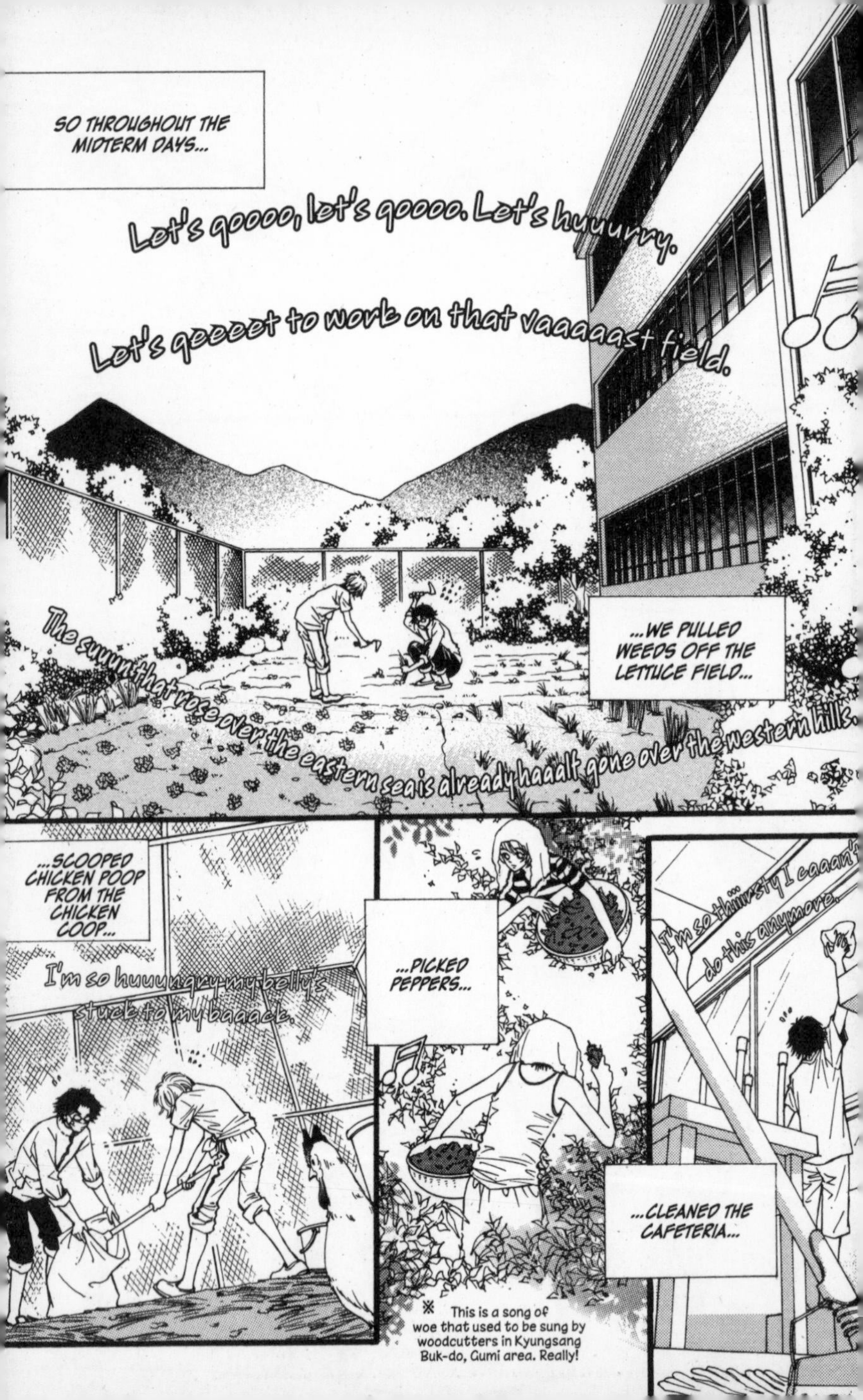
SO THROUGHOUT THE MIDTERM DAYS...
Let's goooo, let's goooo. Let's huuurry.
Let's geeeet to work on that vaaaaast field.
...WE PULLED WEEDS OFF THE LETTUCE FIELD...
The suuun that rose over the eastern sea is already haaalf gone over the western hills.
...SCOOPED CHICKEN POOP FROM THE CHICKEN COOP...
I'm so huuungry my belly's stuck to my baaack.
...PICKED PEPPERS...
I'm so thiiirsty I caaan't do this anymore.
...CLEANED THE CAFETERIA...

※ This is a song of woe that used to be sung by woodcutters in Kyungsang Buk-do, Gumi area. Really!

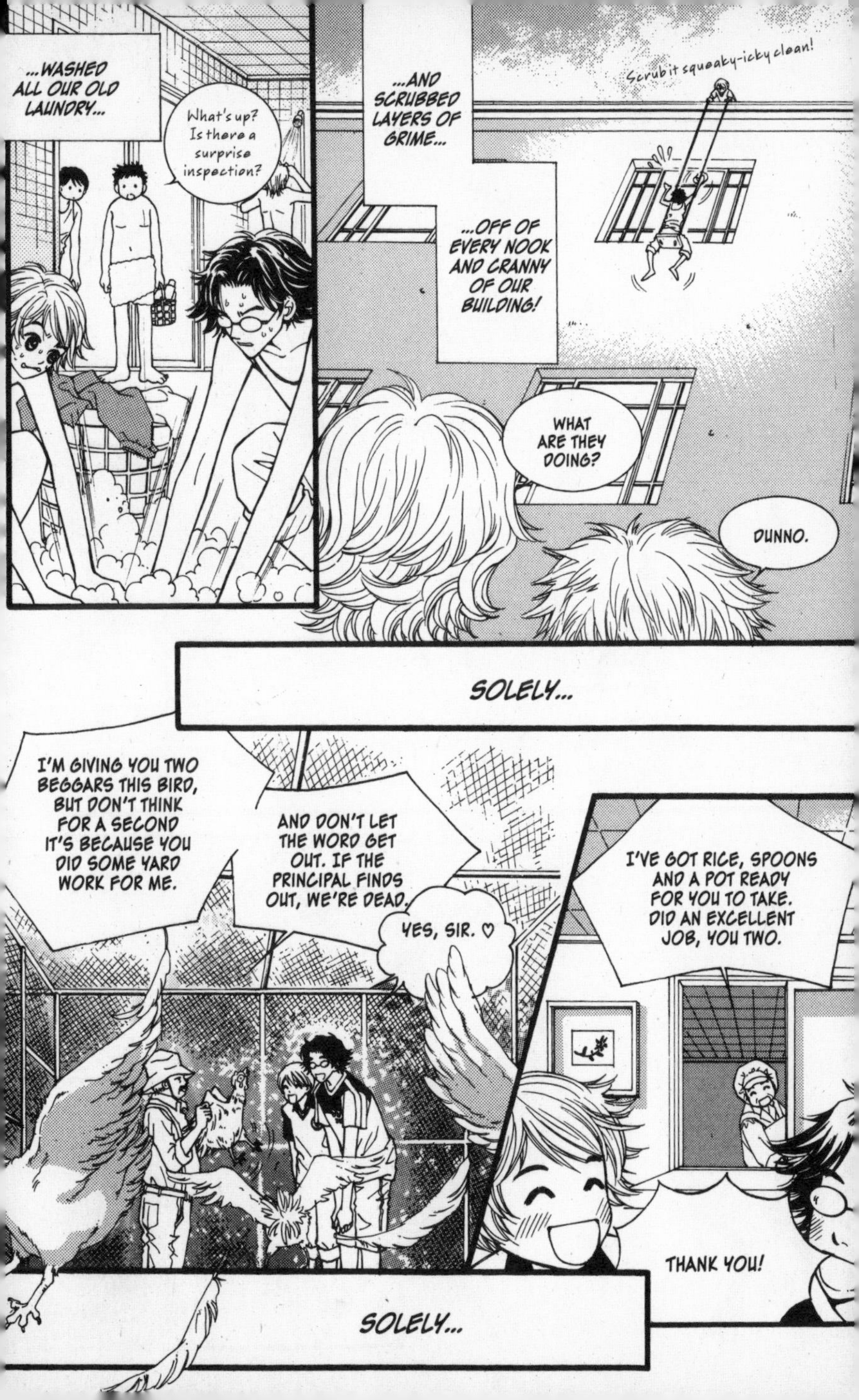

...WASHED ALL OUR OLD LAUNDRY...
What's up? Is there a surprise inspection?
...AND SCRUBBED LAYERS OF GRIME...
...OFF OF EVERY NOOK AND CRANNY OF OUR BUILDING!
Scrub it squeaky-icky clean!
WHAT ARE THEY DOING?
DUNNO.
SOLELY...
I'M GIVING YOU TWO BEGGARS THIS BIRD, BUT DON'T THINK FOR A SECOND IT'S BECAUSE YOU DID SOME YARD WORK FOR ME.
AND DON'T LET THE WORD GET OUT. IF THE PRINCIPAL FINDS OUT, WE'RE DEAD.
YES, SIR. ♡
I'VE GOT RICE, SPOONS AND A POT READY FOR YOU TO TAKE. DID AN EXCELLENT JOB, YOU TWO.
THANK YOU!
SOLELY...

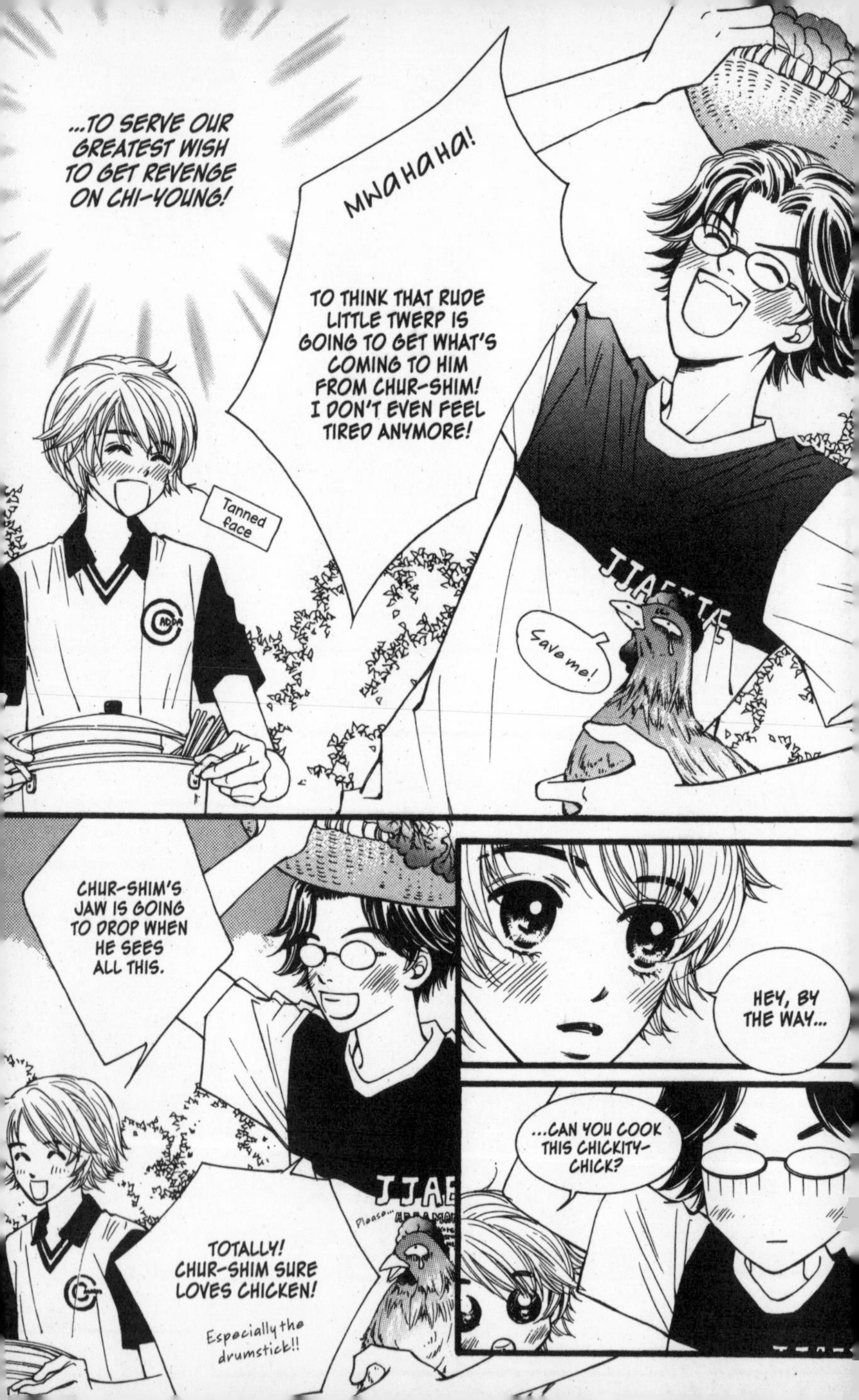
...TO SERVE OUR GREATEST WISH TO GET REVENGE ON CHI-YOUNG!
MWAHAHA!
TO THINK THAT RUDE LITTLE TWERP IS GOING TO GET WHAT'S COMING TO HIM FROM CHUR-SHIM! I DON'T EVEN FEEL TIRED ANYMORE!
Tanned face
Save me!
CHUR-SHIM'S JAW IS GOING TO DROP WHEN HE SEES ALL THIS.
Please...
TOTALLY! CHUR-SHIM SURE LOVES CHICKEN!
Especially the drumstick!!
HEY, BY THE WAY...
...CAN YOU COOK THIS CHICKITY-CHICK?

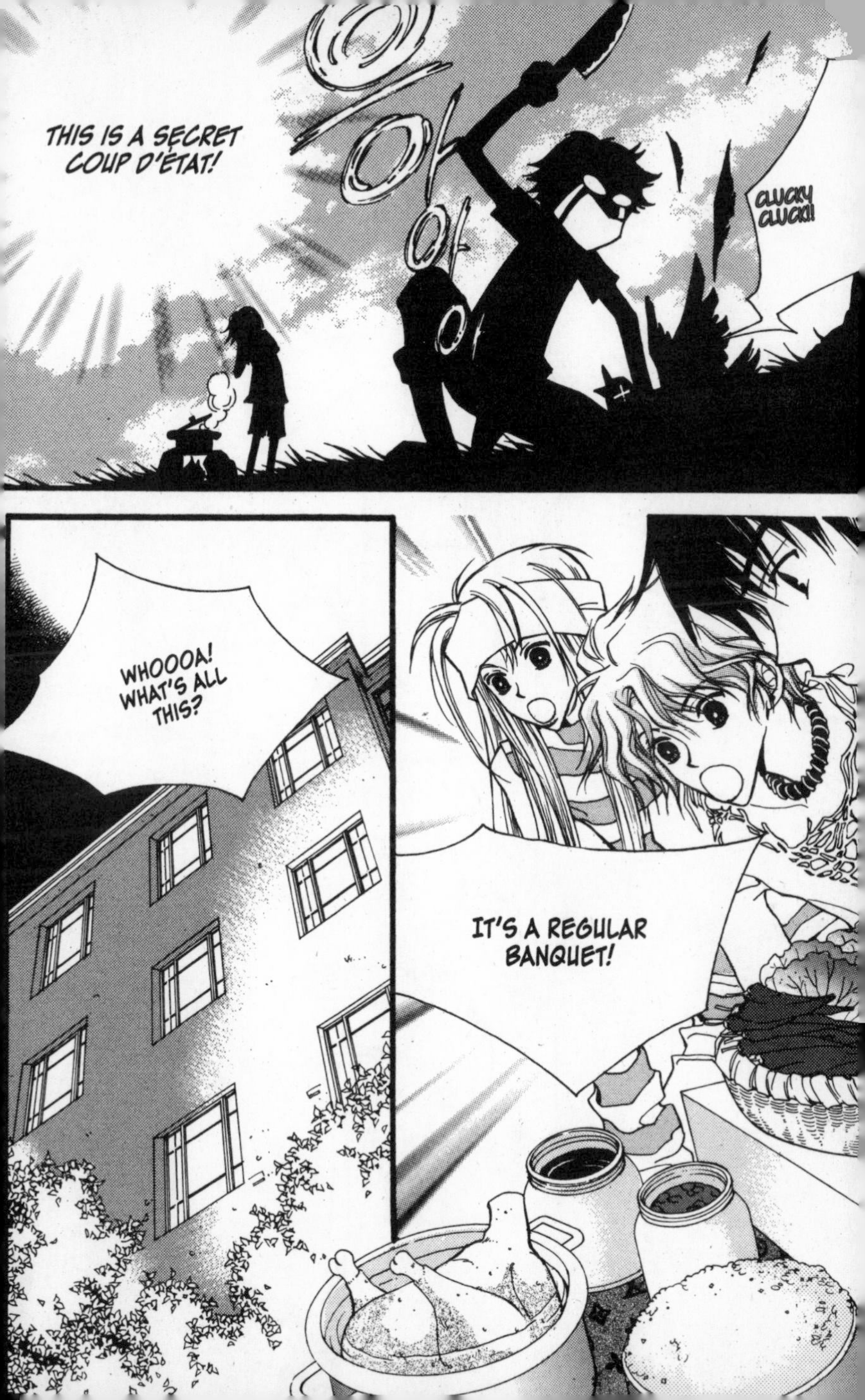
THIS IS A SECRET COUP D'ÉTAT!
CLUCKY CLUCK!!
WHOOOA! WHAT'S ALL THIS?
IT'S A REGULAR BANQUET!

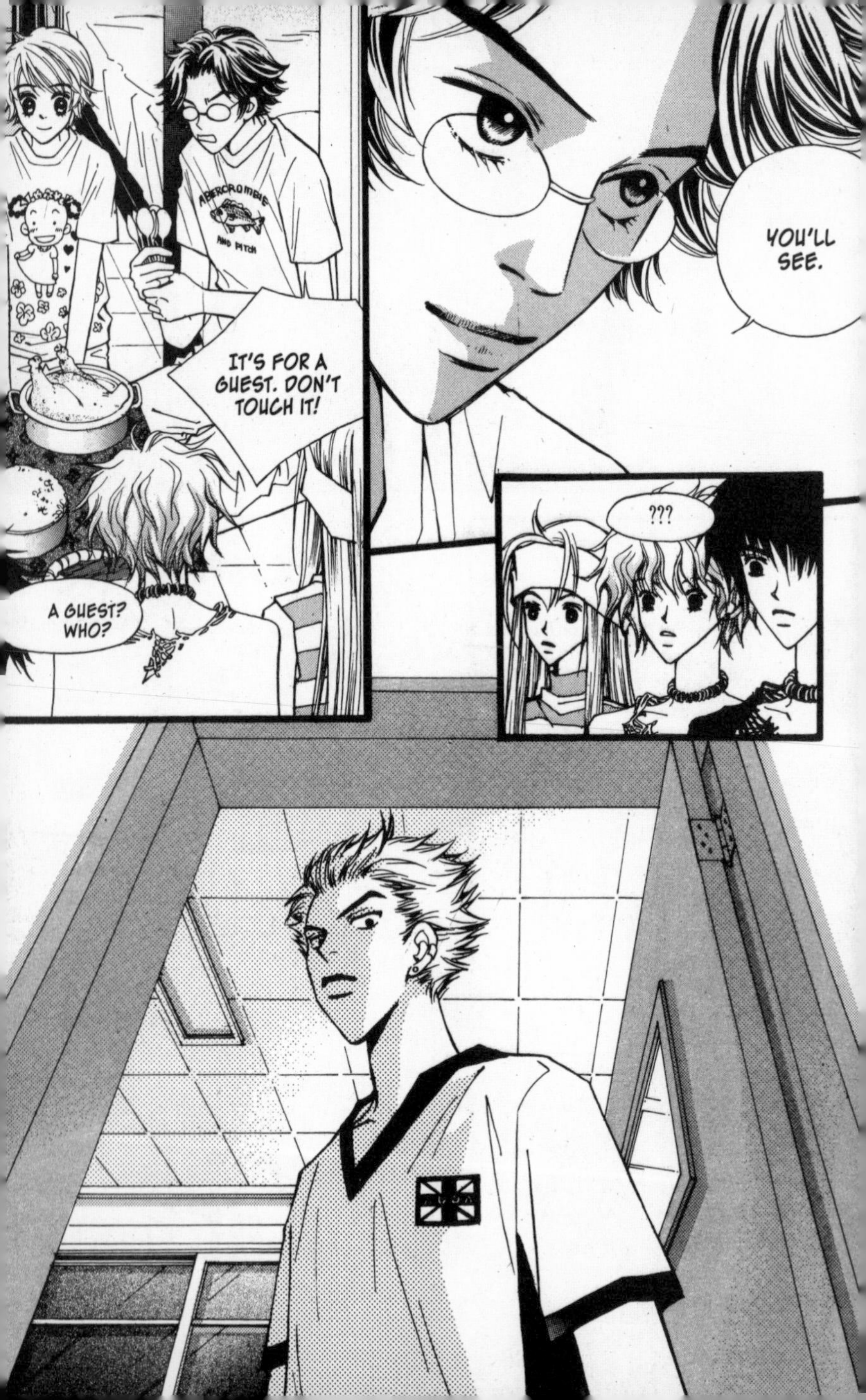
IT'S FOR A GUEST. DON'T TOUCH IT!
A GUEST? WHO?
YOU'LL SEE.
???

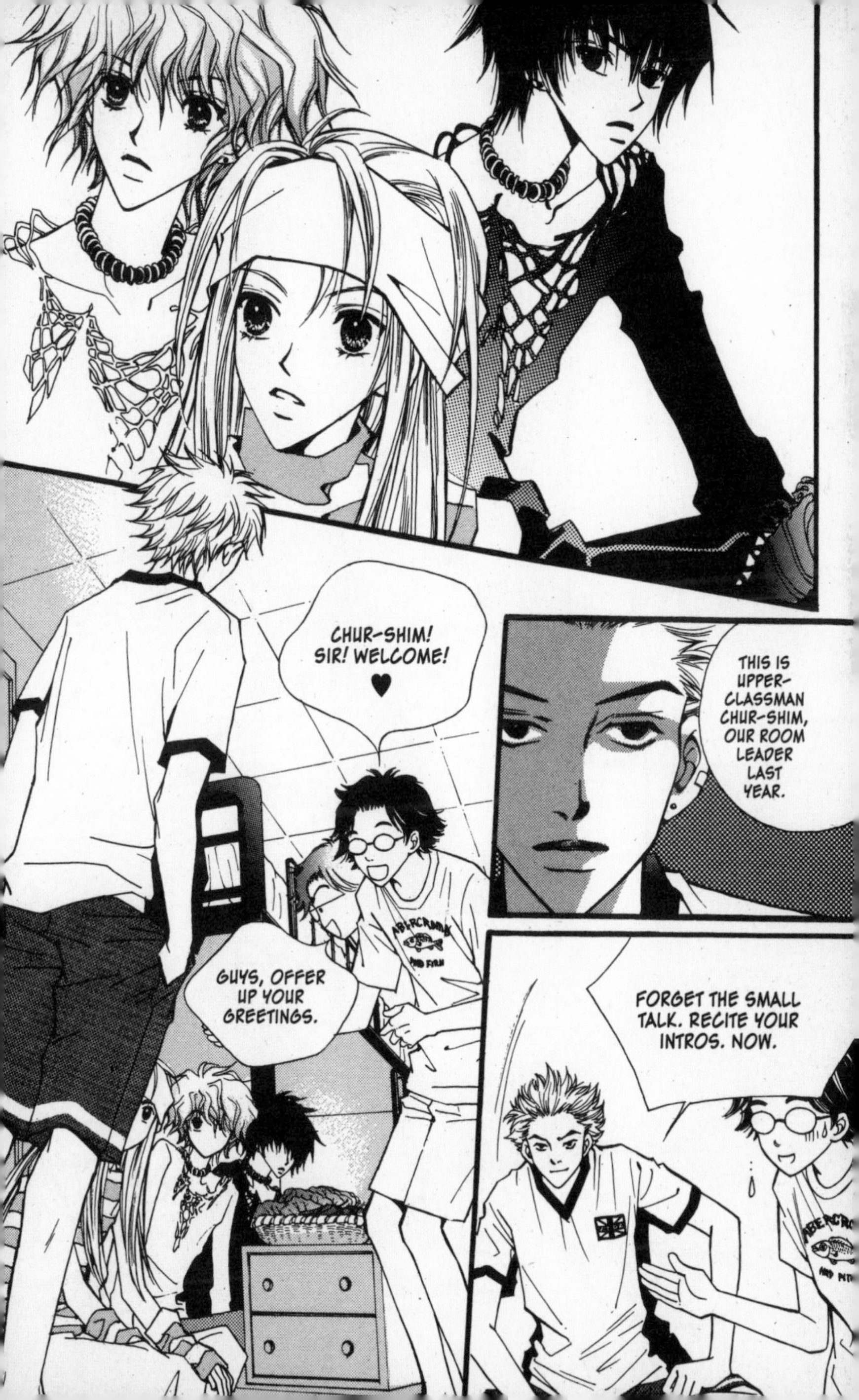
CHUR-SHIM! SIR! WELCOME! ♥
GUYS, OFFER UP YOUR GREETINGS.
THIS IS UPPER-CLASSMAN CHUR-SHIM, OUR ROOM LEADER LAST YEAR.
FORGET THE SMALL TALK. RECITE YOUR INTROS. NOW.

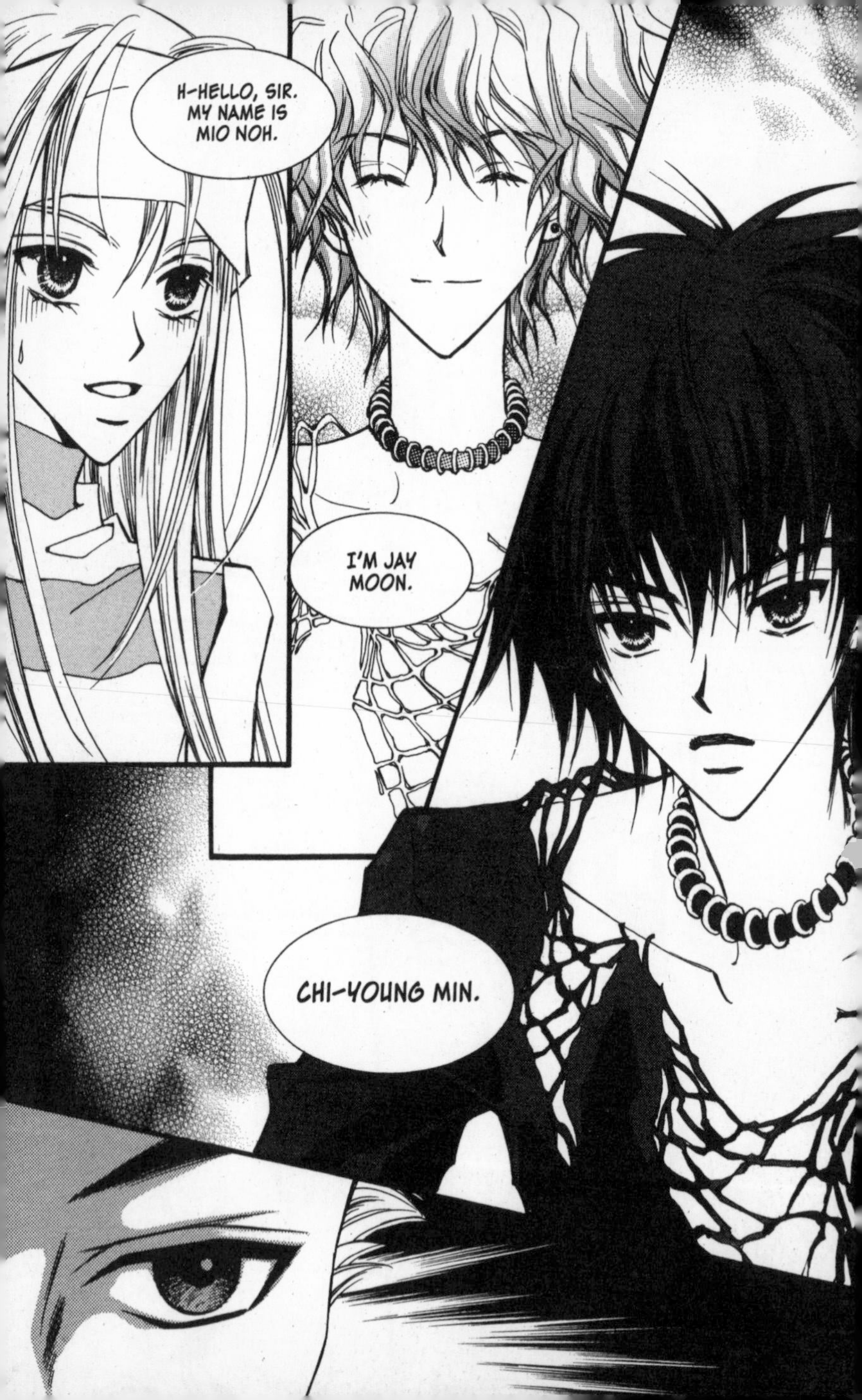
H-HELLO, SIR. MY NAME IS MIO NOH.
I'M JAY MOON.
CHI-YOUNG MIN.

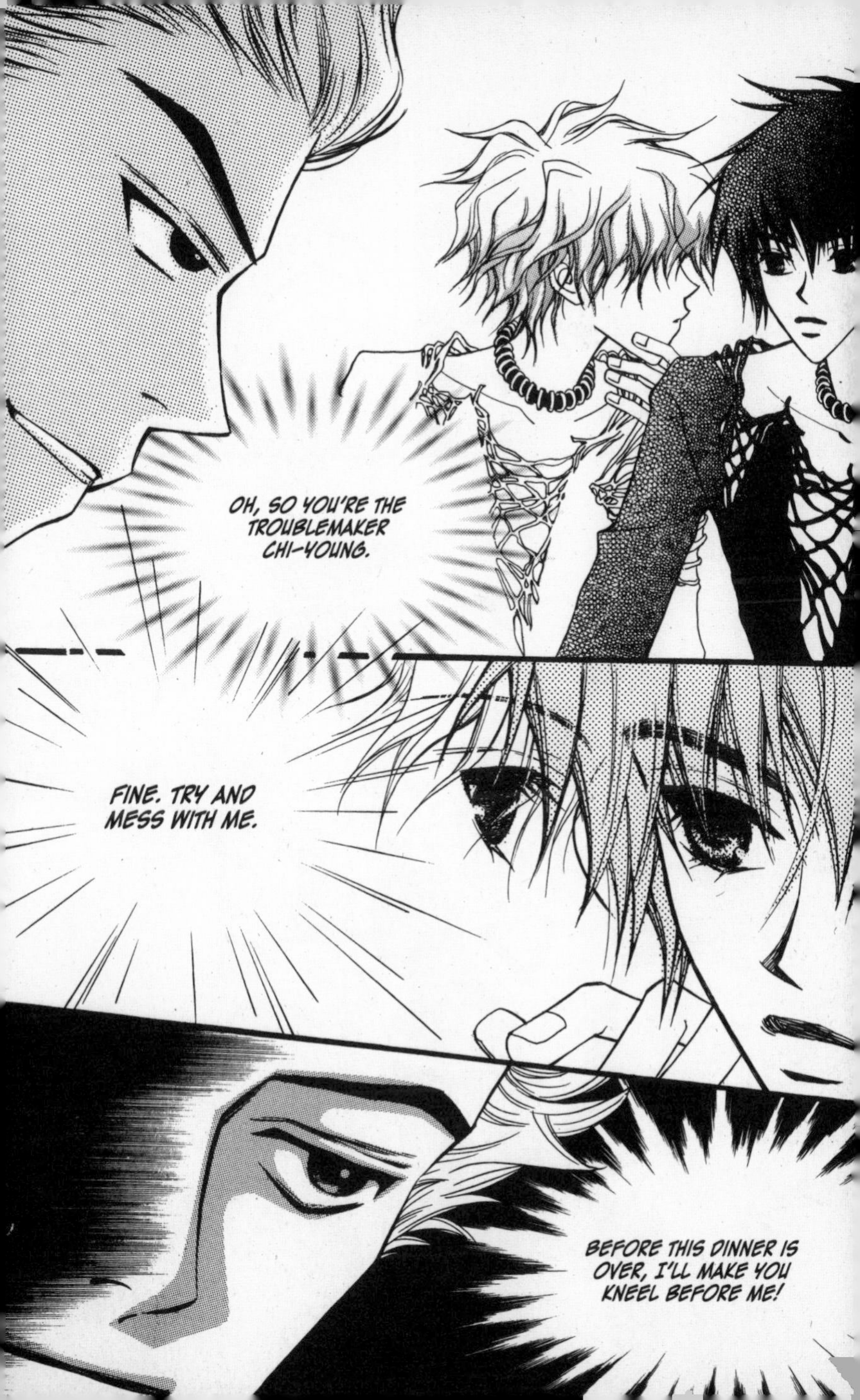
OH, SO YOU'RE THE TROUBLEMAKER CHI-YOUNG.
FINE. TRY AND MESS WITH ME.
BEFORE THIS DINNER IS OVER, I'LL MAKE YOU KNEEL BEFORE ME!

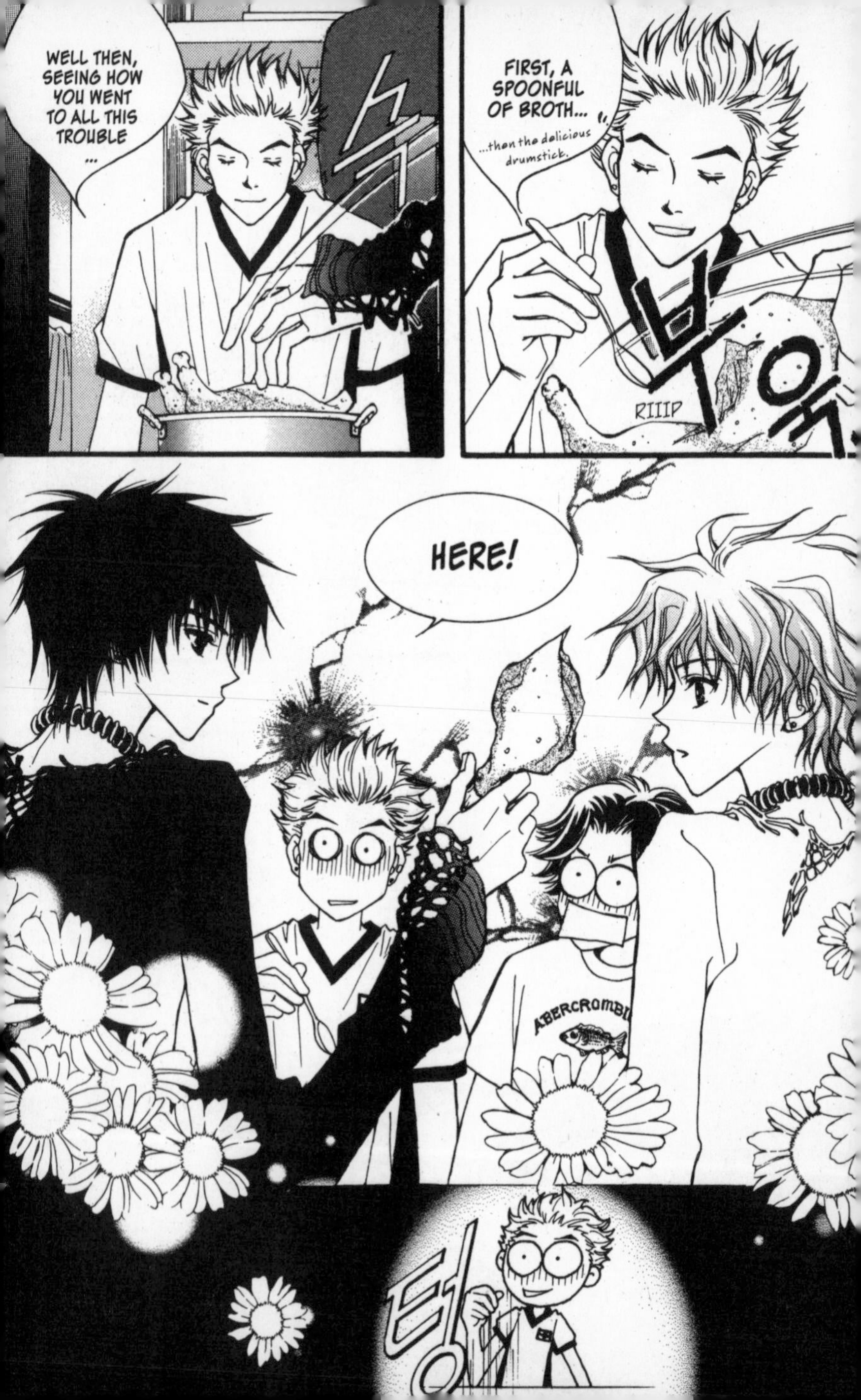
WELL THEN, SEEING HOW YOU WENT TO ALL THIS TROUBLE ...
FIRST, A SPOONFUL OF BROTH...
...then the delicious drumstick.
RIIIP
HERE!
ABERCROMBIE

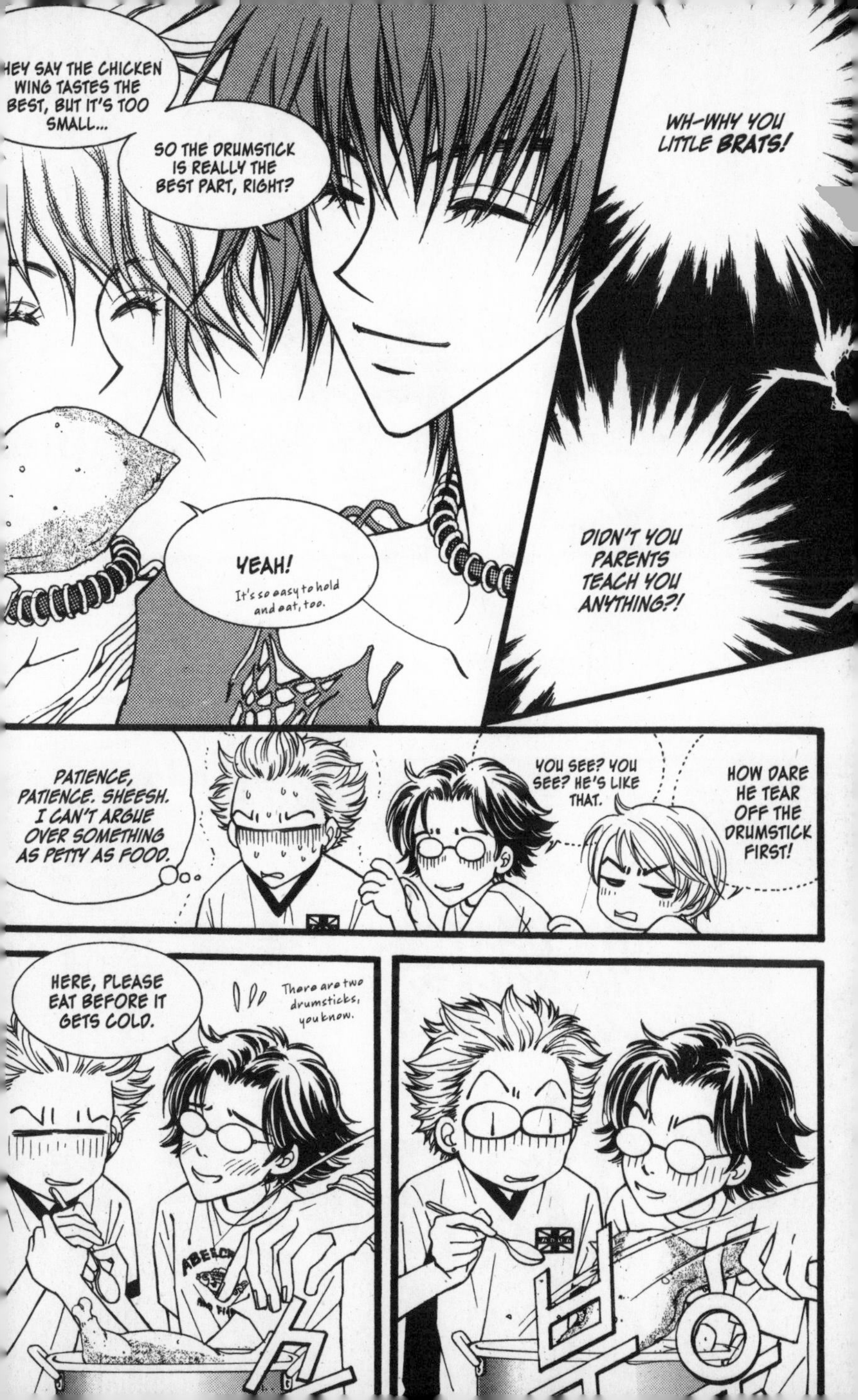
HEY SAY THE CHICKEN WING TASTES THE BEST, BUT IT'S TOO SMALL...
SO THE DRUMSTICK IS REALLY THE BEST PART, RIGHT?
YEAH! It's so easy to hold and eat, too.
WH-WHY YOU LITTLE BRATS!
DIDN'T YOU PARENTS TEACH YOU ANYTHING?!
PATIENCE, PATIENCE. SHEESH. I CAN'T ARGUE OVER SOMETHING AS PETTY AS FOOD.
YOU SEE? YOU SEE? HE'S LIKE THAT.
HOW DARE HE TEAR OFF THE DRUMSTICK FIRST!
HERE, PLEASE EAT BEFORE IT GETS COLD.
There are two drumsticks, you know.

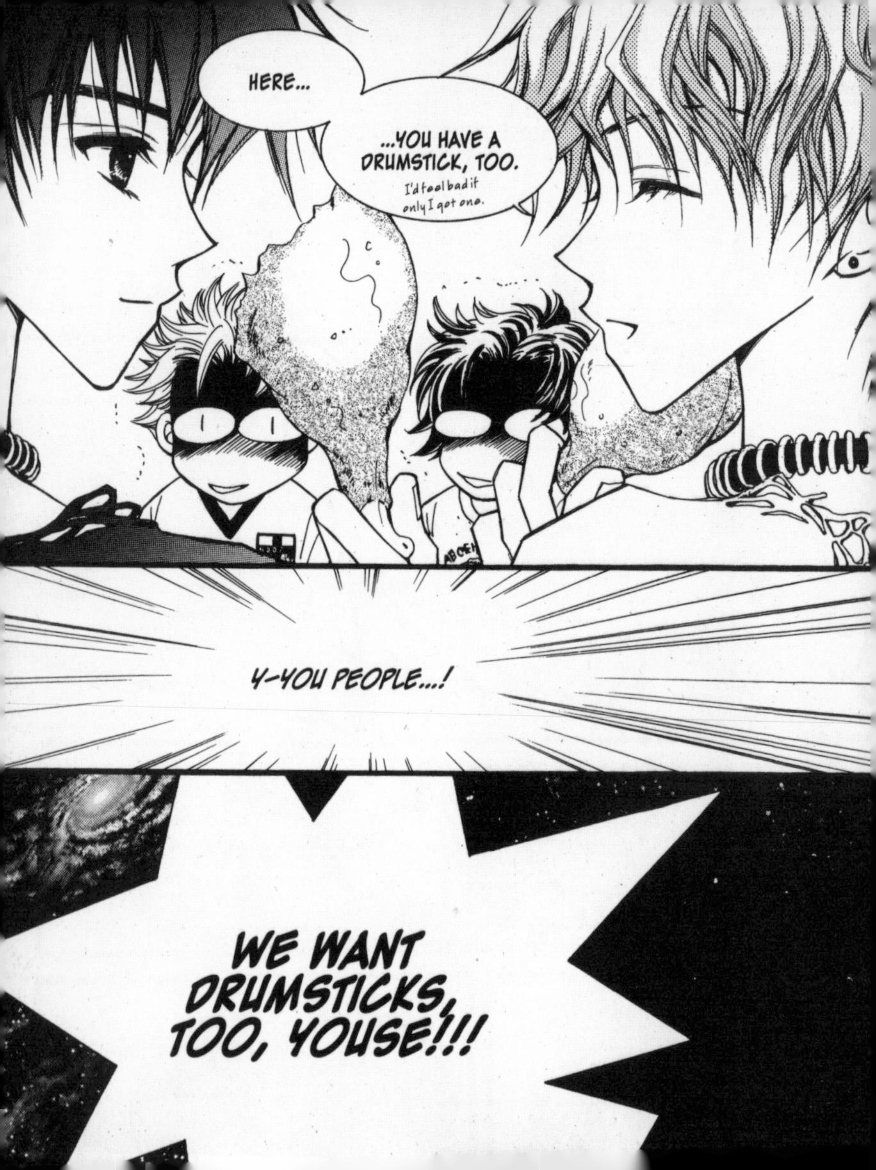
HERE...
...YOU HAVE A DRUMSTICK, TOO.
I'd feel bad if only I got one.
Y-YOU PEOPLE...!
WE WANT DRUMSTICKS, TOO, YOUSE!!!

IF A RATIONAL PERSON FIGHTS WITH AN IRRATIONAL PERSON, THE RATIONAL PERSON IS BOUND TO LOSE.

THIS IS BECAUSE THE IRRATIONAL PERSON INEVITABLY THROWS HIS FIST FIRST.

IF A RATIONAL PERSON ARGUES WITH AN IRRATIONAL PERSON, THE RATIONAL PERSON, AGAIN, LOSES.

THIS IS BECAUSE THE IRRATIONAL PERSON NEVER LISTENS ANYWAY.

SO WHERE THERE IS NO REASONING, THERE IS NO SOLUTION.

I've never been in such a ridiculous situation. ㅠㅠ

State Of Impassivity

WHY AREN'T YOU EATING?

It's good.

HE MUST NOT LIKE CHICKEN.

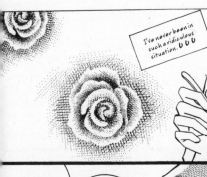

I DO LIKE CHICKEN!

WE LOVE CHICKEN, TOO!!

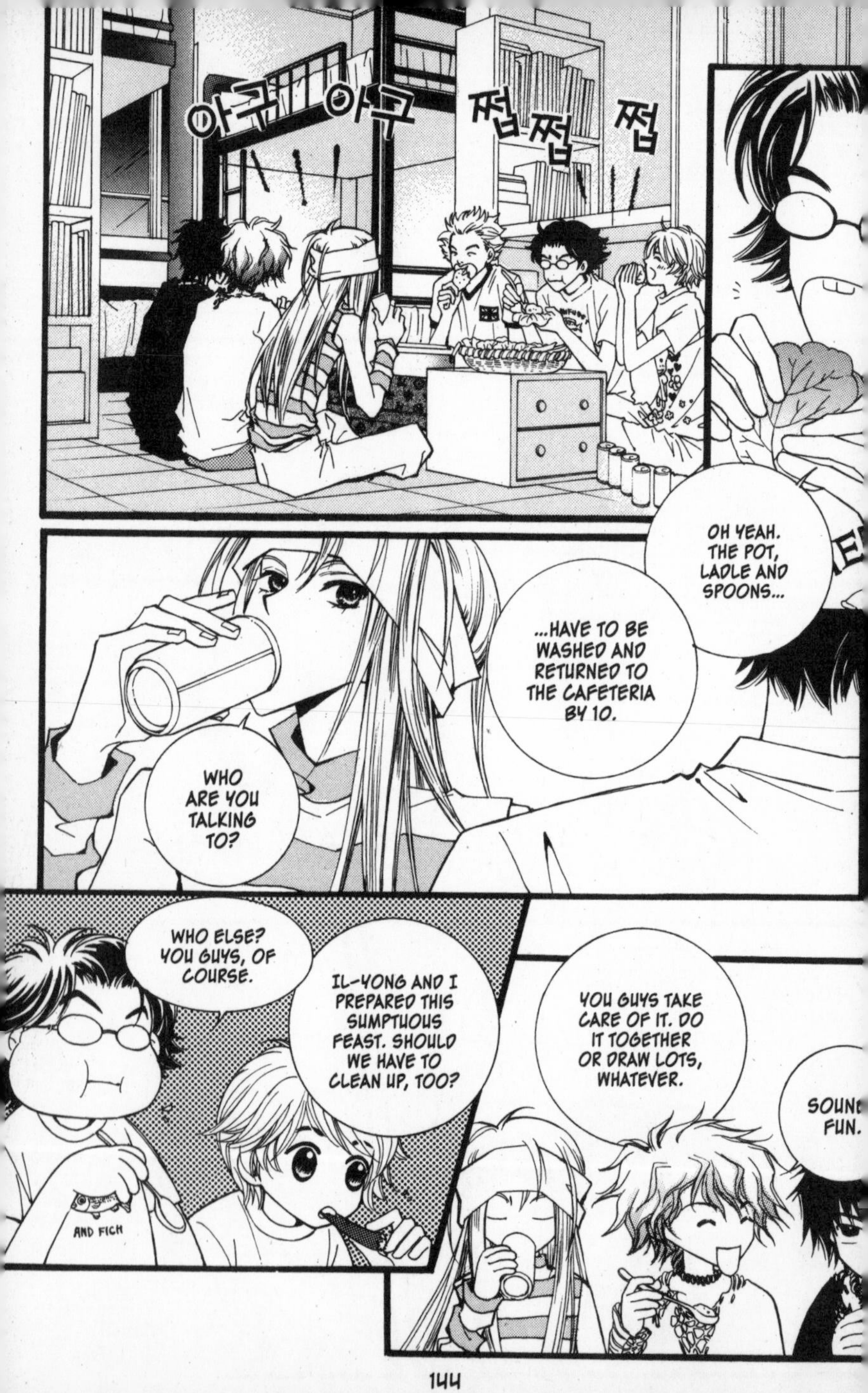
아구 아구 쩝쩝 쩝
OH YEAH. THE POT, LADLE AND SPOONS...
...HAVE TO BE WASHED AND RETURNED TO THE CAFETERIA BY 10.
WHO ARE YOU TALKING TO?
WHO ELSE? YOU GUYS, OF COURSE.
IL-YONG AND I PREPARED THIS SUMPTUOUS FEAST. SHOULD WE HAVE TO CLEAN UP, TOO?
AND FICH
YOU GUYS TAKE CARE OF IT. DO IT TOGETHER OR DRAW LOTS, WHATEVER.
SOUN FUN.

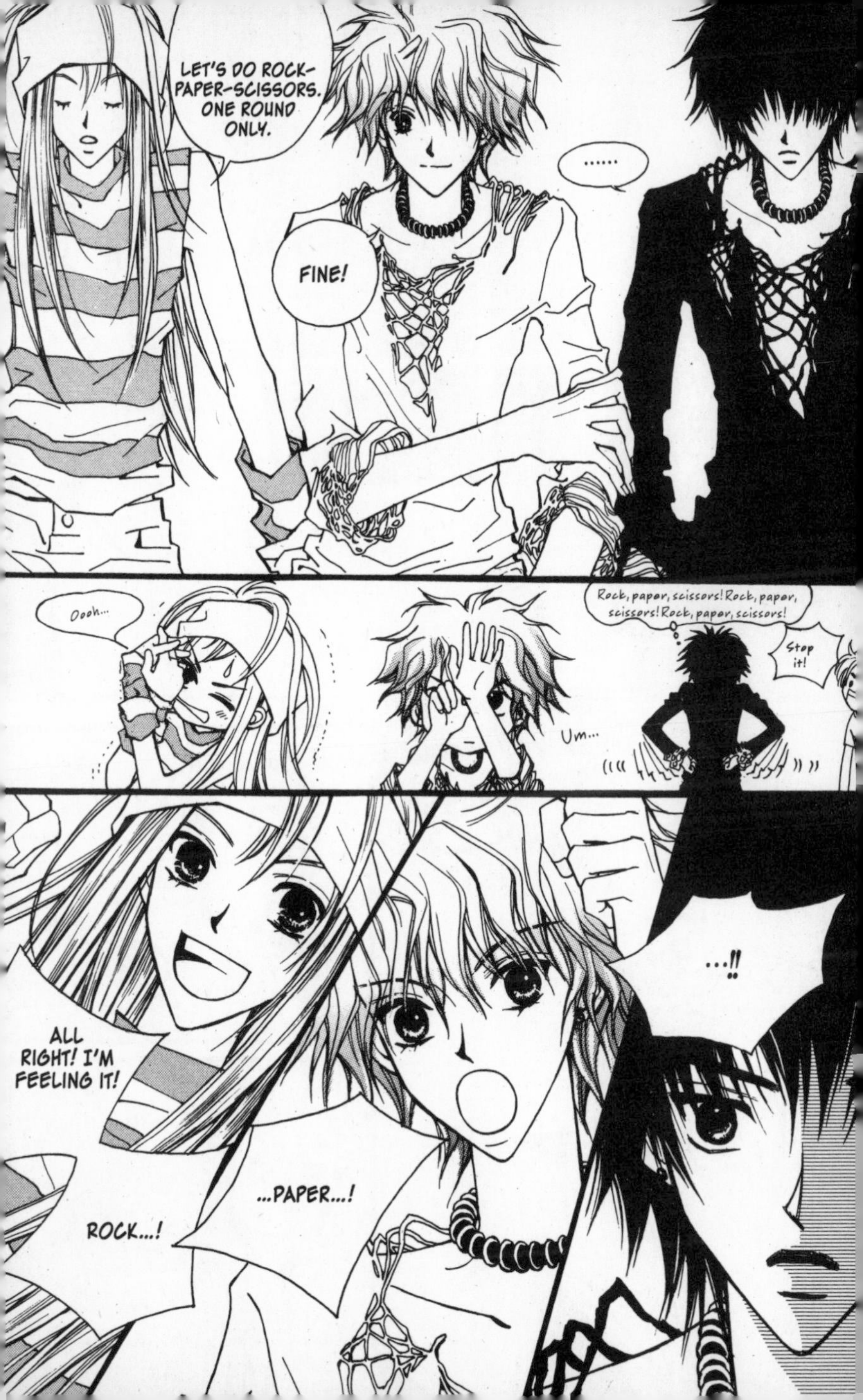

LET'S DO ROCK-PAPER-SCISSORS. ONE ROUND ONLY.
FINE!
......
Oooh...
Um...
Rock, paper, scissors! Rock, paper, scissors! Rock, paper, scissors!
Stop it!
ALL RIGHT! I'M FEELING IT!
ROCK...!
...PAPER...!
...!!

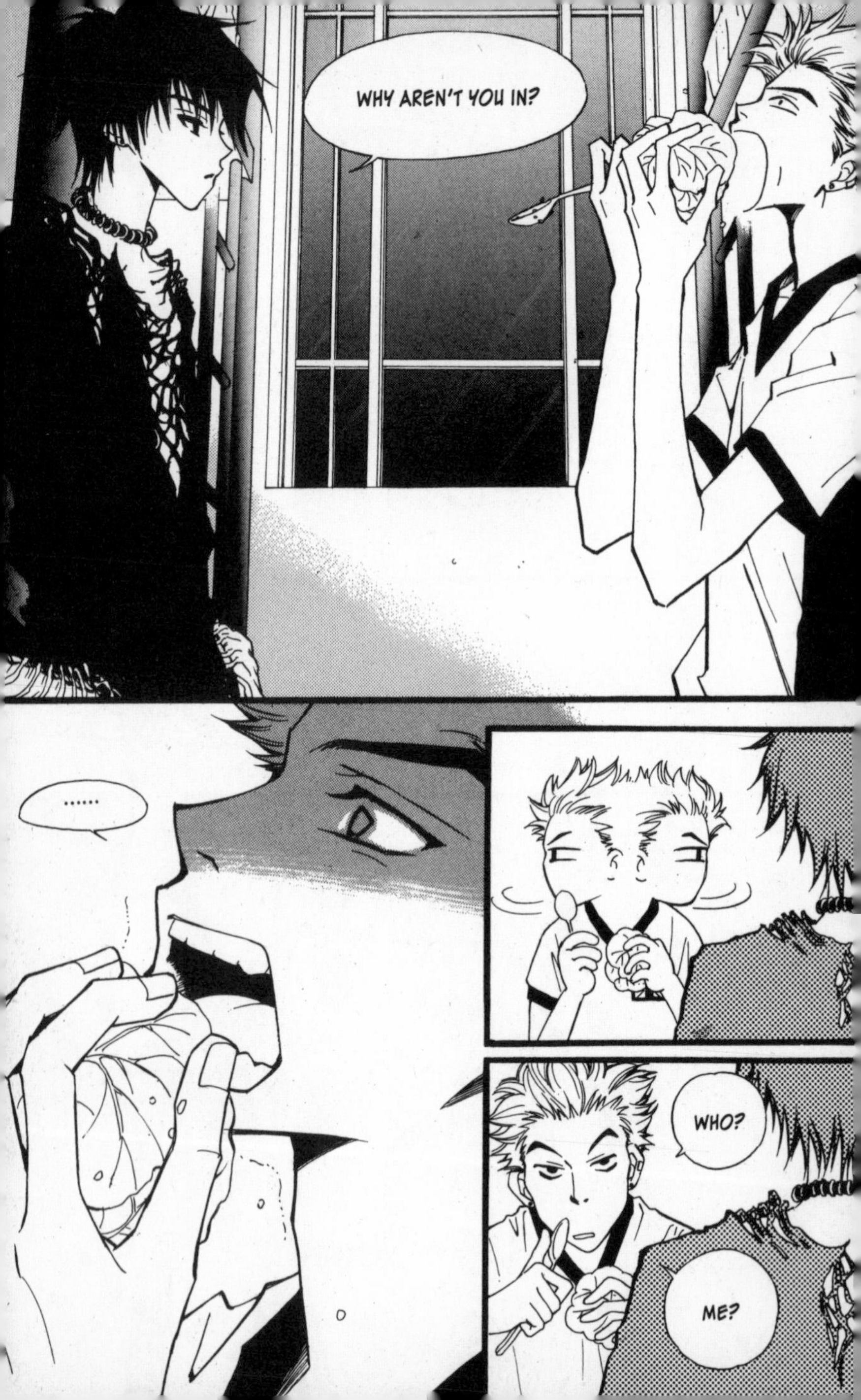
WHY AREN'T YOU IN?
......
WHO?
ME?

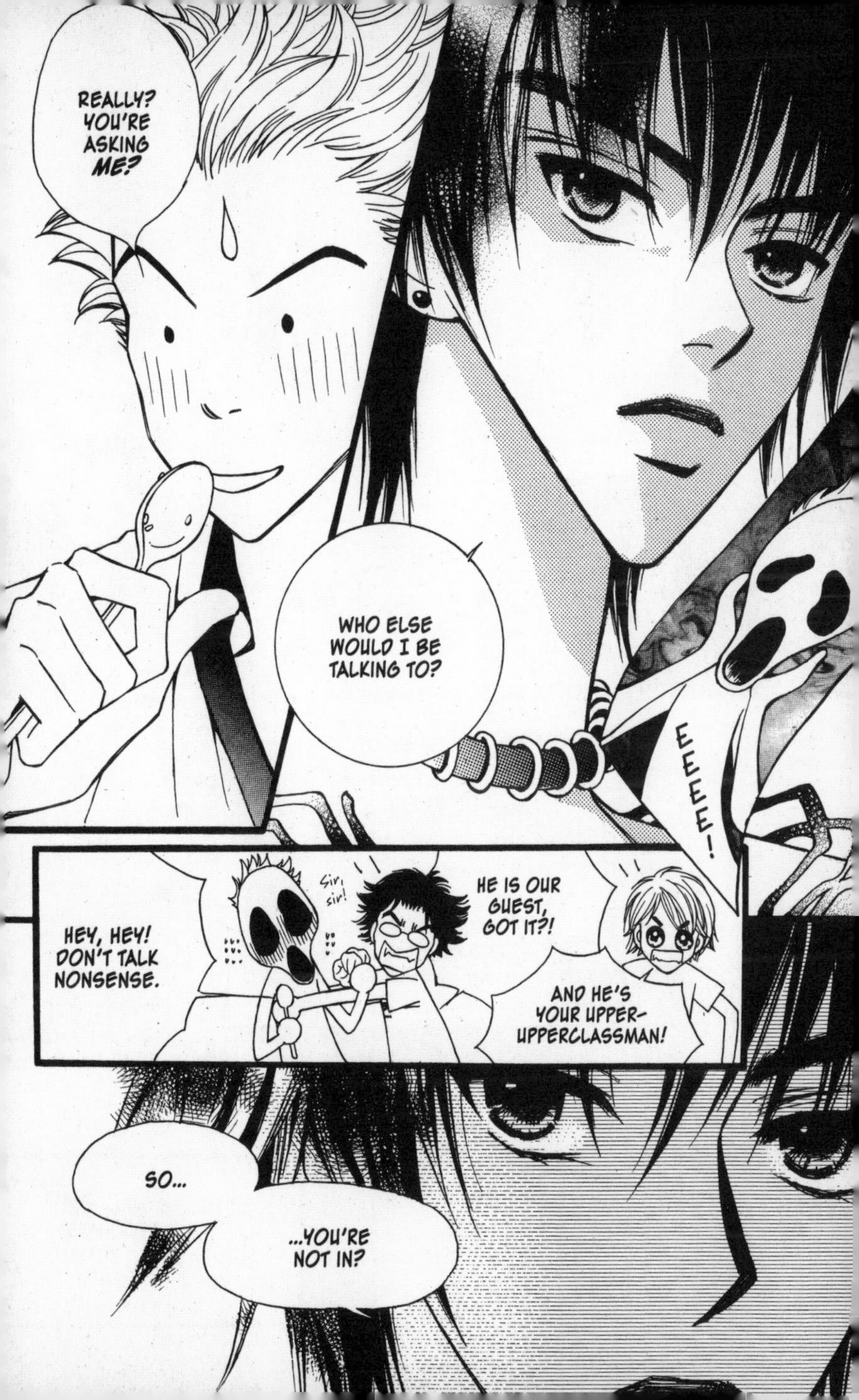
REALLY? YOU'RE ASKING *ME?*
WHO ELSE WOULD I BE TALKING TO?
EEEE!
HEY, HEY! DON'T TALK NONSENSE.
Sir, sir!
HE IS OUR GUEST, GOT IT?!
AND HE'S YOUR UPPER-UPPERCLASSMAN!
SO...
...YOU'RE NOT IN?

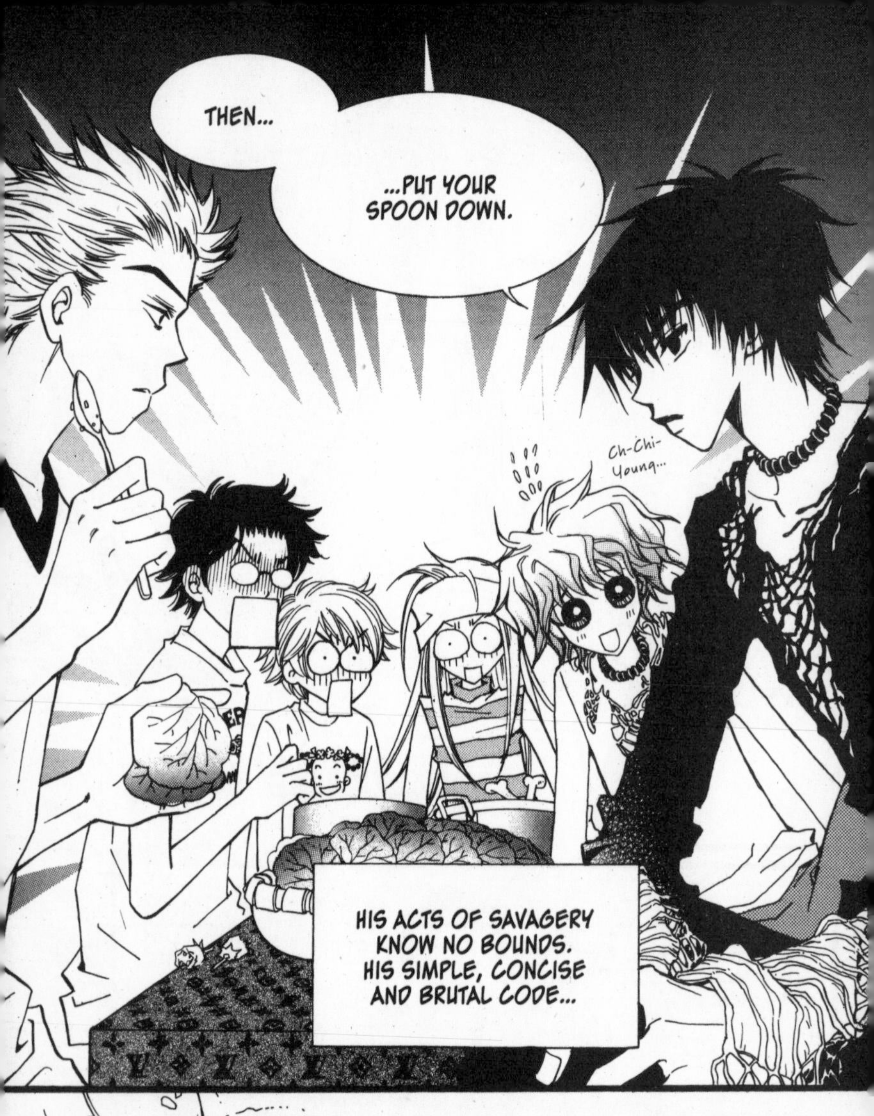
THEN...
...PUT YOUR SPOON DOWN.
Ch-Chi-Young...
HIS ACTS OF SAVAGERY KNOW NO BOUNDS. HIS SIMPLE, CONCISE AND BRUTAL CODE...
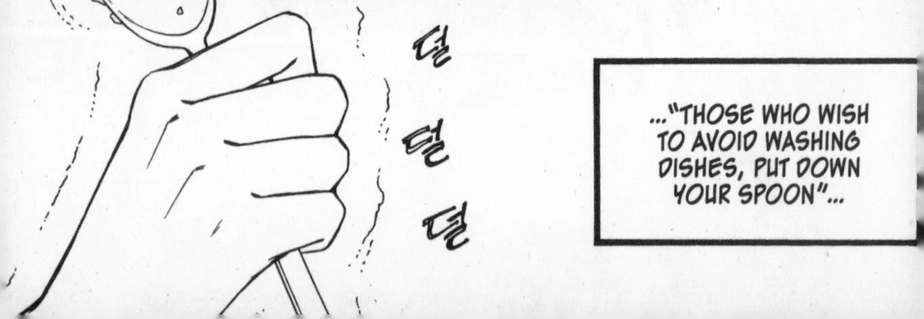
덜 덜 덜
..."THOSE WHO WISH TO AVOID WASHING DISHES, PUT DOWN YOUR SPOON"...

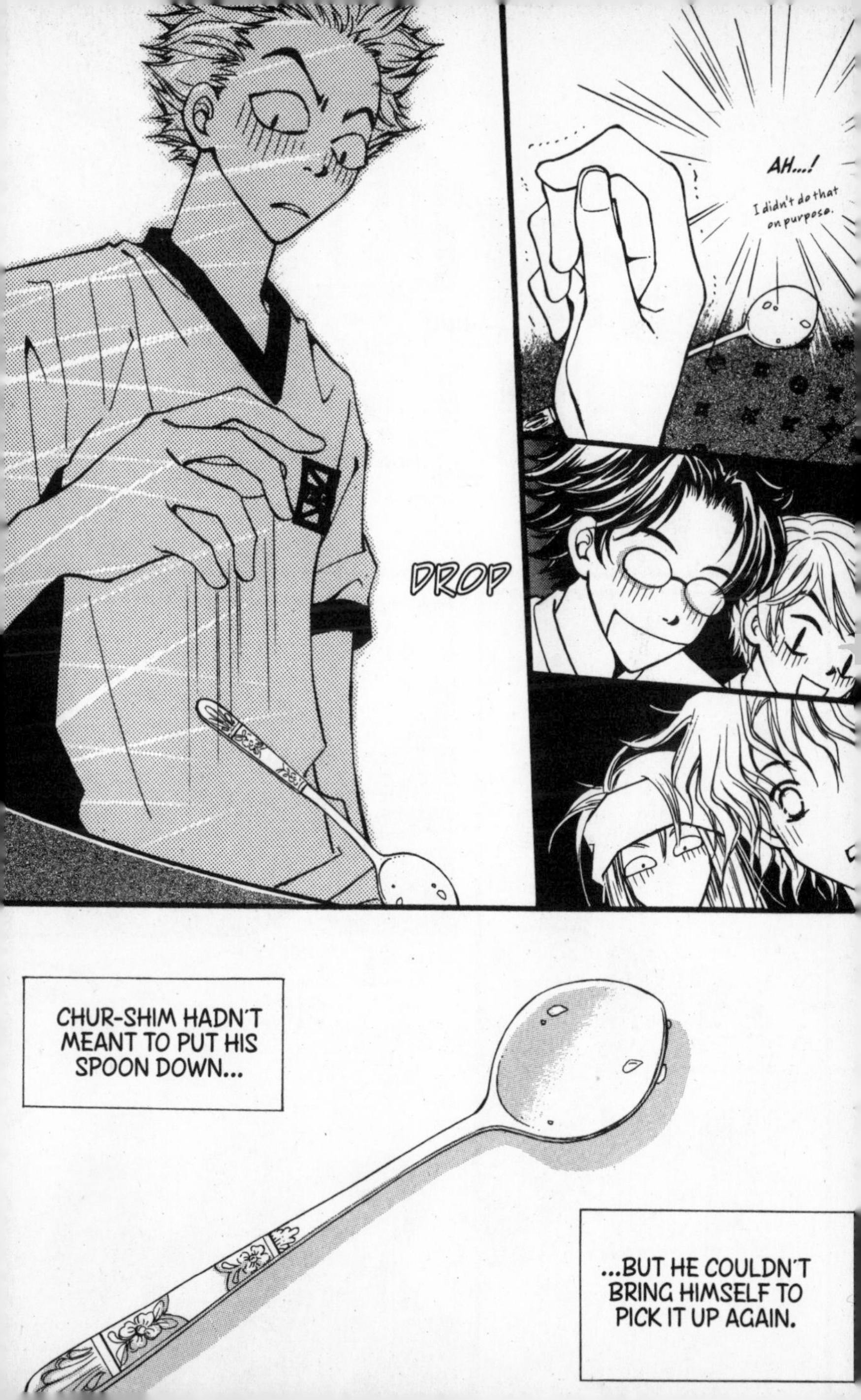
DROP
AH...!
I didn't do that on purpose.
CHUR-SHIM HADN'T MEANT TO PUT HIS SPOON DOWN...
...BUT HE COULDN'T BRING HIMSELF TO PICK IT UP AGAIN.

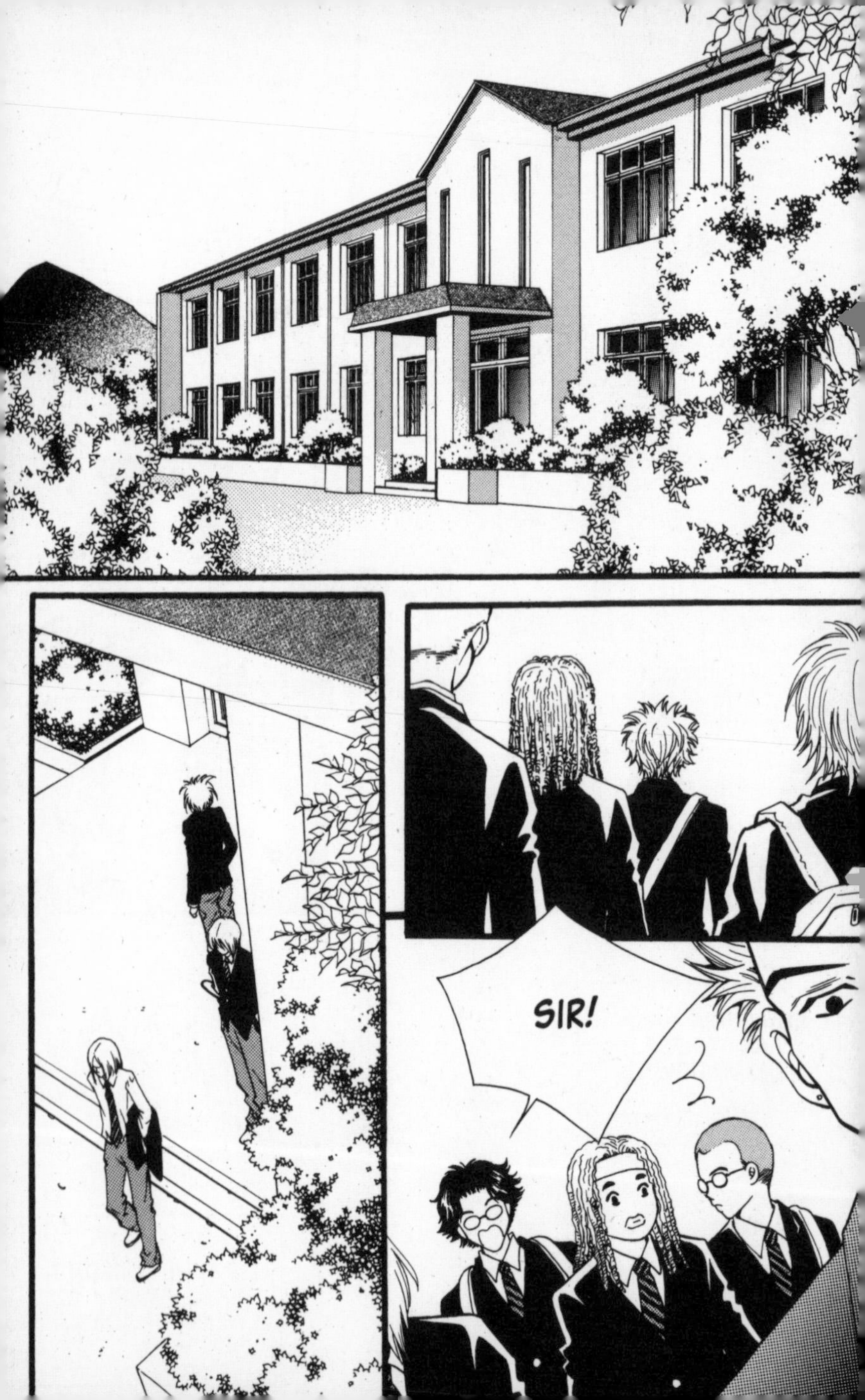
SIR!

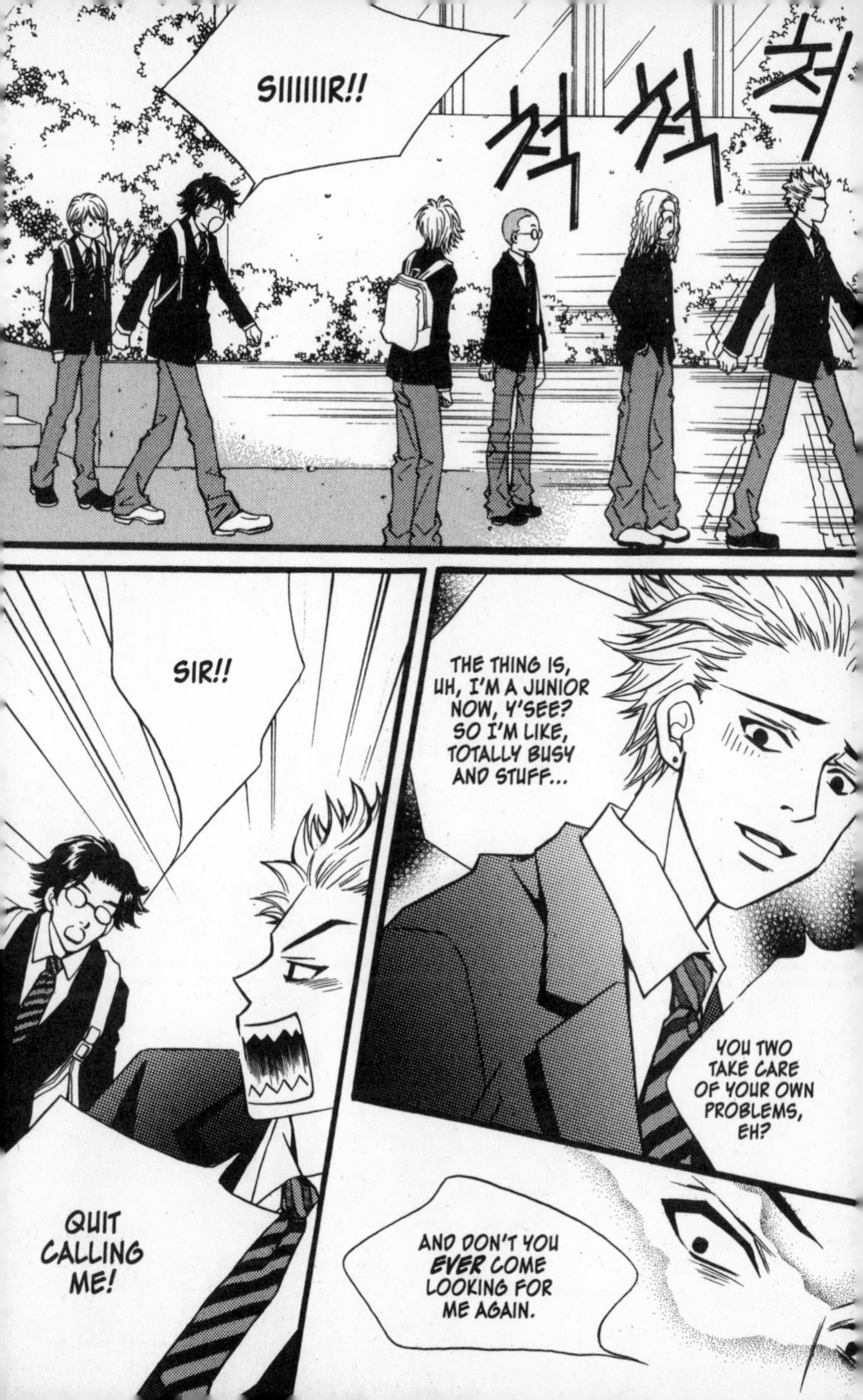
SIIIIIIR!!
척 척 척
SIR!!
QUIT CALLING ME!
THE THING IS, UH, I'M A JUNIOR NOW, Y'SEE? SO I'M LIKE, TOTALLY BUSY AND STUFF...
YOU TWO TAKE CARE OF YOUR OWN PROBLEMS, EH?
AND DON'T YOU EVER COME LOOKING FOR ME AGAIN.

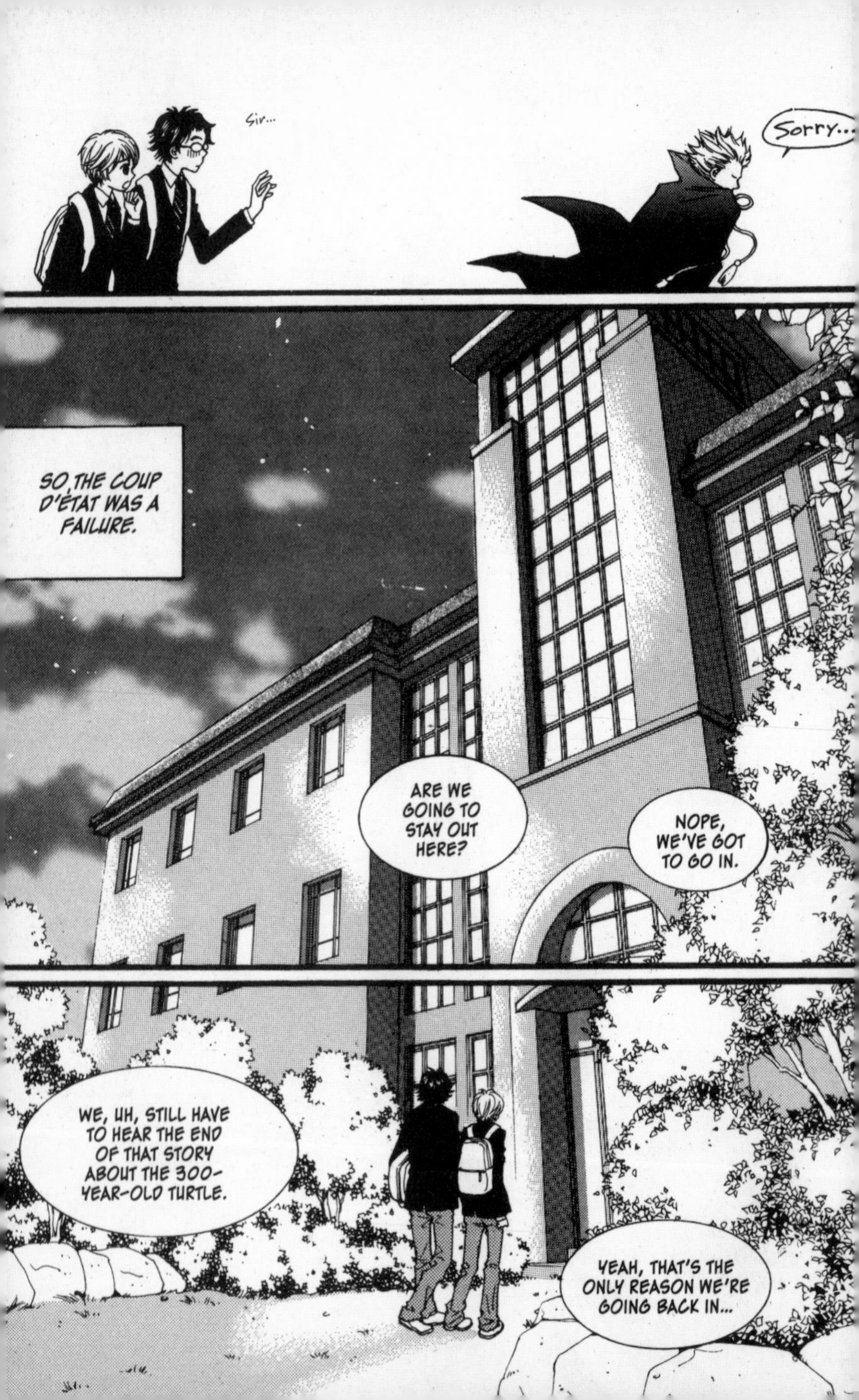
Sir...
Sorry...
SO, THE COUP D'ÉTAT WAS A FAILURE.
ARE WE GOING TO STAY OUT HERE?
NOPE, WE'VE GOT TO GO IN.
WE, UH, STILL HAVE TO HEAR THE END OF THAT STORY ABOUT THE 300-YEAR-OLD TURTLE.
YEAH, THAT'S THE ONLY REASON WE'RE GOING BACK IN...

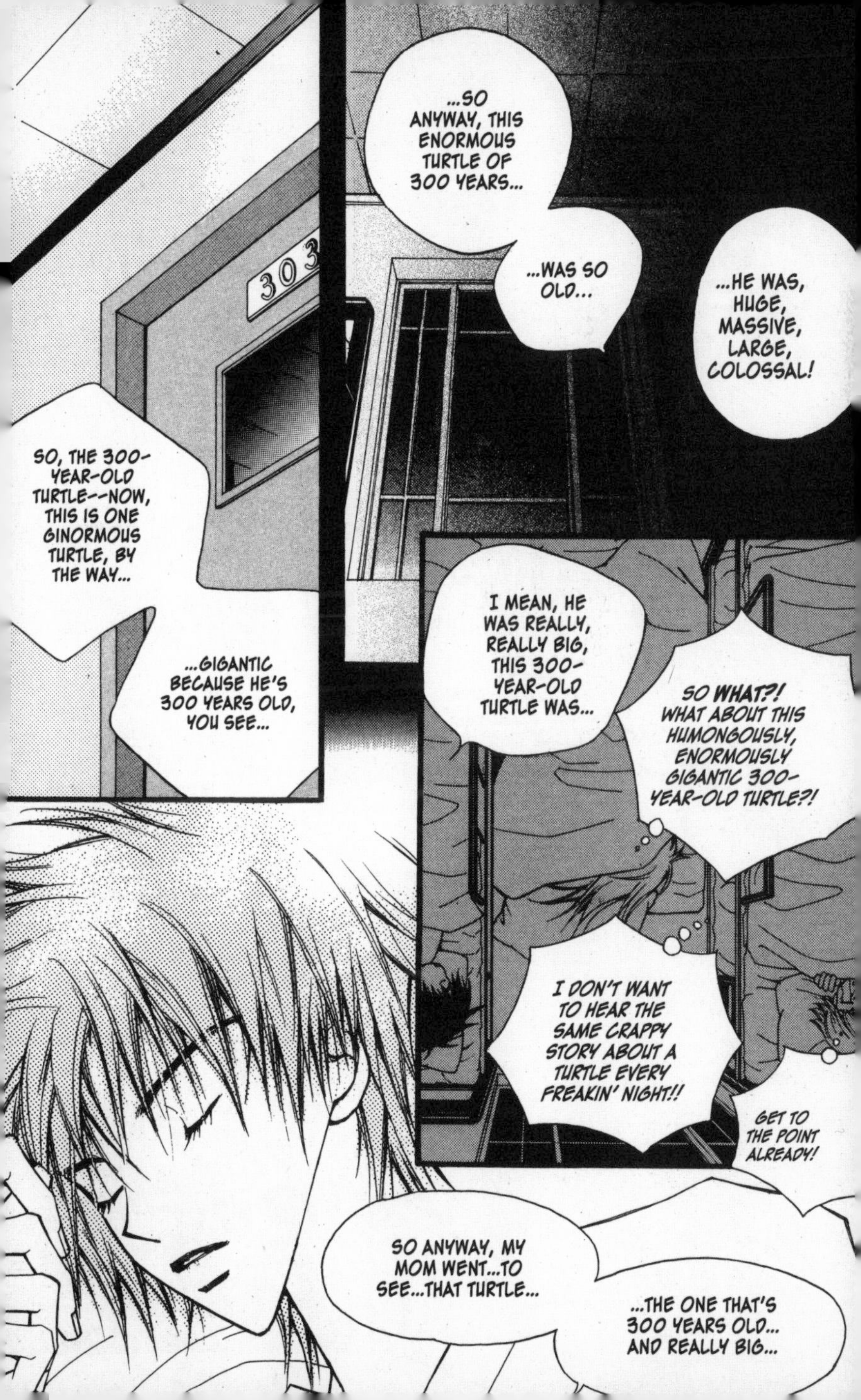
SO, THE 300-YEAR-OLD TURTLE--NOW, THIS IS ONE GINORMOUS TURTLE, BY THE WAY...
...GIGANTIC BECAUSE HE'S 300 YEARS OLD, YOU SEE...
...SO ANYWAY, THIS ENORMOUS TURTLE OF 300 YEARS...
...WAS SO OLD...
...HE WAS, HUGE, MASSIVE, LARGE, COLOSSAL!
I MEAN, HE WAS REALLY, REALLY BIG, THIS 300-YEAR-OLD TURTLE WAS...
SO WHAT?! WHAT ABOUT THIS HUMONGOUSLY, ENORMOUSLY GIGANTIC 300-YEAR-OLD TURTLE?!
I DON'T WANT TO HEAR THE SAME CRAPPY STORY ABOUT A TURTLE EVERY FREAKIN' NIGHT!!
GET TO THE POINT ALREADY!
SO ANYWAY, MY MOM WENT...TO SEE...THAT TURTLE...
...THE ONE THAT'S 300 YEARS OLD... AND REALLY BIG...

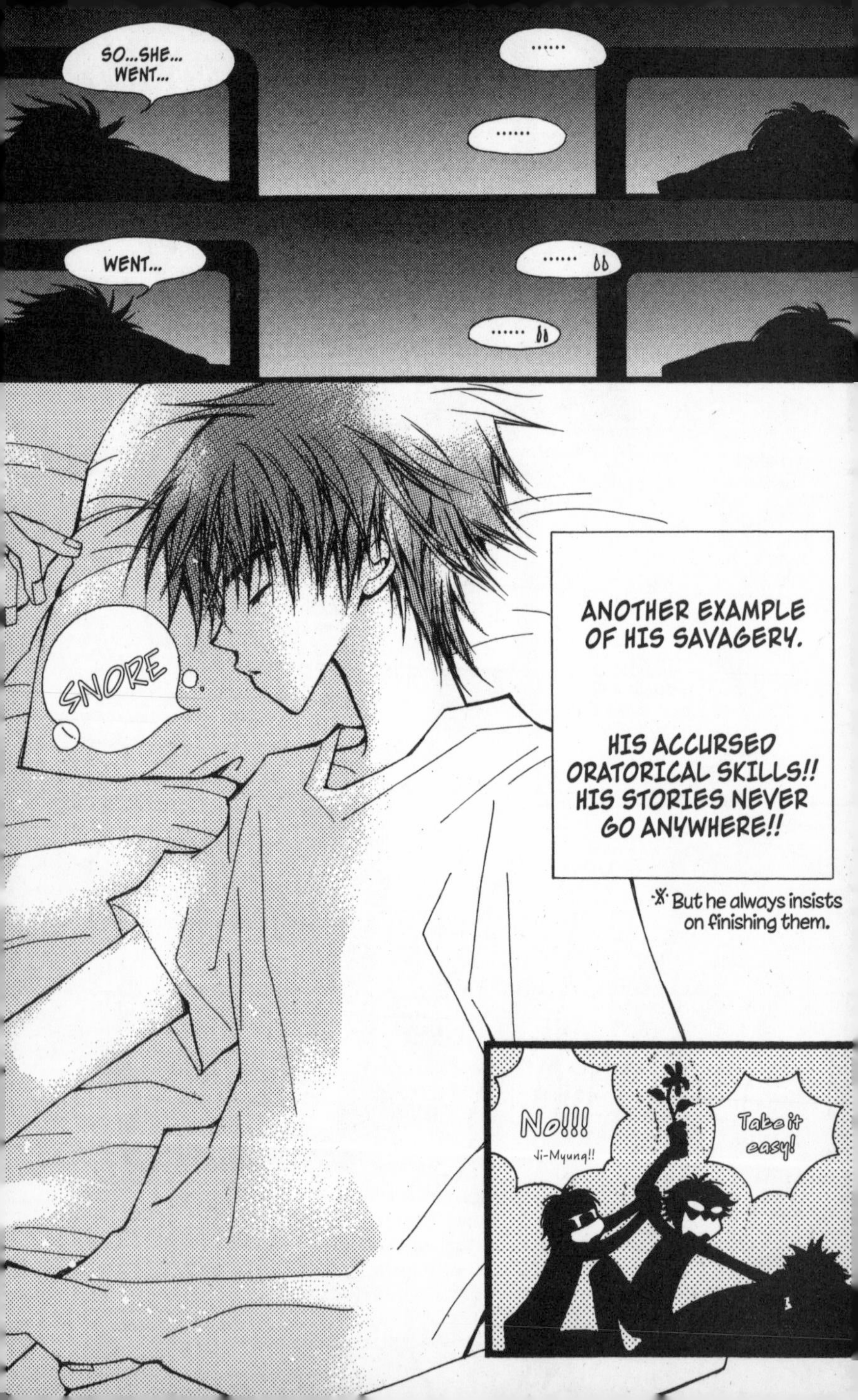
SO...SHE... WENT...
......
......
WENT...
......
......
SNORE
ANOTHER EXAMPLE OF HIS SAVAGERY.
HIS ACCURSED ORATORICAL SKILLS!! HIS STORIES NEVER GO ANYWHERE!!
※ But he always insists on finishing them.
No!!!
Ji-Myung!!
Take it easy!

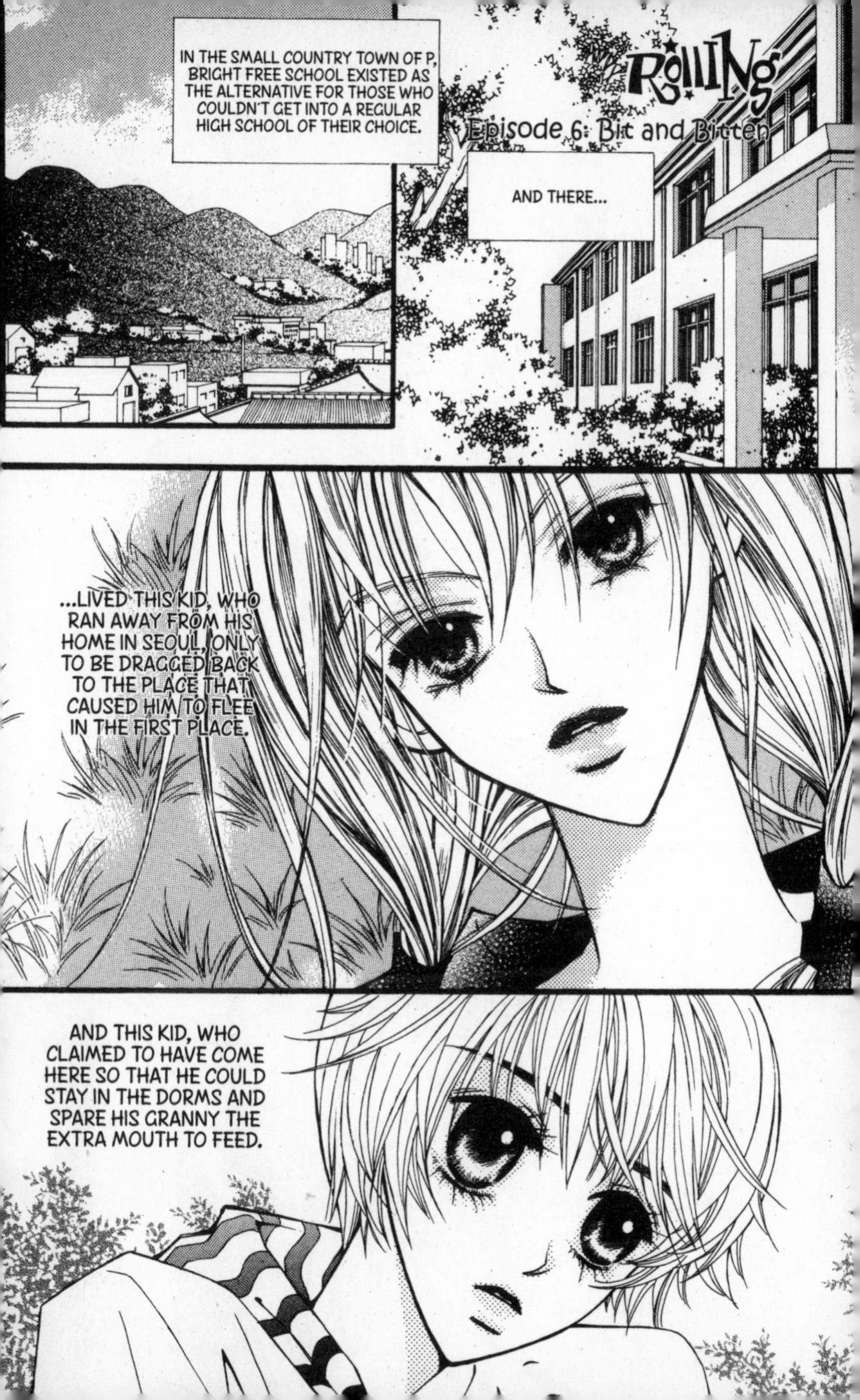
IN THE SMALL COUNTRY TOWN OF P, BRIGHT FREE SCHOOL EXISTED AS THE ALTERNATIVE FOR THOSE WHO COULDN'T GET INTO A REGULAR HIGH SCHOOL OF THEIR CHOICE.
Rolling
Episode 6: Bit and Bitten
AND THERE...
...LIVED THIS KID, WHO RAN AWAY FROM HIS HOME IN SEOUL, ONLY TO BE DRAGGED BACK TO THE PLACE THAT CAUSED HIM TO FLEE IN THE FIRST PLACE.
AND THIS KID, WHO CLAIMED TO HAVE COME HERE SO THAT HE COULD STAY IN THE DORMS AND SPARE HIS GRANNY THE EXTRA MOUTH TO FEED.

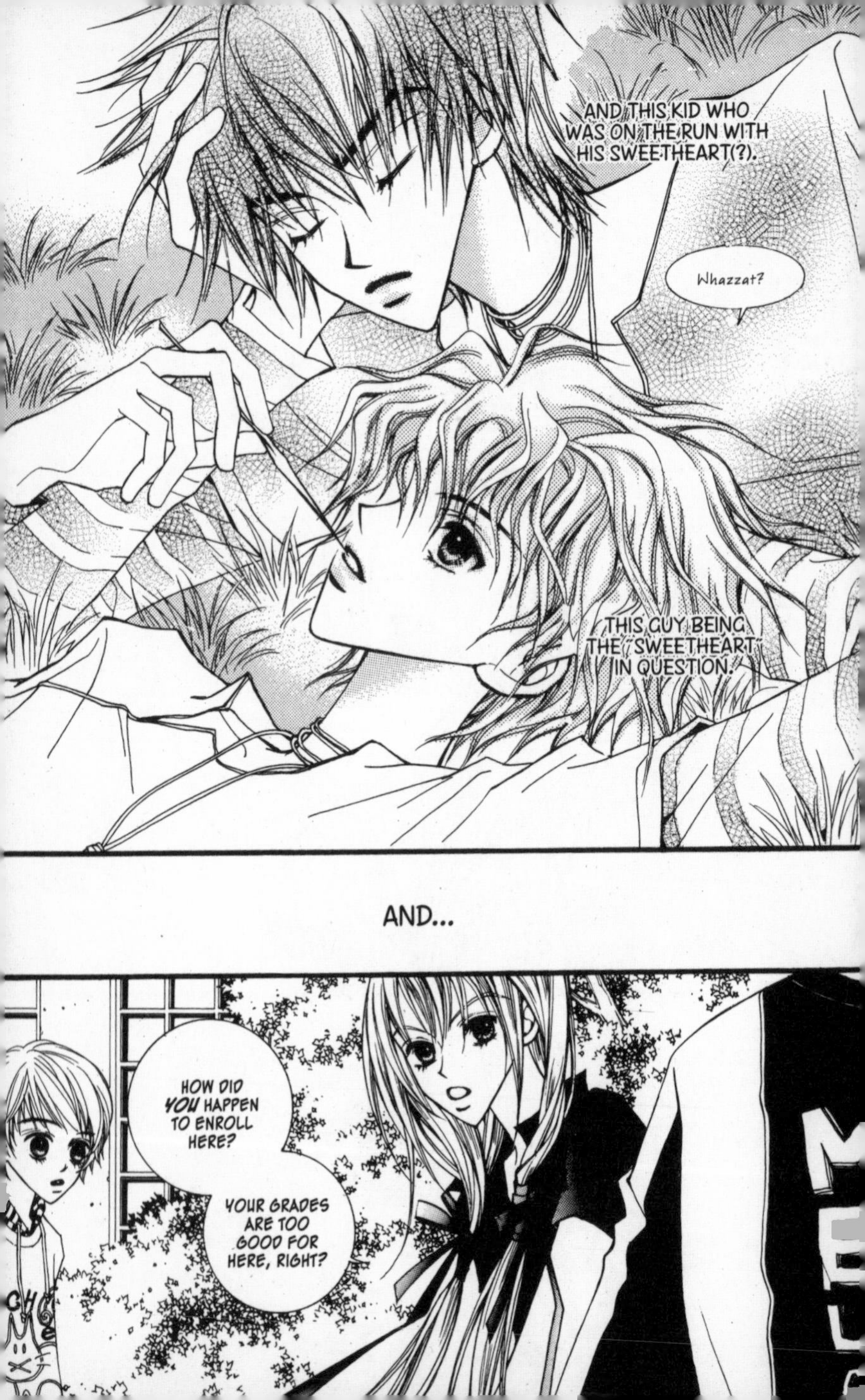
AND THIS KID WHO WAS ON THE RUN WITH HIS SWEETHEART(?).
Whazzat?
THIS GUY BEING THE "SWEETHEART" IN QUESTION.
AND...
HOW DID *YOU* HAPPEN TO ENROLL HERE?
YOUR GRADES ARE TOO GOOD FOR HERE, RIGHT?

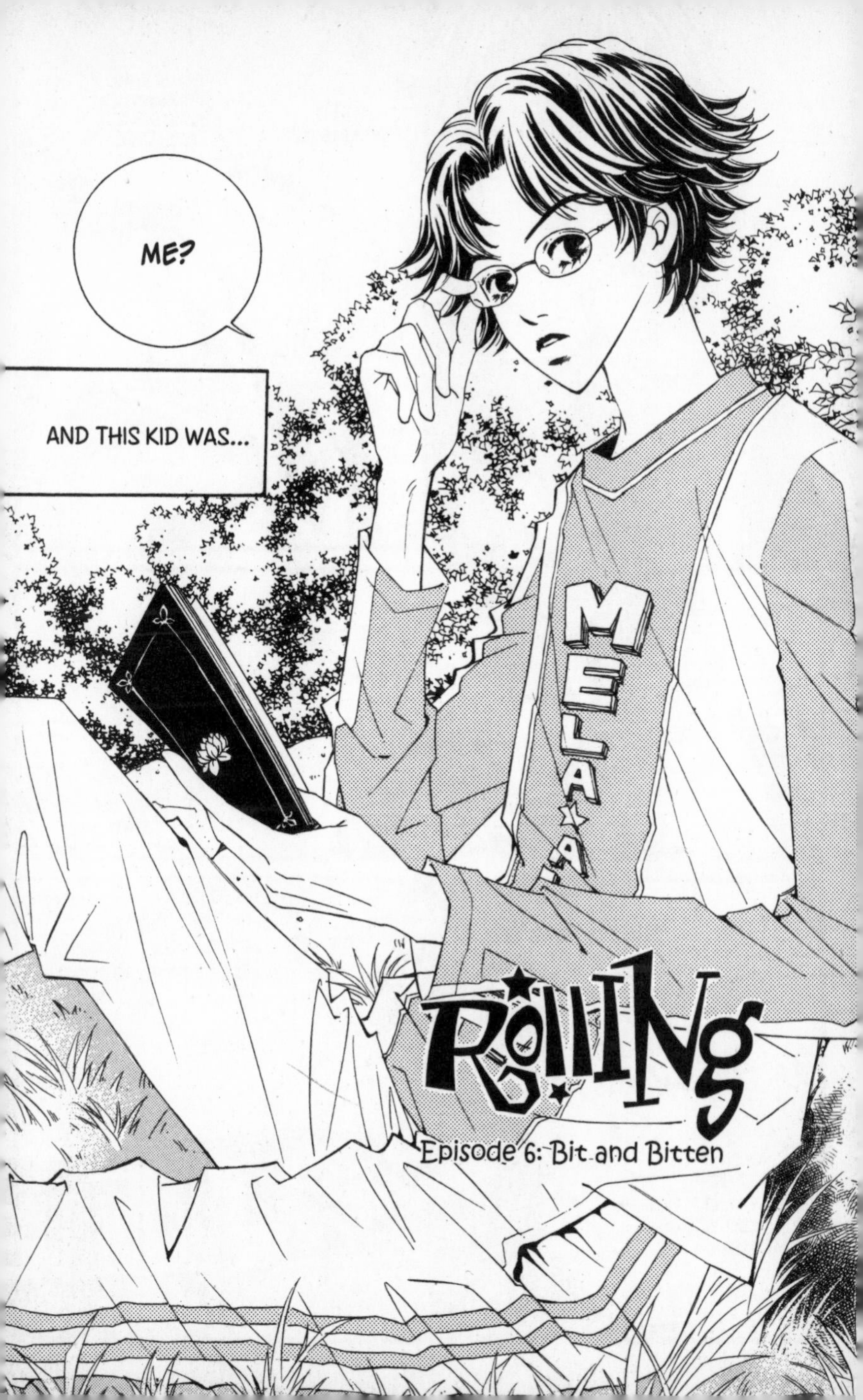
ME?
AND THIS KID WAS...
Rolling
Episode 6: Bit and Bitten

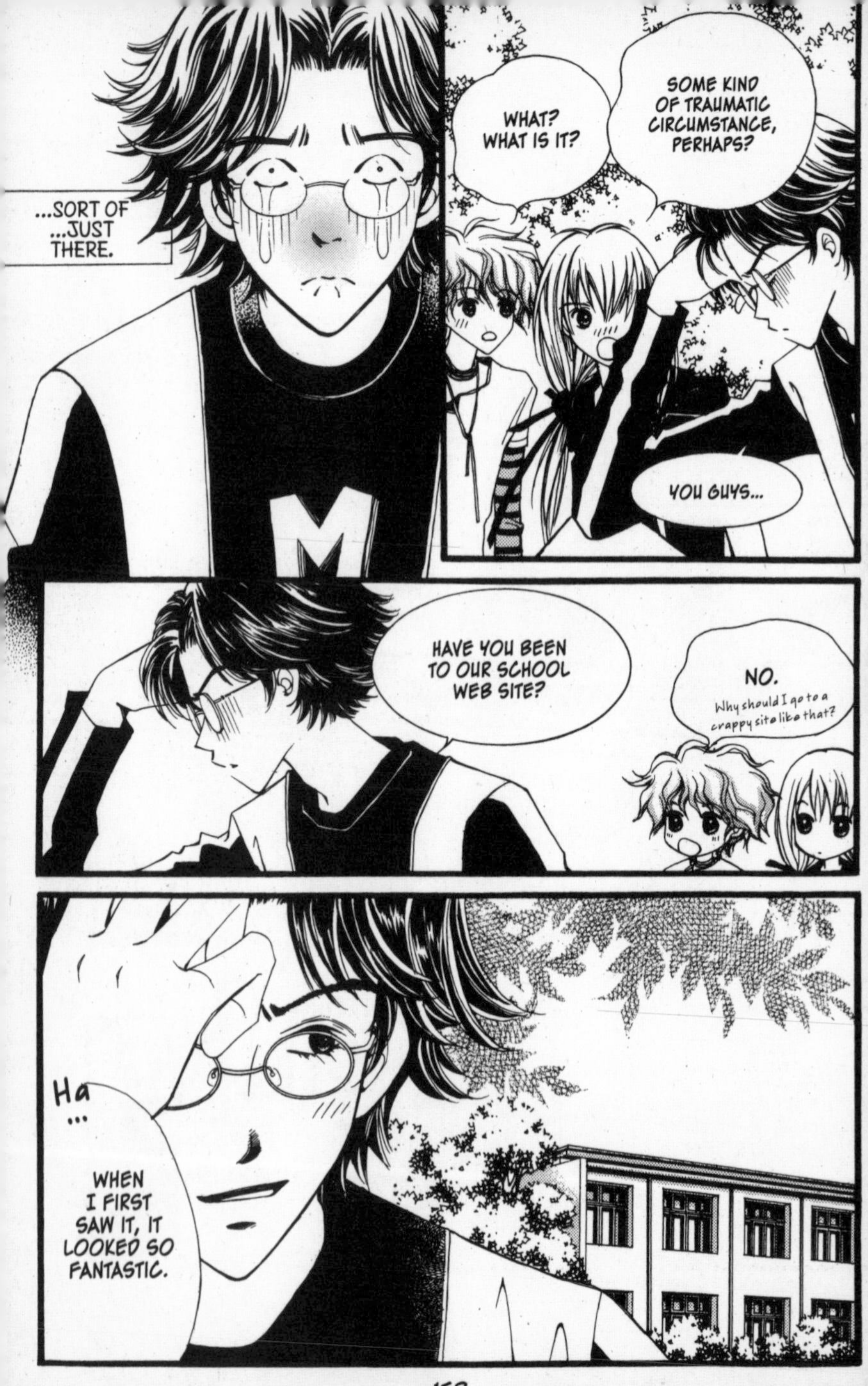
...SORT OF ...JUST THERE.
WHAT? WHAT IS IT?
SOME KIND OF TRAUMATIC CIRCUMSTANCE, PERHAPS?
YOU GUYS...
HAVE YOU BEEN TO OUR SCHOOL WEB SITE?
NO.
Why should I go to a crappy site like that?
Ha ...
WHEN I FIRST SAW IT, IT LOOKED SO FANTASTIC.

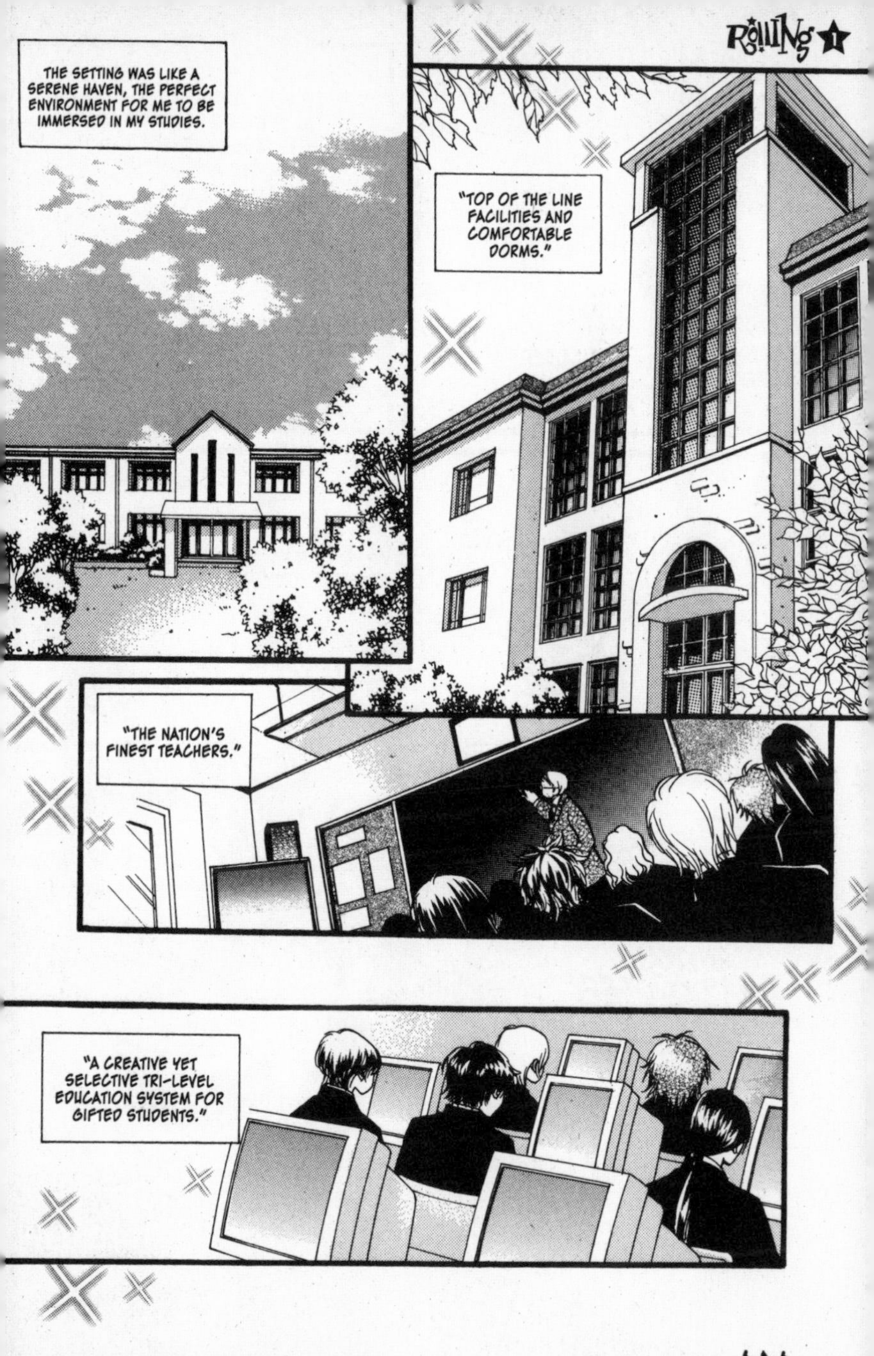
THE SETTING WAS LIKE A SERENE HAVEN, THE PERFECT ENVIRONMENT FOR ME TO BE IMMERSED IN MY STUDIES.
"TOP OF THE LINE FACILITIES AND COMFORTABLE DORMS."
"THE NATION'S FINEST TEACHERS."
"A CREATIVE YET SELECTIVE TRI-LEVEL EDUCATION SYSTEM FOR GIFTED STUDENTS."

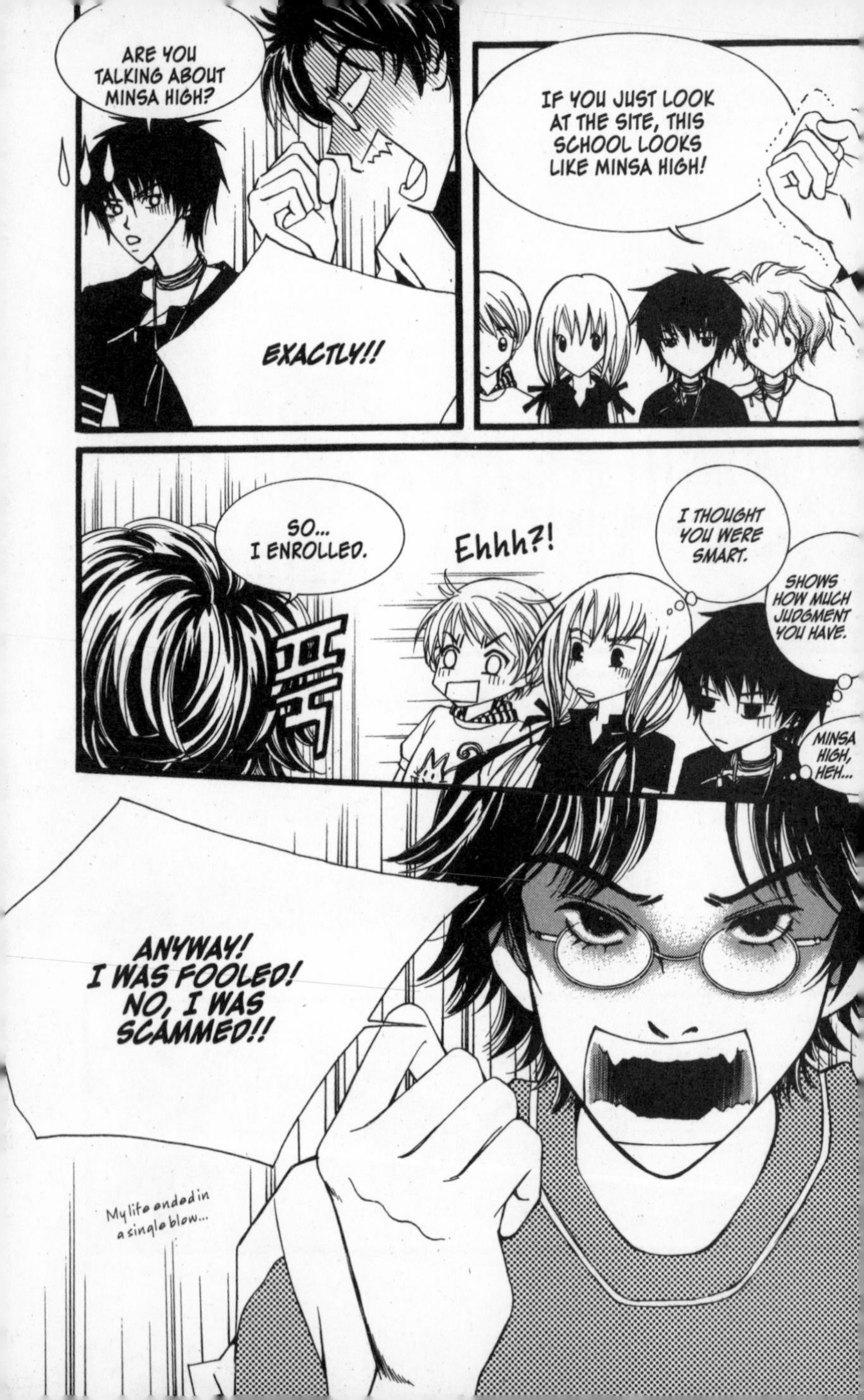
ARE YOU TALKING ABOUT MINSA HIGH?
EXACTLY!!
IF YOU JUST LOOK AT THE SITE, THIS SCHOOL LOOKS LIKE MINSA HIGH!
SO... I ENROLLED.
Ehhh?!
I THOUGHT YOU WERE SMART.
SHOWS HOW MUCH JUDGMENT YOU HAVE.
MINSA HIGH, HEH...
ANYWAY! I WAS FOOLED! NO, I WAS SCAMMED!!
My life ended in a single blow...

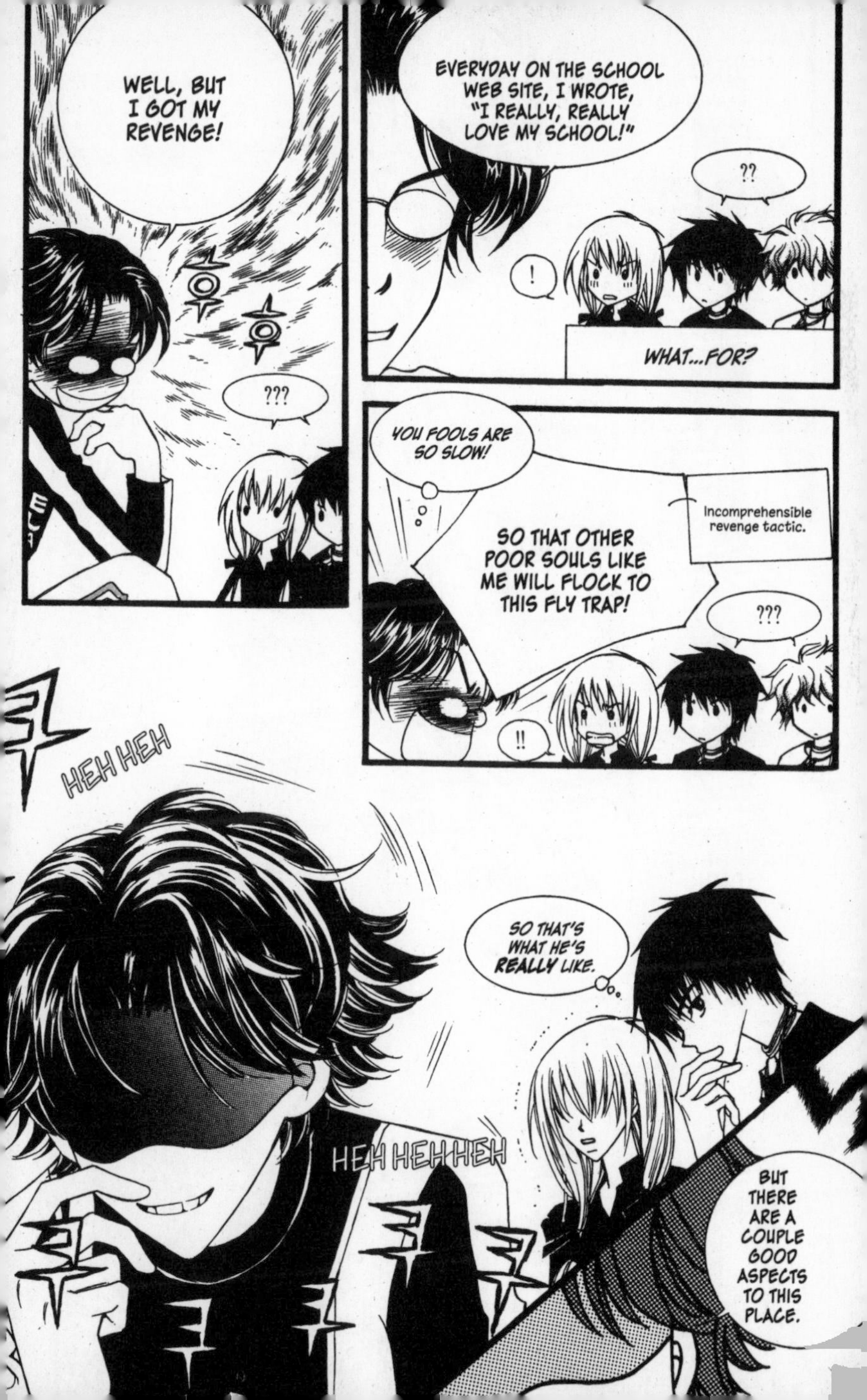
WELL, BUT I GOT MY REVENGE!
???
EVERYDAY ON THE SCHOOL WEB SITE, I WROTE, "I REALLY, REALLY LOVE MY SCHOOL!"
??
!
WHAT...FOR?
YOU FOOLS ARE SO SLOW!
Incomprehensible revenge tactic.
SO THAT OTHER POOR SOULS LIKE ME WILL FLOCK TO THIS FLY TRAP!
???
!!
HEH HEH
SO THAT'S WHAT HE'S REALLY LIKE.
HEH HEH HEH
BUT THERE ARE A COUPLE GOOD ASPECTS TO THIS PLACE.

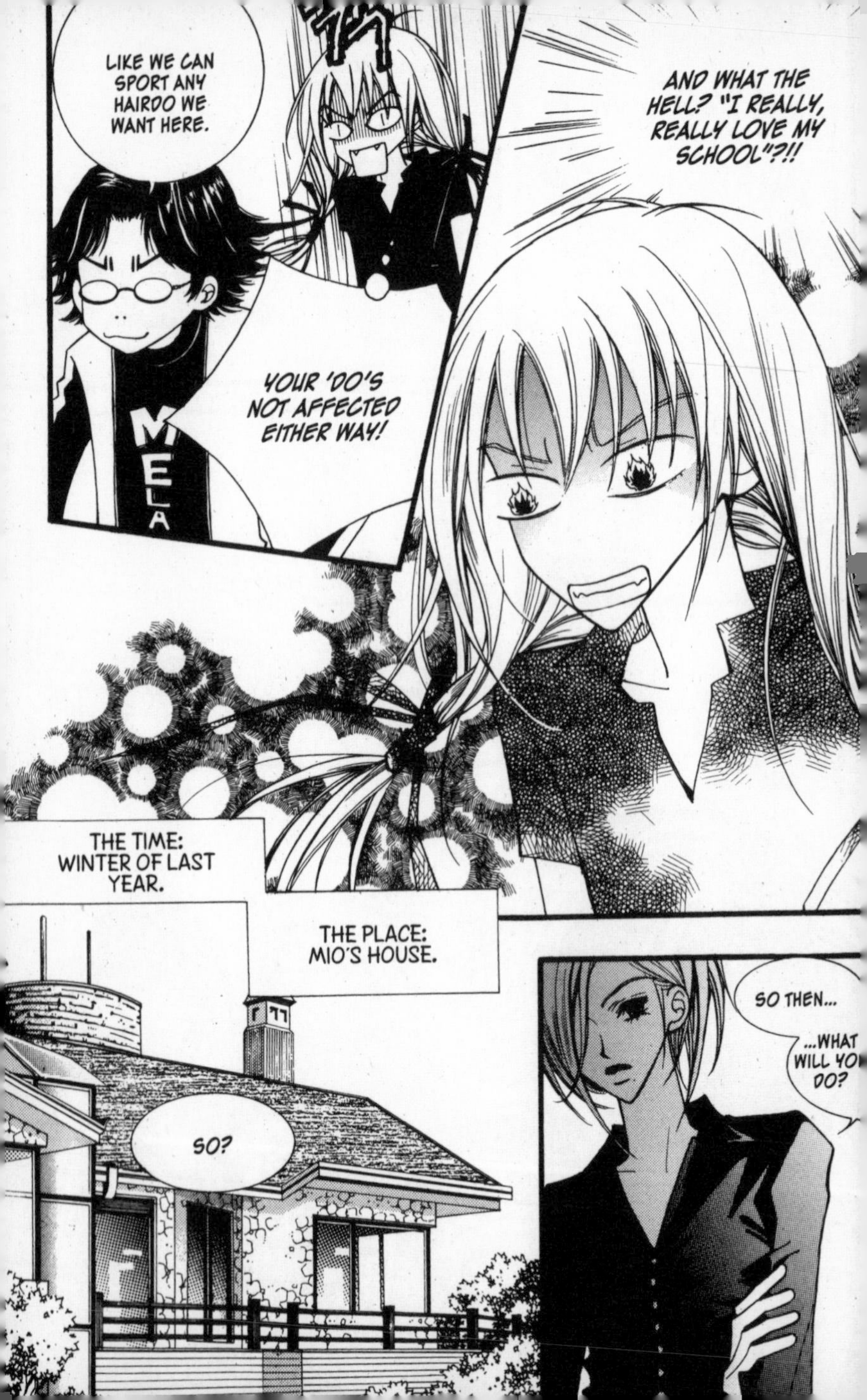

LIKE WE CAN SPORT ANY HAIRDO WE WANT HERE.
YOUR 'DO'S NOT AFFECTED EITHER WAY!
AND WHAT THE HELL? "I REALLY, REALLY LOVE MY SCHOOL"?!!
THE TIME: WINTER OF LAST YEAR.
THE PLACE: MIO'S HOUSE.
SO?
SO THEN...
...WHAT WILL YO DO?

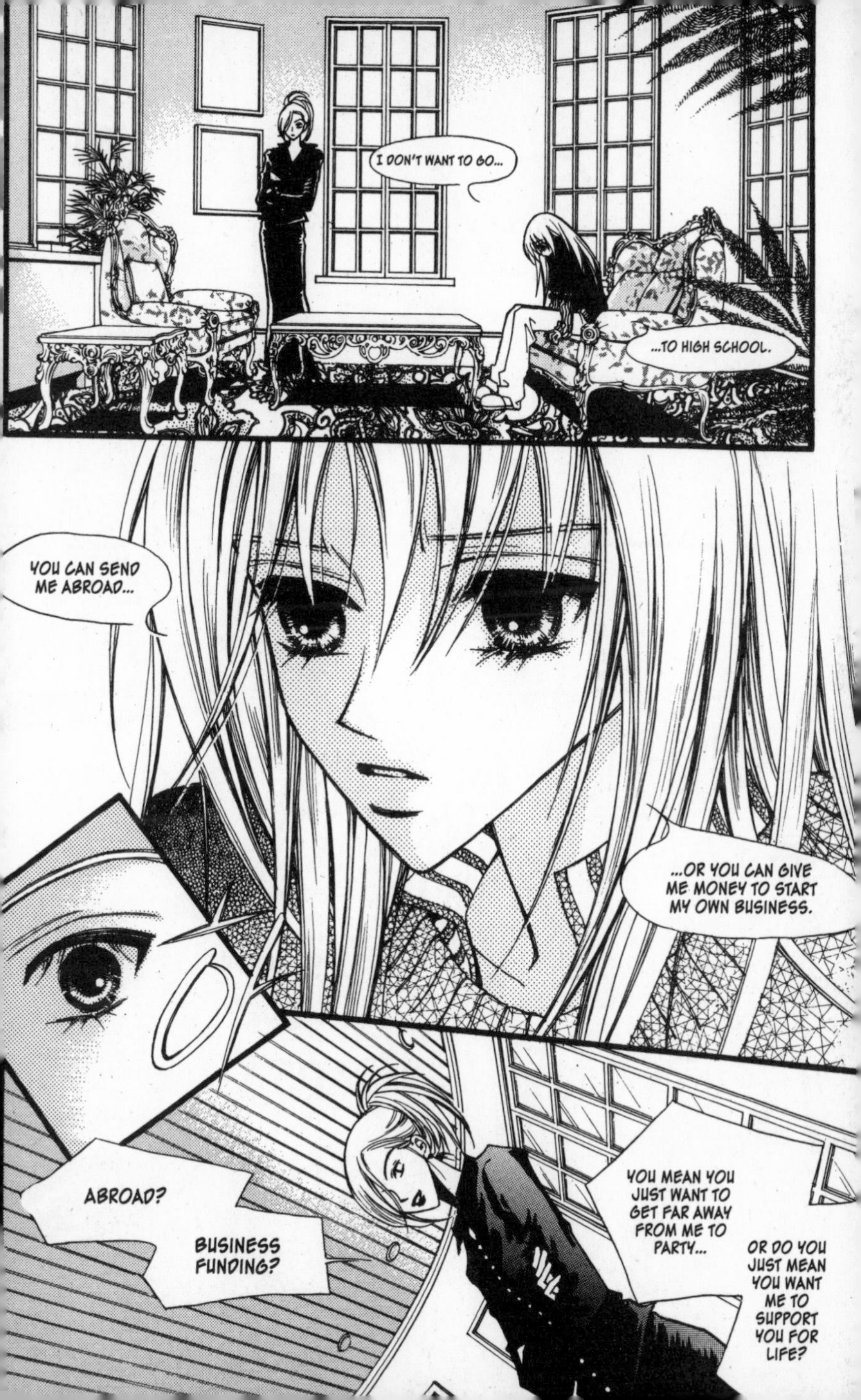
I DON'T WANT TO GO...
...TO HIGH SCHOOL.
YOU CAN SEND ME ABROAD...
...OR YOU CAN GIVE ME MONEY TO START MY OWN BUSINESS.
ABROAD?
BUSINESS FUNDING?
YOU MEAN YOU JUST WANT TO GET FAR AWAY FROM ME TO PARTY...
OR DO YOU JUST MEAN YOU WANT ME TO SUPPORT YOU FOR LIFE?

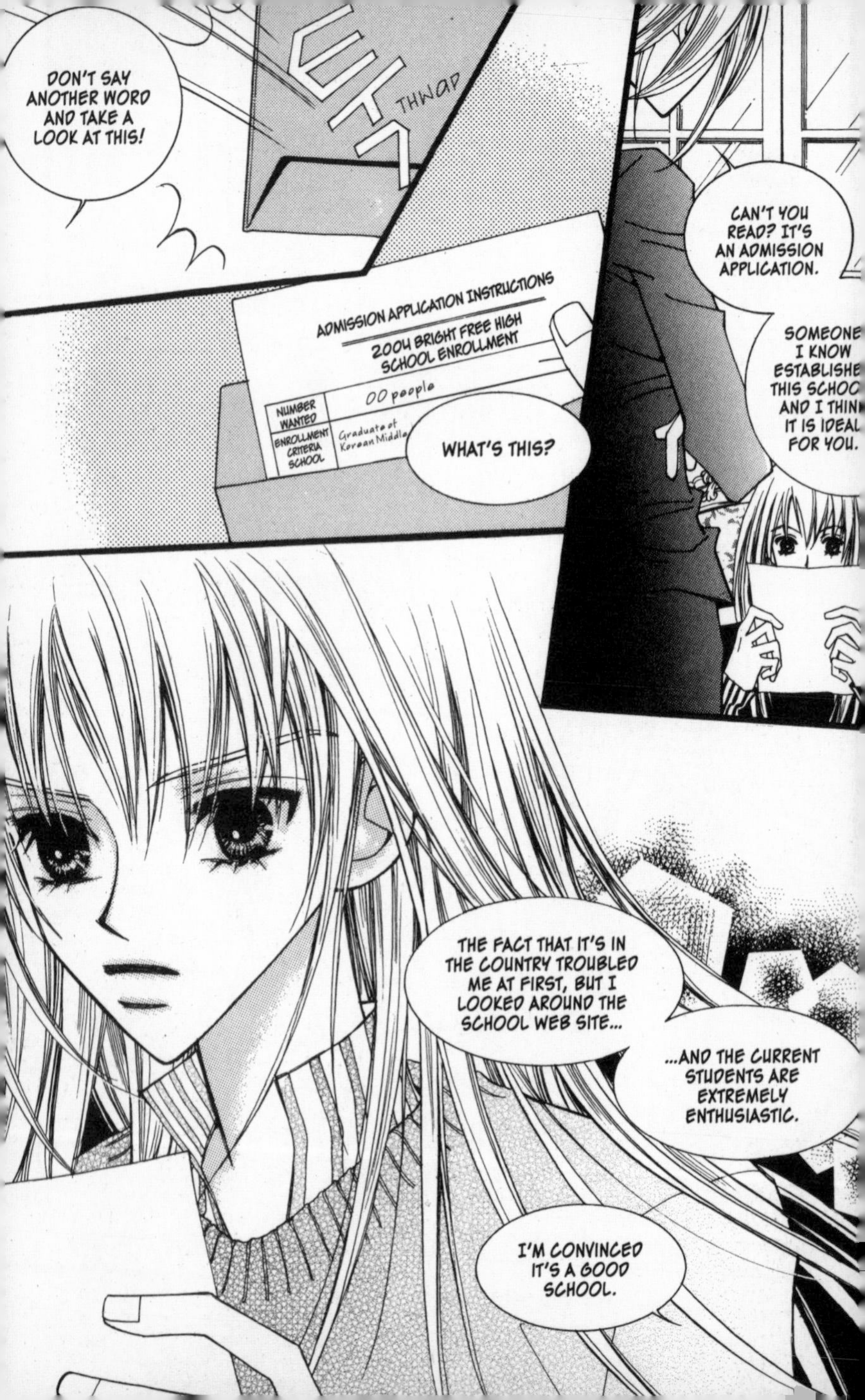
DON'T SAY ANOTHER WORD AND TAKE A LOOK AT THIS!
THWAP
ADMISSION APPLICATION INSTRUCTIONS
2004 BRIGHT FREE HIGH SCHOOL ENROLLMENT
NUMBER WANTED
00 people
ENROLLMENT CRITERIA SCHOOL
Graduate of Korean Middl
WHAT'S THIS?
CAN'T YOU READ? IT'S AN ADMISSION APPLICATION.
SOMEONE I KNOW ESTABLISHE THIS SCHOO AND I THIN IT IS IDEAL FOR YOU.
THE FACT THAT IT'S IN THE COUNTRY TROUBLED ME AT FIRST, BUT I LOOKED AROUND THE SCHOOL WEB SITE...
...AND THE CURRENT STUDENTS ARE EXTREMELY ENTHUSIASTIC.
I'M CONVINCED IT'S A GOOD SCHOOL.

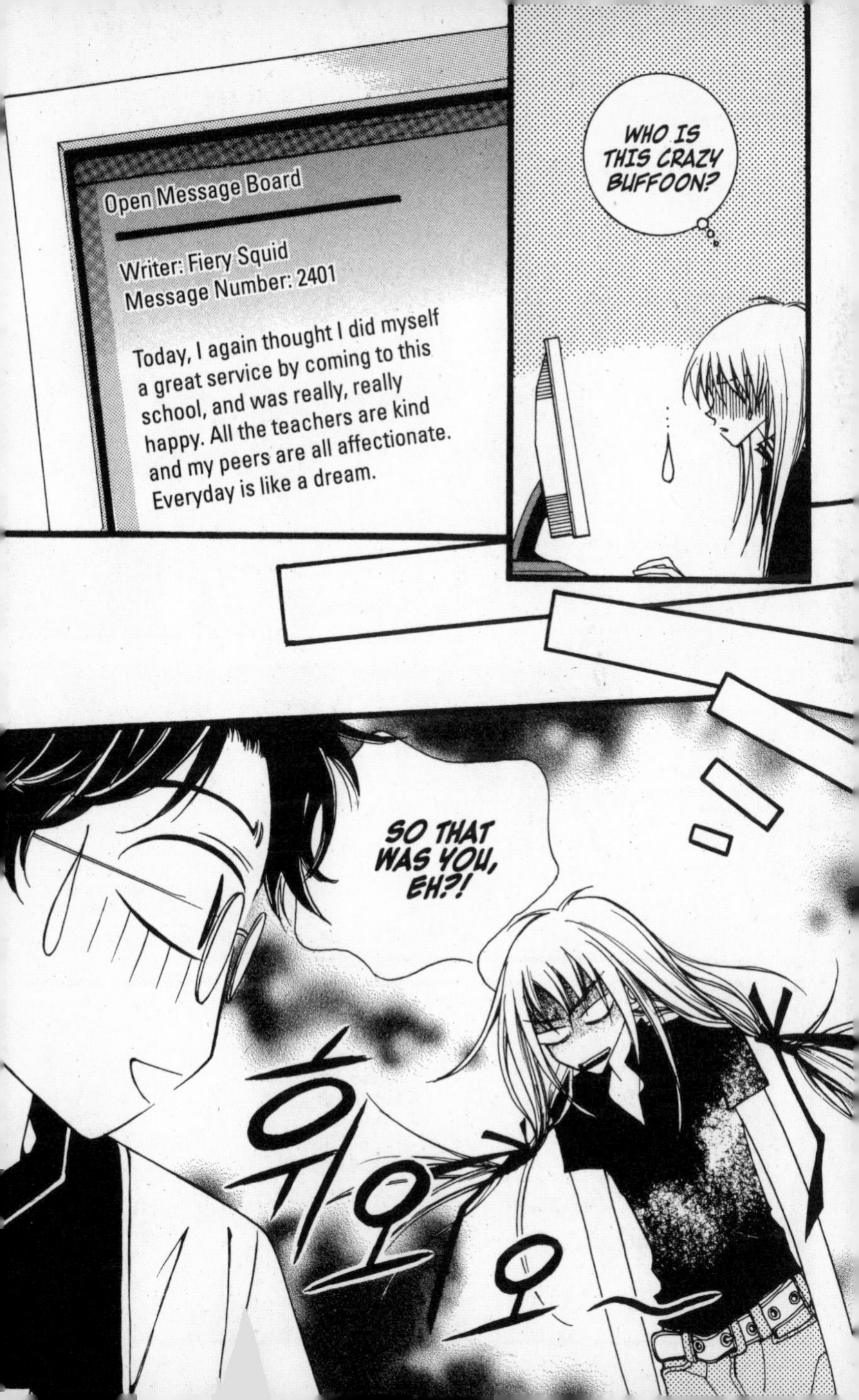
Open Message Board
Writer: Fiery Squid
Message Number: 2401
Today, I again thought I did myself a great service by coming to this school, and was really, really happy. All the teachers are kind and my peers are all affectionate. Everyday is like a dream.
WHO IS THIS CRAZY BUFFOON?
SO THAT WAS YOU, EH?!

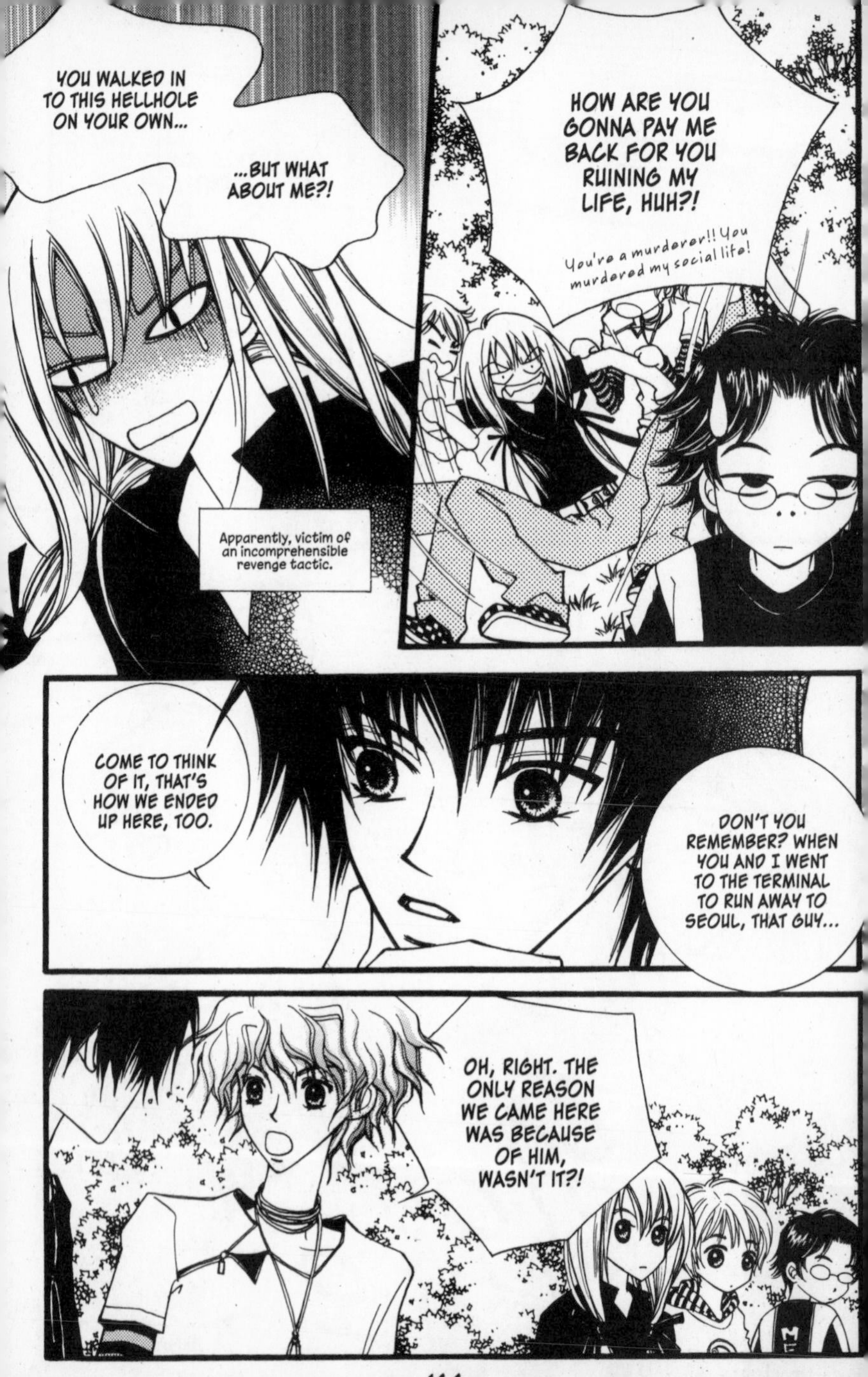
YOU WALKED IN TO THIS HELLHOLE ON YOUR OWN...
...BUT WHAT ABOUT ME?!
Apparently, victim of an incomprehensible revenge tactic.
HOW ARE YOU GONNA PAY ME BACK FOR YOU RUINING MY LIFE, HUH?!
You're a murderer!! You murdered my social life!
COME TO THINK OF IT, THAT'S HOW WE ENDED UP HERE, TOO.
DON'T YOU REMEMBER? WHEN YOU AND I WENT TO THE TERMINAL TO RUN AWAY TO SEOUL, THAT GUY...
OH, RIGHT. THE ONLY REASON WE CAME HERE WAS BECAUSE OF HIM, WASN'T IT?!

THE TIME: LAST YEAR, OF COURSE.
THE PLACE: THE BUS TERMINAL OF P-TOWN.
YOU'RE REALLY RUNNING AWAY FROM HOME?
YUP!
I'M GOING TO CHUCK SCHOOL, TOO...
...AND GO NORTH TO SEOUL AND MAKE MONEY!

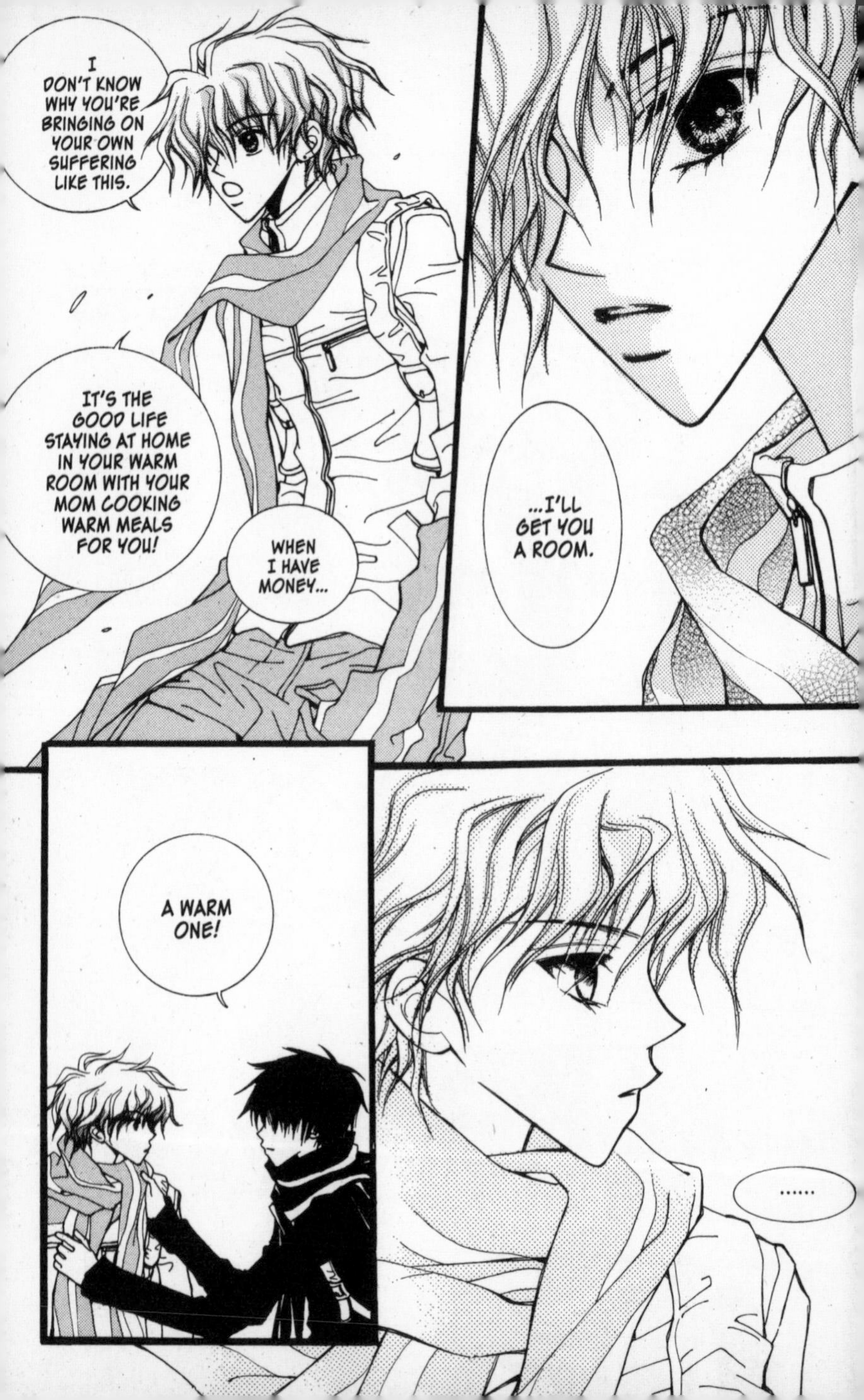
I DON'T KNOW WHY YOU'RE BRINGING ON YOUR OWN SUFFERING LIKE THIS.
IT'S THE GOOD LIFE STAYING AT HOME IN YOUR WARM ROOM WITH YOUR MOM COOKING WARM MEALS FOR YOU!
WHEN I HAVE MONEY...
...I'LL GET YOU A ROOM.
A WARM ONE!
......

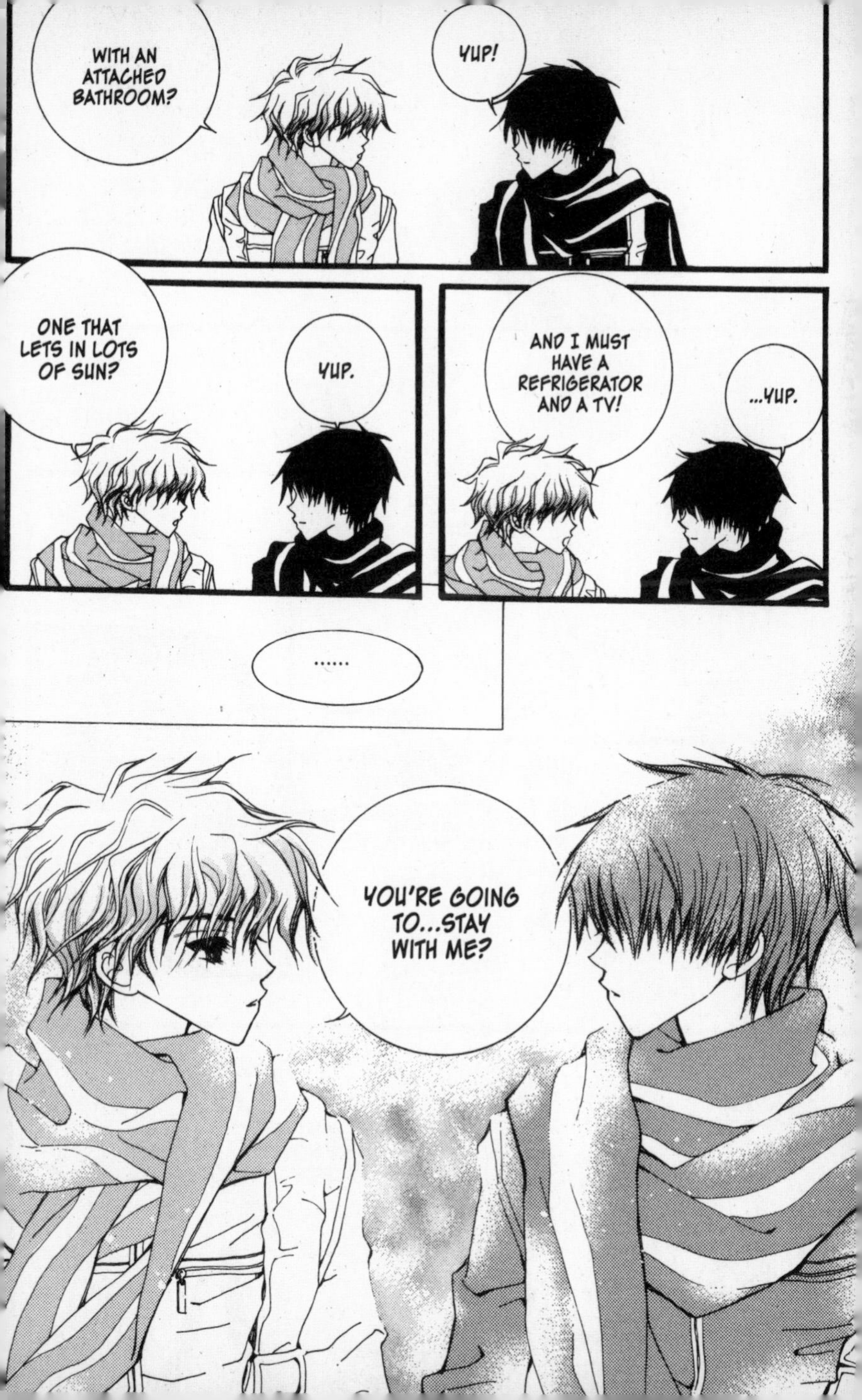
WITH AN ATTACHED BATHROOM?
YUP!
ONE THAT LETS IN LOTS OF SUN?
YUP.
AND I MUST HAVE A REFRIGERATOR AND A TV!
...YUP.
......
YOU'RE GOING TO...STAY WITH ME?

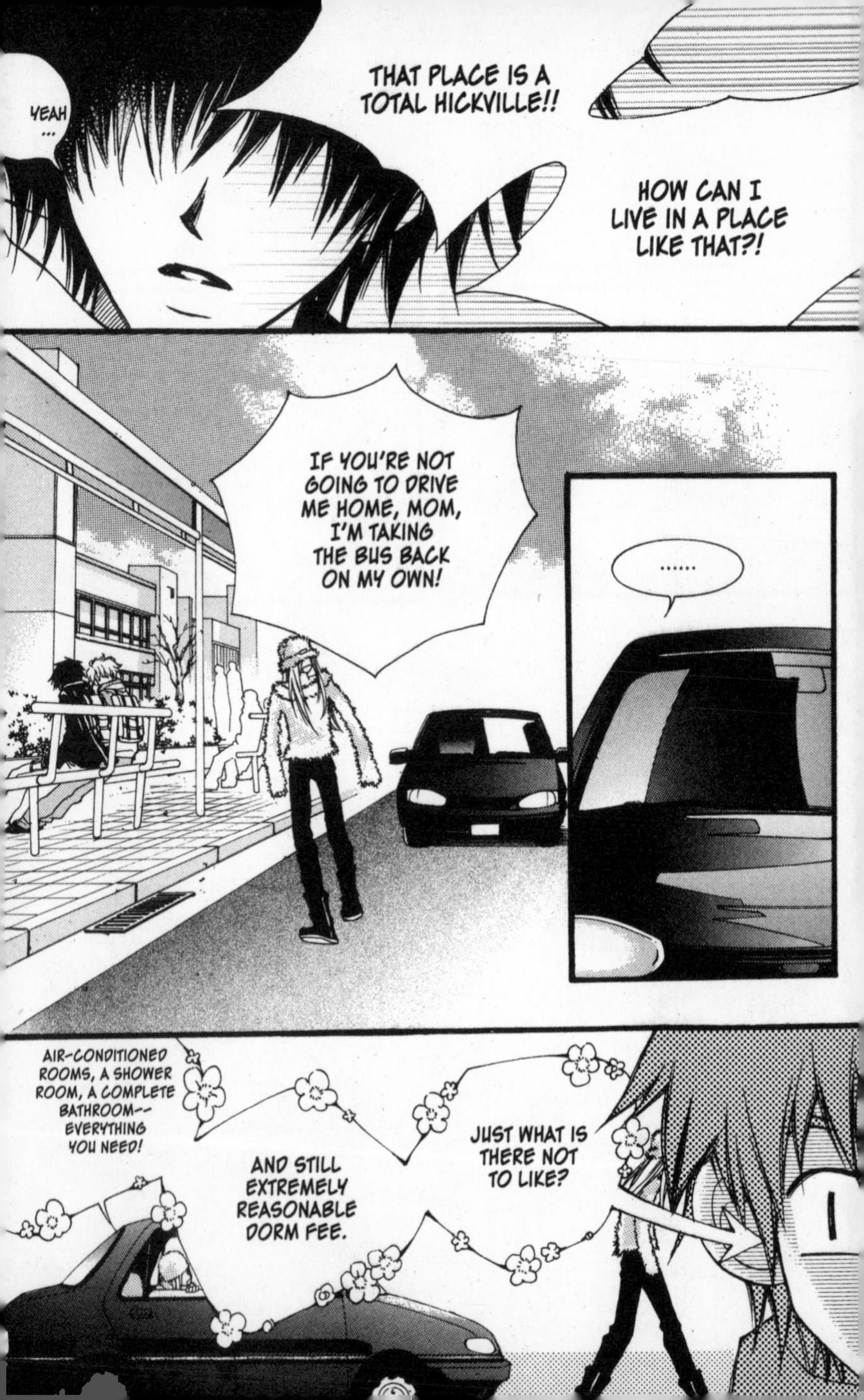
YEAH ...
THAT PLACE IS A TOTAL HICKVILLE!!
HOW CAN I LIVE IN A PLACE LIKE THAT?!
IF YOU'RE NOT GOING TO DRIVE ME HOME, MOM, I'M TAKING THE BUS BACK ON MY OWN!
......
AIR-CONDITIONED ROOMS, A SHOWER ROOM, A COMPLETE BATHROOM-- EVERYTHING YOU NEED!
AND STILL EXTREMELY REASONABLE DORM FEE.
JUST WHAT IS THERE NOT TO LIKE?

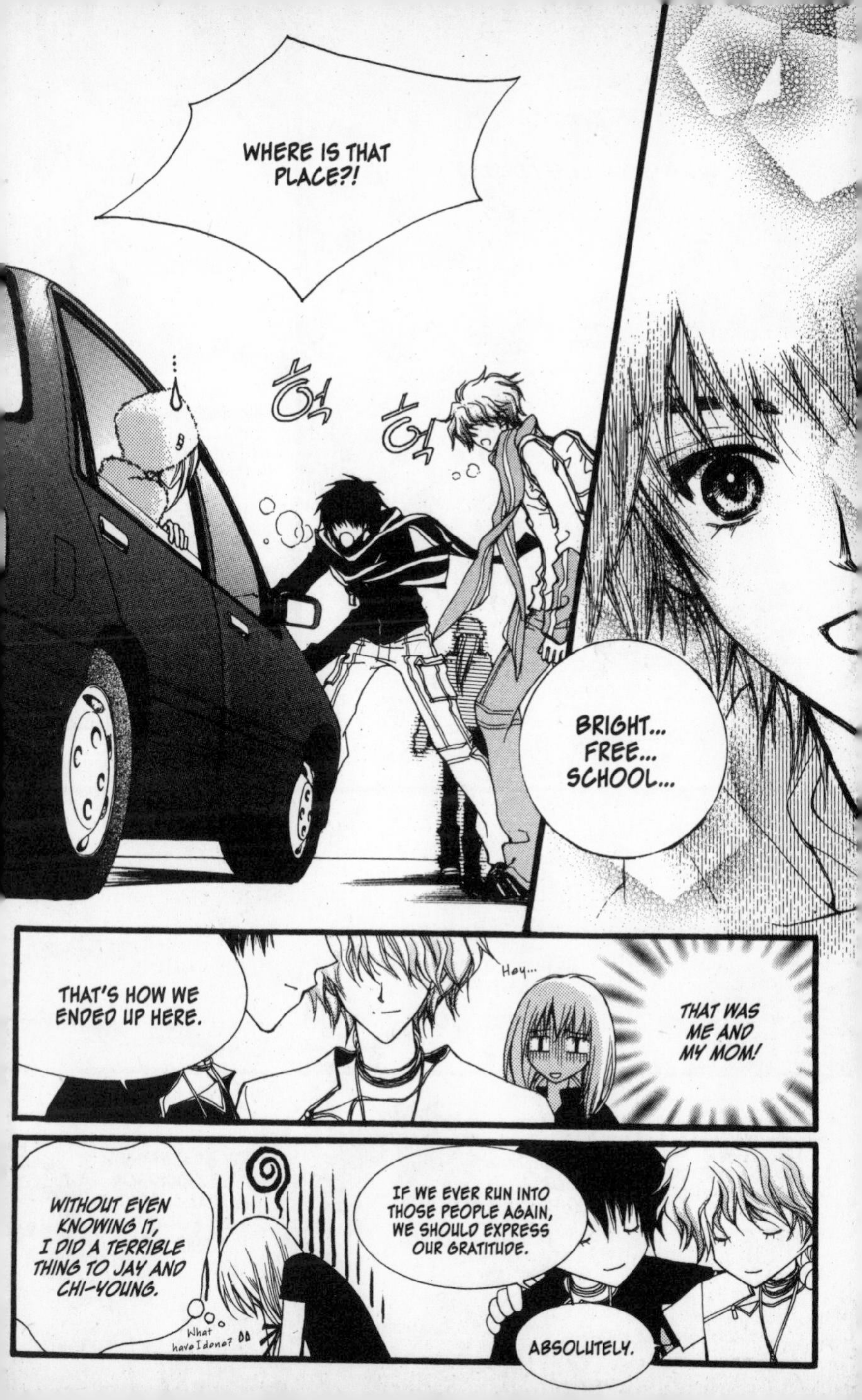

WHERE IS THAT PLACE?!
헉
헉
BRIGHT... FREE... SCHOOL...
THAT'S HOW WE ENDED UP HERE.
Hey...
THAT WAS ME AND MY MOM!
WITHOUT EVEN KNOWING IT, I DID A TERRIBLE THING TO JAY AND CHI-YOUNG.
What have I done?
IF WE EVER RUN INTO THOSE PEOPLE AGAIN, WE SHOULD EXPRESS OUR GRATITUDE.
ABSOLUTELY.

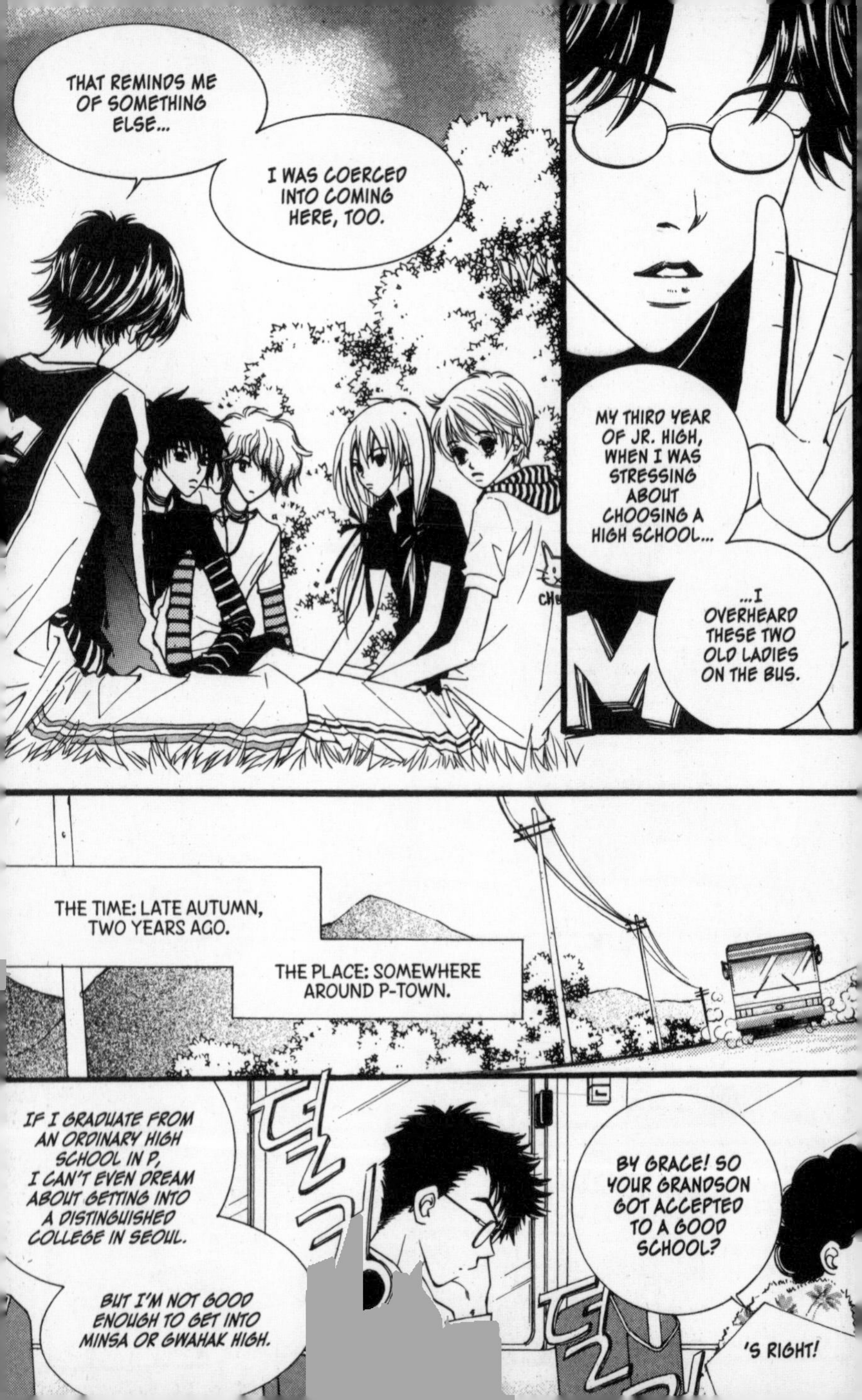
THAT REMINDS ME OF SOMETHING ELSE...
I WAS COERCED INTO COMING HERE, TOO.
MY THIRD YEAR OF JR. HIGH, WHEN I WAS STRESSING ABOUT CHOOSING A HIGH SCHOOL...
...I OVERHEARD THESE TWO OLD LADIES ON THE BUS.
THE TIME: LATE AUTUMN, TWO YEARS AGO.
THE PLACE: SOMEWHERE AROUND P-TOWN.
IF I GRADUATE FROM AN ORDINARY HIGH SCHOOL IN P, I CAN'T EVEN DREAM ABOUT GETTING INTO A DISTINGUISHED COLLEGE IN SEOUL.
BUT I'M NOT GOOD ENOUGH TO GET INTO MINSA OR GWAHAK HIGH.
BY GRACE! SO YOUR GRANDSON GOT ACCEPTED TO A GOOD SCHOOL?
'S RIGHT!

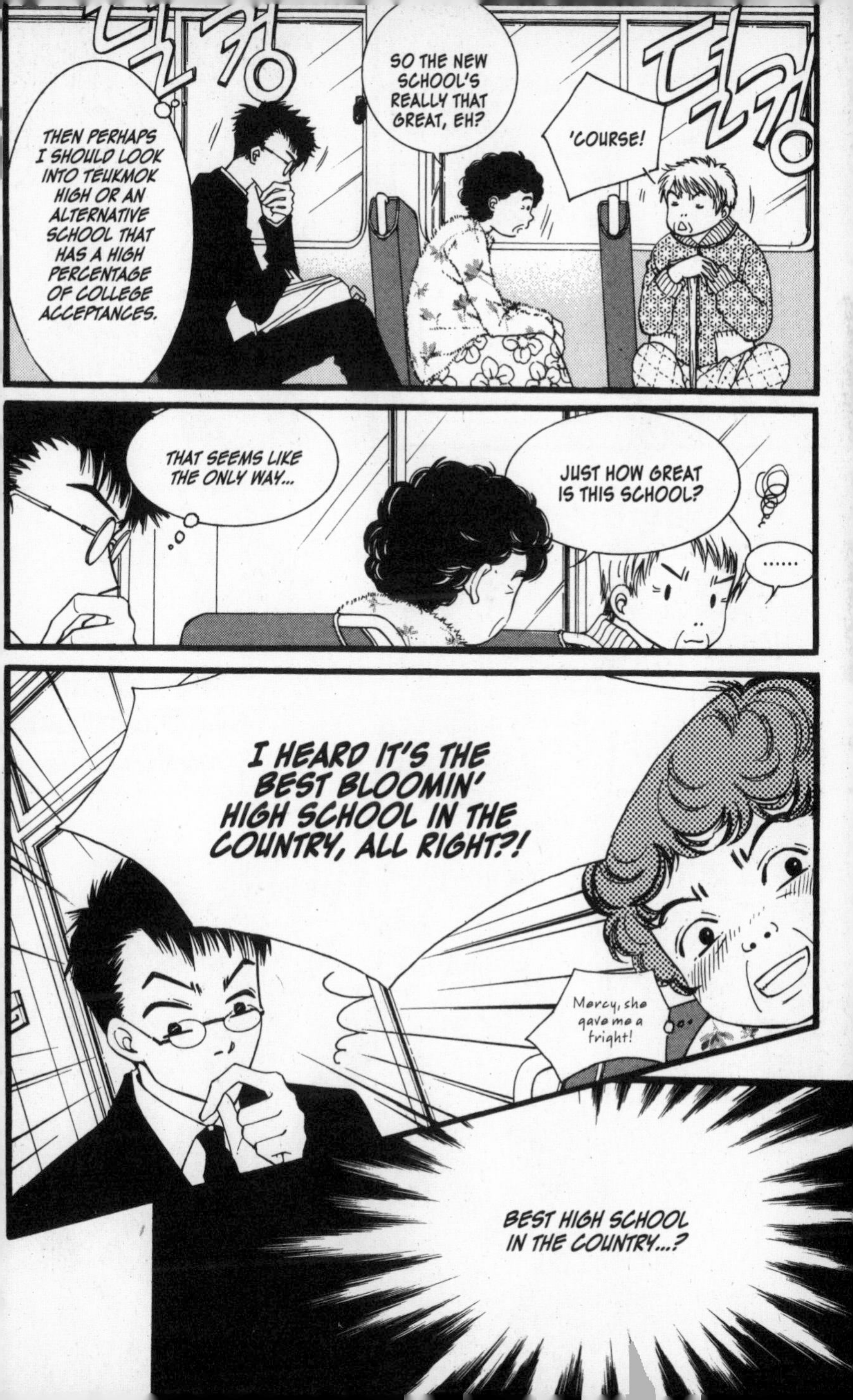
덜컹
THEN PERHAPS I SHOULD LOOK INTO TEUKMOK HIGH OR AN ALTERNATIVE SCHOOL THAT HAS A HIGH PERCENTAGE OF COLLEGE ACCEPTANCES.
SO THE NEW SCHOOL'S REALLY THAT GREAT, EH?
덜컹
'COURSE!
THAT SEEMS LIKE THE ONLY WAY...
JUST HOW GREAT IS THIS SCHOOL?
......
I HEARD IT'S THE BEST BLOOMIN' HIGH SCHOOL IN THE COUNTRY, ALL RIGHT?!
Mercy, she gave me a fright!
BEST HIGH SCHOOL IN THE COUNTRY...?

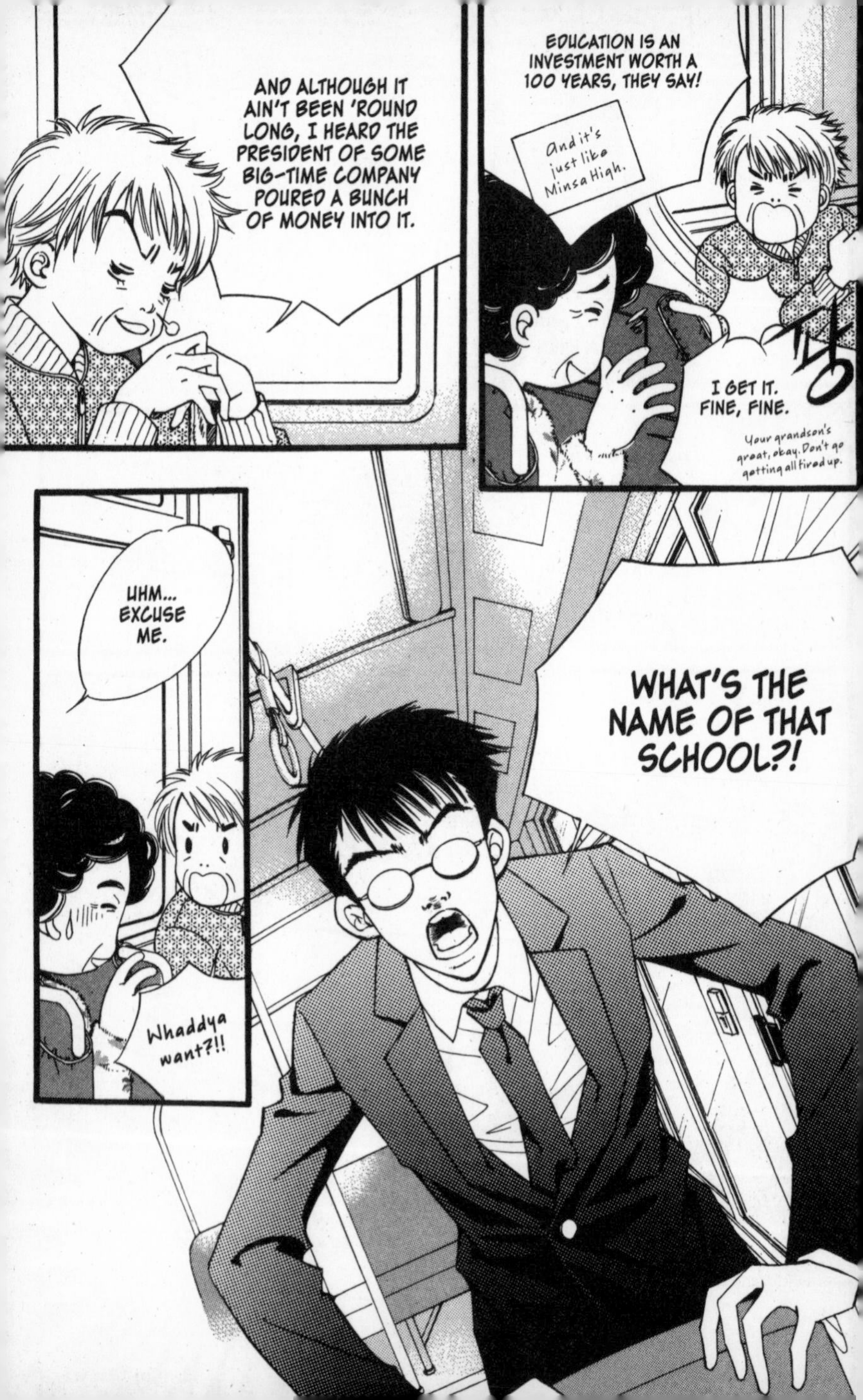
AND ALTHOUGH IT AIN'T BEEN 'ROUND LONG, I HEARD THE PRESIDENT OF SOME BIG-TIME COMPANY POURED A BUNCH OF MONEY INTO IT.
EDUCATION IS AN INVESTMENT WORTH A 100 YEARS, THEY SAY!
And it's just like Minsa High.
I GET IT. FINE, FINE.
Your grandson's great, okay. Don't go getting all fired up.
UHM... EXCUSE ME.
Whaddya want?!!
WHAT'S THE NAME OF THAT SCHOOL?!

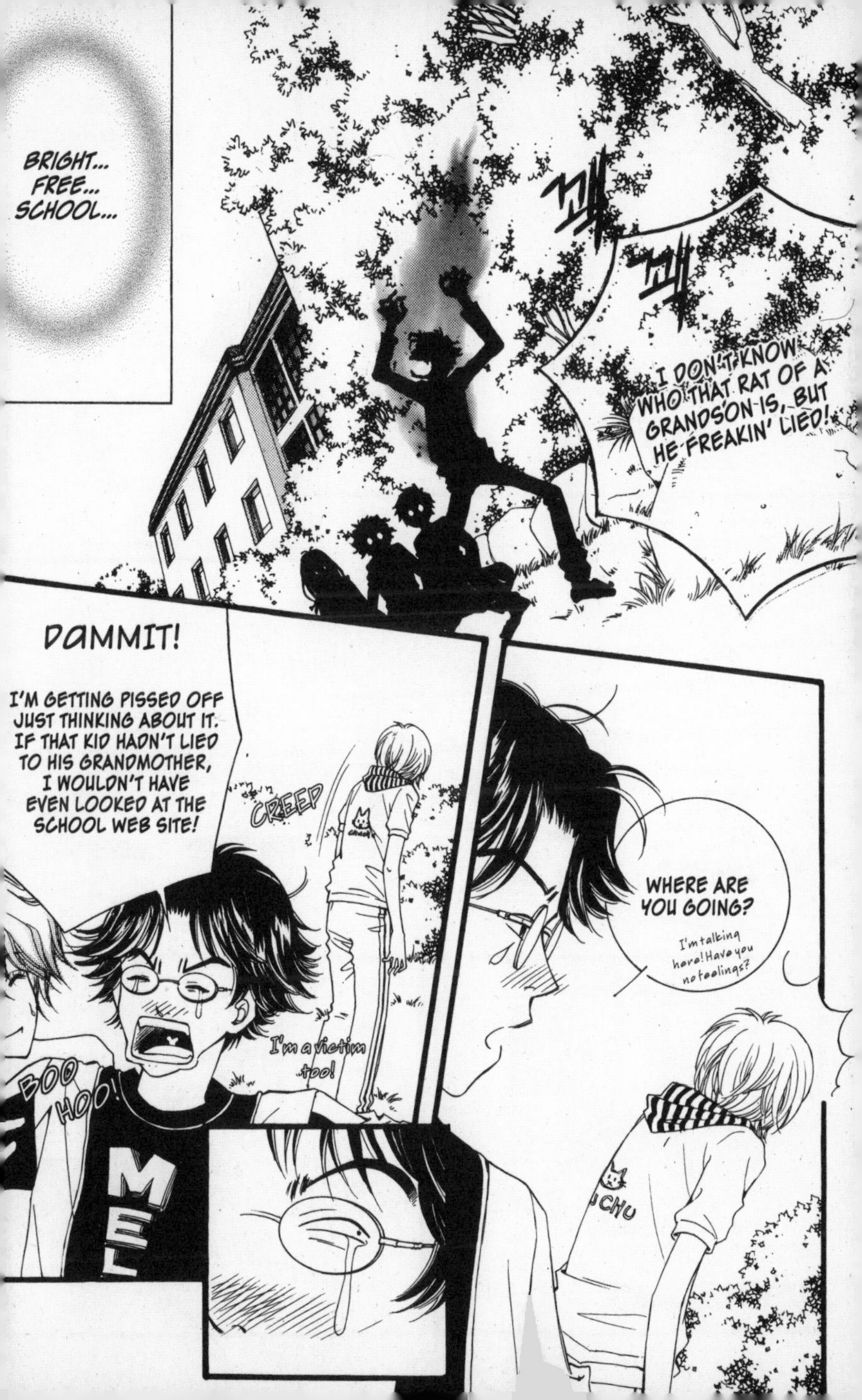
BRIGHT... FREE... SCHOOL...
I DON'T KNOW WHO THAT RAT OF A GRANDSON IS, BUT HE FREAKIN' LIED!
DAMMIT!
I'M GETTING PISSED OFF JUST THINKING ABOUT IT. IF THAT KID HADN'T LIED TO HIS GRANDMOTHER, I WOULDN'T HAVE EVEN LOOKED AT THE SCHOOL WEB SITE!
CREEP
BOO HOO!
I'm a victim too!
MEL
WHERE ARE YOU GOING?
I'm talking here! Have you no feelings?
CHU

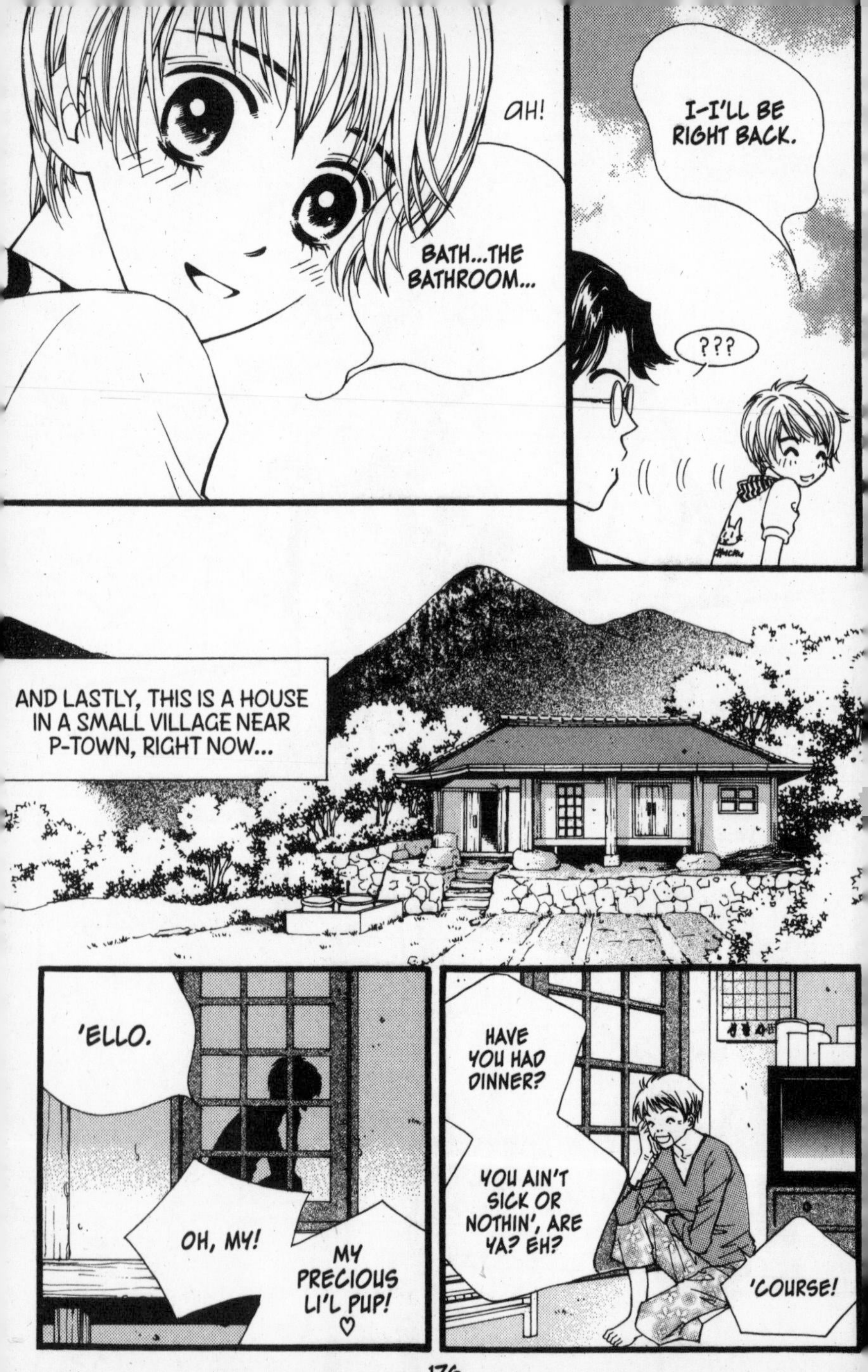
ah!
BATH...THE BATHROOM...
I-I'LL BE RIGHT BACK.
???
AND LASTLY, THIS IS A HOUSE IN A SMALL VILLAGE NEAR P-TOWN, RIGHT NOW...
'ELLO.
OH, MY!
MY PRECIOUS LI'L PUP! ♡
HAVE YOU HAD DINNER?
YOU AIN'T SICK OR NOTHIN', ARE YA? EH?
'COURSE!

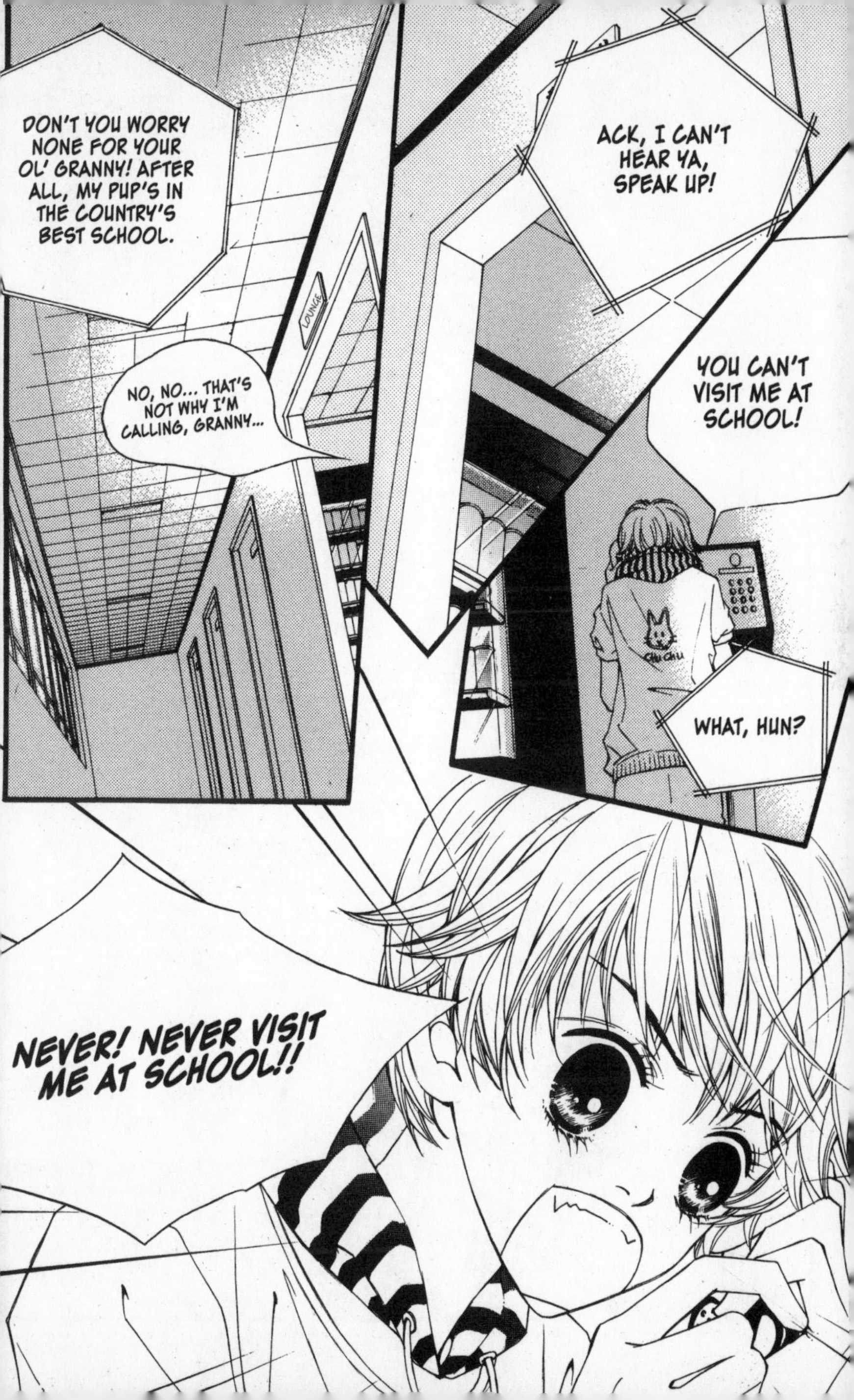
DON'T YOU WORRY NONE FOR YOUR OL' GRANNY! AFTER ALL, MY PUP'S IN THE COUNTRY'S BEST SCHOOL.
LOUNGE
NO, NO... THAT'S NOT WHY I'M CALLING, GRANNY...
ACK, I CAN'T HEAR YA, SPEAK UP!
YOU CAN'T VISIT ME AT SCHOOL!
WHAT, HUN?
NEVER! NEVER VISIT ME AT SCHOOL!!

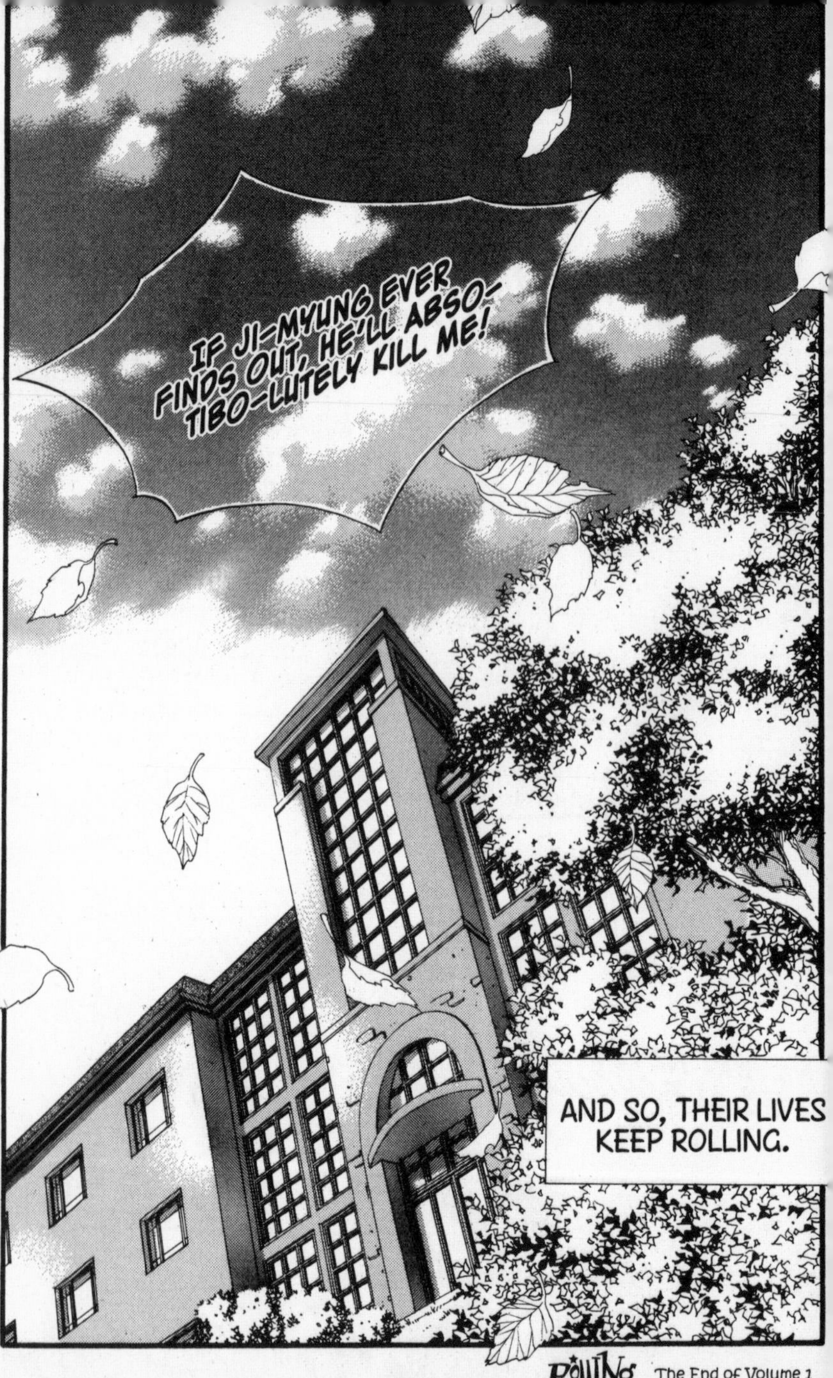
IF JI-MYUNG EVER FINDS OUT, HE'LL ABSO-TIBO-LUTELY KILL ME!
AND SO, THEIR LIVES KEEP ROLLING.

Rolling The End of Volume 1

ROLLING

롤링

More wacky silliness comes rolling your way as Jay gets himself a stalker who follows him everywhere... even to the showers! With Chi-Young on the prowl to find and pummel the stalker's face in, it's not a matter of IF the scoundrel will be found but WHEN! And Ji-Myung emerges as an unlikely hero as he rescues Mio from the devastating "no toilet paper" situation while Il-Yong performs exorcism to cure a dorm mate's indigestion!

Checkitty out volume 2! ♥

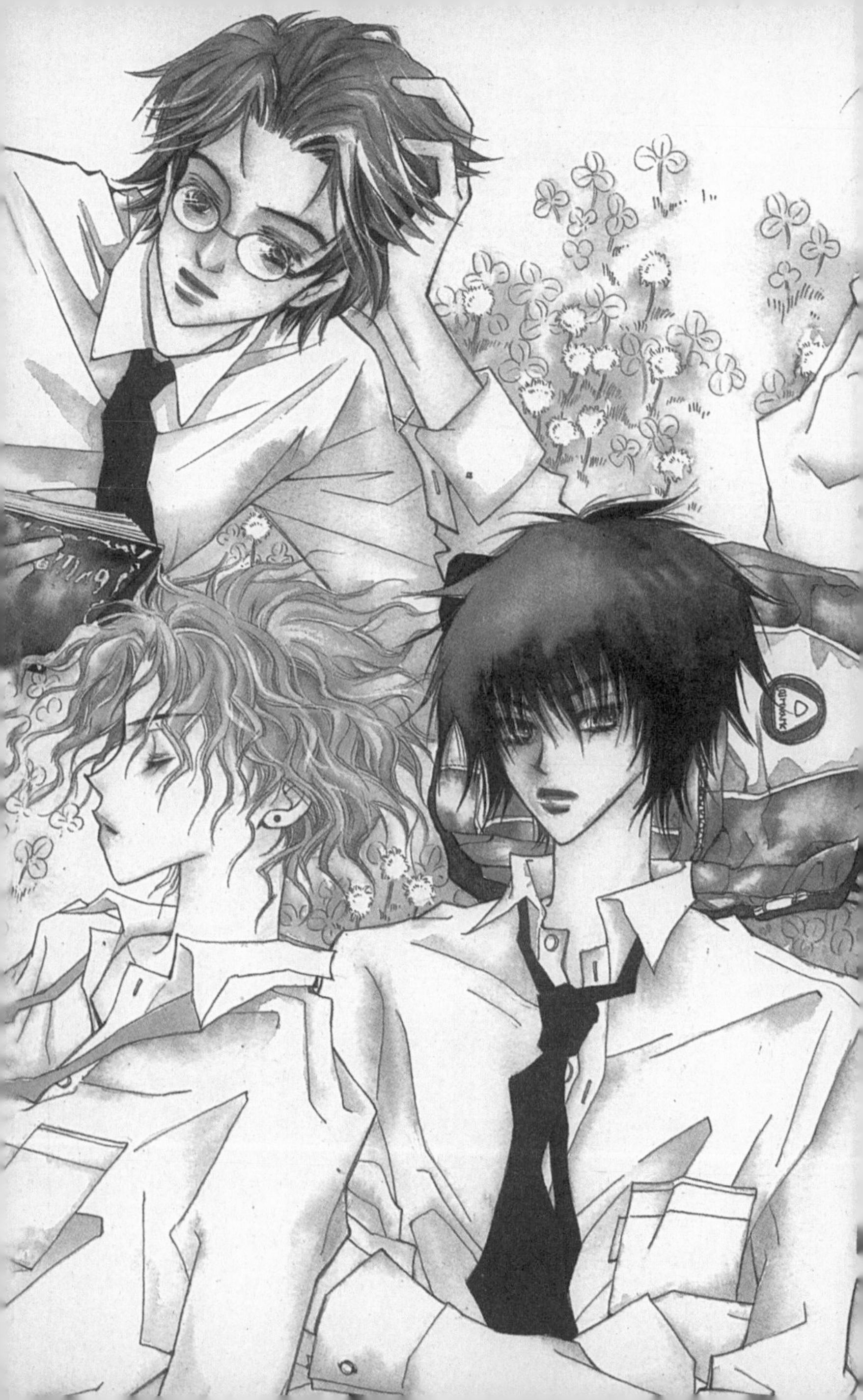

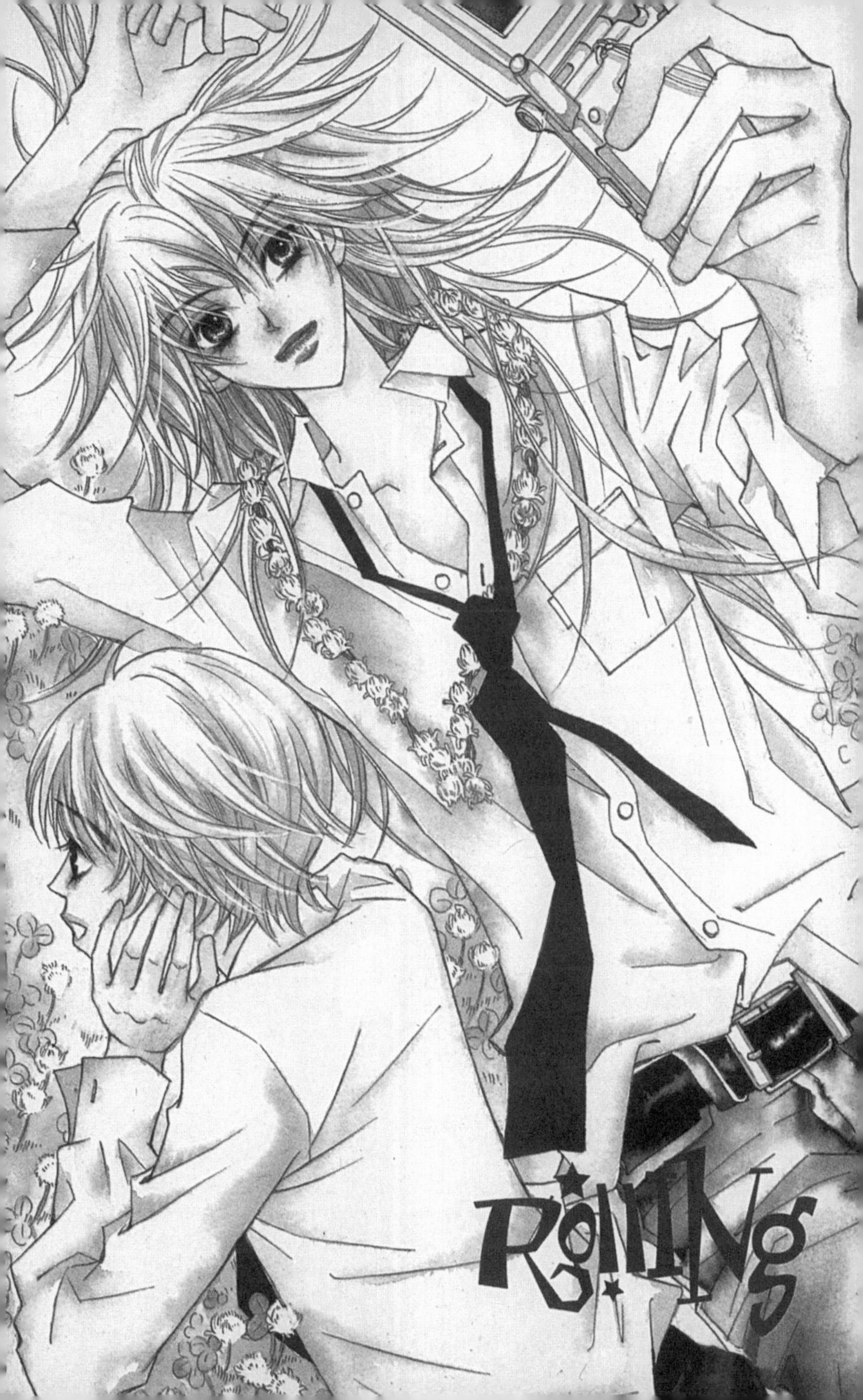
Rolling

TOKYOPOP.com
WHERE MANGA LIVES!
JOIN the TOKYOPOP community: www.TOKYOPOP.com
COME AND PREVIEW THE HOTTEST MANGA AROUND!
CREATE...
UPLOAD...
DOWNLOAD...
BLOG...
CHAT...
VOTE...
LIVE!!!!
WWW.TOKYOPOP.COM HAS:
• Exclusives
• News
• Contests
• Games
• Rising Stars of Manga
• iManga
• and more...
TOKYOPOP :: Leading the Manga Revolution for 10 Years and Beyond
http://www.TOKYOPOP.com/
Where else?
POP-CAST
Now with long lasting flavor!
WATCH HERE!
MOST RECENT
MOST POPPED
TOKYOPOP.COM 2.0
NOW LIVE!
LEADING THE MANGA REVOLUTION
漫画革命
© Branded Entertainment LLC, TOKYOPOP Inc., and Russell Productions, Inc.

Fruits Basket™

By Natsuki Takaya

Volume 20

Can Tohru deal with the truth?

After running away from his feelings and everyone he knows, Kyo is back with the truth about his role in the death of Tohru's mother. But how will he react when Tohru says that she still loves him?

Winner of the American Anime Award for Best Manga!

The #1 selling shojo manga in America!

CHIBI VAMPIRE
MANGA BY YUNA KAGESAKI, NOVEL BY TOHRU KAI AND YUNA KAGESAKI

The HILARIOUS adventures of

As Karin and Kenta's official first date continues, Anju shows up to keep an eye on the clumsy couple. When Kenta tells Karin how he really feels, will it destroy their relationship? Also, the new girl in town, Yuriya, begins snooping around in search of vampires. Why is she trying to uncover Karin's identity, and what secrets of her own is she hiding?

chibi Vampire ™  Inspired the

FOR MORE INFORMATION VISIT: